Danielson
Metropolitan
politics

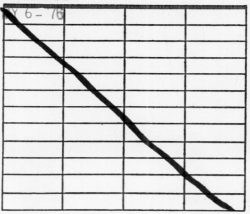

METROPOLITAN POLITICS

SECOND EDITION

METROPOLITAN POLITICS
A Reader

Edited by
MICHAEL N. DANIELSON
Princeton University

LITTLE, BROWN AND COMPANY
Boston

Library of Congress Catalog Card Number: 71–160699

FOURTH PRINTING

Published simultaneously in Canada
by Little, Brown & Company (Canada) Limited

Printed in the United States of America

PREFACE

Five tumultuous years have passed since the first edition of this collection of readings on metropolitan politics appeared. During this half decade, scores of cities have been the scene of riots as tens of thousands of black Americans rebelled against conditions in the social, economic, and political ghettos that stain the urban landscape. A president pledged to rebuild America's cities but lost his (and perhaps his successors') opportunity in the rice paddies of Southeast Asia. A new census confirms what our eyes tell us: that hundreds of thousands more Americans, most of them white, have joined one of the great migrations in history, the exodus to the suburbs; that our older cities continue to lose population while the newer ones of the South and West grow rapidly; and that blacks, the aged, and other disadvantaged groups remain concentrated in the cities. Commissions, task forces, and congressional committees have studied and restudied our urban, suburban, and racial dilemmas, warning against the dire consequences of continuing our present course of fragmentation and segregation, and recommending vast new programs designed to produce a more equitable pattern of urban development and a metropolitan political system better able to serve the welfare of all urban Americans.

This new edition reflects these dynamics, and the impact of the forces of urban growth and change on politics in the American metropolis. Over half the selections are new. More attention is paid to race and ethnicity, to politics in the older cities, and to questions of centralization and decentralization. But the central aim remains unchanged. This volume's primary objective is the analysis of the political system of the metropolis rather than its reform. Therefore, the main focus is political behavior rather than institutional structure. From a wide range of perspectives, the readings examine the distribution of influence in the metropolis and the impact on this distribution of the

vii

forces of urban growth and change. In so doing, considerable attention is given to the attitudes, perceptions, capabilities, and activities of the various participants in the metropolitan political system.

Students of metropolitan politics frequently restrict their attention to political activity arising from efforts to create, maintain, and operate metropolitan governments. In this volume, however, metropolitan politics is not defined in this narrow fashion. Selections cover the entire spectrum of issues and political activity that shapes and is shaped by the patterns of metropolitan politics. Thus, the readings examine the politics of transportation, water supply, planning, race relations, special districts, interlocal agreements, and state and federal involvement in metropolitan problems, as well, of course, as the politics of metropolitan government.

Each of the seven chapters begins with an introductory essay that sets forth the central theme around which the chapter is organized, provides continuity, and underscores matters of particular interest to the student of metropolitan politics. In addition, these introductory sections offer a general analysis of the development, operation, and prospects of the metropolitan political system. Some of the readings document or reinforce the editor's interpretation; others challenge it or introduce discordant notes.

Inevitably a number of debts are incurred in the preparation of a collection of readings. First, I am grateful to the authors and their publishers for kindly permitting me to reprint the material included in this volume. Second, I want to thank the students who have read and evaluated many of these selections in my undergraduate and graduate courses at Princeton University. I also am indebted to Jameson W. Doig and John H. Strange, who read the original manuscript and offered numerous suggestions for improvement. Richard M. Cion provided invaluable assistance in the collection of the contents of the first edition and their preparation for publication. Two undergraduate research assistants, Sanford Greenberg and Arthur Kent, played a key role in the selection of items for the second edition. I also benefited from their criticisms of the first edition, as I did from the comments of other Princeton students and colleagues. My secretary, Lucille Crooks, copied the selections, typed the introductions and original articles, secured the permissions to reprint items, and ran a busy office while I was stealing the time to rework the book. John Andrews, Alfred Browne, and their coworkers at Little, Brown did the rest with their usual good cheer and competence.

Michael N. Danielson

CONTENTS

1

URBANIZATION AND THE POLITICAL ENVIRONMENT 1

5

THE POLITICS OF METROPOLITAN
REFORM   *247*

6

THE METROPOLIS AND THE
FEDERAL SYSTEM   *311*

METROPOLITAN POLITICS

URBANIZATION AND
THE POLITICAL ENVIRONMENT

1

An understanding of political behavior in the American metropolis depends heavily on knowledge of the process of urban growth and change. The social, economic, and technological forces that have produced the sprawling metropolitan areas of the 1970's have indelibly marked urban political systems. We have been transformed into a nation of suburbanites almost before we realized that we had become a nation of urban dwellers. Remnants of older technologies such as the trolley car and the downtown factory loft have been swept away by the automobile and the industrial park. The poor, most of whom are black or Spanish-speaking, have been concentrated in the older cities while the burgeoning middle class has spread far beyond the city limits. Political power in the extended metropolis has been fragmented as geographic and functional units of government have proliferated. Differences in constituency, capabilities, and the impact of urban change have produced a widening gulf between city and suburb, growing conflict among the diverse neighborhoods of the city, and sizable disparities among suburbs. With growth and change have come pyramiding demands on government for more and better services, as well as intensified pressures to resolve conflicts arising from a complex, fragmented, and differentiated urban society.

More and more Americans are becoming aware of the basic dimensions of urbanization in their society. A rapidly growing population is concentrated in metropolitan areas. In 1970, of the 205 million inhabitants of the United States, 140 million lived in the nation's 230 metropolitan areas. The two dozen regions with a million or more residents held approximately half of this metropolitan population. Metropolitan areas accounted for more than four-fifths of the population growth of the United States between 1950 and 1970; and almost all of this increase occurred at the outer reaches of the metropolis. Many of the older cities, particularly in the larger metropolitan areas of the Northeast and Midwest, either failed to grow or lost population during the fifties and sixties. During the 1960's alone, St. Louis lost 142,000 residents for a 19 per cent decline, Cleveland 137,000 for a 16 per cent drop, and Detroit 177,000 for an 11 per cent loss. A massive exodus of white families from the cities and migration to the cities from the black regions of the South and depressed areas such as Appalachia have significantly changed the composition of the population in older urban centers such as New York, Philadelphia, and Chicago.

The underlying causes of the growing dominance of a metropolitan way of life and its spread outward from the traditional urban centers also are readily apparent. The components of a complex, modern economy gravitate to the metropolis. Metropolitan areas account for more than three-quarters of the nation's bank deposits and industrial jobs. Agricultural mechanization generates a steady stream of rural migrants to the city. Economic growth provides an increasing proportion of the population with the capital needed to partake in the outward march from the city. Prosperity also encourages people to have larger families, which quickens the quest for enlarged living space. By liberating urban development from fixed transportation systems, the automobile and the public highway have opened vast tracts of land to new settlement. The movement of jobs also has been centrifugal. Retail and service establishments have followed the population outward. Technological innovation and the transportation revolution have produced voracious demands for space for manufacturing facilities that the older industrial areas have been unable to satisfy. The result has been a new kind of urban society, a world of the housing development, the shopping center, and the industrial park, a world tied together by the automobile and the expressway, and a world increasingly oblivious to the urban core.

Many voices have protested against the outward thrust of the metropolis and the concomitant decay of the inner city. The transformation of the economic, social, cultural, and intellectual centers of the nation into vast slums and tinderboxes of racial conflict is an appalling prospect to partisans of the American city. Social critics decry the conformity and monotony of the mass-produced, homogeneous suburb. Conservationists condemn greedy consumption of land by subdevelopments, shopping centers, and superhighways. Civic leaders despair at the prospect of an auto-dominated "spread city" twice the size of the present 7,000 square mile New York region. California planners nervously watch bulldozers turn orchards and citrus groves into vast, formless "slurbs."

Those who value the city and its culture insist that there are alternatives to the emerging diffused metropolis. Since World War II, planners have sought to revitalize the central city with widely heralded programs for public housing, urban renewal, improved public transportation, and the overhaul of outmoded systems of public education and welfare. An older generation of urban reformers has viewed the decentralized political system as a primary cause of unplanned growth, fiscal inequities, spreading slums, and deteriorating transit systems. To cure these ills, as well as to redirect the development of the metropolis, the traditional reformers have sought metropolitan planning to control land use and coordinate developmental activities, and regional government to tackle areawide problems and equalize the resources of city and suburb. A newer generation of urban activists, on the other hand, emphasizes massive infusions of federal aid and decentralization and community control within the city as the best means of reviving the older urban centers.

What are the prospects of reversing, or even checking, the present trend of urban development? Practically nonexistent, argues York Willbern in his analysis of urban growth and metropolitan dispersal. Once set in motion the forces of decentralization appear inexorable to Willbern. In the absence of evidence that governmental policy can reverse the choices of the marketplace, choices that overwhelmingly favor continued dispersion, he questions the strength of the political system as a major factor in shaping the urban environment. The interplay of the forces of dispersion, Willbern concludes, withers away the city conceived as the center of urban activity.

A strong dissenting note comes from the late Charles Abrams, who argues that a change in public policies and priorities can save the city from further decline. Abrams concedes the attractions of the suburbs and the liabilities of the older core areas. But he contends that the current trends are as much a product of governmental action and inaction as they are the result of the "natural" forces of urban growth and change. Because Abrams sees the city and its culture as unique, indispensable, and irreplaceable, he urges new directions and new commitments to preserve the city as the center of variety, vitality, and creativity in American society.

To Raymond Vernon, an economist who directed the ambitious New York Metropolitan Region Study, assessments such as that of Abrams characterize the wishful thinking of the small minority of Americans who value the city. In Vernon's view, the public by and large ignores the prophets of metropolitan doom because it correctly associates the emerging metropolis with personal betterment. Only the economic, social, and intellectual elites, with their close ties to the traditional city, he contends, have been seriously disadvantaged by the changing pattern of urban growth. Although the protests of a small but articulate minority dominate the debate on the metropolis, the vast majority quietly adjusts and advances. As a result, pressures on the political system for more of the same are likely to be far more influential than the cries for a halt to the outward march of urban development and a rebirth of the city.

Vernon's analysis, like many produced in the late 1950's and early 1960's, underestimates the importance of racial conflict in the increasingly segregated metropolis. Perhaps no factor altering the urban landscape has more significance for metropolitan politics than race. Unlike other Americans, blacks have not shared widely in the benefits that have flowed from the outward spread of urban development. As the report of the National Advisory Commission on Civil Disorders (the Kerner Commission) illustrates, most blacks have participated only in the first stage of urbanization, the movement to the city. Whereas they have followed other immigrants into the oldest and least desirable sections of the city, few have followed their predecessors out to the more attractive neighborhoods on the periphery of the city or to the suburbs beyond. Instead, most blacks have been contained in segregated neighborhoods by inadequate income and racial antipathy, the former itself a product in part of the latter.

Allan Spear's account of Black Chicago reminds us that racial ghettos in American cities are new only in their scale and number. Despite the enormous increase in the number of blacks in Chicago during the past half century, its ghetto has changed little since it developed at the end of the nineteenth century in response to the systematic exclusion of blacks from the mainstream of life in Chicago.

White hostility continues to prevent most blacks from following in the footsteps of the Irish, Italians, Jews, and Poles whose outward trek in search of space, privacy, status, and opportunity has done so much to alter the landscape of the metropolis. Nowhere is such hostility more pervasive than among the white ethnic groups of moderate and low income who are left in the older cities. Once, these groups and their ethnically differentiated neighborhoods provided the base for urban political machines. Today, as Jerome Skolnick points out in his report to the National Commission on the Causes and Prevention of Violence, many white ethnic city dwellers are alienated and insecure, resentful of governmental policies that they see as advancing black interests at their expense, and fearful of apparent threats to their jobs, neighborhoods, and schools. In almost every city, white resistance and black resentment encourage separatists of both races and foster the polarization of politics in the city and the metropolis along racial lines.

York Willbern

THE TRANSFORMATION OF THE URBAN COMMUNITY

The linguistic and historical relationship between the words "city" and "civilization" has often been noted. The present state of American cities and that great part of the civilization of this country which revolves around their functioning and well-being, have provoked a rapidly growing volume of interest and concern.

Most literate people are reasonably familiar with the gross outlines of urban population movements. They know that urban areas have increased in population much more rapidly than rural areas, that the great bulk of this growth has been in areas of metropolitan character, and that suburban areas have been growing much more rapidly than have central cities. None of us, however, yet understands adequately the implications and consequences of these massive redistributions of the population.

We are participating, in my opinion, in two revolutions, one imposed upon the other, and the meaning of the second is partially obscured by the fact that the first, much older, revolution is continuing even as the second develops.

The first of these revolutions, of course, is the rise of an urban way of life. The second is its diffusion and dispersal over the countryside. The first has been in the making in Europe and in this country for several hundred years. It was in nearly full flower when Johnson and Boswell were enjoying the fleshpots of eighteenth century London. This revolution was based on the rise of trade and on the growth of industry. The new technologies which promoted specialization, manufacturing, and great increases in the interchange of goods and services have continued and been accelerated in the last two generations. They are now world-wide in their impact; the non-Western world as well as the West is struggling today with the gains and costs of these changes. Those who are staggered by the problems of urbanization in this country are really shaken when they see Tokyo or Calcutta. Tokyo, the world's most populous city, has no sewerage for eighty per cent of the metropolitan

Reprinted from *The Withering Away of the City* (University, Ala.: University of Alabama Press, 1964), pp. 9–33, with the permission of the author and the publisher.

5

area. In Calcutta two-thirds of a million people have no home but the public streets and alleys.[1]

These urbanizing forces continue unabated in this country. The proportion of the national population living in areas defined by the Census Bureau as "metropolitan" increased from 58 per cent in 1950 to 63 per cent in 1960. The proportions continue to grow and will probably reach 50 or 75 per cent before the Census Bureau decides that it is unable any longer to fabricate definitions to demarcate a population which is almost universally metropolitanized.

The second revolution is much newer and has been much more strongly felt in this country than anywhere else. This is the outward explosion of our urban centers. It has several causes, of course. One is the desire of families, particularly families with children, for detached dwellings on substantial plots of land. Sir Frederic J. Osborn, dean of British planners and editor of *Town and Country Planning*, emphasized this desire in a recent address to American planning officials, and in so doing raised a question of crucial importance to the continuation and welfare of large cities. He indicated that the most disastrous shortcoming associated with city size is "the lack of sufficient space inside cities for good family dwellings with private yards or gardens, for recreation, for industrial efficiency, and for the vegetative surroundings and the quiet and simple beauty man needs and desires for the fullness of life."

> Relative unconsciousness of this aspect of the urban problem surprises me in all countries, including my own, because the most conspicuous cause of the "metropolitan explosion" is the spontaneous quest by more and more urban families, as net incomes rise, for the family house standing in its own yard. The outward movement of the well-off is nothing new; what is new is the spread of wealth to far more numerous classes who can afford what Susannah's husband provided for her in Babylon and great senators took for themselves in ancient Rome — a suburban home in a garden. . . . Such environments reflect a universal natural desire that man indulges wherever and whenever he becomes prosperous and free.

> Admittedly, there are some genuine addicts of high urban culture to whom space and green surroundings make little appeal — types who like to live in city centres with their rich assemblies of theatres, concert halls, art galleries, restaurants, night clubs, snack bars, and hamburger stands — and are reassured by the bustle of crowds, traffic noises, flashing signs, and the insistent impact on their senses of commercial vitality. I do not deplore the existence of these types, though I suspect that their contribution to our culture is over valued. But they are a tiny minority. . . .[2]

[1] *New York Times*, Dec. 17, 1961, p. 40; Paul N. Ylvisaker, address to the World Traffic Engineering Conference, Washington, D.C., Aug. 21, 1961.

[2] Frederic J. Osborn, "The Conqueror City," *Town and Country Planning*, XXIX (Apr., 1961), 141.

This view is, of course, greatly at odds with that suggested by Mrs. Jane Jacobs in a book which is currently attracting a great deal of attention among students of urbanism.[3] If the figures on population movement are an accurate indication of the desires of people for home environments, the evidence certainly supports Sir Frederic's view much more strongly than that of Mrs. Jacobs.

A good many technological developments have made this dispersion of urban housing relatively easy. Reliance upon electric power and the ease of power transmission, telephone lines, septic tanks, and similar developments bring to widely scattered houses many of the conveniences and amenities once possible only in very closely settled cities.

A development of social technology — the long-term, monthly payment mortgage loan with low interest rates — has greatly facilitated the spread of American families into single-family detached dwellings. The growth of credit arangements of this type has certainly been encouraged and fostered by national legislation. It can be argued that the nature of the urban residential patterns of this generation has been shaped very substantially by FHA and similar governmental programs. The overwhelming political support for these programs, however, and the existence of parallel non-governmental developments indicate clearly that these credit socialization devices have probably been more the product than the cause of the social and economic forces at work.

If the basic desire for detached dwellings and space is one cause of the dispersion, another and very important cause is the appearance and practically universal use of the automobile in this country. We now have available, for most individuals, personalized rapid transit. The customary reaction to the automobile of Mrs. Jacobs and others who admire the congestion of dense urban settlement is to wish it would go away.

The impact of the automobile revolution is newer than many of us realize; its outlines are only now beginning to emerge. The last decade was the first in which it was fully operative; the 1960 census returns gave figures which indicate some of the results on a nationwide basis. Automobiles began to be widespread in the 1920's, but too little time had as yet passed for really basic changes in ways of living and spatial relationships. In the 1930's the great economic depression overshadowed and hampered adjustments to the new technology; the 1940's brought another overpowering circumstance, the war and its aftermath, to mask and postpone the basic changes. They hit us full force in the 1950's, but a decade is a short time for a social revolution. The greatest public works enterprise in the history of mankind, our national system of expressways, which will probably give the automobile age its greatest boost since the

---

[3] Jane Jacobs, *The Death and Life of Great American Cities* (New York: Random House, 1961).

Model T Ford, is just beginning. I am indebted to Harlan Cleveland for a statistic which he considered the most interesting of a recent year: we now have enough automotive vehicles in operation in this country for every man, woman, and child in the population to ride comfortably and simultaneously in the front seats.

It is difficult for us to realize that this new revolution may have a social impact comparable to that of the first. The basic purpose of a city is the facilitation of interchange — the interchange of goods through trade and merchandising, of labor and services in industrial and service enterprises, of messages and ideas in financial and political and cultural activities. When the means of interchange are drastically altered, the nature of the city must also be drastically altered.

In the large cities of a century ago, population was tightly concentrated. Concentration was necessary, in order for people to get from home to work and school and shop and engage in the other complex exchanges of a city. When each individual and most of the goods move from place to place within the urban environment in a vehicle weighing more than a ton and capable of moving economically at the rate of a mile a minute, the old patterns of settlement are technologically obsolete and will inevitably be changed. To achieve for a given population the same facility of circulation that the older concentrated cities had for pedestrian, horse-drawn, or even rail traffic, the modern city requires a land area many times greater. When movement and interchange were pedestrian and horse-drawn, an efficient area for a population of 200,000 might be about four square miles,[4] for 200,000 people now, on a one or two persons per car basis (increasingly the normal pattern), the most efficient area might well be 100 square miles.

Many of the great cities of the world outside the United States are experiencing the integrating revolution, with relatively little evidence yet of the disintegrating one. Perhaps they may avoid the second. A Soviet economist, watching Americans coming to work one-in-a-car is supposed to have said "we'll never make that mistake — that is, if we can help it."[5]

In this country, however, disintegrating forces are moving at a rapid pace. The area north of the Ohio River and east from Chicago and St. Louis contains the urban heart of the United States. There were in this area in 1950 a dozen cities with more than half a million inhabitants each. What happened to the population of these cities in the decade of the 1950's, a decade in which urbanization continued apace? Every one of them lost, rather than gained, in population. While the urban area, the metropolitan area, in each case grew very substantially in population, not a single one of the large central cities in this area increased. If this is

4 In 1850 Philadelphia had a population of 121,000 and an area of two square miles.
5 Ylvisaker, p. 18.

what is happening to the oldest, best established American cities, will Birmingham and Indianapolis, or even Houston and Los Angeles, be far behind?

The famous Regional Plan of 1929 for the New York metropolitan area projected a population by 1965 of 21 million people living in approximately 1,000 square miles of the region. In 1960, five years before the projected date, there were actually only 16 million people, but the urbanized area constituted 2,000 square miles, twice the projected amount.[6]

CHANGE IN POPULATION, 1950–1960, MAJOR CITIES IN NORTHEAST AND MIDWEST

	1950	1960	Amount change
Baltimore	949,708	939,024	— 10,684
Boston	801,444	697,197	—104,247
Buffalo	580,132	532,759	— 47,373
Chicago	3,620,962	3,550,404	— 70,558
Cincinnati	503,998	502,550	— 1,448
Cleveland	914,808	876,050	— 38,758
Detroit	1,849,568	1,670,144	—179,424
New York	7,891,957	7,781,984	—109,973
Philadelphia	2,071,605	2,002,512	— 69,093
Pittsburgh	676,806	604,332	— 72,474
St. Louis	856,796	750,026	—106,770
Washington, D.C.	802,178	763,956	— 38,222

Source: *Statistical Abstract of the United States*, 1962, pp. 22–23.

The most recent major study of the New York metropolitan area, which Raymond Vernon and his associates made for the same Regional Plan Association, came to the following conclusion:

As one surveys the outward shift of the population in the New York Metro-politan Region and of the consumer activities tied to them, the forces behind the shift seem near-inexorable. Basic technological developments in trans-portation and deepseated changes in consumer wants appear to lie behind the phenomenon. Here and there one sees evidences of preferences which breast the main tide; the occasional reappearance of a disillusioned exur-banite in his former city haunts, the gradual growth of apartments-in-the-city for the very rich — these are phenomena whose impact cannot be overlooked. The bigger risk, however, is that their implications for the future will be ex-aggerated rather than overlooked. Short of some fundamental alteration in consumer outlook or in urban environment, the trends for the future seem

[6] Paul Windels, "The Region — Past, Present, and Future," *Metropolis 1985*, a report from a conference held at Arden House, March 1, 1961.

likely to represent a continuation — even a speed up — of the dispersive tendencies of the past.[7]

This is what they predict in the text of the book. After coming to this conclusion, however, Mr. Vernon inspected the 1960 census returns and found that he had been short of the mark. The city core has declined in population more than he anticipated, and the outlying areas have expanded more rapidly. In a footnote attached after the report was completed, but before the volume was finally published, he confessed that "in general, the dispersive population forces in the Region seem even stronger than those built into our model."[8]

Even the census figures summarizing the growth in the outlying portions of metropolitan areas and the losses or much slower growth in the urban core may understate the dispersion. For example, the Census Bureau defines the Indianapolis metropolitan area as Marion County. This area increased in population by 24 per cent between 1950 and 1960, a very substantial rate of growth. But the counties immediately to the north, east, south, and west of Marion County, not included in the census-defined metropolitan area, had rates of growth of 40, 30, 67, and 65 per cent, respectively. The growth of these counties immediately beyond the census metropolitan area limits is not considered in the statistics to be suburban growth, but the percentage growth has often been even greater than that of the suburban areas *within* the official metropolitan area.

During the decades when the urbanizing forces were strongest, and before the forces of dispersal had begun to accumulate, the percentage of the population living in the central city of an urbanizing area increased substantially. This percentage has tended to decrease as the second revolution has become mixed with the first. In the accompanying chart are some representative figures from three cities at which I have been looking intensively.

In each of the three cities the central city reached its peak percentage in 1920 or 1930, along with the initial surge of the automobile revolution, and has since declined at a rapid and ordinarily accelerating rate. New York City constituted the largest percentage, in population, of the counties composing its metropolitan area in 1910; the percentage has been dropping ever since. The peak in Birmingham was 1930.

In gross national figures the greatest concentration of metropolitan population inside central cities occurred between 1920 and 1930. Until 1920 the central cities were growing faster than their metropolitan rings;

[7] Raymond Vernon, *Metropolis 1985* (Cambridge: Harvard University Press, 1960), p. 165.
[8] *Ibid.*, p. 222.

PERCENTAGE OF COUNTY POPULATION IN CENTRAL CITY
THREE CITIES, 1850–1960

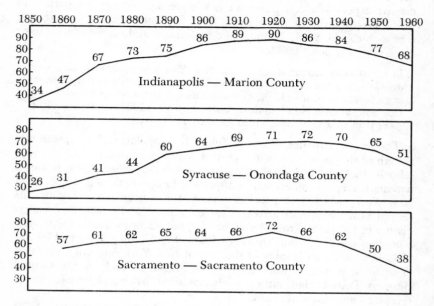

beginning with the census of 1930, the fringe growth has been faster than the central growth, and the gap widens with each census. During the 1950–1960 decade, the central cities of the 212 metropolitan areas of the country increased 1.5 per cent in population within their 1950 boundaries, and added another 9.2 per cent by annexation, for a total increase of 10.7 per cent, and, as I have indicated, many of the biggest and oldest actually lost population. The remaining, or fringe portion of the metropolitan areas, increased 48.6 per cent. The more than 90 per cent of the land area outside the metropolises saw its population increase by 11 per cent.

It is roughly accurate to say that one-third of the American population is within the central cities of metropolitan areas, and this segment is increasing at the rate of 1 per cent per year, almost entirely by annexation. (This increase, as we shall see, is concentrated in a few states.) Another third is in the metropolitan fringes, and here the rate of increase is 4 per cent per year, in spite of the bites taken from it by annexation into the central cities. The remaining third of the population is in the rest of the country, and this segment also is increasing at the rate of about 1 per cent per year.

Nor is this diffusion of urban life over the countryside to be limited by the commuting range, expanding though that range may be through massive expenditures on expressways. We are not witnessing a pattern in which people seek out spaciousness for living, but return to a congested core each day for work. The jobs also seek space, and manufacturers want space as well as home builders.

In recent years, manufacturers in the New York Metropolitan Region have dramatically increased their use of land. Our surveys indicate that the amount of plot space per worker in the post war suburban plants of the Region is over four times as great as in suburban plants built before 1922. In the new plants more than an acre of land is used for every ten workers.[9]

The service activities, of course, follow the population. The spectacular growth of shopping centers, the great demands for extensive sites for new schools, the need to locate all kinds of enterprises where there is ample parking space, are indications of dispersion in economic activity. Even in New York, which has peculiar reasons for concentration because its central business district serves in large measure as the central business district of the nation, the jobs are moving out about as fast as the people, according to the Vernon studies.[10] Frank W. Herring, Deputy Director of Comprehensive Planning of the Port of New York Authority, says that "growth in journey-to-work travel is no longer focused on the Central Business District, but rather is characterized by intersuburban travel, reverse commuting and the like."[11]

The net flow of commuting is, of course, still toward the center, and it will probably continue to be for a long time. The Vernon studies indicate that the core of the New York area now has about half the population of the region and two-thirds of the jobs. According to their projections, by 1985 the core will have only one-third the population but will probably still have half the jobs.

The dispersion of employment may be greater in other centers than in New York. In the Chicago area (where the city of Chicago constitutes a larger portion of its metropolitan area than does New York), the city's share of manufacturing employment in the area fell from 84 per cent in

9 *Ibid.*, pp. 116–117.

10 New York is to be contrasted to London and Tokyo, its two largest competitors as the world urban centers. In both of these, the population increase is at the edges while the jobs continue to be relatively concentrated in the center. Paul Ylvisaker reports that land in the heart of Tokyo is four times as expensive as land in the heart of Manhattan. The chief reason for the difference is almost certainly the difference in the state of the automotive revolution.

11 "Metropolitan Growth and Metropolitan Travel Patterns," a paper presented at the annual meeting of the Highway Research Board, Committee on Urban Research, Jan. 12, 1961.

1920 to 81 per cent in 1940 and to 72 per cent in 1957.[12] A continuation of this accelerating trend would suggest that the city of Chicago now has less than 70 per cent of the industrial jobs in the area, compared to about 58 per cent of the people.

Dispersal of manufacturing activity from the inner zones of the central city was the dominant trend in plant location throughout the United States in 1950–1960. In Chicago, typically, the greatest gains in activity took place in an arc ten to fifteen miles from the central business district. The greatest losses occurred within five miles of the core. Warehouses, in particular, moved from inner zones to the periphery, situating themselves close to areas of population growth and expanded manufacturing activity. To call this process suburbanization may be too much of a simplification.[13]

In many cities of smaller size, the great developments in industrialization, and in jobs, occur beyond the city limits. The new industries tend to locate in industrial parks, or on spacious sites well outside the cities. In Syracuse, New York, for example, the city's proportion of the population of Onondaga County has been declining for more than twenty years, but its proportion of the assessed valuation of the county has been declining even more rapidly than its proportion of the population, indicating that productive property, which has higher assessments than residences, has been growing faster outside the city than inside.[14]

Some observers argue that the tide of movement out of central cities into suburban and rurban areas can be checked and reversed by improved mass transit, renewal of the older urban areas, and various other remedial measures. Efforts in this direction may be expected to continue. It seems likely that policy changes may affect the character of the movement somewhat, but the overwhelming bulk of the evidence makes the outward movement seem, as Vernon and his associates put it in their study of New York, "inexorable."

Most of our accumulated physical capital is in urban areas. The sweeping changes in the technology of settlement and interchange which have resulted in the shifting populations have a great impact on the maintenance and utility of these accumulated investments. The existence of these great investments, both in physical facilities and in skills and habits, constitutes a great drag upon adaption to technological innovation. Farm homes and land holdings and habits of work have continued

---

[12] Northeastern Illinois Metropolitan Area Planning Commission, *Social Geography of Metropolitan Chicago* (Chicago, 1960), p. 20.

[13] Mark Reinberg, *Growth and Change in Metropolitan Areas and Their Relation to Metropolitan Transportation: A Research Summary* (Evanston, Ill.: The Transportation Center, Northwestern University, 1961), p. 10.

[14] Roscoe C. Martin, Frank Munger, and others, *Decisions in Syracuse* (Bloomington: Indiana University Press, 1961), pp. 23 and 29.

long after becoming technologically obsolescent; this is the basic cause of our so-called "farm problem." We now have similar lags because of the investments in outmoded urban plants. We live, however, in a relatively affluent age, an age when we can make massive continuing new investments, even at the price of losing full use of much of the old. Furthermore, our society is increasingly mobile, not only geographically but in capacity to shift patterns of behavior. Substitution of investment for many reasons, in addition to the changing technology of communication and movement, goes on continually.

With new investments being made as a matter of course, the investors (whether in productive plant, or in patterns of service, or in housing and ways of life) are able to locate in better conformity to the technological patterns of the present and future. The pressures to maintain and adapt and renew the center which have characterized European cities for many generations are far less demanding here. A merchant who sees opportunities for growth in an expanding urban environment, and who has or can get capital to invest, is much less likely to use it in rebuilding or refurnishing and improving a downtown store location. Instead he will join a new regional shopping center near a freeway interchange where there can be six square feet of parking space for every square foot of selling space.

So far, in this country the forces of the second, suburbanizing revolution have been balanced in large measure by the continuing forces of the first, urbanizing revolution. The massive forces for dispersal of investment have been accompanied by such great need for the use of all the possible capital available in urban areas that both the new and much of the old have been necessary.

The physical decay and obsolescence of the older investment have not yet resulted in great decreases in property values. In the last thirty years the rate of investment in new housing units and new industrial and business sites in urban areas has not exceeded the rate of influx from the remote rural communities. To be more explicit, although over a million housing units a year have been built in urban fringe areas for the last decade, as yet comparatively few vacancies have appeared in the deteriorating housing units of the central cities. The new units serve as additions to the total urban supply, not as replacements. The accumulated overcrowding of the depression and war years and the continuing immigration from rural parts of the country have kept the demand for housing units at a sufficient intensity that rental income from slum property is still highly remunerative. As fast as the inhabitants of the gray area (or "mice country," as Robert Wood calls it) have moved out to the suburbs, the Negro, Puerto Rican, and hill country farm people have crowded in to the decaying houses of the old city. Reductions in population of the central cities, now definitely begun, have made it possible so far only to clear some land to provide more room for automobiles to maneuver and be stored and to reduce somewhat the doubling up and overcrowding; vacancy rates in slum housing are still not high enough to worry the landlords. There are some indications that new housing construction has begun to catch up with the urban population growth. As to the deteriorating central city housing in New York, Vernon suggests that "no projection which we would consider realistic contemplates an increase in the demand for such housing in the Region anywhere near as great as the prospective increase in supply."[15] If vacancies in the slums begin to mount (as is already true in some decaying commercial and industrial properties) reductions in income potential may cause the values of the decaying central city properties to fall significantly.

Some forces do exist which tend to offset the disintegrated effects of transportation changes and the desire of people for detached dwellings. One is the great value for many small enterprises of what the economists call "external economies." These are the specialist services which a large enterprise may provide for itself but which a small enterprise can best get from other suppliers. Although these may be interchanged even in a dispersed, less congested locational pattern, there remain some advantages in the greater proximity of denser locations.

Second, and much more important, some activities in our complex society are best carried on where there is frequent and convenient opportunity for face-to-face contact with a variety of other people: the financial institutions, for example; the central corporate offices; the advertising business. Here, intelligence is perhaps the chief item of exchange, and it can best be exchanged on the basis of frequent conferences, luncheons, and personal contacts. For this reason the shining towers of central Manhattan continue to rise although much of the surrounding area is deteriorating.

The central business district of New York has peculiar advantages, of course, because it performs so many of these functions for the whole nation and even the world. At the same time, the proportion of our society engaged in the white-collar, highly interpersonal communication activities is increasing so extensively that there are good economic prospects for the core of central business districts of many of our cities, even though the fabrication and distribution of goods may be continually dispersed.

Third, some industries need large quantities of relatively low-wage labor. Since the lowest income groups tend to live in the central city, and relatively near the center, and since these groups are somewhat less mobile, it is sometimes advantageous for lower-wage industries to stay near the population and transit center. In Chicago the industries showing the lowest decentralizing tendencies (though even here the net movement was outward) were textiles and apparel, lumber and furniture, and food products, all of which are comparatively low-wage operations.[16]

A fourth centralizing factor may be suggested, but its actual impact is not easy to predict. This is the almost certain great increase in the number of two-house families. Two-car families are now commonplace in this country, and two-house families are expected to become so. Already perhaps a million of the fifty million family units have more than one place of residence, and these million tend to be the high-income, high-status families whose patterns of life are copied by others as quickly as they can afford it. If one residence offers almost complete isolation, many families may plump in favor of the attractions and conveniences of high-density living for the other residence and use their automobiles as much or more for week-end as for daily commuting. The apparent preference of people with children for detached dwellings, however, along with the continually growing reliance upon the automobile even for frequent movements during the day, leads to considerable doubt that the rise in dual dwellings will result in more than a marginal integrating force.

How much can public policy shape and guide and direct these patterns of investment and of settlement? Was it government's cheap land policy which led to the rapid agricultural expansion of the early nineteenth century, or did migration and settlement force the government to follow the policy it did? Was it governmental promotion of the transcontinental railroads later in the century, and the Panama Canal early in this century, that linked the two coasts into an economic unit, or did the economic ties and links make the governmental public works enterprises necessary? Was it the massive public water system that made possible the settlement of so many people in and around New York, and the development and operation of the subway system that enabled them to focus such a concentration of economic activity in Manhattan, or were these great public enterprises produced rather haltingly to meet the necessities of the developing situation? No simple answer is possible to such chicken-and-egg priority questions, but recent searching economic studies of metropolitan regions suggest very strongly that, as Charles Adrian summarizes it:

> Both local and regional (metropolitan) governments tend to follow the economic pattern rather than to lead it. Governmental innovations that complement the decisions of the market place are likely to succeed; others are not.[17]

---

[16] Reinsberg, pp. 18–19.

[17] Charles R. Adrian, "Metropology: Folklore and Field Research," *Public Administration Review*, XXI (Summer, 1961), 155.

. . . [T]he evidence seems clear that . . . our farms and small towns are being abandoned in a great movement into an urban way of life. At the same time the city, in the sense of a tightly knit corporate community with a clear distinction between its high-density living and the rural countryside, is fast becoming so blurred at the edges as to be incapable of operational definition. There seems little to block an endless expansion of urban or semi-urban ways of life over vast areas of the countryside outside our traditional city limits. Instead of distinct cities with distinguishable centers and edges somewhat like a fried egg, we seem likely to be approaching in large segments of our country a condition somewhat like that of a thin layer of scrambled eggs spread over much of the platter. The more urban we become, the more shaky become both the concept and the reality of the city.

Charles Abrams

THE CITY AT BAY

The history of civilization from Memphis, Egypt, to Memphis, Tennessee, is recorded in the rise or demise of cities. It is the story of Rome and its million people in the first century reduced to a city of 17,000 in the fourteenth; of the scourges and famines of Paris and the Renaissance that made it the intellectual capital of Europe; of the heap of ruins that was London fifty years after the Roman evacuation, its rise under mercantilism, its desolation by war, and its resurgence to the London of today.

In our own era, the world's cities are witnessing their greatest surge in man's history. Everywhere, hordes of people are leaving the hinterlands in

From pp. 3–18 in *The City Is the Frontier*, by Charles Abrams. Copyright © 1965 by Charles Abrams. Reprinted by permission of Harper & Row, Publishers, Inc.

quest of the city's opportunities, its excitements, and its way of life. From 1800 to 1950, the proportion of people living in cities with more than 20,000 people leaped from 2.4 per cent to 21 per cent. Our civilization is becoming urban, and the advance into cities is one of the most spectacular social phenomena of our time. The city has become the frontier.

The United States is also experiencing the impact of urbanization. Whether they live in the city proper or a few miles from its borders, the nation's people are becoming an urban people. But while 70 per cent of the nation's population now lives in urban areas, most of its great cities, which are the cores of these areas, have been declining both in population and influence. This, too, is a phenomenon, and no other country in our time or at any time has experienced a similar contradiction.

In 1937, Congress authorized a small housing program, and in 1949, it supplemented this with a program aimed at renewing its cities. These were the first real signs of a federal responsibility for the improvement of America's urban environments. In terms of money, the two programs were of minor significance. But in political terms, they were revolutionary, for under the nation's unique political system, cities were always the creatures of the states, and for the federal government to deal directly with their problems — even if undertaken with the states' technical consent — was an innovation and a significant exercise of the federal government's new and still undefined welfare power.

That the urban renewal program, moreover, should have gained both its name and its current impetus in the United States is an anomaly, for the attitudes toward cities that prevail in the Old World had never expressed themselves in the American story. Almost from its beginnings as a nation, America's cities fell into low esteem. Thomas Jefferson feared they would harbor Europe's rabble and become "pestilential to the morals, the health and the liberties of man." During the century that followed Jefferson's death, cities and political corruption were held to be virtually synonymous. It was in the cities that nativism and anti-alien movements rose with each immigrant influx. The farmer inveighed against the city's rising power, while the fledgling West blasted the city's capitalists as the enemies of American progress.

Nor had our cities won more honor in our own era. An O. Henry or an E. B. White might be sensitive to the city's values, Carl Sandburg might chant of Chicago as the city with the big shoulders, while H. L. Mencken could see New York as "the icing on the pie called Christian civilization." But they have been a small voice in the anticity clamor — and as new minorities keep pouring into the central cities, they are again being defamed as the nests of mobs, the seats of slums, and the dens of crime. The important role they played in the nation's development and the role they still play in its progress are being obscured as the strong undercurrents generated by the racial problem are making themselves felt.

The American attitude toward cities contrasts sharply with attitudes in the Old World. For thousands of years, man had built cities and idealized them. Aristotle could find the common life for the noble end only in Athens, and Socrates would never leave it for the trees. Voltaire could see the London of his time as the rival of ancient Athens. Europe's culture and progress continue to this day to be reflected in its Paris, Rome, Geneva, Amsterdam, and Vienna. Urbanity was always associated with urban life, while suburban and suburbanity were contemptuous slams at the inferior ways of the provinces. But the flight to suburbia in America has taken on the semblance of a flight from scourge.

This contrast in attitudes toward cities between the Old World and the New might be partly explained by the existence of a European urban culture that had been well rooted long before the industrial revolution had blemished it. The words city, civility, and civilization shared a common root. Antiquity and tradition in Europe stood their ground against the contaminations of industrialization, and when social problems festered, they were met by social reforms, not flight. People from all walks of life shared the adventure of living in the city and continued seeing its virtues above its blight, its surviving grace over its rising slums. Similar traditions and cultural ties to a past never gained root in an America whose cities were springing up almost overnight. Most of its buildings are of recent origin and were built for speculation, not use. For more than a century, the city's elite had been terrified by the ever-flowing hordes of foreigners who kept edging toward their moorings. A lasting pride in place could not exist for long in a country constantly washed by massive waves of an unwelcome poor and by a society on the move.

What, therefore, are the reasons behind the current effort to renew American cities? Are they earning a new acknowledgment of their values comparable to those of London or Paris? Can the current urban renewal effort salvage them? Or is it just another passing flare in the political spectacle, to be forgotten when it has run its course?

American cities embrace a variety of categories. They are large and small, trade centers and industrial centers, rich and poor. They are as heterogeneous as the people who inhabit them. In assessing the state and fate of American cities, one should distinguish between polymorphic cities like New York or Chicago and cities like Gary, Detroit, Grand Rapids, or Fall River that owe their lives mainly to one or two industries and might die with their departure. There are American capital cities that never change anything but their governors, cities that are no more than languid milltowns, cities that have more cows than people, cities dominated by the aging, cities with most of their houses on wheels, cities

like Los Angeles that spread for miles and are still spreading, and one city
in California that supports its quick on the burial fees of its dead.

The Declining Central City

There are, however, a large number of cities in the United States that are
more or less similar in their troubles. They are principally the older
central cities that grew up in the first flush of America's industrial
revolution, have now aged, and are being challenged by the suburban
push on their peripheries. They are seeing the emigration of some of
their industries, their more affluent taxpayers, and their institutions.
Together they are still the pulse of America but a pulse that falters.
These cities include not only New York, Baltimore, Cleveland, Chicago,
San Francisco, Boston, Cincinnati, St. Louis, and Philadelphia, but also
hundreds of smaller cities such as Newark, New Haven, Trenton,
Norfolk, and Knoxville. They represent billions in investment and are
still the centers around which the surrounding populations and their new
communities are polarized.

For more than a century, these older cities were able to hold their own
against the invasion of Europe's poor, the anticity propaganda, the shift
of population to the west, and the gathering flesh on their peripheries.
They were small compact units, geared to foot and hoof, which happened
to be the only means of bringing people together. Immigration and births
met their labor needs and fed them more recruits than they lost by
exodus. Class patterns in these cities were not only buoyant but ebullient;
while the slum was disdained, the slum dweller was no captive to his
environment, and the Horatio Alger stories were not all fiction — a slum
immigrant or his boy, by taking an American haircut and learning the
language, could rise in a single generation from bootblack to owner of the
shoe company. Indeed, many did. Despite anti-alien movements, graft,
and corruption, these cities spawned the brain and brawn of the country.
The streak of vibrant land from Boston to Chicago not only became the
haven for the oppressed and hungry of Europe but America's great
belt-line that carried the fruits of its minds and machines to the world's
four corners.

The dawn of the twentieth century saw these cities spreading outward
to accommodate their swelling complement of rich and poor. The slums
which housed their poor were not always isolated from the main stream
of city life; and some, in fact, were at the city's center where the poor
could more conveniently serve their betters — fire their furnaces, launder
their cuffs, and fix their plumbing. Others were an hour or more from
work, the slum dweller paying the penalty of distance for his poverty.
City life contrasted sharply with the rural and village life in America's
hinterlands and with the peasant environment from which most immi-

grants came. Its impersonality was now a characteristic of the American milieu both in the city's center and on the fringe. Lord Bryce in 1921 described the American city as:

> a huge space of ground covered with houses, two or three square miles appropriated by the richer sort, fifteen or twenty, stretching out into the suburbs, filled with the dwellings of the poorer. . . . They [the poorer] were not members of a community, but an aggregation of human atoms, like grains of desert sand, which the wind sweeps hither and thither.[1]

The Effluent Society

The shift from reins to ignition had sparked more than the spark plug. As roads were cut into the farmlands, the peripheries overreached the poorer settlements on the outer precincts. Cities changed from self-contained trade centers into the cores of ever-expanding regions girded by independent suburban formations which the city could no longer swallow up. These outer areas were soon occupied by the burgeoning middle- and upper-income classes who sought its more open spaces, its free-standing houses, and its new life-styles. Forty years after Bryce's description, population in the suburban areas was increasing almost five times faster than in the central cities; and from 1950 to 1960, more than three-fourths of metropolitan growth had taken place outside the central areas. But forty-one out of sixty-two northeastern central cities had lost population, with fourteen of them losing more than 10 per cent. Among those losing population were nine central cities in the nation's eleven largest metropolitan areas. In the single decade 1950–1960, metropolitan counties outside such central cities showed a population increase of 61.7 per cent, while the central cities showed a population growth of only 1.5 per cent. It was apparent that the nation had become urban-suburban. It was apparent also that the central cities were becoming urban islands in an ever-expanding sea of suburban satellites. This spread of living areas and work locations is only an extension of a trend that started and accelerated with urbanization itself. It takes no longer to travel from the old city to the new suburb today than it once took to cover the distance between the city's central business district and some of its residential areas. But the disorganized pattern of the many small, political jurisdictions that surround the central cities is a relatively new and perplexing complication. Though dependent on the city, these formations have developed their own government apparatus and have been isolating themselves from the stream of problems that beset the region of which they are a part.

As the suburbs continued fanning out, some industries began to follow

[1] *Modern Democracies*, Macmillan, 1921, II, 108.

the population trend by settling where land was cheaper and where efficient one-story factories could be built. Skilled and white-collar workers bought homes there; the air was cleaner, and the surroundings better. Soon churches followed their parishioners, discount houses hawked their bargains on the freeways, and department stores moved into huge regional shopping centers on the roadsides, where a housewife could buy all her goods and gadgets with a minimum tax on her energies.

In the population reshuffle, some among the rich have preferred to remain ensconced in their urban mansions or in expensive new apartments safely insulated against unwelcome intrusions. The old big city also continued to harbor the elderly, the slum tenant, the single person, the widowed, the confirmed city dweller, the reclaimed exurbanite, and the atypical folk. In general, however, a new class formation had begun to transform America's social pattern. With few exceptions, Lord Bryce's generalization of the richer sort inhabiting the city and the poorer the outskirts was no longer true. The poor now live predominantly in the central city areas left behind by the once poor, the rising middle class, or the more opulent. Their ranks are being swelled by hordes of minorities, particularly Negroes, in quest of haven and a better break in life.

Other Causes of Central City Decline

The central cities are the products of the burgeoning system of private enterprise. Profit conditioned planning and housing standards; whatever city planning there was, was geared to the speculation urge. (The gridiron plan for New York City, which still dominates it more than 150 years later, had been chosen because "straight-sided and right-angled houses are the most cheap to build.") What the private builder built also had to fit the immigrant's purse, which meant crowding the land, providing no heat and only a single toilet for a whole tenement. But as higher standards were imposed in response to social pressures, the costs of new buildings rose, too; and the older run-down houses hung on because they were the only shelter the poor could afford. As for recreational facilities, a swath might be cut out here or there for a park or play space after private developments and people had already established their crude settlements.

The central cities had also been built for limited populations and services. The same three-man commission that had been set up in 1807 to plan New York City, for example, had thought it would be a "source of merriment" that it had planned for a "greater population than is collected on any spot on this side of China"; but only forty years later, the city's population had already doubled the estimate.

In laying out the cities, lots had been divided into small parcels of 20 or 25 by 100 feet. But with the advent of steel construction and the need for larger plots, assembling land for an economic parcel became a costly exercise in patience, luck, and cunning. It is no surprise, therefore, that the million or more acres being added to the urbanizing areas every year for homes and new settlements are mostly outside the central cities. There, a developer can more easily acquire 50 suburban acres from a single farmer-owner and develop his land as a unit. He might also build without more costly union labor, offer better mortgage terms, and find a ready market for the middle and upper class fleeing the cities.

There are a number of other problems that intensify the quest for the suburban alternative. Cities handle a daytime population 30 to 50 per cent greater than their residential population. During the rush hours, the automobile flow is often slowed down on the old city streets to the pace of the horse and sometimes the snail. Traffic snarls, lack of parking space, difficulties in loading and unloading, and lack of storage facilities add to business and personal frustrations. One estimate puts the cost of traffic jams at $5 billion annually in time and wages lost, extra fuel consumption and vehicle depreciation, and in lower tax yields and other costs. Besides being troublesome to business, traffic has also accentuated the fear of accidents to children. Sidewalks that were always inadequate for play are being narrowed to make room for the car, and the child tends dangerously to share its assigned preserve. The long distance to a safe recreational area, the trek to the local school past automobiles, and the specter of a child under a truck are enough to speed the exodus to the cul-de-sacs of suburbia.

It is, however, the influx of Negroes and other minorities into cities that has added a dimension to the problem which cannot be reckoned with easily. The Negro concentration in central cities is changing their social atmosphere and altering the racial composition in public schools. The white child is often a minority in the classroom, and the quality of teaching is not keeping pace with the growing imperatives. The increase in break-ins, muggings, and rioting and the failure of police action to cope with them has made more sections of the city unsafe, particularly at night. Other fears also play a part in the changing compositions of population and the flight from cities — fear of loss of social status, of neighborhood associations, and of property values.

Meanwhile the Hegira to the suburbs has drained from the city some desperately needed civic leadership, the presence of which had not only stabilized neighborhoods but had brought essential pressures on official-dom for reform. With continued immigration of the less privileged, mediocrity and corruption are again fixing their holds on some of the political apparatus; the poorer and the in-migrant are again becoming fair game for the opportunist.

While the city's social problems and its educational needs, pensions, and payrolls are rising, its springs of revenue are drying up. Only a generation ago, municipalities were collecting more taxes than the national and state governments combined. Their take, 52 per cent of the total in 1932, had dropped to 7.3 per cent by 1962. The capacity of the city's real estate to support the rising costs is becoming more limited with the outflow to the suburbs. From 1930 to 1963, for example, Boston raised its tax rate from $31 per thousand dollars of real estate assessment to almost $100, but in the same period, its real estate valuations had shrunk from $1.8 billion to $1.3 billion. A sharp rise in the real estate tax brings proportionate diminutions in value, while local sales taxes required to supplement property levies take about a billion dollars a year from taxpayers. Retail sales in the core of New York dropped from 69 per cent of the New York region in 1929 to 55 per cent in 1954. Suburban competition is a main reason, but the difference of $80 on a car or $12 on an air conditioner is not overlooked by the shopper. Limited in their capacity to tax, the cities are borrowing heavily, and thanks to the federal tax exemptions extended to the bond buyers, the volume of borrowings has soared.

The Fabulous Invalid

With all its troubles, the ailing central city is anything but dead. Some suffer more than others, while big cities like New York, San Francisco, Atlanta, or Chicago can take a beating and still show remarkable staying power. Although eight out of ten people are electing to settle on the fringe, some dwellings continue to rise in the center, and despite its troubles, New York City even experienced a spurt in apartment building in the 1960s; hotels, factories, executive offices, and new enterprises still see the central city's special advantages. The central city is changing, losing retail trade and manufactures; but it is still the primary source of skills, the main market for goods and ideas. It is the seat of business services, can still boast a large built-in consumer market, is a magnet for visitors, salesmen, and buyers; it provides a central place for banking, subcontractors, bargains, and for the spare parts without which the machine wheezes and goes dead. In an era of expanded government intervention, it provides more intimate contact with officials, proximity to import and export licenses, consuls, lawyers, banks, and accountants. Life insurance companies, wholesale trade, and newspapers continue in the city, and not all industries can afford to pull up stakes, move costly machinery, and gamble on recruiting talents in their new surroundings.

If the central city no longer attracts most of the newcomers, it serves a vital function for some of them and for many others. It has lights as well as shadows, savants as well as bums, and a host of attractions that include not only cabarets, twist emporia, and race tracks but opera, coffee houses, and theaters. The universities, fixed to the city, provide a cache of research and brain power. The museums, art galleries, and the central library are there, too. Though the sumptuous roadside inn is offering challenge, some talented chefs still practice their alchemy on the main streets. Many a fringe-dweller still looks to the central city for his job, and the variety of jobs in cities adds to his sense of confidence and independence. The rising young housewife turns to the city when she needs old andirons or a painting; and for the curious, a ramble past a Victorian mansion or an old Greek Revival loft may call up richer conversation than the best recipe for suburban icebox cake. Though age in America is still equated with obsolescence, some city sections are still capable of aging gracefully, if given the chance.

If the city's chaos is part of its planlessness, its contrasts and variety still offer relief from the sameness of suburbia and its greater exposure of one's personal life and idiosyncrasies. People still seek escape to the metropolises, crave contrast, look for occasional anonymity, and want to see more people without being seen. They do not get all this at three families to the acre, and there is a limit to what a round of cocktail parties can do for the suburban spirit. If the nation was just one sprawling network of suburbias, it would be a bore.

Fringe living does offer many advantages for families — home ownership, better air, more play space, and fewer tensions. But it is not so free of infirmities as to offer a lasting guarantee that the confirmed exurbanite may never return. The American family likes to move about and moving is not always the one-way trip suburbanward. The commuter railroad, with its waning schedules and service, is turning many an out-dweller inward; while toll bridges, highways, tunnels, and parking problems have become a heavier drag on him than on the city dweller, and if it is still tolerable today, it may be intolerable by 1975 when more than 225 million people will be weaving in and out of our urban areas in some 80 million automobiles. Add the dearth of maids and day laborers to make life easier (a by-product of suburban exclusion devices) and the housewife may yet be driven back to the city after the child is off to college or boarding school and the seven-room split-level has become a splitting headache. There is already some evidence that this is happening in a few of our larger cities.

Many a suburb, moreover, has still to pay for its new schools and services, and a suburbanite may give up the lawn in despair after looking at the tax bill. Nor are suburbanites immune against the social distortions and infiltrations of the very minorities who have driven them out of the city. They will try hard to remain exclusive but the availability of jobs for minorities in the suburbs, their yearning for home ownership, and the improvement in their incomes may well make the minority problem a factor in some suburbs as it is now a factor in the cities. The urbanization of the suburb may, therefore, bring some of the city's vexations to it without the compensations of the central city and its greater ability to take social challenges in stride.

In thirty-five years, 160 million people will be added to the population, and most of them will probably try to stake out a niche in the suburbs. Our urban and suburban population will double, and the land it occupies will double too. But the time is not far off when travel will have reached the maximum of human endurance, when a multiple dwelling may be all that is offered, and when many a suburb will be just another city with all of its headaches.

The pace of the continued drift outward will also hinge on whether each suburb can retain its exclusiveness, continue building good schools, hold its taxes down, and provide good services and social advantages. It will also depend on whether the fringe can provide enough of the amenities and interests the central city offers — theaters, efficiency units, more interesting people, more relief from dullness, and a larger sense of anonymity when one needs it. In short, the future of the fringe may depend on whether it can itself acquire some of the amenities of the core city or itself produce a big city replica that can cope with some of the same problems the big city faces. Thus, the core city, new or existing, will be on hand — to house the menials and the poor (if there will still be any), the migrant and the transient, the city's working mothers, the nondrivers and walkers, and the millions of nonconformists and nonaverage folk who live in the cities today and will have nothing else.

The salvation of the existing core cities, in turn, will depend on whether they can provide better schools, make their own environments healthier, more interesting, more recreational, more suitable for children and the family, more useful and more opportune for a job. This, too, will depend on the American will to keep the central city among the electives available to its people, and on whether we are willing to pay the price of making the city a sound component of the nation's social structure. In an era in which life is becoming urban and human behavior becoming the behavior of people in an urban setting, we may be producing the most ingenious machines but computing and commuting are routines, not civilization. If we lack the capacity for creating the social ideas for the new life and the variety of environments and opportunities which human beings need for human progress, we may decline as a nation.

Despite its setbacks and its new concentrations of minority families, the central city is still the heart of American life and still shapes its more vital institutions. It is still the confluence of diversities, and when a nation has many cities and many types of cities, the diversities and alternatives are multiplied. It is still the precinct of many faces, the vast mobile in an ever-shifting human landscape. If it brings loneliness to some, it guarantees privacy for others. It has maintained its ancient role as a refuge for the oppressed. It is even the unspoken refuge of those who try to escape from the city to the outskirts — for they are within its magnetic field though not at its pole. If the city is presently the seat of new social conflicts and new group tensions, it continues to be the melting pot in which ways of life are blended, the training ground of the poor in search of a better life, the crucible in which will be tested our ability to endure the fatigue which democracy exacts.

A city, even an American city, is the pulsating product of the human hand and mind, reflecting man's history, his struggle for freedom, his creativity, his genius — and his selfishness and errors. It is the palimpsest on which man's story is written, the record of those who built a skyscraper or a picture window, fought a pitched battle for a play street, created a bookshop or bakeshop that mattered. It is a composite of trials and defeats, of settlement houses, churches, and schoolhouses, of aspirations, images, and memories. A city has values as well as slums, excitement as well as conflict; it has a personality that has not yet been obliterated by its highways and gas stations; it has a spirit as well as a set of arteries and a voice that speaks the hopes as well as the disappointments of its people.

If American cities do not bear the mark of the generations of craftsmen who built Europe's churches and works, most of them, barring atomic destruction, are destined to last as long — for better or worse. If it is to be for the better, there must be a national will to make it so. For the nation's strength is that we are a nation of diverse people — 35 million of us move annually from and into cities, suburbs, farms, villages, mobile parks, warm and cold climates, and every variety of house and environment. Much of the nation's strength and freedom exist because of the concentration of job choices in cities; the variety of places in which people live or may choose to live — those who seek the fringes and those who will settle for nothing less than the collision of minds in an ever-changing medley of faces and people.

The physical patterns available to people, however, and the existence of alternatives no longer rest exclusively on the decisions of private industry or of individuals. For in our time, public policy has become one of the most important forces in determining whether the city improves or wanes, the suburb stagnates or grows, the farm survives or disappears. Public policy for slum clearance, housing, race discrimination, zoning, road building, community facilities, transportation, suburban development, recreation, relief of poverty, and for spending and taxation is a main lever in manipulating the patterns of the society and the choices available to its members.

If we are to be committed to retaining the city as one of the choices in our national life, real urban renewal therefore calls for something more than tearing down a few slums, putting up another string of public projects, or another row of apartment houses. It will entail more than a few isolated and unintegrated programs hailed as a war on poverty or a token federal appropriation for a skirmish against ignorance or an unimplemented declaration of the need for equal opportunity. It will hinge also on whether the central city with all its problems is acknowledged as one of the vital options in American life.

It is only if the national purpose is known and defined that the value of the present renewal effort and the other federal programs directed toward achieving of great society can be measured. It is only if the central city is accepted as one of the living forces in the American scene and the problems of the people who live in it become part of the nation's concern, that meaningful specifications can be framed for the city's regeneration.

Raymond Vernon

URBAN CHANGE AND PUBLIC OPINION

As the 20th century opened, the number of people in America's urban areas who could afford to buy living space was growing at a tremendous pace. New streets and speculative subdivisions were opening up at the edges of every big city as fast as the curbing could be put into place. Electric trolley lines were appearing all over the country, complete with parks at the end of the run to generate the week-end traffic. America's cities were spreading out.

The new subdivisions, it is true, continued to shun the extravagant use of land. The automobile, after all, was still a novelty and most breadwinners had to assume that their daily trek to office, store, or

Reprinted by permission of the publishers from Raymond Vernon, *The Myth and Reality of Our Urban Problems* (Cambridge, Mass.: Harvard University Press, Copyright 1962, 1966, by the President and Fellows of Harvard College), pp. 28–54.

factory would begin with a walk to the nearest public conveyance. So the style of the era continued to be the three- or four-story tenement, the triple decker, the row house, or the private dwelling on a handkerchief-sized lot.

As we follow this middle-income group through the decades of the 20th century, we see an almost continuous process of movement. By the 1920's, some of the more adventurous settlers at the edges of the urban mass were beginning to take the automobile into account as a fixed feature of their existence. By that time, some were willing to choose their living space on the assumption that they would ride, not walk, to a trolley or train; or, more daring still, that the trip to the office, plant, or store would be made regularly by car. As a result, building sites became much more plentiful — more plentiful in the sense that larger areas became accessible to the urban mass. Subdivisions began to break away from the public transportation lines and locate in open country. With the car becoming an indispensable part of the family's possessions, more households elected to live in private homes, even in areas where the prevailing style up to that time had been the multifamily dwelling.

The 1930's, though a period of depression, postponed marriages, and undersized families, still saw a continuation of the trend. The craving of most people for a place of their own in the suburbs was reflected in Federal programs, such as the FHA guaranteed-mortgage program, to meet the financing problems of home-buying. Hand in hand went the proliferation of consumer credit devices to ease the purchase of the ubiquitous family car and all the other hard goods of the home owner.

The period after World War II witnessed an even swifter acceleration of the trend. Now, single-family dwelling units were overwhelmingly important in the new construction undertaken each year within the big urban areas of the country. There were, of course, exceptions to the pattern — exceptions which make much more impact on the eye than on the cold and impersonal statistical totals. Each year, some tens of thousands of dwelling units in new low-cost public housing structures were built for operation under government subsidy. Each year, too, there were some hundreds of thousands more of private apartment units, though some involved land-acquisition subsidies or credit subsidies from one arm or another of government. But the overwhelming bulk of new housing in the post-war period was the ranch-house-in-the-suburb, in one variant or another, complete with one- or two-car garage.

America's middle-income group seems hungry for land — for quarter acres, half acres, or more, well removed from the crowded urban centers where their parents may have lived. And the nation has managed to provide them with the land they seem to want, by a process which can continue to go on for quite some time to come. The spreading national system of highways and superhighways has had two effects on the supply of land. First, of course, it has placed more land in reach of the urban mass — that is, within a radius of the thirty or forty minutes which most people seem prepared to spend in going from home to work. Thirty minutes, after all, was two miles to a swift and steady walker, and eight or ten miles on a speedy electric trolley; and it now represents 15 to 25 miles of distance on the road system of the 1960's.

At the same time, the highways have had a profound effect on the land-using propensities of the farmers who surround the big cities. As the roads drew the cities closer to the land, the farmers discovered that hired help was getting costly; either help could not be had at all in the periods of planting and harvest or else it was demanding a wage equivalent to that offered in the city nearby. So the farmers at the edges of most urban areas began to make adjustments to their new problems. Some gave up serious farming and lived on the sale of land parcels to the city folk. Others altered the lines of agriculture in which they were engaged; they abandoned their land-extensive pursuits such as raising grain and grass and began to feed their cooped-up cows and chickens with commercial feeds. Considerable acreage reverted to scrub pine and weedy pasture, awaiting the day when the suburban developer would appear.

As a result, though developers grouse about the mounting cost of land, no dearth of land has developed around the margins of the big urban masses. No dearth has developed, that is, if we take into account the fact that every urban area now can reach much further outward along its various spokes than was possible a decade or two ago. True, neighborhoods that were once potato fields are now covered with the spread of urban growth. But the land taken up each year with the new split-level, the Cape Cod, the Colonial, and the ranch house amounts to less acreage in most parts of the country than the added land made congruent to the urban mass by the improvement of the highway system.

And there is no reason to suppose that this process is at an end. Here and there, the edge of some urban area may merge with the spreading reaches of another, or may back up into some natural barrier such as a mountain range or seaside. But for a quarter century or more, the land around Boston, New York, Chicago, Washington, Philadelphia, St. Louis, and most of the other great urban clusters of the country will easily absorb their growing populations.

The process of spread which we have been at such pains to describe in the last few paragraphs has not merely affected the growing edges of the urban mass. It has also had its effects — profound effects — on the older neighborhoods left behind inside the mass. In simple terms, the children with middle-class incomes have chosen not to live where their parents lived; they have chosen not to refurbish their parents' homes, even if their parents enjoyed an income level not unlike their own in its relative position on the national income ladder. As a result, one can detect a cycle which appears again and again in many older middle-class neighborhoods. The new compact neighborhood of 1920, filled with its close-drawn homes of young families, has now become 30 or 40 years old. The children have grown up and departed, but the older folks have stayed on. The sidewalks have heaved and cracked over the roots of overgrown trees; the shrubbery has got out of hand; the lawns have been choked off by the heavy shade; the retail trade of the neighborhood, living off the declining purchases of the aging households, has begun to shrivel.

Why? Why have the children not stayed on, trimming the shurbbery, wielding the brush and paintpot, maintaining the walks, and providing themselves with decent shelter at half the price? The answers are not obscure. For one thing, the middle-income family today enjoys a real income which is close to double the absolute level of 30 or 40 years ago. It can afford two cars where its parents had one; a dozen electric appliances in lieu of a day worker; a television set instead of a neighborhood movie. Could the old house have been made to do for these needs? Sometimes, yes; more often, no. No, partly because the old houses were set up on plots so small that space for the second car — or the first one for that matter, as long as it sported the tailfins of the 1950's — could not have been provided on the site.

But another factor has discouraged the refurbishing of the older houses — the fact that the cost of skilled labor comes so high in the United States, as an unavoidable by-product of our high productivity and high living standards. This last point is worth a moment's more consideration. The cost of wiring a new home for the heavy electrical loads of modern living sometimes amounts to a good deal less than the cost of rewiring an old one to carry modern loads. The cost of installing the sleek, aseptic trim of the 1960's in a newly constructed house is less than the price of ripping out and replacing the dust-catcher moldings and Dutch shelves of the 1920's. To steam the ancient paper off crumbling plaster a third-of-a-century old, to patch, size, and repaint the walls, costs more than the pristine decoration of the newbuilt home. In short, in a nation whose economy places a heavy price on hand labor and a low price on materials, the cost of repairs and remodelling can easily outrun the cost of new construction. Like economic men, therefore, the children of the middle class have moved to the modernity of the split-level-in-the-suburbs, leaving many of the older middle-income neighborhoods to stagnate or decline.

This process of spread, to be sure, might not have gone on forever if the jobs of our metropolitan areas had not evidenced a similar tendency to spread outward. The reasons for this spread of jobs are not hard to find. Of every twenty jobs in urban areas, about four are in the consumer trade lines and another five or six in local governments, local utilities, local business or professional services, and local construction; these jobs, making up about half the urban labor force, more or less automatically follow the drift of the population as it spreads outward from the old city.

The other half of the job market is subject to a more complicated calculus of location. In a word, however, most of the labor force employed in manufacturing — the lighter manufacturing plants as well as the abattoirs and chemical plants — have joined the outward move. The kind of site required for the modern space-hungry plant simply cannot be found in the older portions of an urban area. The time-cost and money-cost involved in assembling an industrial site in some ossified district already encumbered by structures are extremely high — so high as to make that kind of operation simply out of the question, at least without summary public powers and extensive public subsidy. And even when public powers and the public subsidy are at hand, they are not swift enough or flexible enough or generous enough to match the offerings of private land on the outskirts.

Besides, with the advent of the truck, the erstwhile attraction of the railroads and rivers for industrial plants has grown weaker. With the ubiquitous use of the automobile, the labor force of the city no longer offers a unique attraction to the factory employer. Power, water, and sewage can now be had over much wider areas, a by-product of the spread of the homes. So industry has followed the trek to the suburbs, gobbling up land at the rate of about ten employees to the acre.

In fact only one major cluster of employment has resisted the outward move. This is the complex of frenetic economic activities . . . whose elite are overwhelmed with uncertainties, demanding face-to-face communication, and dependent for their effective operation upon swift access to various other enterprises. Most of these activities are in offices, some are in showrooms, and some are in manufacturing lofts. All told, they account for perhaps one-fifth of the urban areas' labor force and represent the critical nub of employment in the central business districts of most major cities.

Even in these activities, however, one can see a certain loosening of ties to the old city center. After all, the needs for swift and easy access and face-to-face communication do not apply to more than a tiny fraction of the office workers in the downtown area. In fact, the locational needs of the average stenographer or billing clerk can scarcely be said to differ very much from the locational needs of the mechanic or warehouseman. The unique requirements of many offices are confined to the office elite — to the vice president and treasurer, to the sales manager, the house counsel, and so on.

As offices have grown, therefore, and as the line of authority between the billing clerks and the treasurer has become more and more attenuated, one company after another has reconsidered whether the billing department and functions like it ought to remain in the central business district. Here and there, the decision has been made to peel off some of these functions and to locate them in the suburbs.

The trend to suburban locations for the billing clerks, if not the bosses, has been accelerated by two factors. One has been the appearance of the first generation of young women who drive cars more naturally than they walk; to recruit a workforce of young women office workers it is no longer necessary to sit astride a public transportation facility. The second factor has been the growing remoteness of the daughters of the middle class from the old city centers. In weighing the attractiveness of alternative job opportunities, a significant fraction of these young women have preferred a job in the suburbs near home to one in the more remote, albeit more ebullient, city centers.

As far as the middle class is concerned, therefore, there has been little to impede the outward movement of homes and jobs. Both have drifted outward, sometimes for independent reasons, sometimes as a mutually reinforcing phenomenon. Except for the minority — the declining minority — who work in the central business district, travel from home to office is probably no more difficult for the middle class than it was twenty years ago. There is nothing to suggest that the outward drift of the middle class will not continue. There is no rubber band being stretched to the breaking point, no growing pressure which cannot be contained.

For the poor of the urban areas, the story of the last fifty or sixty years has been rather different. Each urban area has had its own particular brand of poor, each stamped with some ill-fitting mass label. In the South and West, the cities have housed large numbers of Mexicans and Oakies; in the Southeast and Midwest, hillbillies and southern Negroes; on the Eastern Seaboard, Italians and Jews from Eastern Europe, then Puerto Ricans and more southern Negroes.

Each immigrant group has developed on a slightly different pattern from any other. Nonetheless, most immigrants have made a swift adjustment to their new urban life. When I say "swift," however, I am speaking in terms of decades, not of years. In the first decade or so, it has been enough for most newcomers to cling to the slim security of friends and relatives, and to take the hand-me-downs in jobs and living space that came along. Typically, therefore, these groups have settled on the edges of the neighborhoods where they first found shelter and have taken jobs that their friends have found for them.

By the first part of the 20th century ... the newcomers had little choice but to settle in the oldest parts of the older cities. Barred from shacktowns in the suburbs, they crowded such structures as had been already surrendered by the middle class in the older neighborhoods.

Incredible living densities were recorded in some cities; in New York, where such densities were at their highest, some 300,000 people could be found living in one square mile of lower Manhattan.

But neighborhoods such as these did not retain their peak densities for many years. After a time, they began to show population declines. For if the parents could abide such brutal crowding, the children could not. So the children of the poor, like the children of the middle class, moved on, leaving their parents to luxuriate in the moldering space of the ancient neighborhoods. Some of the offspring acquired income sufficient to buy new housing, and became a part of the extensive middle-income group. Others used their growing knowledge of the city to ferret out less ancient structures, structures which in turn were at the stage of being surrendered by the middle class.

In many large cities, therefore, the location of the most notorious slum neighborhood of today is different from that of a generation ago. More likely than not, the current slum is in a "newer" portion of the city. The chances are very high, too, that it is rather less crowded. In addition, it is typically less compact and covers a good deal more acreage than the slums of a generation or two ago.

It is in this last characteristic — the extensive acreage covered by the modern slum — that we find one key to the heightened public interest in the slum phenomenon. As long as the slum was contained in a small congested mass within the old center of the city, most of the middle- and upper-income inhabitants of the urban area could live out their lives without being acutely aware of its existence. As the slum-dweller has taken to less dense living, however, the manifestations of his existence have not been quite so easy to suppress. In more recent decades, slum neighborhoods have come to ring the business districts of the city and have even begun to reach out into the less congested fringes of some urban areas. As they have reached out into the newer areas, their march has driven the middle-income groups before them, giving still more space to the poor. In some degree, therefore, the poor have created their own housing supply, simply by ostentatiously bidding for it.

The latest phase of this outward spread of low-income families is one which is especially calculated to draw attention to their existence. In this phase, low-income families have begun to discover that structures ripe for downgrading are to be found not only in the ancient central city of the urban mass but in nearby suburban towns as well. Sometimes these are suburban towns with an old industrial core of their own; but sometimes they are residential satellites, built for the rail- or trolley-riding commuters of 1900 or 1910, with a supply of obsolete housing just about ready for the low-income market. Discovering these caches of obsolescent structures, low-income families have begun to appear in little ghettos in some of the most "exclusive" suburban communities of the country. The signs of their coming are evident from a close reading of the 1960 population census data, which show widespread population declines in the slum areas of the old cities and substantial increases among the identifiable low-income groups in many suburban cities. And this is only the beginning.

The spread of the low-income groups outward from the old city center has been sparked not only by the spread of obsolescent housing but also by the redistribution of low-income jobs. As a rule, the jobs of the low-income groups have consisted of common labor on streets and docks, stevedoring in warehouses, factories, or yards, and menial help in the consumer trades. Practically every sector of employment in which low-wage labor has predominated is to be found drifting outward away from the old slum neighborhoods. The warehouses, factories, and consumer trades have followed the trend; and while the docks have remained anchored to their waterside locations, they have been giving up their economic function to trucking terminals located further out from the center. The low-income groups, therefore, have been faced with a growing need to keep up with their peripatetic jobs.

It is evident, however, that many have not yet looked for newer living space or have not succeeded in their search. This grows apparent as one views the changes in the commuting streams that are beginning to appear in many cities. Outcommuting — the movement each morning of people from homes in the center portions of the urban area to jobs on the periphery — is growing fast. The spectacle of groups of blue-collar workers, travelling outward by car pool against the flow of incoming traffic, is now a common sight on the roads of many large cities. In fact, the spotty and fragmentary information of this phenomenon suggests that it may be one of the fastest-growing streams of traffic among the complex currents of our urban areas.

As far as the low-income groups are concerned, therefore, one sees a process of a constant turnover, a constant pushing outward to take possession of the housing hand-me-downs of the middle-income group. This is the trickle-down theory of progress in its most graphic form.

Distasteful as the trickle-down theory may be in the abstract, it seems to have worked in some measure to improve the housing of the poor in recent years. Between the 1950 housing census and the 1956 housing census, the number of so-called "substandard dwellings" in our major urban areas underwent a rather considerable decline. Of course, statistics which purport to measure any such abstraction as "substandard housing" are rarely invulnerable; and so it is with these. But there is no serious doubt that there has been a substantial upgrading in the housing stock available to the poor as the middle-income groups have fled to the suburbs from the advancing salients of the poor. In those urban areas where new home construction has been highest, the upgrading has been most apparent. As an added measure of the improving situation for the poor, the number of available vacancies in the major urban areas also seems to have gone up rather considerably between the two housing censuses.

In our concentration upon the *trend* in housing for the poor, however, we must never lose sight of the *level*. One needs only his eyes, his nose, and a willingness to walk through the slums of America's great cities to be aware that we are many leagues away from the goal of tolerable housing for all Americans. Besides, the disconcerting statistics of the 1956 housing census remind us that Negroes and other recognizable minority groups are suffering from a systematic economic discrimination in the housing market, paying more for comparable space than white families. On top of all this, the aspirations of the low-income groups may well be expanding faster than their actual living conditions.

Nonetheless, it is important to be aware that the trend is not clearly retrogressive. Once more there is no clear evidence of the taut stretching of a rubber band close to its breaking point, no indication of the building up of pressure to levels which the political vessel can no longer contain.

The medium-income group and the poor, according to our argument, have made some kind of adjustment to the changing urban structure. But the well-to-do — that small but critically important group which is in a position to pay whatever may be demanded for the living space it desires — seem not to have fared as well.

At the turn of the century ... the well-to-do urban dweller had a number of satisfactory living choices. One possibility was to take a mansion on Fifth Avenue, the Gold Coast, Nob Hill, or Rittenhouse Square. Here, one could have propinquity to the office and the theater, the easy use of the city streets in the evening or on weekends, and only a minimum of exposure to the relatively localized and compact slums. Alternatively — or in addition — one could maintain a home in an exclusive suburb, barely thirty or forty minutes from an office in the central city by way of the new suburban trains.

In the past fifty or sixty years, however, these comparatively idyllic arrangements have gradually been threatened. As the mansions of the downtown areas have grown obsolete, it has not been easy to replace them with equally adequate quarters in the same neighborhoods. Apartment houses, office buildings, parking lots, and slums have swallowed up the accessible land; and even if money was no object, in a country in which the Protestant ethic still prevails it would be unconscionable to pay $500,000 or so for a site on which to locate a private residence.

Besides, the city streets were no longer quite so easily used in off-hours. The middle class was gradually abandoning the use of mass transit as a means of off-hour travel in the central business district and was crowding the downtown streets with private cars and taxi-cabs. The slums were gradually ringing the central business district in neighborhoods many miles deep. The possibility of a mansion in town was no longer anywhere nearly as attractive as it had been in America's Age of Innocence.

At the same time, the exclusive suburban location was falling prey to another kind of outside pressure. The inexorable tide of the middle class was surrounding the elite suburb, infiltrating the empty land where it could, crowding the little shopping centers, undermining the air of exclusivity and remoteness which had once prevailed.

There were two escapes available to the well-to-do, and they availed themselves of both. One was to abandon the town house for the exclusive flat in an expensive apartment house. In many big cities, therefore, elaborate apartments began to appear in or very near the central business district — overlooking a park or a river, or dominating a hill. This compromise was not an altogether felicitous one, of course. Though it allowed the rich to remain close to offices and theaters, it did not deal with the problems of comfort and security on the public streets.

Another alternative — one especially attractive to families with children — has been to flee from the sound of the subdivision steamshovel into even more remote settlements in the country. Instead of spending 30 or 40 minutes on the daily suburban trains to downtown offices, the well-to-do have taken to spending an hour or more on their way to or from the office. To heap difficulty on difficulty, the services of the suburban trains . . . have deteriorated in quality and frequency.

These problems might have been mitigated in some degree if the jobs of the elite, like the jobs of the middle-income groups and the poor, had shown any tendency to move out rapidly toward the suburbs. Some, of course, did. A number of insurance companies and a few large central offices, responding to the pressures of their commuting executives, moved from their downtown locations to more felicitous surroundings in the suburbs. For the most part, however, the compulsion of executives to remain in the central business district has been very strong. The delicate problems of face-to-face communication to which we earlier referred have prevented them from moving very far from the tight-woven mass of which they are a part. Typically, therefore, the executive suites of the large manufacturing enterprises, the advertising agencies, the banks, and the law firms have remained firmly anchored to the central business district.

There is still another reason why the plight of the central city is calculated to draw more response from the elite of the urban area than from the rank and file of the middle-income groups or of the poor. In every major city, there is a group of substantial business interests which are immobilized in the city — prevented from sharing in the swifter rates of suburban growth. Under many state laws, the chartered banks of the central city are prohibited from opening branches freely in the suburbs. In other cases, the public utilities of the central city are prevented from extending their franchises into the suburbs. In still others, department stores with heavy investments sunk in their central city locations are eyeing with concern the need to make new investments in the growing suburban areas. And there are cases, as well, in which central city newspapers fear an irretrievable loss of circulation and advertising from the drift of homes and jobs to outside locations. One can safely predict, therefore, how the articulate and influential elite of the urban areas is likely to react to the problem of increasing remoteness between the central business district and the suburbs.

The attachment of the rich to the central city, however, is not based solely upon the need for shortening the journey-to-work or upon business interest. At least in equal measure, the attachment derives from sentiment, tradition, and avocational ties. These latter are made up of many strands. One, for instance, is the uniqueness of the institutions to which the rich tend to belong. Few urban areas can support more than one Harvard Club, one Council on Foreign Relations, one Union Club. Given only one such institution in the area, its location is bound to be at the center of the urban mass. In this respect, therefore, the rich who want both the exclusivity of the suburbs and propinquity to their clubs are less well-situated than the middle class who can find their bowling league, their VFW post, or their bridge club reproduced in any suburban area close to home.

Another strand in the tie to the central city is created by the role of the rich as supporters of the cultural activities of the city. No list of sponsors for the leading orchestra or the leading art museum of any urban area fails to include a generous sampling of the leading families. Often the sponsorship goes back in an uninterrupted chain over many generations. Once again, therefore, the rich are the victims of the urban area's spread, pulling them from the neighborhoods in which their absorbing interests lie.

To understand today's growing literature of protest against the metropolis, however, we have to take cognizance of the reactions of elite who do not derive their status from wealth. They are typified, perhaps caricatured, by the man who, when asked why he felt the need to settle in a metropolis of seven or eight million, said with all sincerity and accuracy, "I need seven or eight million from whom to select my 70 or 80 friends." They are people who find the mass media and the mass forms of amusement inadequate for their needs. Commonly, they include the individuals who are more than casual onlookers in their relation to the cultural institutions peculiar to the established city — the museum, the symphony orchestra, the art galleries, the foreign policy clubs, the social workers' organizations, the public hospitals. Sometimes they are not well-to-do. And when they are not, their bitterness against the spread of the urban areas is greatest of all. For they do not have the ability of the rich to maintain propinquity to their interests in the city by buying luxury downtown space.

Add to these groups the influential sectors of the opinion-forming elite of the community: the political organizations, built up on a carefully developed structure of city political clubs; the older church parishes, rich in tradition, yet reliant for their support on neighborhood parishioners; the director of the symphony orchestra, the curator of the public or private museum, the superintendent of the adult education program. The wonder of it is that the cry for the preservation of the old city or for improved access to its center is not even louder and more insistent than it is.

And yet, if my analysis has any validity at all, we may have an answer to the riddle of the curious passivity of America to its urban problems. To most Americans, the personal experience of urban living seems not one of personal retrogression but of continuous improvement. By moving out of the slag heaps of the worked-out city, they have improved their surroundings sufficient for a generation. The worries of a Riesman, the strivings of a Mumford, are inarticulate, scarce-comprehensible murmurings. Let the central city weep; let the sociologists fume; except for such intractable problems as death, war, and taxes, things are getting slightly better all the time.

The National Advisory Commission
on Civil Disorders

THE FORMATION OF THE RACIAL GHETTOS

The Migration of Negroes from the South

THE MAGNITUDE OF THIS MIGRATION. In 1910, 91 per cent of
the Nation's 9.8 million Negroes lived in the South. Twenty-seven per
cent of American Negroes lived in cities of 2,500 persons or more, as compared to 49 per cent of the Nation's white population.

By 1966, the Negro population had increased to 21.5 million, and two
significant geographic shifts had taken place. The proportion of Negroes
living in the South had dropped to 55 per cent, and about 69 per cent of
all Negroes lived in metropolitan areas compared to 64 per cent for
whites. While the total Negro population more than doubled from 1910
to 1966, the number living in cities rose over fivefold (from 2.7 million
to 14.8 million) and the number outside the South rose elevenfold (from
885,000 to 9.7 million).

Negro migration from the South began after the Civil War. By the
turn of the century, sizable Negro populations lived in many large
Northern cities — Philadelphia, for example, had 63,400 Negro residents
in 1900. The movement of Negroes out of the rural South accelerated
during World War I, when floods and boll weevils hurt farming in the
South and the industrial demands of the war created thousands of new
jobs for unskilled workers in the North. After the war, the shift to
mechanized farming spurred the continuing movement of Negroes from
rural Southern areas.

The Depression slowed this migratory flow, but World War II set it in
motion again. More recently, continuing mechanization of agriculture
and the expansion of industrial employment in Northern and Western
cities have served to sustain the movement of Negroes out of the South,
although at a slightly lower rate. . . .

IMPORTANT CHARACTERISTICS OF THIS MIGRATION. It is useful to recall
that even the latest scale of Negro migration is relatively small when
compared to the earlier waves of European immigrants. A total of 8.8

Reprinted from the *Report* of the National Advisory Commission on Civil Disorders (Washington, D.C.: U.S. Government Printing Office, 1968), pp. 116–120.

million immigrants entered the United States between 1901 and 1911, and another 5.7 million arrived during the following decade. Even during the years from 1960 through 1966, the 1.8 million immigrants from abroad were almost three times the 613,000 Negroes who departed the South. In these same 6 years, California alone gained over 1.5 million new residents from internal shifts of American population.

Three major routes of Negro migration from the South have developed. One runs north along the Atlantic Seaboard toward Boston, another north from Mississippi toward Chicago, and the third west from Texas and Louisiana toward California. Between 1955 and 1960, 50 per cent of the nonwhite migrants to the New York metropolitan area came from North Carolina, South Carolina, Virginia, Georgia, and Alabama; North Carolina alone supplied 20 per cent of all New York's nonwhite immigrants. During the same period, almost 60 per cent of the nonwhite migrants to Chicago came from Mississippi, Tennessee, Arkansas, Alabama, and Louisiana; Mississippi accounted for almost one-third. During these years, three-fourths of the nonwhite migrants to Los Angeles came from Texas, Louisiana, Mississippi, Arkansas, and Alabama.

The flow of Negroes from the South has caused the Negro population to grow more rapidly in the North and West, as indicated below.

Period	Total Negro population gains (millions)		Percentage of gain in North and West
	North and West	South	
1940–50	1.859	0.321	85.2
1950–60	2.741	1.086	71.6
1960–66	2.119	0.517	80.4

As a result, although a much higher proportion of Negroes still resides in the South, the distribution of Negroes throughout the United States is beginning to approximate that of whites, as the following tables show.

PERCENTAGE DISTRIBUTION OF THE POPULATION
BY REGION — 1950, 1960, AND 1966

	Negro			White		
	1950	1960	1966	1950	1960[a]	1966
United States	100	100	100	100	100	100
South	68	60	55	27	27	28
North	28	34	37	59	56	55
Northeast	13	16	17	28	26	26
Northcentral	15	18	20	31	30	29
West	4	6	8	14	16	17

[a] Rounds to 99.

NEGROES AS A PERCENTAGE OF THE TOTAL POPULATION
IN THE UNITED STATES AND EACH REGION — 1950,
1960, AND 1966

	1950	1960	1966
United States	10	11	11
South	22	21	20
North	5	7	8
West	3	4	5

Negroes in the North and West are now so numerous that natural increase rather than migration provides the greater part of Negro population gains there. And even though Negro migration has continued at a high level, it comprises a constantly declining proportion of Negro growth in these regions.

Period:	Percentage of total North and West Negro gain from southern in-migration
1940–50	85.9
1950–60	53.1
1960–66	28.9

In other words, we have reached the point where the Negro populations of the North and West will continue to expand significantly even if migration from the South drops substantially.

FUTURE MIGRATION. Despite accelerating Negro migration from the South, the Negro population there has continued to rise.

Date	Negro population in the South (millions)	Change from preceding date Total	Change from preceding date Annual average
1940	9.9		
1950	10.2	321,000	32,100
1960	11.3	1,086,000	108,600
1966	11.8	517,000	86,200

Nor is it likely to halt. Negro birth rates in the South, as elsewhere, have fallen sharply since 1957, but so far this decline has been offset by the rising Negro population base remaining in the South. From 1950 to 1960, southern Negro births generated an average net increase of 254,000 per year and, from 1960 to 1966, an average of 188,000 per year. Even if Negro birth rates continue to fall they are likely to remain high enough to support significant migration to other regions for some time to come.

The Negro population in the South is becoming increasingly urbanized. In 1950, there were 5.4 million southern rural Negroes; by 1960, 4.8 million. But this decline has been more than offset by increases in the urban population. A rising proportion of interregional migration now consists of persons moving from one city to another. From 1960 to 1966, rural Negro population in the South was far below its peak, but the annual average migration of Negroes from the South was still substantial.

These facts demonstrate that Negro migration from the South, which has maintained a high rate for the past 60 years, will continue unless economic conditions change dramatically in either the South or the North and West. This conclusion is reinforced by the fact that most Southern states in recent decades have also experienced outflows of white population. From 1950 to 1960, 11 of the 17 Southern states (including the District of Columbia) "exported" white population — as compared to 13 which "exported" Negro population. Excluding Florida's net gain by migration of 1.5 million, the other 16 Southern states together had a net loss by migration of 1.46 million whites.

The Concentration of Negro Population in Large Cities

WHERE NEGRO URBANIZATION HAS OCCURRED. Statistically, the Negro population in America has become more urbanized, and more metropolitan, than the white population. According to Census Bureau estimates, almost 70 per cent of all Negroes in 1966 lived in metropolitan areas, compared to 64 per cent of all whites. In the South, more than half the Negro population now lives in cities. Rural Negroes outnumber urban Negroes in only four states: Arkansas, Mississippi, North Carolina, and South Carolina.

Basic data concerning Negro urbanization trends . . . indicate that:

Almost all Negro population growth is occurring within metropolitan areas, primarily within central cities. From 1950 to 1966, the U.S. Negro population rose 6.5 million. Over 98 per cent of that increase took place in metropolitan areas — 86 per cent within central cities, 12 per cent in the urban fringe.

The vast majority of white population growth is occurring in suburban portions of metropolitan areas. From 1950 to 1966, 77.8 per cent of the white population increase of 35.6 million took place in the suburbs. Central cities received only 2.5 per cent of this total white increase. Since 1960, white central-city population has actually declined by 1.3 million.

As a result, central cities are steadily becoming more heavily Negro, while the urban fringes around them remain almost entirely white. The proportion of Negroes in all central cities rose steadily from 12 per cent in 1950, to 17 per cent in 1960, to 20 per cent in 1966. Meanwhile, metropolitan areas outside of central cities remained 95 per cent white from 1950 to 1960 and became 96 per cent white by 1966.

The Negro population is growing faster, both absolutely and relatively, in the larger metropolitan areas than in the smaller ones. From 1950 to 1966, the proportion of nonwhites in the central cities of metropolitan areas with 1 million or more persons doubled, reaching 26 per cent, as compared with 20 per cent in the central cities of metropolitan areas containing from 250,000 to 1 million persons and 12 per cent in the central cities of metropolitan areas containing under 250,000 persons.

The 12 largest central cities — New York, Chicago, Los Angeles, Philadelphia, Detroit, Baltimore, Houston, Cleveland, Washington, D.C., St. Louis, Milwaukee, and San Francisco — now contain over two-thirds of the Negro population outside the South and almost one-third of the total in the United States. All these cities have experienced rapid increases in Negro population since 1950. In six — Chicago, Detroit, Cleveland, St. Louis, Milwaukee, and San Francisco — the proportion of Negroes at least doubled. In two others — New York and Los Angeles — it probably doubled. In 1968, seven of these cities are over 30 per cent Negro, and one, Washington, D.C., is two-thirds Negro.

FACTORS CAUSING RESIDENTIAL SEGREGATION IN METROPOLITAN AREAS. The early pattern of Negro settlement within each metropolitan area followed that of immigrant groups. Migrants converged on the older sections of the central city because the lowest cost housing was located there, friends and relatives were likely to be living there, and the older neighborhoods then often had good public transportation.

But the later phases of Negro settlement and expansion in metropolitan areas diverge sharply from those typical of white immigrants. As the whites were absorbed by the larger society, many left their predominantly ethnic neighborhoods and moved to outlying areas to obtain newer housing and better schools. Some scattered randomly over the suburban area. Others established new ethnic clusters in the suburbs, but even these rarely contained solely members of a single ethnic group. As a result, most middle-class neighborhoods — both in the suburbs and within central cities — have no distinctive ethnic character, except that they are white.

Nowhere has the expansion of America's urban Negro population followed this pattern of dispersal. Thousands of Negro families have attained incomes, living standards, and cultural levels matching or surpassing those of whites who have "upgraded" themselves from distinctly ethnic neighborhoods. Yet most Negro families have remained within predominantly Negro neighborhoods, primarily because they have been effectively excluded from white residential areas.

Their exclusion has been accomplished through various discriminatory practices, some obvious and overt, others subtle and hidden. Deliberate efforts are sometimes made to discourage Negro families from purchasing or renting homes in all-white neighborhoods. Intimidation and threats of violence have ranged from throwing garbage on lawns and making threatening phone calls to burning crosses in yards and even dynamiting property. More often, real estate agents simply refuse to show homes to Negro buyers.

Many middle-class Negro families, therefore, cease looking for homes beyond all-Negro areas or nearby "changing" neighborhoods. For them, trying to move into all-white neighborhoods is not worth the psychological efforts and costs required.

Another form of discrimination just as significant is white withdrawal from, or refusal to enter, neighborhoods where large numbers of Negroes are moving or already residing. Normal population turnover causes about 20 per cent of the residents of average U.S. neighborhoods to move out every year because of income changes, job transfers, shifts in life-cycle position or deaths. This normal turnover rate is even higher in apartment areas. The refusal of whites to move into changing areas when vacancies occur there from normal turnover means that most of these vacancies are eventually occupied by Negroes. An inexorable shift toward heavy Negro occupancy results.

Once this happens, the remaining whites seek to leave, thus confirming the existing belief among whites that complete transformation of a neighborhood is inevitable once Negroes begin to enter. Since the belief itself is one of the major causes of the transformation, it becomes a self-fulfilling prophecy which inhibits the development of racially integrated neighborhoods.

As a result, Negro settlements expand almost entirely through "massive racial transition" at the edges of existing all-Negro neighborhoods, rather than by a gradual dispersion of population throughout the metropolitan area.

Two points are particularly important:

"Massive transition" requires no panic or flight by the original white residents of a neighborhood into which Negroes begin moving. All it requires is the failure or refusal of other whites to fill the vacancies resulting from normal turnover.

Thus, efforts to stop massive transition by persuading present white residents to remain will ultimately fail unless whites outside the neighborhood can be persuaded to move in.

It is obviously true that some residential separation of whites and

Negroes would occur even without discriminatory practices by whites. This would result from the desires of some Negroes to live in predominantly Negro neighborhoods and from differences in meaningful social variables, such as income and educational levels. But these factors alone would not lead to the almost complete segregation of whites and Negroes which has developed in our metropolitan areas.

THE EXODUS OF WHITES FROM CENTRAL CITIES. The process of racial transition in central-city neighborhoods has been only one factor among many others causing millions of whites to move out of central cities as the Negro populations there expanded. More basic perhaps have been the rising mobility and affluence of middle-class families and the more attractive living conditions — particularly better schools — in the suburbs.

Whatever the reason, the result is clear. In 1950, 45.5 million whites lived in central cities. If this population had grown from 1950 to 1960 at the same rate as the Nation's white population as a whole, it would have increased by 8 million. It actually rose only 2.2 million, indicating an outflow of 5.8 million.[1]

From 1960 to 1966, the white outflow appears to have been even more rapid. White population of central cities declined 1.3 million instead of rising 3.6 million — as it would if it had grown at the same rate as the entire white population. In theory, therefore, 4.9 million whites left central cities during these 6 years.

Statistics for all central cities as a group understate the relationship between Negro population growth and white outflow in individual central cities. The fact is, many cities with relatively few Negroes experienced rapid white-population growth, thereby obscuring the size of white outmigration that took place in cities having large increases in Negro population. For example, from 1950 to 1960, the 10 largest cities in the United States had a total Negro population increase of 1.6 million, or 55 per cent, while the white population there declined 1.4 million. If the two cities where the white population increased (Los Angeles and Houston) are excluded, the nonwhite population in the remaining eight rose 1.4 million, whereas their white population declined 2.1 million. If the white population in these cities had increased at only half the rate of the white population in the United States as a whole from 1950 to 1960, it would have risen by 1.4 million. Thus, these eight cities actually experienced a white outmigration of at least 3.5 million, while gaining 1.4 million nonwhites.

---

[1] The outflow of whites may be somewhat smaller than the 5.9 million difference between these figures, because the ages of the whites in many central cities are higher than in the Nation as a whole, and therefore the population would have grown somewhat more slowly.

THE EXTENT OF RESIDENTIAL SEGREGATION. The rapid expansion of all-Negro residential areas and large-scale white withdrawal have continued a pattern of residential segregation that has existed in American cities for decades. A recent study[2] reveals that this pattern is present to a high degree in every large city in America. The authors devised an index

PROPORTION OF NEGROES IN EACH OF THE 30 LARGEST
CITIES, 1950, 1960, AND ESTIMATED 1965

	1950	1960	Estimate,[a] 1965
New York, N.Y.	10	14	18
Chicago, Ill.	14	23	28
Los Angeles, Calif.	9	14	17
Philadelphia, Pa.	18	26	31
Detroit, Mich.	16	29	34
Baltimore, Md.	24	35	38
Houston, Tex.	21	23	23
Cleveland, Ohio	16	29	34
Washington, D.C.	35	54	66
St. Louis, Mo.	18	29	36
Milwaukee, Wis.	3	8	11
San Francisco, Calif.	6	10	12
Boston, Mass.	5	9	13
Dallas, Tex.	13	19	21
New Orleans, La.	32	37	41
Pittsburgh, Pa.	12	17	20
San Antonio, Tex.	7	7	8
San Diego, Calif.	5	6	7
Seattle, Wash.	3	5	7
Buffalo, N.Y.	6	13	17
Cincinnati, Ohio	16	22	24
Memphis, Tenn.	37	37	40
Denver, Colo.	4	6	9
Atlanta, Ga.	37	38	44
Minneapolis, Minn.	1	2	4
Indianapolis, Ind.	15	21	23
Kansas City, Mo.	12	18	22
Columbus, Ohio	12	16	18
Phoenix, Ariz.	5	5	5
Newark, N.J.	17	34	47

[a] Except for Cleveland, Buffalo, Memphis, and Phoenix, for which a special census has been made in recent years, these are very rough estimations computed on the basis of the change in relative proportions of Negro births and deaths since 1960.

Source: U.S. Department of Commerce, Bureau of the Census, BLS Report No. 332, p. 11.

[2] *Negroes in Cities*, Karl and Alma Taeuber, Aldine Publishing Co., Chicago (1965).

to measure the degree of residential segregation. The index indicates for each city the percentage of Negroes who would have to move from the blocks where they now live to other blocks in order to provide a perfectly proportional, unsegregated distribution of population.

According to their findings, the average segregation index for 207 of the largest U.S. cities was 86.2 in 1960. This means that an average of over 86 per cent of all Negroes would have had to change blocks to create an unsegregated population distribution. Southern cities had a higher average index (90.9) than cities in the Northeast (79.2), the North Central (87.7), or the West (79.3). Only eight cities had index values below 70, whereas over 50 had values above 91.7.

The degree of residential segregation for all 207 cities has been relatively stable, averaging 85.2 in 1940, 87.3 in 1950, and 86.2 in 1960. Variations within individual regions were only slightly larger. However, a recent Census Bureau study shows that in most of the 12 large cities where special censuses were taken in the mid-1960's, the proportions of Negroes living in neighborhoods of greatest Negro concentration had increased since 1960.

Residential segregation is generally more prevalent with respect to Negroes than for any other minority group, including Puerto Ricans, Orientals, and Mexican-Americans. Moreover, it varies little between central city and suburb. This nearly universal pattern cannot be explained in terms of economic discrimination against all low-income groups. Analysis of 15 representative cities indicates that white upper and middle-income households are far more segregated from Negro upper and middle-income households than from white lower income households.

In summary, the concentration of Negroes in central cities results from a combination of forces. Some of these forces, such as migration and initial settlement patterns in older neighborhoods, are similar to those which affected previous ethnic minorities. Others — particularly discrimination in employment and segregation in housing and schools — are a result of white attitudes based on race and color. These forces continue to shape the future of the central city.

Allan H. Spear

BLACK CHICAGO

In the summer of 1966, Chacigo's racial problems were front-page news throughout the country. Martin Luther King and his followers dramatized the persistence of segregation and discrimination in the city by marching into white neighborhoods, where they were greeted by taunts, insults, and physical violence. King's activities in Chicago coupled with the riots that have erupted in a score or more American cities since 1964, shifted the focus of the race problem in the United States from the South to the North. By 1966, no domestic problem seemed more complex, more fraught with danger to the social fabric of the nation, than the confrontation in our major cities between Negroes, frustrated by generations of oppression, and whites, battling against what they conceive to be a threat to their way of life. Chicago, with its seething ghetto and its rigid pattern of housing segregation, had come to exemplify the urban racial conflict of the 1960's.

At first glance, Chicago's racial problem in 1966 seemed vastly different from the problems of the late nineteenth and early twentieth centuries. Quantitatively there had been enormous change. Over ten times as many Negroes lived in Chicago in 1966 as in 1920; instead of 4 per cent of the population, they now constituted almost 30 per cent. The ghetto occupied large sections of the city that had been all-white just two decades before. The Cottage Grove Avenue and Fifty-fifth Street boundary lines, successfully defended for a generation, fell after World War II, as Negroes, their ranks swelled by continued migration from the South, moved east into Kenwood and Hyde Park, south into Woodlawn, Park Manor, and Chatham, and southwest into Englewood. In the 1950's, the formerly Jewish section of Lawndale became solidly Negro, and a ghetto grew on the West Side soon to rival in size the South Side black belt.

On the surface, too, white attitudes toward the Negro's struggle seemed far different in 1966 from what they had been early in the century. Between 1890 and 1920, Negroes had fought against an almost solid wall of white resistance; white Chicagoans had stood virtually united in their belief in Negro inferiority and their conviction that Negroes must forever occupy a subordinate status in the city's social structure. The

Reprinted from *Black Chicago*. © 1967 by The University of Chicago, pp. 223–229, with the permission of the author and the publisher.

conflict in the summer of 1966, on the other hand, came in the wake of ten years of almost continual civil rights activity. Nationally, the Negro plight had been recognized as the country's most pressing domestic problem. The President had committed himself to the Negro Revolt, the Supreme Court had upheld the legitimacy of the Negro's claim to full citizenship rights, and the Congress had passed four civil rights bills in eight years. On the local level, too, Chicago's politicians, newspapers, clergymen, and civic leaders had proclaimed their support of the Negro's struggle for equality. Unlike the situation fifty years earlier, Chicago's Negroes seemed to be moving with the wind at their backs.

Nevertheless, in many significant ways, remarkably little had changed since 1920. Increased numbers had vastly expanded the ghetto, but had not changed its basic structure. Negroes were still unable to obtain housing beyond the confines of the ghetto, and within the black belt the complex of separate institutions and organizations that had first developed between 1890 and 1920 continued to serve an isolated Negro populace. The same restrictions that had limited Negro opportunities in the early twentieth century still operated in 1966. In fact, four civil rights bills, dozens of court decisions, and thousands of brave words about Negro rights had barely touched the life of Chicago's Negroes. It remained as constricted as it had been two generations earlier. And the bitter hostility of the residents of Gage Park, Belmont-Cragin, and Cicero toward Dr. King's marches demonstrated that thousands of white Chicagoans were still determined to preserve the status quo.

No other ethnic enclave in Chicago had changed so little over the past fifty years. While the city's Irish, Polish, Jewish, and Italian sections had broken down or developed new forms in the suburbs, the Negro ghetto remained much as it had been — cohesive, restrictive, and largely impoverished. Some historians and sociologists have suggested that the persistence of the Negro ghetto is simply the result of the steady influx of Southern Negroes into the city. While European immigration almost ceased in the 1920's, Negro migration continued, augmenting the ghetto and strengthening its internal structure. In its inception, they have argued, the Negro ghetto was no different from other ethnic neighborhoods; only the difference in population patterns over the past fifty years has made it so. Oscar Handlin, for instance, maintains that the Negroes of the urban North, like the Irish, Germans, Italians, and Yankees, "chose . . . to live in communities of their own because they could thus best satisfy their social and cultural needs." In his view, the Negro ghetto, like the immigrant enclaves, was established "by adjustment — largely voluntary . . . to the conditions of metropolitan life."[1]

[1] Oscar Handlin, *Fire-Bell in the Night* (Boston: Little, Brown and Company, 1964), p. 97.

Much of the rhetoric that accompanied the rise of the Chicago Negro ghetto in the early twentieth century seems to support Handlin's contention that Negroes voluntarily chose separate development as a positive good. Both Negro and white leaders extolled the move toward separatism. Many Negroes spoke proudly of self-help, Negro achievement, and racial solidarity. White leaders hailed the growth of a self-sufficient Negro community as proof that Negroes not only recognized the realities of a biracial society, but preferred to be "with their own." In brief, the growth of the Negro ghetto often seemed, from the statements of both Negro and white leaders, less a manifestation of proscription than a mark of Negro progress.

The rhetoric contained a certain degree of truth. Separate community development in the urban North provided Negroes with new opportunities for independent action. In the rural South, despite legal segregation, Negroes did not really act on their own. The white landowner told them what crops to plant and when to plant them, provided them with tools and living quarters, gave them what few welfare benefits they might expect, and possessed sole political power. Only in their churches and lodges did the rural southern Negroes manage their own affairs. In Chicago, on the other hand, Negroes acted independently in many ways. They were on their own in seeking homes and jobs, and their employers exercised no control over their lives once they left the factories and yards. They supported Negro civic institutions and a Negro hospital, read Negro newspapers, and participated in a Negro political organization headed by Negro politicians. Paradoxically, Negroes were more independent of whites in the integrated North than in the segregated South.

The importance of this self-sufficiency should not be minimized. First, it provided Negroes with opportunities for leadership that hitherto they had never enjoyed. In the rural South, only the church and the fraternal orders provided training for Negroes with leadership ambitions. Chicago's black belt, on the other hand, afforded Negroes the opportunity to become leaders in politics, business, journalism, and civic life. Second, the idea of an independent black belt provided Negroes with a new sense of pride. Whatever the real achievements of Negro businessmen, politicians, and civic leaders, the sight of Negroes participating independently in fields that had previously been monopolized by whites became a source of race pride. Jesse Binga, Oscar De Priest, and George Cleveland Hall were more than Negro leaders; they became race heroes. Their accomplishments seemed to prove that Negroes could succeed, just as whites had succeeded, even with the odds arrayed against them.

Most important, even the man who could never hope to own a bank, go to Congress, or run a hospital could attain a degree of self-respect in Chicago that was often impossible in Natchitoches, Louisiana, or Macon County, Alabama. In Chicago, there was no omnipresent white man demanding obeisance. "The man," to be sure, was still there — the boss on the job, the cop on the beat, the Jew that ran the clothing store, but he was further removed from the intimacies of everyday life. Moreover he was an impersonal figure who, unlike the southern white, expected no fealty from "his niggers." In an almost all-Negro community, with no white man supervising every decision, manifesting his superiority in status at every opportunity, the northern Negro was able to develop a new sense of self-reliance and, to some degree, self-respect.

Nevertheless, much of the rhetoric of Negro achievement rings false when compared with the reality of Negro life in Chicago. The advantages of separate development were far outweighed by the disadvantages. In the first place, the Negro community was never truly independent. Only a handful of Negroes worked for Negro firms. The vast majority continued to rely upon white employers for their livelihood. The Negro civic institutions were run by Negroes, but white philanthropists provided them with the necessary financial support. White merchants controlled most of the retail businesses in the black belt, and even the most successful Negro businessmen often operated at the sufferance of white interests. This was most graphically illustrated in the late 1920's when Jesse Binga became a vassal of Samuel Insull, the utilities magnate, and the Binga State Bank became the first in Chicago to fall in the wake of the stock market crash, because Insull, preoccupied with his own interests, was unable to help.[2] Negro politicians came closest to exercising truly independent power. With Edward Wright's election as ward committeeman in 1920, Negroes gained control of the Second Ward Republican machinery. Still, the Thompson organization could break the Negro politicians, as Wright ruefully learned later in the decade.[3]

Second, no amount of rhetoric could obscure the inferiority of Negro community institutions and facilities. Probably the only Negro venture with a solid claim to excellence was Provident Hospital in its early days under Daniel Hale Williams; but once Williams and his white associates resigned, Provident could no longer compete with other hospitals in quality of medical care. Although Negro leaders were reluctant to recognize it, the indisputable fact remained that they had neither the experience nor the resources to create an adequate community life of their own. Moreover whites stood in their path at every turn. The inability of Negro businessmen to obtain credit from white banks, the inferior municipal services provided by the city to Negro districts, and the

2 "A Negro Bank Closes Its Doors," *Opportunity* (New York), 8 (September, 1930): 264; W. E. B. DuBois, "Binga," *Crisis* (New York), 37 (December, 1930): 425–26; *Chicago Defender*, April 6, 1935; interview with Joseph D. Bibb, March 29, 1963.

3 Lloyd Wendt and Herman Kogan, *Big Bill Thompson* (Indianapolis: Bobbs-Merrill & Company, 1953), pp. 249, 256–57.

refusal of many white agencies to take Negro community projects seriously all made the task of creating a separate but equal Negro community nearly impossible. Negro businesses were, by white standards, small, unstable, and underfinanced. The Wabash Avenue YMCA was but a shadow of the superbly equipped, lilywhite YMCA in the Loop, and Negro welfare organizations were inadequate to meet the needs of the underprivileged and maladjusted. The Second Ward political organization could determine the outcome of a mayoralty election, but it had neither the talent nor the will to face realistically the black belt's most pressing problems. In sum, the idea of a Negro city on the South Side, providing its inhabitants with all of the facilities from which they were excluded in the white community, remained a dream. Instead, the South Side was no more than a woefully inadequate, vastly inferior version of White Chicago.

Finally, despite their emphasis on the positive aspects of separate development, Negro leaders did not make a free choice when they opted for separatism. Their action was necessitated by white hostility and oppression. They built the institutional ghetto only after whites had created the physical ghetto, after Negroes had been barred from white neighborhoods and from the facilities of white Chicago. The architects of the "black metropolis" merely made the best of a bad situation. Many of them realized this and expressed an ambiguous attitude toward the developments they themselves encouraged. A few, perhaps, may have been wholeheartedly committed to the idea of a Negro metropolis on the South Side. Some probably saw an immediate advantage — both for themselves and for the Negro community — in separate development and never considered long-range objectives. Others saw no alternative, given the hostility of white Chicagoans. And still others looked upon separatism as merely a temporary expedient, never losing sight of the ultimate goal of an integrated society. In Drake and Cayton's analysis, "the very preachers, editors and politicians who did the most to keep the dream of Black Metropolis alive only half believed in its ultimate realization."[4]

The Chicago experience, therefore, tends to refute any attempt to compare Northern Negroes with European immigrants. Unlike the Irish, Poles, Jews, or Italians, Negroes banded together not to enjoy a common linguistic, cultural, and religious tradition, but because a systematic pattern of discrimination left them no alternative. Negroes were tied together less by a common cultural heritage than by a common set of grievances. Even those who made a major effort to emphasize the positive aspects of separate Negro development were hard-pressed. The Garveyites, for instance, were forced to glorify an African past that had no

---

[4] St. Clair Drake and Horace Cayton, *Black Metropolis* (New York: Harcourt, Brace & Company, 1945), p. 82.

relationship to the historical experience of American Negroes. Racial solidarity was a response rather than a positive force. It was an attempt to preserve self-respect and foster self-reliance in the face of continual humiliations and rebuffs from white society.

The persistence of the Chicago Negro ghetto, then, has been not merely the result of continued immigration from the South, but the product of a special historical experience. From its inception, the Negro ghetto was unique among the city's ethnic enclaves. It grew in response to an implacable white hostility that has not basically changed. In this sense it has been Chicago's only true ghetto, less the product of voluntary development within than of external pressures from without. Like the Jewries of medieval Europe, Black Chicago has offered no escape. Irishmen, Poles, Jews, or Italians, as they acquired the means, had an alternative; they could move their enclaves to more comfortable environs or, as individuals, leave the enclaves and become members of the community at large. Negroes — forever marked by their color — could only hope for success within a rigidly delineated and severely restricted ghetto society. No physical wall has encircled the black belt. But an almost equally impervious wall of hostility and discrimination has isolated Negroes from the mainstream of Chicago life. Under such conditions, Negroes have tried, often against impossible odds, to make the best of their circumstances by creating a meaningful life of their own. But they have done so, not out of choice, but because white society has left them no alternative.

Jerome Skolnick

WHITE MILITANCY IN THE URBAN NORTH

They have learned from the black people that the squeaky wheel gets the grease, so they're going to squeak, too.

— Tony Imperiale

It should be abundantly clear that violent white militancy has not been confined to the South. At present, although there has been relatively little private violence by whites in the North, the potential exists for a substantial amount of urban violence directed against blacks. There are a number of indications that militancy is increasing among some segments of the population of the Northern and Western cities. The immediate precipitants seem to have been black civil-rights activity, the ghetto riots, and a perception of the increasing danger of black criminality, but the increasing militancy of these groups reflects a larger problem that has received less attention than its importance warrants; the situation of the working-class and lower-middle-class white living in what may be called the white ghettos of the cities.

The leading edge of the growing Northern militancy lies in the largely working-class, generally ethnic neighborhoods of the cities. Given a national context in which the representatives of all three major political parties felt compelled to issue remarkably similar demands for "law and order," it is not surprising that a similar, but more strident, demand is made by those who are most directly threatened by the disorder attendant on contemporary social change. In short, the new militancy of the urban working-class must be seen in proper perspective. The militancy of those in the white ghettos differs principally in being more urgent.

This urgency is anchored in a set of real and pressing problems. As Robert Wood of HUD has put it:

> Let us consider the working American — the average white ethnic male: He is the ordinary employee in factory and in office. Twenty million strong, he forms the bulk of the nation's working force. He makes five to ten

Reprinted from *The Politics of Protest: Violent Aspects of Protest and Confrontation*, a staff report to the National Commission on the Causes and Prevention of Violence, prepared by Jerome Skolnick (Washington, D.C.: U.S. Government Printing Office, 1969), pp. 170–175, with permission of the author.

thousand dollars a year; has a wife and two children; owns a house in town —
between the ghetto and the suburbs, or perhaps in a low-cost subdivision on
the urban fringe; and he owes plenty in installment debts on his car and appliances.

The average white working man has no capital, no stocks, no real estate
holdings except for his home to leave his children. Despite the gains ham-
mered out by his union, his job security is far from complete. Layoffs, reductions, automation, and plant relocation remain the invisible witches at every
christening. He finds his tax burden is heavy; his neighborhood services, poor;
his national image, tarnished; and his political clout, diminishing . . . one
comes to understand his tension in the face of the aspiring black minority. He
notes his place on the lower rungs of the economic ladder. He sees the movement of black families as a threat to his home values. He reads about rising
crime rates in city streets and feels this is a direct challenge to his family. He
thinks the busing of his children to unfamiliar and perhaps inferior schools
will blight their chance for a sound education. He sees only one destination
for the minority movement — his job.

As has been the case historically, American social and political
institutions have not found ways of accommodating both the legitimate
grievances of aspiring minorities and the grievances of those who feel the
threat of displacement. Nor have those institutions succeeded in substantially lessening the danger of physical violence or criminal victimization
which accompanies life on the fringes of the slums. The result has been a
pervasive insecurity for the white urban dweller, which, while frequently
exaggerated, nevertheless has a basis in the rather grim realities of
contemporary urban life. Under present conditions, property values may
indeed be threatened when blacks move in numbers into white areas;
whites living near black ghettos do have to cope directly with the
problem of "crime in the streets;" and the failure of American
institutions to commit themselves decisively to the eradication of racial
injustice means that the root causes of white insecurity as well as black
discontent are likely to remain with us. It is in the context of these
conditions that urban white militancy is nourished. Politically ineffective,
educationally limited, and uncommitted to the finer distinctions regarding civil liberties and minority rights, the urban white of ethnic
working-class background is increasingly disposed to resistance.

One indication of the depth of the new militancy is the body of
evidence showing that a sizable segment of the urban population is
willing to use violence to defend itself against black disorder. Not only do
many Northern whites organize in support of harsh police measures
against rioters, many urban whites express a willingness to use private
violence. A Harris poll taken in September, 1967, indicated that 55 per
cent of a sample of white gun owners said they would use their gun to
shoot other people in case of a riot, a later Harris survey in March, 1968,
found the same question answered affirmatively by 51 per cent of white

gun owners. In the 1967 survey, 41 per cent of whites with incomes under $5,000 expressed the fear that their own home or neighborhood would be affected in a riot, as compared with 34 per cent of all whites. A study of white reaction to the Los Angeles riot of 1965 indicates that the willingness to use guns and personal fear of the riot are related. Twenty-three per cent of a sample of whites said that they had felt a great deal of fear for themselves and their families during the riot, and 29 per cent said that they had considered using firearms to protect themselves or their families. However, nearly half of those who had considered the use of firearms were also among those who had felt a great deal of fear. Willingness to use guns was highest in lower income communities and in integrated communities at all income levels; among whites living in close proximity to Negroes; among men, the young, the less-educated, and those in three occupational categories — managers and proprietors, craftsmen and foremen, and operatives.

In general, these findings support the conception of the white working- and lower-middle-class on the ghetto fringe as the most violence-prone wing of the growing white militancy, but the fact that higher-income whites living close to blacks express a high degree of willingness to use violence emphasizes the point that it is the situation — rather than the character or culture of the working-class — which is critical. The perception of threat appears to be a great equalizer of class distinctions.

Expressing willingness to use guns in the face of a riot, of course, is not the same as actually doing so. Since the recent riots have been contained within the black ghettos themselves, no information exists which directly matches white behavior with white opinion on the use of guns. However, the Los Angeles study found that 5 per cent of their sampled whites did in fact buy firearms or ammunition during the riot to protect themselves and their families. In Detroit, more than twice as many guns were registered in the first five months of 1968 — following the riots in August of 1967 — than in the corresponding five months in 1967, prior to the riot, and a similar trend is evident in Newark. It must be remembered that white neighborhoods were not significantly threatened during these riots. Speculation on what might result if white areas were directly threatened is not reassuring.

Further light on the potential for white violence is shed by a study prepared for the Kerner Commission which attempted to pinpoint the "potential white rioter." A sample of whites was asked whether, in case of a Negro riot in their city, they should "do some rioting against them" or leave the matter for the authorities to handle. Eight per cent of male whites advocated counter-rioting. Suburban whites were slightly less inclined to advocate a counter-riot than were city whites. Less educated whites tended to support counter-rioting, and there was a striking degree of advocacy of counter-riot by teenage males, 21 per cent of whom agreed that they should riot against Negroes. This percentage was slightly higher than the percentage of Negro teenagers who said they would join a riot if one occurred in their city.

Again, the degree to which these attitudes are, or might be, expressed in behavior is not clear. Nevertheless, studies of recent riots indicate that a significant number of "riot-related" arrests of whites have taken place. Occasionally, as in the Detroit riot of 1967, whites have been arrested on charges of looting, apparently in cooperation with blacks. More frequently, however, white males have been arrested beyond or near the perimeters of riot areas for "looting outside the riot areas, riding through the area armed, refusing to recognize a police perimeter, shooting at Negroes." Such incidents were particularly apparent in the New Haven, Plainfield, Dayton, and Cincinnati riots of 1967. The white counter-riot, of course, has historical precedent; most of the Northern race riots before 1935 involved pitched battles between whites and blacks, with working-class white youth particularly in evidence.

The historically prominent role of youth in militant white violence has received less attention than it deserves. A similar pattern has been evident in more recent years, as the figures above would suggest. Participation of white working-class youth in violence against civil-rights activity and against blacks moving into white neighborhoods has been noted in many Northern cities. In Chicago, for example, white youth were especially prominent in the Trumbull Park housing disturbances of the late 1950's, the assault on civil-rights activists attempting to integrate South Side beaches in the early 1960's, and the violence accompanying Martin Luther King's West Side campaign in 1966. Militant white youth have been active in several racially troubled areas of Chicago in 1968. In Blue Island, for example, sixty-seven white youths were arrested after harassing and beating Negroes following an incident in which two young whites were shot. Schools in many areas have been disrupted by conflict between black and white youth. The new militancy of black high school students is being countered in some areas by a corresponding white student militancy. In Trenton, N.J., for example, militant white high school students, many carrying signs reading "White Power," boycotted classes protesting incidents of "roughing-up" by black students.

Although youth have been prominent in relatively disorganized instances of militant white violence, the major efforts at organized militancy have been made by the adults who comprise the leadership of the various neighborhood defense organizations which have appeared in the North and West. Some of these, like the "Breakthrough" organization in Detroit, urge members to "study, arm, store provisions and organize"; a similar group called "Fight Back" in Warren, Michigan, argues that "The only way to stop them is at the city limits." Others focus less on arms training and storage, concentrating on community patrols to discourage black intrusion. The most significant of these urban vigilante groups is the North Ward Citizens Committee of Newark, whose leader, Anthony Imperiale, has recently been elected to the Newark City Council.

Newark's North Ward is a primarily Italian-American neighborhood with a large and growing black population, adjacent to the predominantly black Central Ward, which was the scene of the Newark riot of 1967. The strident nativism of the North Ward Citizens Committee reflects the ironies of the process of ethnic succession in America. Not too long ago,

> The Italians were often thought to be the most degraded of the European newcomers. They were swarthy, more than half of them were illiterate, and almost all were victims of a standard of living lower than that of any of the other prominent nationalities. They were the rag-pickers and the poorest of common laborers; in one large city their earnings averaged forty percent less than those of the general slum-dweller. Wherever they went, a distinctive sobriquet followed them. "You don't call an Italian a white man?" a West Coast construction boss was asked. "No sir," he answered, "an Italian is a Dago." Also, they soon acquired a reputation as bloodthirsty criminals. Since Southern Italians had never learned to fight with their fists, knives flashed when they brawled among themselves or jostled with other immigrants. Soon a penologist was wondering how the country could build prisons which Italians would not prefer to their own slum quarters. On the typical Italian the prison expert commented: "The knife with which he cuts his bread he also uses to lop off another 'Dago's' finger or ear . . . he is quite as familiar with the sight of human blood as with the sight of the food he eats."

Today, of course, the situation has shifted considerably, and the North Ward Italians feel themselves beleaguered by a horde of criminal blacks, instigated by radicals. The North Ward Citizens Committee operates patrols of the neighborhood, and members train in karate. Their militant quest for law and order is rooted in a set of severe insecurities attendant on life in Newark, where all the problems of the urban white North exist in extreme form. Newark is over half black; it leads all cities of its size in crime rates. It was the scene of one of the most disastrous episodes of black disorder and violent official response in the Sixties. The sense of fear pervading the white ghetto is reflected in Imperiale's words: "When is it gonna stop? Everybody says, 'don't bother 'em now. Leave 'em alone, and they'll calm down.' Well, it took riots that burned down half of a town before we learned."

Accompanying the fear of black violence is a strong sense of relative injustice. The citizens of the North Ward, conscious that their own neighborhood is deteriorating, strongly resent the concentration of state and Federal monies being poured into the black community.

Are there no poor whites? But the Negroes get all the antipoverty money. When pools are being built in the Central Ward, don't they think the white kids have got frustration? The whites are the majority. You know how many of them come to me, night after night, because they can't get a job? They've been told, we have to hire Negroes first.

The sense of special and unjust treatment for whites with grievances is compounded by what Imperiale regards as unfair discrimination against his organization:

The Mayor says he is going to try to get funds to start civilian patrols in the Central Ward. He claims this should be done for the so-called ghetto area. I went to Washington to get federal funds to set up a civilian patrol program in the North Ward and the other areas of the city, black as well as the white, and I was pushed from pillar to post. It is all right for the Central Ward but not for the North Ward where I am called a para-military organization.

In August, Imperiale's headquarters was bombed, and Imperiale has been highly critical of the lack of response by the law and city officials. "What makes me mad is that if the bombing had happened in the Central Ward, there would have been all kinds of FBI agents and authorities. When we get bombed, neither the mayor, the governor nor anyone else said it was a bad thing to have happened. No statement whatsoever was made in the papers."

This sense of injustice and of exclusion from political concern could lead to a heightened political alienation. The citizens of Newark's North Ward are largely correct in feeling that the polity has ignored them. At present, the Imperiale organization remains involved in traditional political action through the electoral process. Imperiale has insisted on this: "The Anti-Vigilante bill will do nothing because I am not a Vigilante. I am one-hundred per cent for a para-military law because that would outlaw people dressed in uniforms getting together and practicing sabotage and overthrow of the government. I love the government and am trying to save it. Should legitimate politics bear few significant results in terms of the grievances of the white ghetto, the North Ward Citizens Committee and similar groups may feel driven beyond politics. . . .

THE POLITICAL SYSTEM
OF THE METROPOLIS

2

Seventy years ago the political system of the metropolis was the city, a legal entity whose boundaries enclosed most urban development. As population increased and transportation improvements moved residences outward in the years between the Civil War and World War I, most cities expanded to encompass the urban growth spilling over their borders, usually by annexing adjacent unincorporated territory. Less frequent, but more dramatic, was expansion by merger or consolidation. The most notable of these amalgamations was the joining in 1898 of the nation's biggest city, New York, with its fourth largest, Brooklyn. The politics of annexation often fostered bitter strife, especially when city governments used their utility systems as a lever to force annexation on reluctant suburbs. In arid Southern California, this strategy has been pursued with considerable success by Los Angeles, which developed the area's major water supply system.

With few exceptions, cities have failed to keep pace with the spread of urban development in the twentieth century. Natural barriers checked their growth in some metropolitan areas. State and county boundaries also halted some cities. In addition, city administrations occasionally declined to annex because the costs of servicing the new territory exceeded the anticipated benefits to the city. But the overriding reason for the containment of the central cities, as Sam Bass Warner, Jr., points out in his analysis of Boston during the second half of the nineteenth century, has been the drive for suburban autonomy. Independence through incorporation or the prevention of annexation provides the residents of the new neighborhoods of the metropolis with a degree of personal control over taxes, zoning, and the educational system that is unavailable to the city dweller. Autonomy divorces the Republican suburbanite from the political system of the

Democratic city, a government usually perceived by the middle class as corrupt and unresponsive. By living in a separate political jurisdiction, the suburbanite tries to insulate himself from the social welfare burdens, racial problems, and crime of the city. He may also evade responsibility for maintaining the city's educational, cultural, recreation, and transportation facilities, which serve a broader population than that of the city alone.

The Boston case illustrates that the struggle between the annexationists and the autonomists, like most local political conflicts, was resolved in the state capital. As usually occurs in the triangular city-suburban-state relationship, the state legislatures were responsive to the suburbs but thwarted the cities. Annexation was made more difficult in most states, particularly when incorporated municipalities were the target. Regulations governing incorporation were eased in many states, stimulating the creation of municipalities by suburbanites seeking to avoid annexation. In the two decades before World War II, most of the larger cities, and many of the smaller ones, were ringed by independent suburban governments. With the great urban exodus of the postwar years came a vast proliferation in the number of suburban municipalities. Only in the newer metropolitan areas of the Southeast, Southwest, and Northern plains has annexation kept pace with urban growth. City-suburban disparities and antagonisms tend to be less significant in these younger and usually smaller areas. In the absence of strong pressures for autonomy, states in these sections of the nation have facilitated rather than blocked the expansion of cities. Texas, for instance, permits annexation without the consent of the residents of the territory to be acquired. Elsewhere, a few cities have stubbornly clung to their irredentist dreams. But as David Gladfelter indicates in his account of Milwaukee's attempts in the 1950's to induce incorporated suburbs to accept annexation in return for city water, the durability of the suburban-state house alliance probably forecloses a revival of imperialism in the cities.

The effects of the political separation of city and suburb are not immediately apparent to the casual observer of the metropolis. Rarely does the city line mark a sharp change in the pattern of urban development. Instead, as one moves outward from the urban core, there is a gradual transformation from the densely populated working class dwellings of the city's older neighborhoods to the low density single family housing typical of the suburban middle class. Since every city has some of the latter, city and suburb tend to blend together in the outer neighborhoods of the city. The amount of low density development within the city varies greatly. Old cities like Boston which were completely settled before the automobile revolution have relatively few "suburban" residents within their borders. Much of the development of newer cities like Miami and Los Angeles, on the other hand, was strongly influenced by the forces of dispersion. As a result, large areas of these cities are "suburban" in character.

Although the change in the pattern of development is gradual, political separation nonetheless produces important differences in the aggregate population of the city as compared with that of the suburbs. Regardless of when or where the city stopped growing, it encompasses far more of the older residential, commercial, and industrial development of the metropolis than suburbia. Especially in the larger and older metropolitan areas, a relatively high proportion of city residents are in the lower socioeconomic ranks. The average city dweller occupies less living space, is older, has had fewer years of school, and earns a lower income than the suburbanite. In addition, he is more likely to be unemployed or impoverished, or to be black, Spanish-speaking, or foreign born. Most residents of the suburbs are members of the broad strata we call the middle class. Compared to their neighbors in the city, they are more likely to be managers or professionals, to be married, to have school-age children, and to own a home and an automobile. Among the rapidly growing number of working-class suburbanites, skill levels and incomes tend to be higher than among working-class residents of the city.

The political separation of the city and suburb was not the basic cause of these socioeconomic variations among the residents of the metropolis. Long before the city ceased to grow, urban Americans had sorted themselves into neighborhoods differentiated along ethnic, class, and income lines. What the decline of annexation and the growth of independent suburbs did produce, as the excerpt from the report of the Advisory Commission on Intergovernmental Relations indicates, is a fragmented metropolis in which political boundaries reinforce social and economic differences. Once, the many components of an urban society lived within a single political jurisdiction which crosscut the socioeconomic diversity of its population. The nineteenth century city also was a regional taxing unit, enclosing within its boundaries all significant forms of wealth in the metropolis. Thus, it had the geographic scope — although it often lacked either the will or the capability — to perform two of the most fundamental functions of a political system: the moderation of conflict among diverse groups; and the redistribution of wealth to advance the general welfare.

Performance of these functions is much more difficult in the fragmented contemporary metropolis. Instead of encompassing diversity, the jurisdictional lines between the city and suburbia on the one hand and among the suburbs on the other institutionalize the conflicts that arise from ethnic, racial, class, income, and territorial differences. A welter of independent taxing jurisdictions replaces a political system whose revenue base includes all sectors of the urban economy. These jurisdictions vary widely in resources and needs, with little direct relation between the two. The older cities and suburbs with the greatest needs typically have the most meager resources available on a per capita basis.

As important as the political separation of city and suburb to an understanding of metropolitan politics is the fragmentation of the suburban political system. The property tax, the chief fiscal resource available to the governments of suburbia, is the primary source of this fragmentation. Robert C. Wood's analysis reveals how the suburban dependence upon local property taxes encourages competitive neomercantilist policies based on maximizing high-value development and minimizing inexpensive residential development. Suburbia's tireless pursuit of a favorable balance between resources and demands produces differences in public service, reinforces the social and ethnic homogeneity of individual suburbs through segregation by home value, and fosters the creation of new suburban units of government.

The processes of separation and differentiation have produced a fragmented metropolitan political system. This system institutionalizes the diversity of the metropolis, separates numbers and wealth, and enhances the many differences within the metropolitan population. These divisions, in turn, ensure that the differential impact of urban growth and change on the various sectors of the metropolis will continue to be reflected in the political system. In most metropolitan areas, fragmentation and differentiation have foreclosed the development of areawide government. General purpose governments with metropolitan constituencies exist only in Miami, Nashville, Indiana,᷒ ᷒ lis, Baton Rouge, and in the handful of cities, mostly in Texas, whose boundaries encompass the metropolis. The absence of central instrumentalities means that public policy for the metropolis is made either by the area's many jurisdictions acting unilaterally or by surrogates for metropolitan government such as special districts, the states, and the federal government.

Norton E. Long indicates that the fragmented institutional base shapes the perceptions, attitudes, resources, and goals of all the participants in metropolitan politics. Aside from the central city business and civic leaders who seek to save the city through reunification, few contestants in the political arenas of the metropolis are oriented toward the problems or the interests of the metropolitan area as a whole.

The decentralized metropolitan system makes widespread use of special districts and public authorities to perform functions that transcend local governmental jurisdictions. Unlike metropolitan government, special purpose agencies are not perceived as a threat to local control. Because they usually are financed by user fees, they do not raise the threat of unequal costs and benefits implicit in proposals to create metropolitan institutions with general taxing powers. The jurisdiction of the special district can be tailored to fit a particular problem, the boundaries of the participating communities, or the desires of the technicians involved. Districts and authorities are free from the state-imposed tax and debt restraints that limit the activities of local government practically everywhere in the United States. Finally, the image of the "businesslike" special district that is "out of politics" with its "pay as you go" revenue-financing strikes a responsive chord in the average resident of the metropolis who vaguely distrusts both politicians and the normal processes of local government.

To secure the advantages of the special district, however, the communities of the metropolis must pay a price. The growth of functional autonomy erodes a central function of government — the allocation of limited resources to meet the many demands for public goods and services. As independently financed and politically insulated special districts and authorities acquire responsibility for an enlarging area of public policy, the range of choice available to the local elected official dwindles. The problem is further complicated, as Jameson W. Doig illustrates, because self-supporting, revenue-financed authorities skim the cream off the top of the public economy of the metropolis. Although the onerous task of raising taxes to finance those programs that incur deficits is left to the general purpose governments, special districts like New York's Port Authority are free to pursue policies designed to maximize their revenues. Far from removing sectors of the public's business from politics, authorities create their own insulated political worlds, adding to the decentralization and diffusion of responsibility that characterize the metropolitan political system.

Sam Bass Warner, Jr.

STREETCAR SUBURBS AND THE
END OF ANNEXATION IN BOSTON

Two qualities mark off the Boston of 1900 from all preceding eras: its great size and its new suburban arrangement. In 1850 the metropolitan region of Boston encompassed a radius of but two or three miles, a population of two hundred thousand; in 1900 the region extended over a ten-mile radius and contained a population of more than a million. A change in structure accompanied this change in scale. Once a dense merchant city clustered about an ocean port, Boston became a sprawling industrial metropolis. In 1850 it was a fairly small and unified area, by 1900 it had split into two functional parts: an industrial, commercial, and communications center packed tight against the port, and an enormous outer suburban ring of residences and industrial and commercial subcenters. . . .

In Roxbury, West Roxbury, and Dorchester the parade of 23,000 new houses arranged by grid streets and frontage lots, the regular progress from one architectural style to the next, the constancy of basic house design, and the clustering of buildings by the income levels of their owners witness uniformity of behavior among individual decision makers.

Both positive and negative factors contributed to the uniformity of decisions of the 9,000 private builders. Positively, these middle class homeowners and amateur investors shared a sympathy for the suburban style of living which was then developing in metropolitan Boston. There existed a consensus of attitude which made each decision maker to some degree favorable to the new shingle and later colonial revival styles of architecture. This same consensus caused each man to build houses much like those of his neighbors and to seek to locate in a neighborhood or on a street which was popular with families of an income similar to his own. Finally, this same consensus encouraged each man to seek and to perpetuate the new suburban environment which emphasized the pleasures of private family life, the security of a small community setting, and the enjoyments of an increased contact with nature. The strength of this consensus grew with the passage of time. Every year more and more

Excerpted by permission of the publishers from pp. 153–166 of Sam B. Warner, Jr., *Streetcar Suburbs: The Process of Growth in Boston*, 1870–1900. Cambridge, Mass.: Harvard University Press, copyright, 1962, by the President and Fellows of Harvard College and the Massachusetts Institute of Technology.

middle class families lived in the suburbs. Every year, too, the streetcar and utility networks brought a steady increase in land available for settlement so that successively closer approximations to the desired environment became possible.

Negatively, suburban builders were repelled by conditions in the central city. The unending immigrant invasion, the conversion of old houses and the encroachment of industry and commerce heightened the contrast between the new suburbs and the central city. Negatively, too, the limited financial position of homebuilders disciplined their choices of houses and neighborhoods and controlled their methods of land division.

The policies of the large institutions concerned with building supported and disciplined these individual choices. The role of the larger agents was essential. At the municipal scale, utilities had to be laid before most men would be willing to build. Adequate streetcar service also preceded homebuilders and their customers. At the neighborhood scale the arrival of new families attracted by a new improved transportation service, or the expansion of adjacent neighborhoods, or the departure of old families because of housing obsolescence, all encouraged one kind of building and discouraged others. At his peril a man built cheap rental units in outer suburbs, or expensive singles in old inner suburbs. The patterned spread of various kinds of new construction bears witness to the power of the informal neighborhood regulation of building. It was a power based upon the sensitivity of individual landowners to the economic standing of their neighbors.

The behavior of the large institutions concerned with suburb building also encouraged individual landowners to repeat in their building the popular suburban architecture, engineering, and economic grading of neighborhoods. Late nineteenth century Boston was a fast-growing metropolitan society made prosperous by the new industrial technology and propelled by the energy of thousands of individual capitalists. The middle class was one of the principal beneficiaries of this prosperity, and its well-being and rapid enlargement gave this large segment of Boston society the confidence to stress its equalitarianism and the willingness to exploit each new technological device. The rise of thousands of families of the most diverse ethnic backgrounds to a middle class competence, like their quick adoption of each new invention, was taken as proof of the success of the society.

The City of Boston and the later metropolitan boards enthusiastically adopted the new sanitary engineering. These institutions undertook to see that all new neighborhoods would be built to the latest standards, and at great expense attempted to service the old parts of the city. This enormous undertaking not only made the new devices available to Boston's homeowners, but also stimulated the universal acceptance of middle class criteria for home services. In the suburbs all the new regulations for plumbing, gas fitting, and building and fire safety were perhaps more important as official affirmations of middle class norms than for policing an occasional offender. With the cooperation and example of the large institutions almost all new suburban building from 1870 to 1900 included safe construction, indoor plumbing, and orderly land arrangement. From the prosperity of the middle class and its enthusiastic acceptance of the new sanitation and transportation technology came the popular achievement of the late nineteenth century suburbs: a safe environment for half the metropolitan population.

The orientation of the large institutions toward the benefit of the suburban builders also assisted the small landowners. The street railways and other utilities rapidly extended their service to outlying metropolitan villages. In so doing they encouraged private development of distant land. This policy was aimed at taking advantage of the general growth of the city, but it also reflected a belief that public agencies should assist private undertakings. Similarly, the Park Department carefully avoided land which was thought to be suited to private construction, taking instead the marshes and uplands at the edge of areas then building. In effect, the Park Department landscaped the margins of private developments. In the new neighborhoods the City of Boston built schools at a very rapid rate and its official architecture and landscape design mirrored the fashions of private builders. Public policy held installation charges for new utilities and streets to below cost, much of the expense being borne by general taxation and general rates. When the city bargained with gas and electric companies for the extension of its lighting it often bargained in behalf of residential users as well, endeavoring to see that they too would be connected to the new lines and served at reasonable rates. The combined effect of all these policies was to greatly assist the individual builder to develop the vacant land outside the old city. . . .

The suburb, the home of property owners and settled family life, was thought by contemporaries to be an environment that encouraged individual participation in community life. Compared to transient conditions in older parts of the city the suburbs were more conducive to integration of the individual into some sort of community activity. Their physical arrangement, however — the endless street grids and the dependence upon the downtown for work and shopping — failed to provide local centers where all the residents of a given area might, through frequent contact, come to know each other and thereby be encouraged to share in community-wide activities.

Aside from class segregation there was nothing in the process of late nineteenth century suburban construction that built communities or neighborhoods: it built streets. The grid plan of the suburbs did not concern itself with public life. It was an economically efficient geometry which divided large parcels of land as they came on the market. The arrangement of the blocks of the grid depended largely upon what farm or estate came on the market at which time. The result was not integrated communities arranged about common centers, but a historical and accidental traffic pattern. . . .

As a result of the centerless character of most suburbs, community life fell into fragments. Groups formed about particular churches, clubs, schools, and ward club rooms; rarely did any large fraction of the population of a suburban area participate in any joint endeavor. When, through accident, the historic political boundaries of a town coincided with the building pattern of a new suburb local politics provided a framework for community activities. Nevertheless, even these conditions were unfavorable to the development of meaningful community life. The limited subject matter of town politics, and the frequently narrow income band of the residents of new bedroom suburbs, together generated an enervating parochialism which hung heavy over such community life as existed.

In 1900 the new metropolis lacked local communities that could deal with the problems of contemporary society at the level of the family and its immediate surroundings, and it lacked a large-scale community that could deal with the problems of the metropolis. As a result Boston community life fell into a self-defeating cycle. Each decade brought an increase in the scale and complexity of economic and social life; each decade's problems demanded more wide-scale attention, more complex solutions. Because of the physical arrangement of the new metropolis, each decade also brought an ever greater fragmentation of community life into town and ward politics, church groups, clubs, and specialized societies of all kinds. The growing parochialism and fragmentation resulted in a steady relative weakening of social agencies. Weakness, in return, convinced more and more individuals that local community action was hopeless or irrelevant. From this conviction came the further weakening of the public agencies. The self-defeating cycle, begun by the streetcar metropolis, has continued with increasing severity to this day. It has proved, both for the metropolis and its constituent political units, an iron cycle, a cycle which once established, is difficult to break.

The inattention of late nineteenth century Bostonians to the fragmentation of their community life was not an accidental oversight, it was a matter of principle, the principle of individualistic capitalism. Above all else the streetcar suburbs stand as a monument to a society which wished to keep the rewards of capitalist competition open to all its citizens. Despite ignorance and prejudice, during this period of mass immigration, the suburbs remained open to all who could meet the price.

By 1900 about half the families of metropolitan Boston had come to share this new environment. The wealth brought to the society by its industrial technology, and the special practices of suburban building, made this mass achievement possible. The manner in which the nineteenth century building process physically separated the metropolitan population into two sections — the middle class section of families who could afford new construction, and the lower class section of families who could not — assisted some of the open equalitarian goals of the capitalist society. In the suburbs families of similar economic standing lived next to each other, and their similarity of economic position helped them to learn to ignore their differences of religion and national background. The great extent of the new suburbs, moreover, left room for fine graduations of the middle class population. Middle class families were free to choose among hundreds of possible locations, free to find a neighborhood which suited both their ethnic feelings and their progress up the economic ladder.

The infrangible and enduring problems of the suburbs also derive from the principle of open capitalist competition. At any moment in the late nineteenth century half the metropolitan society was not successful, half the society remained apart from the achievements of the suburbs. The process of new construction, since it was tied to the abilities of individual builders erecting houses for their own immediate use or profit, took no effective responsibility for the lower income half of the society. As a result, contemporary progress in housing for lower class families was slow and uncertain, limited to slight improvements in sanitation, structural safety, and fire prevention.

By sheer enlargement of their numbers, and by the obsolescence of middle-income structures, low-income groups could and did reach the new suburbs. Most often, however, they could occupy them only by destroying much of what the suburb had achieved. Because the late-comers possessed but small sums for rent, secondhand houses in the suburbs often had to be divided and redivided so that a single became a double or a triple, to a two-family house was added an attic apartment, and so forth. Even where slightly higher incomes made division of structures unnecessary the cost of maintaining old wooden houses often prevented the newcomers from keeping up their houses and lots to the level originally intended. Though not included in their rent bills, the progressive deterioration of their environment was one of the prices of low-income tenancy.

Neither the architecture nor the land planning of the new suburbs took any account of the possible subsequent users. A satisfactory single-family house brought, when divided, two or three cramped and mean apartments, each one often well below the building's original standards for light, air, and sanitation. The reduction in floor area per person brought an immediate and obvious retreat from the norms of the first owner. The garden setting of the street often disappeared under the feet of running children; back yards and porches filled with the overflow and trash from the houses; planted playgrounds required tar to support increased use; and the large country parks grew to weeds because of lack of time and interest among their new users.

By assigning building to the activities of thousands of individual middle class landowners the metropolitan society allowed itself to build a physical environment which would become, by its own terms, the unsatisfactory home of half its members. By this means also the society received a physical plan which was destructive to its democratic processes. The essence of the new metropolitan plan was the separation of the vast areas of new construction from the old central city.

The literature of late nineteenth century reformers tells the consequences of this division. For the middle class the inner area of low-income housing became an unknown and uncontrolled land. Here, in one ward vice and drunkenness flourished out of reach of middle class supervision; in another ward nationalist demagogues, institutionally isolated from the rest of the metropolis and responsible only to the majority of the ward, held free rein in the search for their own profit. Such troublesome manifestations of the divided society gave much concern to contemporaries. They were but symptoms of the serious consequences of the physical division of classes.

Most important, the concentration in a solid two-mile area of foreign languages, poverty, sweatshops, and slum housing gave the suburban middle class a sense of hopelessness and fear. Much of the work of reformers in the twentieth century progressive era had to be devoted to the task of educating the middle class to the conditions of modern industrial cities. It was a task undertaken with the middle class faith that through knowledge would come a willingness to take action.

Opposing reformers' goals of knowledge and action stood the structure of the streetcar metropolis which had damaged the fabric of the society. In part the rural ideal bore responsibility for the arrangement of the metropolis, for it had encouraged middle class families to seek escape from the conditions of modern industrial life into an isolated family environment. More important, the dominant ideal of individualistic capitalism with its accompanying unwillingness to bring private profit to account had caused the economic division of the society. The slums and the suburbs were the physical expression of this division. The conditions of the central city which so dismayed the middle class were the product of its failure to control the distribution of income, its failure to regulate housing and working conditions, its failure to develop an adequate welfare program for the sick and unfortunate, and its failure to devise a community program for integrating the thousands of new citizens who every year moved to the metropolis. These things, neglected, bore a harvest of middle class fear. From fear came the late nineteenth century paradox of the growth of an economically integrated regional city of over a million inhabitants accompanied by an increase in the parochialism of its political and social units.

In 1870 many middle class suburbanites regarded Boston as their achievement, something they wished to join in order to create a political union of homes, jobs, and community. Such sentiment gave popularity to the mid-century annexation movement. From about 1850 to 1873 almost every city and town around Boston had an annexationist group, and the question of the advantages and disadvantages of union with Boston was seriously debated. In 1868 Roxbury joined Boston; in 1870 Dorchester, and in 1873 Charlestown, Brighton, and West Roxbury, voted for unification.

The year 1873 marked the end of the annexation movement. That year the residents of Brookline voted to remain separate. This political defeat, and the Depression of 1873–1878 ended public concern over the metropolitan expansion of Boston. With the return of prosperity, however, the movement never revived. Instead, the legislature created in the late 1880's and early 1890's three specialized state-managed agencies which undertook to serve metropolitan needs for water, sewer, and park building.

The sudden and permanent collapse of the annexation movement had two causes: the first concerned municipal services; the second, the idea of community. During the middle years of the nineteenth century some of the larger and more prosperous of the peripheral towns and cities had built their own waterworks and expanded their street and educational services so that they approximated some of the high standards of Boston. In 1870 Charlestown, Cambridge, and Brookline had satisfactory independent waterworks. These same towns and Dorchester and Roxbury possessed advanced educational facilities. Other towns, however, lacked the tax base and access to the rivers and lakes necessary for high-quality municipal service. The metropolitan agencies, by building a unified drainage and water supply for the whole metropolis, put all the region's towns in a position to meet modern municipal standards.

The motive of services having been withdrawn, there remained only the idea of community. Annexation debates had always concerned themselves with this question. Annexationists appealed to the idea of one great city where work and home, social and cultural activities, industry, and commerce would be joined in a single political union. Boston, they said, would share the fate of Rome if the middle class, which heretofore had provided the governance of the city and the force of its reforms, abandoned the city for the suburbs.

Opponents of annexation countered with the ideal of small town life: the simple informal community, the town meeting, the maintenance of the traditions of rural New England. They held out to their audience the idea of the suburban town as a refuge from the pressures of the new

industrial metropolis. Nor were the opponents of annexation slow to point out that the high level of city services maintained by Boston meant higher taxes, and further, they frankly stated that independent suburban towns could maintain native American life free from Boston's waves of incoming poor immigrants.

As early as 1851 West Roxbury estate owners led a successful move to separate the rural part of the town of Roxbury from its industrial half. In 1873 middle class Boston commuters who had moved to West Roxbury reversed this decision by a close vote, and the town joined Boston. The new commuters wanted the high level of services offered by Boston, and they were confident that the middle class could govern the enlarged city to its own satisfaction.

By the 1880's, with but one exception, no suburban town ever again seriously considered annexation. The segregation of the metropolitan population brought about by the interaction of the expansion of street railway transportation and the suburban building process had by the mid-1880's given a permanent set to political life. In the face of the continually expanding size of the metropolis, by contrast to the continual waves of poor immigrants that flooded the central city and destroyed its old residential neighborhoods, the new suburbs offered ever new areas of homogeneous middle class settlement. Here, most immigrants spoke English, most were Americanized, and here the evenness of income lessened the scope of political conflict. It was already apparent in the 1880's that to join Boston was to assume all the burdens and conflicts of a modern industrial metropolis. To remain apart was to escape, at least for a time, some of these problems. In the face of this choice the metropolitan middle class abandoned their central city.

Very soon the middle class began to reap the harvest of its action. Already by 1900 Boston was something to be feared and controlled. Many of its powers of self-government had been taken from it by the state or voluntarily abandoned by tax-conscious voters to put a check on demands for public improvements. Beyond Boston the special suburban form of popularly managed local government continued to flourish. In suburbs of substantial income and limited class structure, high standards of education and public service were often achieved. Each town, however, now managed its affairs as best it could surrounded by forces largely beyond its control. New transportation, new housing, new industries, new people, the great flow and vigor of the metropolis, lay beyond the knowledge and competence of these individual agencies. In the years to come World Wars and depressions would unleash antidemocratic forces that threatened the foundations of the society: its democratic institutions, its property, its ethnic harmony, the chance of each citizen to prosper through capitalist competition. Confronting these challenges stood a metropolitan society physically divided by classes, politically divided by about forty parochial institutions. So divided, the society denied itself the opportunity to end, through common action against common problems, the isolation of its citizens and the fear they held toward each other. So divided, the metropolis was helpless to solve its own problems.

During the years 1870 to 1900 industrial capitalism was, comparatively, a new thing, and a mass suburban metropolis like Boston had never existed before anywhere in the world. To rely on individual capitalists, to expect that each man building for himself would build a good environment for a democratic society was perhaps a reasonable error to have made. Today, some of the problems confronting the streetcar city have been solved or passed by. Except for the American Negro, immigration conditions are over. The automobile allows a less rigid class arrangement and less dense housing than was possible under streetcar transportation. Zoning, large-scale subdivision planning, and new financial institutions have made suburban building somewhat more orderly, and have opened homeownership to a greater proportion of the society. Most important of all, the great twentieth century national reforms of progressive taxation and labor, factory, and welfare legislation have allowed more widespread participation in the profits of industrialism.

Despite these changes the two great problems first met in the streetcar city remain unsolved. Even by popular standards one enormous segment of the population still lives in an unsatisfactory physical environment. More serious, because it is a condition which affects all others, the growing metropolitan society as a whole remains shut up in an ever larger number of specialized social and political units, its citizens isolated from one another, its society needlessly uncontrolled because of the weakness of its agents.

David D. Gladfelter

THE POLITICAL SEPARATION OF CITY
AND SUBURB: WATER FOR WAUWATOSA

The Setting

In 1954, the city of Wauwatosa, Wisconsin, a suburb adjoining Milwaukee to the West (see map), suddenly developed a serious problem of water supply. The suburb had often experienced shortages during summer droughts and periods of heavy use, and it had been warned for over ten years that its water table was steadily falling. Engineers, however, considered the independent Wauwatosa water system, a utility which drew upon eight artesian wells, adequate to meet the needs of users within the suburb's original area of 4 square miles.

When the suburb annexed 8.5 square miles from the town of Wauwatosa in 1954, it was suddenly faced with the responsibility of supplying water to that rapidly growing residential and industrial area which already contained some 12,000 inhabitants. The suburb had made no provision for new sources of water before carrying out the annexation.

Wauwatosa officials took this problem to a firm of consulting engineers for study and recommendations. In December, 1954, Samuel J. Gates, one of the firm's executives, recommended that Wauwatosa purchase water from Milwaukee to supplement its supply of well water. Unless the suburb could obtain Milwaukee water, Gates said, it would be forced either to sink additional wells or to join in forming a suburban utility with other suburbs. Gates did not consider the former alternative to be good engineering. To drill additional wells in Wauwatosa would only accelerate the rate of decline of the water table. Regarding the latter, he advised that Wauwatosa not participate in a new cooperative venture until the availability of water from the Milwaukee utility was thoroughly examined. It was Gates' impression that Milwaukee would be able to serve its neighboring suburb by means of existing plant and mains.

Gates then addressed a letter to Edward F. Tanghe, Superintendent of the Milwaukee Water Works, asking whether the city would be willing to sell water to the suburb. Gates thought that Milwaukee could furnish this water "at a profit" during off-peak periods, and added that

Richard T. Frost, Editor, *Cases in State and Local Government*, © 1961. Reprinted by permission of Prentice-Hall, Inc., Englewood Cliffs, New Jersey.

THE AREA INVOLVED IN THE WAUWATOSA WATER CASE

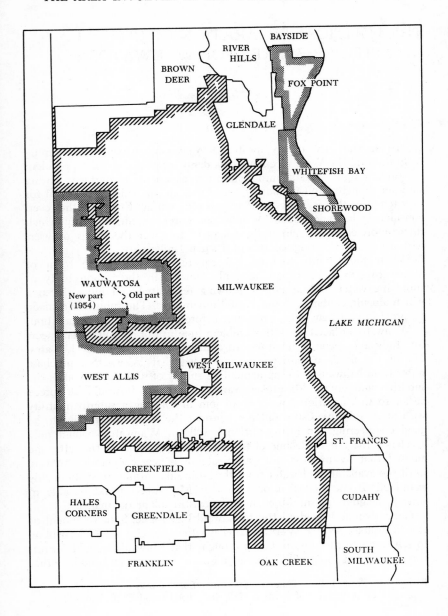

Wauwatosa would be ready to cooperate "in the details" of building storage tanks for the city water.

But Tanghe had other ideas. Referring the letter to the Milwaukee Common Council, whose policy he, as water superintendent, was bound to follow, Tanghe said, "The Common Council is on record and has been for a long time against selling water outside the city." It was his opinion, moreover, that Milwaukee did not have sufficient facilities to provide water to Wauwatosa, since it was then having trouble serving its own users adequately.

Actually, Tanghe's categorical statement concerning Common Council's water service extension policy was not correct. Milwaukee had had the authority to sell its water outside the city limits since 1887, had done so since 1902, and was doing so to six suburbs in the year 1954. It was true, however, that Council had opposed *further* extensions of service, not only because the city lacked the facilities to provide it, but because Council had always considered water service to be related to a larger political problem, that of annexation and consolidation.

The Milwaukee Council has long assumed that by withholding city water, it could induce suburbs needing water to become a part of Milwaukee. Conversely, it has feared that to give suburban users Milwaukee water without requiring their commitment to annexation would be to lose the opportunity to draw them into the city. Why should the suburbs receive a vital city service without incurring the higher city taxes? Council felt that to provide the suburbs with water would be tantamount to inviting city industry to migrate to the suburbs. Consequently, Council's attitude toward Gates' request for more water was negative. Alderman Milton J. McGuire, Common Council president in 1954, suggested that suburbs desiring city water "join the city, and then they'll get it."

After receiving Gates' letter via Tanghe, the Common Council did what was expected. Early in January, 1955, after the Council's utilities committee had voted 3–2 to reject, Milwaukee killed the proposal. This ended Wauwatosa's first attempt to secure a supply of Milwaukee water.

Interim Measures

For the year and a half following the Milwaukee Council's decision, Wauwatosa relied on stopgap measures to meet its water problem. During that time, further engineering studies were made, and the two alternative plans suggested by Gates — well drilling and membership in a suburban utility — were investigated further. During that time also, the water problem became more and more acute, affecting homeowners and to a lesser extent industry. When the suburb again turned to the city, in May of 1956, it was prepared to do serious battle; for the problem had reached the point where residents were aroused and were "behind their government one hundred per cent." This is the way the Wauwatosa City Attorney phrased it.

Water needs were greatest in the newly annexed areas on Wauwatosa's west side. The suburb had not yet provided these areas with piped water; existing homes located there relied upon relatively shallow private wells for water. The development of the area had led to an increase in the number of wells being sunk, which had lowered the water table and had caused some wells to fail or become polluted. On one occasion when a "cooperative well" serving the neighborhood went dry, the suburb had to haul water by tank truck to supply an entire subdivision on an emergency basis for a week. The well had been constructed thirty years earlier to supply a much smaller number of families.

And, on another occasion, about a dozen homeowners protested to the Wauwatosa Board of Public Works that their wells were polluted and that action must be taken at once. As a stopgap, Wauwatosa considered drilling a ninth public well in an area of particular hardship, the Park Ridge area, and supplying the homes directly; but later developments made this project, which would have cost an estimated $175,000, unnecessary.

Other interim measures taken by the suburb included a requirement that subdividers, before receiving approval of proposed plats, sink cooperative wells to serve the homes until a public supply were available. New industries also, specifically Harley-Davidson, Briggs and Stratton, and the Mayfair shopping center, were assigned the responsibility of providing their own water until such time as the suburb could furnish it.

Three months after the Milwaukee rejection, Gates' firm "reluctantly" recommended that Wauwatosa drill two deep wells immediately to meet supply problems. The cost of the wells and necessary mains and storage facilities was estimated at $2 million. The firm also recommended that efforts to obtain water either from Milwaukee or from a suburban utility be renewed, and that unless such a supply could be obtained, the suburb would need three additional new wells. This second Gates report was critical of the water policy of the Milwaukee Common Council; saying:

> It would seem to us that public convenience and necessity, plus the oppor-
> tunity to profit, would determine utility policy, but they [Milwaukee officials]
> are concerned about annexation and other considerations which in our opinion
> are not relevant. Under the present circumstances we are forced to look else-
> where for water.

Meanwhile, other suburbs of Milwaukee were considering increasing their own water supply by creating independent water districts. But none of these suburbs (Oak Creek to the south and Whitefish Bay, Fox Point, and Glendale, to the north) was contiguous in boundaries to Wauwatosa.

This discouraged the Wauwatosa government from participating, because expensive easements would be required at substantial costs in money and time. The suburbs decided not to join in these efforts.

Back to the City

In May, 1956, Wauwatosa directed its attention once again to Milwaukee as a source of water. Wauwatosa Mayor William B. Knuese, in a letter to his common council, urged that the suburb start a proceeding "in the proper state commission (the Public Services Commission — PSC) or in the courts" to force Milwaukee to supply water to Wauwatosa. His position was simply this — since the Milwaukee water department was a public utility already selling water outside the Milwaukee city limits, it could not legally refuse to sell water to Wauwatosa. Knuese's letter said in part:

> With the single exception of the City of Wauwatosa, the water department of the City of Milwaukee now furnishes water to every incorporated city or village immediately adjacent to its boundaries. It also furnishes water to other communities and people. It has been in the public utility business beyond its own corporate limits for a long period of time.

The mayor further recommended that, should action through the PSC or the courts be unsuccessful, Wauwatosa should seek state legislation establishing a metropolitan water district. "If Milwaukee won't sell water," he said, "it should step aside and permit creation of an authority that will."

The Wauwatosa council did not dally. It referred Knuese's letter to its Board of Public Works, which reported back a week later with recommendations for a council resolution. Before another ten days were past, the council had unanimously passed the resolution, its first formal action taken in its quest for Milwaukee water.

The resolution, addressed to the Milwaukee Council, requested permission to connect Wauwatosa mains with those of the city, and further authorized the Wauwatosa attorney to start proceedings with the State or in the courts if Milwaukee continued to refuse. On May 29 the resolution was delivered to the Milwaukee Common Council.

Milwaukee's reaction was unsympathetic. Alderman Matt Schimenz, chairman of the Council's utilities committee, emphatically stated:

> The City's water will go to Wauwatosa over my dead body unless there is a political consolidation of Milwaukee and Wauwatosa.

Mayor Frank P. Zeidler added:

> Wauwatosa wants city services without paying city taxes. When a city like

Wauwatosa holds itself out as a city, it takes on the obligation of supplying all services from its own sources. . . . If we extend our water to everyone outside the city, we will lose industry itself just as we have lost the captains of industry.

The utilities committee referred Wauwatosa's resolution to a special nine-member study committee composed of aldermen and administrative officials. Toward the end of June the committee recommended that Milwaukee not serve any new municipal customers until it could take adequate care of its present customers in the City and in six suburbs. On July 10 the Common Council again rejected Wauwatosa's demand.

This action brought a prompt decision by Wauwatosa to appeal to the State PSC. Herbert L. Mount, special counsel for Wauwatosa, said that even if the city did not have the plant capacity to begin service to the suburb, the PSC could fix a schedule of expansion to meet Wauwatosa's needs. He announced that he would ask the PSC for such an order. In the months ahead, Wauwatosa prepared its testimony and briefs with the aid of engineering consultants and special counsel, and on November 14, 1956 the suburb filed its petition with the state agency.

The State Agency

The Public Service Commission's authority to require public utilities to extend service was explicit in the 1931 statute that created it. The temper of that regulatory body, up to the time of Wauwatosa's petition, had been opposed to Milwaukee's policy of using water to attain other ends. Earlier, for example, in a 1937 test case, the Commission had gone on record as favoring water service extension with a minimum of hardship and delay wherever needed in metropolitan areas.

In this first test case, Milwaukee protested an order of the Commission requiring it to extend service to an adjacent unincorporated town. The city claimed it was not a water utility for the metropolitan area, but sold only by contract; thus it had no obligation to serve outside the city limits and the PSC had no jurisdiction over it. After a rehearing, the Commission had ruled:

The contracts indicate that the city has voluntarily taken upon itself a public utility obligation of supplying water to various municipalities. Once undertaken the public utility may not arbitrarily discontinue it. . . . Nor may the public utility arbitrarily select its customers. The city of Milwaukee holds itself out as a public utility in a metropolitan area to render service by sundry methods to all contiguous municipalities or to individuals; the position of the city that it is under no obligation to serve another potential customer outside its limits creates an intolerably discriminatory situation.

The circuit court to which Milwaukee appealed dismissed the case on stipulation agreeable to both parties, so the PSC's finding was not actually reviewed by a court of law.

The outcome of a similar case, decided by the PSC in 1940 and by the Wisconsin Supreme Court in 1942, modified somewhat the PSC's 1937 opinion. In this case, the Commission ruled that Milwaukee, having contracted to serve a few areas in an unincorporated town, had incurred an obligation to serve the entire town. In its order, the Commission reasserted its authority to require extension of service by the city within the metropolitan area. But the Surpeme Court held that the question at issue was much narrower than the PSC had assumed, and refused to comment as to whether Milwaukee could be obligated to serve the entire metropolitan area. The Court did rule that the city had not "held itself out" to serve the whole unincorporated town by agreeing to serve a part of it, since in its contracts, the city had made express limitation upon the extent of its service. The court disallowed the Commission's order.

The upshot of the Supreme Court's ruling was this: The PSC's statutory power to require extensions of service had not been actually denied, nor had the Court defined the area which the Milwaukee utility could be required to serve. The court *had* ruled that the city was not obligated to extend water service within *un*incorporated areas, thereby leaving the city free to continue to use water as a club to promote annexation of such areas. It had *not* ruled upon Milwaukee's obligation toward incorporated suburbs already possessing water utilities.

The Current Controversy

Hearings before the PSC on Wauwatosa's new application for service were held throughout 1957 and early 1958.

Wauwatosa's counsel, City Attorney Milton F. Burmaster and Special Attorneys Herbert L. Mount and Maxwell Herriott, concentrated their efforts on proving the Milwaukee had an obligation to provide water service. They used two lines of argument: first, that since Milwaukee supplied water to six suburbs, its refusal to serve another was "unjustly discriminatory and in violation of the statutory obligation of the Milwaukee water utility"; and second, that Milwaukee had obligated itself to serve because of a contract made in 1908 to supply water to several Milwaukee County institutions in Wauwatosa.

The 1908 contract did not enter into the PSC's findings of fact, but it did present a technicality. The city of Milwaukee had contracted with the county to supply its hospitals, homes, and asylums via a main through Wauwatosa. In the contract the city had agreed to permit the county to sell water to persons along the pipeline. The county then had obtained an easement from Wauwatosa, upon which Wauwatosa had imposed the condition that in the future "the city of Wauwatosa and the citizens thereof may and shall be eventually supplied with water" from the main. The city of Milwaukee never protested this provision in the contract between Wauwatosa and the county, and by 1956, 236 inhabitants of the suburb were being served by the county from its main. Wauwatosa's lawyers claimed that although the suburb had made no contract directly with the city, the city was nevertheless obligated to the suburb by virtue of both Milwaukee's and Wauwatosa's contracts with the county.

Milwaukee's counsel, First Asst. City Attorney Harry G. Slater, replied to both of Wauwatosa's arguments with a motion to dismiss the petition. Regarding the first argument, Slater contended that the city had not held itself out to serve Wauwatosa and could not be compelled to enter a contract against its will. As for the second, he asserted that the PSC had no jurisdiction in determining the existence of a contract; such a finding was a matter for the courts. The city lost the motion, however, and the PSC ordered hearings to proceed on the merits of the case.

In presenting Milwaukee's petition, Slater reiterated the city Council's viewpoint that Milwaukee would be unable to serve a new customer because it was having trouble serving its present users. To compel Milwaukee to serve additional outside areas "would result in aggravated service deficiencies, substantial engineering difficulties, hardship to our present customers and inequitable burdens to rate payers," he said.

To this, Wauwatosa replied that Milwaukee could supply Wauwatosa reservoirs during off-peak periods without having to add more than a "comparatively small capital outlay" to that already contemplated by Milwaukee. Wauwatosa would pay for needed improvements in its own system, its counsel said.

Slater emphasized the point that Wauwatosa's troubles stemmed directly from its own previous annexations. He said:

> Milwaukee should not be required . . . to meet the problems which the city of Wauwatosa has created for itself . . . through annexations. . . . If Wauwatosa has problems as a result of its annexation policies, the city of Milwaukee offers its sympathy. But Milwaukee should not be expected to take over Wauwatosa's responsibilities.

Slater argued that all of the areas in which Wauwatosa had pressing water needs were in the newly annexed part of the suburb, and that Wauwatosa's well system had been quite adequate to serve the older part. As Slater put it, Wauwatosa officials "bit off more than they could supply with water."

The suburb's attorney, Herriott, replied, "This is a case of the pot calling the kettle black." By this he meant that Milwaukee's difficulties in serving its present customers had resulted from its own recent annexations.

Even during the most bitter moments, the hearings yielded occasional humor. In the stormy final session, Wauwatosa Attorney Mount emphasized the inadequacy of his suburb's water facilities and again doubted the feasibility of Wauwatosa's joining an independent suburban water system. "It would be a duplication of Milwaukee's facilities," he said. Attorney Slater rejoined that the whole network of suburbs surrounding Milwaukee was a "duplication of Milwaukee's facilities." He said he was amazed that Wauwatosa officials would admit, after operating a water utility for 50 years, that they had bad tasting, polluted water, insufficient pressure, and that only Milwaukee could solve these problems.

The PSC Decides

The Commission handed down its order on April 2, 1958. It was in two parts. The first part ordered Milwaukee within 60 days to provide temporary service of up to 2 million gallons a day to Wauwatosa "on an off-peak basis." The second part ordered Milwaukee to "proceed with due diligence" to provide additional plant and facilities as are necessary to supply Wauwatosa permanently.

The Commission, after recapitulating the history of Milwaukee's extension of water service to its suburbs, concluded that the city had held itself out as a water utility by supplying six suburban municipal customers. Because of this, it continued, Milwaukee "thereby assumed an obligation as a water public utility to provide such a service to any municipal water utility" located in Milwaukee County and contiguous to the city. Therefore, Milwaukee could be required to supply Wauwatosa. The PSC's findings as to the capacity and needs of both Milwaukee and Wauwatosa were that Milwaukee would be able to furnish Wauwatosa with 2 million gallons a day with its present plant, such service being "necessary as a temporary measure."

The gist of the case was summarized in the printed abstract:

A municipal utility's obligation to furnish . . . service to adjacent municipal utilities, while not inherent in its public utility status, may be assumed by legislative authority or by voluntary acts of the utility. Having acquired such obligation to serve refusal to serve a contiguous municipal utility is discriminatory between it and other similarly situated utilities now served.

Wauwatosa officials were elated by the news. Mayor Knuese praised the decision as "of the greatest importance and benefit to the entire metropolitan area, including the city of Milwaukee . . ."

To Milwaukee the decision was no surprise, but neither was it welcome. Mayor Zeidler said that if Milwaukee's water works were to take on all applicants, as the PSC had hinted it might require, an extra cost of $50 million for expansion, over and above the $54 million already budgeted, would be needed over the next 20 years.

The Commission's ruling confronted the Milwaukee Common Council with a dilemma. If it accepted the ruling it would be no longer able to use water service extension as a bargaining tool with which to negotiate adjustment of city-suburb controversies. If the city successfully challenged the ruling in court, then the state legislature might act to force Milwaukee to serve Wauwatosa and other suburbs or might create a metropolitan water district for the area. Council met on April 14 to decide which course to follow. A resolution calling for a court appeal was presented and passed.

But Mayor Zeidler vetoed this resolution four days later, explaining that he had concluded that acceptance of the order would be the "least injurious course" for the city "however unjust and contrary to our original defense it may seem." He warned that if the city should continue the battle further, it might lose control of its water works. The Council sustained the mayor's veto, and on April 30, in a tradition-breaking vote, it was decided to sell water to Wauwatosa without a further legal fight. A chastened Alderman Schimenz, who had made the "dead body" statement two years earlier, now remarked:

> Isn't it better for some of us to eat a little crow around here, rather than go into the courts? The water works will be taken away from us.

POSTSCRIPT 1. The friction between Wauwatosa and Milwaukee did not end with the PSC order. Sixty days came and went, and not a drop of water crossed the Milwaukee-Wauwatosa border. Each side accused the other of delaying; the city charged that the suburb's storage tanks were not ready, and the suburb claimed that the city's connections were not in order. When Milwaukee water tardily began to flow to Wauwatosa, the suburb alleged that the city was not providing the full two million gallons a day. Milwaukee Attorney Slater replied that he construed the order to mean that Wauwatosa could draw water from Milwaukee "if we have any water left after meeting our own needs."

2. Early in 1959, Wisconsin Governor Gaylord Nelson submitted the name of Alderman Matt Schimenz to the State Senate for confirmation as Chairman of the Public Service Commission of Wisconsin.

An immediate protest was sent to the Governor by the Municipal League of Milwaukee County (an organization of the suburban governments). State Senator Allen Busby (R-West Milwaukee, one of the suburbs) announced that he would vote against confirmation of Schimenz because the Milwaukee Alderman was "an advocate of the suburbs' adversary — the city."

Other state legislators indicated no particular interest in blocking the nomination at first, but one of the suburban representatives was reported in the *Milwaukee Journal* to have said, "Our only hope of blocking the appointment is to make it a Republican Party issue, one of party loyalty." The vote on the confirmation showed the success of the suburban effort. The Governor's candidate was rejected, 14 to 18. Republicans voted 18–2 against, while Democrats voted 12–0 for confirmation. Another rural legislature had done its work.

Advisory Commission on
Intergovernmental Relations

POLITICAL FRAGMENTATION AND FISCAL IMBALANCE

Prior to the great post-World War II exodus of the middle and upper income families to suburbia, our system for governing urban America appeared to conform to Aristotle's view of the "most perfect" way to shield the community from the perils of political extremism.

> In every city the people are divided into three sorts: the very rich, the very poor and those who are between them. . . . The most perfect political community must be amongst those who are in the middle rank, and those states are best instituted wherein these are a large and more respectable part, if possible, than both the other; or, if that cannot be, at least than either of them separate; so that being thrown into the balance it may prevent either scale from preponderating.[1]

Within the city's boundary were found the relatively few rich, the preponderant middle class, and the poor who often lived on "the other

Reprinted from *Urban America and the Federal System* (Washington, D.C.: U.S. Government Printing Office, 1969), pp. 9–10, 12–13.

[1] Aristotle, *Politics*, Book VI, Chapter XI, pp. 126–127. Madison advanced essentially the same thesis in *The Federalist Papers*, Number 10.

side of the tracks." The great cities of America, however, were more than social "melting pots." They were also balanced economically in the sense that they encompassed within their boundaries virtually all of the urban area's residential, commercial, and industrial development.

Because they possessed social and economic unity, our municipalities were also generally characterized by fiscal balance. The municipality's "deficit" areas — the low-income residential areas — were offset by the "surplus" areas — the high tax producing districts associated with the central business area, the industrial section, and the high income residential neighborhoods.

By far the most important social function performed by the great "balanced" municipalities was political in the Aristotelian sense — that of keeping the public peace by moderating the competing demands of the various classes that comprise the urban body politic.

The Rise of the Lopsided Communities

In many of our metropolitan areas the twin forces of urban expansion and social segregation have combined to burst the shell of the old "balanced" community and in the process have profoundly altered the social and political character of the urban municipality. Whereas the old municipality was socially and economically balanced, the new municipalities are "lopsided," i.e., the wealthy estate and industrial enclaves and the upper, middle, and lower income bedroom communities. While the sprawling and subdivided metropolitan area still has a central or "core" city, typically it is becoming smaller, poorer and blacker when compared to the burgeoning economy of white suburbia.

The political leadership of the old "balanced" municipality was under constant pressure to blur and moderate the conflicting demands of the urban rich, poor and middle class. In contrast, the leaders of the new "lopsided" municipalities are virtually forced by their narrow-gauged constituencies to sharpen and reinforce the divisive elements within our uptight urban society.

This political transformation becomes even more ominous because our highly decentralized system of government historically has relied almost entirely on the cohesive powers of the municipality to hold together the highly segregated components of our urban population. Moreover, the nation has leaned heavily on the local tax base in general and the property tax in particular for financing its domestic needs. It is ironic that the political balkanization of our urban areas occurs in the face of a growing need for social cohesion in an increasingly interdependent society.

The tendency for metropolitan areas to split politically along their income and racial seams is most apparent in the Northeast and Midwest, and least noticeable in the Southwest. More and more rare in the Northeast quadrant of the United States, is the large city that still encompasses within its boundaries most of the residential areas occupied by the white middle class let alone those of the wealthy. In striking contrast stand Houston, San Antonio, and Phoenix. Their vigorous annexation policies may be prompted by the spectacle of the older Eastern cities slowly being choked to death by the "white noose" of suburban municipalities.

Grim Fiscal Outlook for Central Cities

A few successful annexations, however, cannot mask the grim fiscal prospects for most of the nation's great cities. The findings of a recent Advisory Commission study of metropolitan fiscal disparities clearly substantiate the widespread belief that most of our major cities are now in a desperate situation.

1. The central cities, particularly those located in the industrial Northeast and Midwest, are in the throes of a deepening fiscal crisis. On the one hand, they are confronted with the need to satisfy rapidly growing expenditure requirements triggered by the rising number of "high cost" citizens. On the other hand, their tax resources are increasing at a decreasing rate (and in some cases actually declining), a reflection of the exodus of middle and high income families and of business firms from the central city to suburbia.

2. The concentration of high cost citizens in the central city is dramatically underscored by public welfare statistics. For example, 27 per cent of Maryland's population is located in Baltimore, yet 72 per cent of Maryland's AFDC expenditures is to be found in that city. By the same token, Boston, with 14 per cent of Massachusetts' population, accounts for 40 per cent of that State's AFDC expenditure.

3. A clear disparity in tax burden is evident between central city and outside central city. Local taxes in the central cities are 7.5 per cent of income; outside the central cities only 5.6 per cent of income. Higher central city taxes are reinforcing the other factors that are pushing upper income families and business firms out of the central city into suburbia.

4. On the educational or "developmental" front, the central cities are falling farther behind their suburban neighbors with each passing year. In 1957 the per pupil expenditures in the 37 metropolitan areas favored the central city slightly — $312 to $303 for the suburban jurisdictions. By 1965, the suburban jurisdictions had forged far ahead — $574 to $449 for the central cities. This growing disparity between the central city and suburban school districts takes on a more ominous character in light of the fact that the central city school districts must carry a disproportionately heavy share of the educational burden — the task of educating an in-

creasing number of "high cost" underprivileged children. Children who need education the most are receiving it the least!

5. On the municipal service or "custodial" front, the presence of "high cost" citizens, greater population density, and the need to service the needs of commuters force central cities to spend far more than most of their suburban neighbors for police and fire protection and sanitation services. The 37 largest central cities had a non-educational (municipal) outlay of $232 per capita in 1965 — $100 greater than their suburban counterparts.[2]

The situation for most central cities takes on an even more dismal cast because there is little prospect for a *voluntary* solution arising from within the metropolitan area. Suburban political leaders can generally be counted upon to oppose stoutly any proposal that would call for a significant redistribution of resources such as an area-wide tax with a strong equalization twist to aid the central city. By the same token, suburban leadership can be expected to view with a jaundiced eye any major redistribution of burdens, i.e., the rezoning of suburban land to permit low income central city families to obtain public or low cost housing in suburbia.

Cracks in Suburbia's Picture Window

Comparing the fiscal behavior of the central city with the entire suburban area, however, tends both to obscure and to distort the disparity story because it lumps together diverse suburban jurisdictions. Anyone familiar with the fiscal landscape of suburbia is keenly aware of the fact that it does not present a uniform picture of affluence. On the contrary, suburbia fairly bristles with contrasts between rich, poor, and middle income jurisdictions.

In most metropolitan areas, the range between the most affluent and impoverished suburban jurisdiction is considerably greater than that between central city and suburbia in general. For example, elementary school districts in Cook County, Illinois, reveal a range of about 30 to 1 in their property tax base per pupil in 1964 and various studies have reported ranges of 10 to 1 or more in the per capita tax base of municipalities within various metropolitan areas.[3]

2 This analysis was conducted by Professor Seymour Sacks of Syracuse University and appears as a part of the Advisory Commission's study *Fiscal Balance in the American Federal System* (A-31; October 1967), Vol. 2.

3 Dick Netzer, *Economics of the Property Tax* (Washington, D.C.: Brookings Institution, 1966), pp. 24–25. See also, Advisory Commission on Intergovernmental Relations, *Fiscal Balance in the American Federal System*, Vol. 2, Appendix D.

Because they lack a diversified tax base, most of the lower to middle income residential suburbs can also expect a steady deterioration in their fiscal prospects.

There is evidence which indicates that, as the suburban expansion grows, it is increasingly the lower middle class white collar worker and the blue collar worker who is fleeing the central city for suburbia, giving increasing rise to the demand for suburban development which caters to the economic capabilities of these groups. The composite of these trends all seems to indicate that the newly developed suburban community of the future will be developed with tax bases which fail to provide adequate fiscal capacity for the support of municipal and educational services.[4]

A Few Winners and Many Losers

Because the concept of local fiscal disparities is of necessity a relative matter, the political splintering of Urban America along income and racial lines produces its share of municipal winners as well as losers. While difficult to measure with precision, it nevertheless appears possible to detect several gradations along the disparity spectrum ranging from the big winners at one end (i.e., Scarsdale, New York, and Lake Forest, Illinois) to the big losers at the other end (Newark and East St. Louis). Most metropolitan communities can be placed in one of five categories:

1. *Highly disadvantaged* — A community that falls far short on the public service side even though it makes an extraordinary tax effort.
2. *Disadvantaged* — A community that must make an extraordinary tax effort to break even or provide an average level of public service.
3. *Balanced* — A community that can bridge the gap between resources and needs by providing an adequate level of service with an average tax effort.
4. *Advantaged* — A community that can provide a superior level of service with an average tax burden.
5. *Highly advantaged* — A community that can provide a superior level of service with a minimal tax effort.

If most or all of the communities within metropolitan areas fell in the "balanced" category there would be little cause for concern with the fiscal health of the nation's cities, or little need for State and National governments to enact fiscal equalization measures. But that is not the case. Serious widespread disparities do exist. Many of the largest central

---

[4] James M. Banovetz, W. John Pembroke, and Peter J. Fugiel, "Fiscal Disparities in the Chicago, Illinois Metropolitan Area," in *Fiscal Balance* . . . , Vol. 2, p. 243.

cities are in the "highly disadvantaged" category. And some of these disparities continue to grow.[5]

Beggar Thy Neighbor

Ever mindful that no community within the metropolitan area "stands still' in relation to its neighbors, local policymakers are under unremitting pressure to adopt a highly aggressive policy in order to maintain or obtain a favorable competitive position. As it enters the metropolitan arena, each governmental unit has three prime weapons — the power to tax, the power to spend, and the power to determine land use.

This fiscal contest among municipalities in the same metropolitan area might be described as the local Tax and Zoning Game. In order to hold down education costs, suburban legislators are under strong temptation to use a low density approach to residential zoning. Although the one-acre suburban lots can be denounced as an example of "snob" or restrictive zoning, they are also hailed as an act of local financial prudence — the only sure way of placing a lid on school costs and property tax rates. The zoning of great stretches of suburban land for commercial and/or light industrial purposes is another example of fiscal zoning. There is always the hope that a large share of the local tax burden can be exported to neighboring communities by snagging the giant shopping center, the industrial research park or the massive public utility installation. In brief, the name of the game is cutthroat intergovernmental competition, and the object of the game is to "zone in" urban resources and to "zone out" urban problems.

Operating under a logic that goes back to the Domesday Book of William the Conqueror, each autonomous principality has the unchallenged and exclusive right to protect and to exploit all taxable resources within its domain. While this "winner take all" philosophy makes good sense in terms of the old "balanced" community, it takes on a harsh and inequitable color in a sprawling metropolitan area inhabited by aggressive and lopsided governmental units. One jurisdiction can reap all the tax benefits of an industrial location while the neighboring communities are often required to pay the costs of educating the children of the new employees.

"Staying in Line": An Exquisite Tax-Expenditure Calculus

Local policymakers competing in a metropolitan arena are keenly sensitive to inter-community tax rate differentials. There is a constant fear that an

5 Ibid., p. 2.

above average tax rate will act as a powerful deterrent to economic development within the local jurisdiction. While this fear may be exaggerated, the local concern for a "competitive" tax position is very real; it cannot be dismissed as foolish. The effect of local tax differentials upon industrial location within a metropolitan area was underscored in a recent Advisory Commission report.

The relative importance of the tax differential factor in industrial location decisions appears to increase as the location process narrows down to a particular jurisdiction within a general region. As among regions of the country, the non-tax factors such as access to markets and to labor and comparative transportation and supply costs stand out as the primary location considerations. As between neighboring States, there appears to be no direct relationship between industrial growth and tax differentials due largely to the fact that States are careful not to get "too far out of line" with their immediate neighbors. As among local governments within a State and especially within a metropolitan area, tax differentials exert discernible plant location pull — the industrial tax haven stands out as the most conspicuous example. *In almost every metropolitan area there exists wide local property tax differentials — a cost consideration that can become a "swing" factor in the final selection of a particular plant location.*[6]

Because of the desire to "stay in line," the relatively low level of taxation that is possible in the more affluent jurisdictions tends to serve as a brake on higher taxes throughout the metropolitan area. This braking action takes place despite the fact that higher taxes may be urgently needed in other jurisdictions.

Inter-community fiscal competition, however, is not restricted to the tax side of the equation. "Staying in line" with neighboring jurisdictions also forces each municipality and school district to re-examine constantly its expenditure policies.[7] Whereas municipalities are fearful lest their tax rates become too high, they also are concerned lest their public service standards in general and their education standards in particular fall too far below those set by their neighbors. This keen concern for maintaining a competitive educational position often results in local school boards being played off against one another when it comes time to negotiate revised pay scales for teachers.

The fortunate fiscal position of the more affluent jurisdictions within the metropolitan area, therefore, creates a bitter dilemma for their less well endowed neighbors. The below average tax rates of the affluent jurisdictions provide aid and comfort to those persons advocating a tough,

[6] Advisory Commission on Intergovernmental Relations, *State-Local Taxation and Industrial Location* (A–30; April 1967), pp. 78 and 79. (Italics added)
[7] *Ibid.*, p. 79.

"hold-the-line" tax position. On the other hand, the high educational standards of the more fortunate jurisdictions provide heavy ammunition to those persons advocating larger appropriations for the schools.

Caught in this crossfire, the policymakers in the less fortunate jurisdictions must attempt to frame both a tax policy that will underwrite a "fairly decent" brand of public services and an expenditure policy that will not force taxes to "confiscatory" levels — a painfully exquisite form of political-fiscal calculus.

Robert C. Wood

SUBURBIA:
THE FISCAL ROOTS OF POLITICAL
FRAGMENTATION AND DIFFERENTIATION

For the suburbs as a whole, the problem involved in their tax system is less the evils of the property tax as such than the inflexibility of their general tax structure implied by the heavy reliance on property taxes. While other local governments, particularly large cities and independent cities with a rural hinterland, have been able to broaden their tax base considerably, suburbs, with notable exceptions, have not. Municipal income taxes, sales and gross taxes, tobacco and admission taxes, levies on earnings, are not well suited to suburban governments. For one thing, they are difficult to administer, requiring a bureaucratic sophistication, an array of financial power, an assurance that their residents cannot shop elsewhere, and a variety of land uses that few suburbs possess. For another, they often place a suburb at a competitive disadvantage with its

Reprinted from *Suburbia: Its People and Their Politics* (Boston: Houghton Mifflin Company, 1958), pp. 208–225, with the permission of the author and the publisher.

neighbors so far as the attraction of presumably desirable business and commercial activity is concerned. Although, as we will see later, suburbs have shown great ingenuity in discovering and inventing new sources of revenue, by and large they are excluded from the big money earners. While nonproperty taxes accounted for 27 per cent of all local revenues in the 481 cities over 25,000 population in 1956, and multiplied six times in the years between 1950 and 1955, it is doubtful that suburban governments — municipalities, school districts, and towns — figured prominently in the increase.

The heavy reliance on property taxation is the first fiscal liability of the suburbs. The second is the fact that, contrary to popular opinion, the property to be taxed is becoming less lucrative. The comfortable assumption that residential property values are almost always higher in outlying districts of the metropolitan areas — and, therefore, the suburban tax base is proportionately larger than that of the core city — justified many family migrations to the metropolitan fringe. In prewar years this was to a considerable degree correct, but for the last fifteen years suburban real estate has lost a great deal of its comparative advantage over that in the central city.

Almost 50 per cent of the dwelling units constructed between 1940 and 1950 were in the suburbs, and, typically, the values of the new residences were higher than the values of residences built before 1940. But the differences between old and new values are not nearly as great as they were fifteen years ago, and so far as the more expensive residential construction is concerned — houses costing over $15,000 — two important developments have taken place. First, in this category there is no significant difference between old and new suburban houses, and second, median values for new housing in the central cities are almost 30 per cent higher than in the suburbs. Moreover, the faster a metropolitan area grows, the lower the median value of residential housing constructed. In short, when housing values new or old are compared, there is a persistent tendency for the central city to have higher residential values and to retain them, and the faster the suburb grows, the lower is the average residential value. Suburbs are not attracting the high value development of our decade.

Even more important, general averages are likely to be misleading in suburbia, where land uses tend to cluster in the same way different occupations bunch together. Unlike the median values of a large city that encompasses all types of property, the limited jurisdiction of each suburb means that usually only one type of property value predominates. The search for homogeneity carries its inevitable corollary in property values, and suburbs differentiate themselves sharply in their financial resources when they segregate themselves by social status. For the suburbs taken collectively, this range has great significance, for it means that the cheaper construction now underway, especially in rapidly growing areas, is not spread throughout each suburb. Instead, it is concentrated in particular suburbs, heightening their fiscal crises while others take the lion's share of the more expensive residential property to provide the base for their public services.

The continuing dispersion of industrial and service activity may well tend to supply additional resources for the suburbs as a class and provide a welcome cushion to the tax base. But here again the question of variations among suburbs arises. Despite the newly favorable attitude many fringe communities are exhibiting toward light industry, there is, as yet, little evidence that industry locates where it is most needed in terms of tax resources. Most observers believe a contrary pattern is at work, in which "industries tend to locate in one suburban community and the workers locate in another community, with the result that the problem of financing services to the employees, and their families, of those industries, gets very serious indeed."

Nor are shopping centers likely to relieve the plight of low housing value suburbs. They tend to locate where incomes are higher and their aim is to draw together a number of businesses in a concentrated space. Thus their very success reduces the likelihood that neighborhood stores will scatter themselves throughout the suburbs, in physically unattractive but financially rewarding string developments along major streets. With the rich getting richer and the poor poorer, those suburbs with lower value housing and probably a greater need for services may have to depend more and more on residential property value to support their governments.

The continued shift in the labor force from agricultural and manufacturing occupations to "service" industries — and the consequent spread of trade establishments — may well alleviate the tight fiscal situation. And if the diffusion of industry accelerates in the next generation as many expect, more suburbs will find additional revenue sources. Stern reassessments, bringing tax valuations more in line with market price, may also increase the yield of present resources. But these trends are still in the making; at the present time, suburbs in general and in particular seem to face an uphill fight.

Yet the critical factor is not the present difficulties of suburbs as a class, the shortcomings of the property tax as such or the inability of most suburbs to develop other resources. Even the relative decline in suburban residential property value as compared to the central city may not be serious. Rather, it is the haphazard pattern of distribution of property resources among political jurisdictions, and the effect of the property tax upon that distribution, that spells real trouble.

Specifically, financial trouble lies ahead for the metropolitan regions because the property tax system works to encourage a further political fragmentation of the areas. It sets off a game of musical chairs which coincides with social and political proclivities for exclusiveness, and although the process carries with it the seeds of self-destruction, the logic of maintaining the separate status of each such suburb is inescapably reinforced. This is the real significance of the present financial pattern which, in the face of snowballing new demands, works to keep the suburbs divided.

The internal workings of the property tax within suburbia are complicated, and it exists only because the region is already fragmented. But it is the policy induced by the financial system — not the tax itself, not the real wealth of the communities in relation to public expenditures — that is the key to understanding the so-called suburban financial crisis. George Duggar has provided the theoretical framework that explains the suburban maneuvers in their self-imposed battle for resources. He reasons that suburbanites tend to judge governmental expenditures according to whether or not the services they provide add to the land values, or, more specifically, whether their benefits for the individual land owner add to the total value of his property more than his taxes detract from it. Given this tendency, the logical tax policy for any local government is to maximize the benefits of public services and minimize their tax costs. Thus the objective it must seek is to entice high-value property within its borders and prevent the intrusion of low-value construction.

The rationale for this policy of "financial efficiency," so far as residential construction is concerned, is, of course, that expensive properties pay high taxes while they typically require the same level of public services as any other type of property of equal size. For high-value residences, the value of the land itself is proportionately higher and the share of private improvement value in the total value is lower than for low-value property. Thus the total taxable value is greater, compared to the services required, the higher a community climbs up the scale of residential quality. The suburban government of better-class neighborhoods finds itself in a happy position of being able to receive tax returns considerably in excess of the cost of services it must offer.

Moreover, because there is a monopolistic element involved in land prices, arising from the relative scarcity of good sites, the prestige value associated with exclusive neighborhoods, and the reduced importance of money for those who are able to live in them, the suburban government can exact higher prices for the services it provides. In actual practice, it can, of course, reduce the tax rate to the point where revenue equals expenditures, but in theory it behaves like a firm engaged in monopolistic competition — receiving revenues for each unit for service considerably higher than the cost of providing the service. By offering a special type of land advantages, it is able to extract taxes that are considerably larger than those received by other suburbs which do not have choice property but which have the same service needs.

On the other hand, suburbs in which very inexpensive development has taken place cannot hope to receive revenues commensurate with costs. In these municipalities, the value of a typical home is a much larger proportion of total real estate value — house and site taken together. Since the costs for government services are more closely related to the number of houses than the value of the land they are built upon, as construction becomes cheaper and cheaper, the capitalized costs of services per house or square foot of land come to exceed the capitalized taxable value, or even the market value per house or foot of land. Without the cushion which high site values give, the suburban government is forced to increase the tax rate to as high a level as possible, or to cut services. Even then, if total residential values are very low, it may not be able to make ends meet. Its financial position becomes progressively worse, for the ratio between tax burdens and benefits is reduced, each additional unit of service costing more on a capitalized basis than the corresponding unit of revenues the property produces, with the inevitable result of a rising tax rate. In these municipalities property values are not enhanced by government services; instead, they are adversely affected.

Thus, the overall policy implication of the property tax, as Duggar points out, is that suburban governments are led inevitably into an effort to achieve "financial efficiency by a policy of value differentiation" — that is, using local government powers to attract expensive improvements or to repel lower-cost improvements. This drive for high values may take the form of exclusive residential development or it may induce suburbs into the now fashionable search for "light industry," breaking down earlier attitudes antagonistic to industrial development. As these financial problems increase, as the amount of undeveloped land dwindles, many municipalities become actively engaged in enticing industry, regardless of the intrinsic economic value of their particular sites. Unwilling to trust the operation of market forces, they engage in "a sort of mercantilist interplay between municipalities, each fighting to keep its taxes down and its notables up."

Whether residentially or industrially inclined, however, from the point of view of any suburban government the sensible aim is to attract and maintain as large a concentration of high values as possible. Such a policy not only assures an excess of revenues over normal local government expenditures; in the end, it enhances property values even more, since the individual owner finds indirect benefits accruing from the "monopolist" position his government has attained — the value of "exclusive" neighborhoods, the provision of services that add to site value.

These value differentiation policies have obvious injurious effects on particular individuals. For the property owner the implication is, of

course, that total property values are increased among expensive properties and reduced for less costly properties. The owner of a $10,000 Cape
Cod house on a quarter acre lot has little economic incentive to build an
extra room or add a garage. These "improvements" not only reduce the
value of his site in a theoretical sense by distorting it from its "best and
most economically desirable purpose" but they increase his taxes more
than they increase the benefits he receives from local public services.
While, from the municipality's point of view, his total tax burden does
not exceed the cost of services rendered, the additional taxes on his new
improvements reduce the total value of his property, for in effect they
impose expenses greater than benefits. In extreme cases, the after-tax
value of low-value property can even be reduced below the level of value
of the improvements on the land alone, the market prices of the cheaper
houses will fall, and expenditures for proper maintenance and further
improvements will be discouraged.

In short, value-differentiation policies, when in full swing in a
metropolitan area, work against the provision of reasonably inexpensive
homes for the majority of Americans, handicap national policies designed
to further home ownership, and encourage high-value construction rather
than low for prudent investors. The further down the income scale a
family is located, the less likely it is that a suburban house is a good
investment. The more improvements made, the less the portion of
investment which goes into land alone, the harsher are the tax burdens.

Individual inequities aside, an even more significant effect of these
policies from the governmental perspective is the reinforcement of
suburban autonomy. Inevitably, the drive for value-differentiation sets in
motion a continued process of segregation of high-value property and
continued depression of low-value property prices below the market price.
Suburban governments, by any doctrine of prudent fiscal management,
are forced to prefer expensive construction; such property returns more
than it costs in services. The owners of high-value property are then
rationally inclined to encourage their governments to resist invasion by
owners of lower-value property. Even though the latter pay more than
their proportionate share, the presence of cheaper homes may depress
prices of the older, more expensive residences, and certainly it will
increase overall municipal costs. A process is triggered off by which the
suburb initially seeks high value because of the financial advantages
accruing to the government and then is led into restrictive practices
because these appear to be the only way to preserve the initial
investments in the area.

Some authorities find the scramble for resources that goes on in
metropolitan areas ethically questionable. Henry Fagin, for example,
complains that "the very cities that can most easily afford to carry the
burdens of inexpensive homes are the ones which most vigorously resist

such homes and are the most successful in avoiding them." Certainly the drive for high-value and only high-value property buttresses the social and ethnic exclusiveness which suburbanites display in their search for small town homogeneity.

Yet, given the nature of the property tax, it is difficult to criticize suburban officials who are fortunate enough to have desirable locations for exploiting their position. To do otherwise when government costs are rising steadily — to be liberal in their attitude toward lower-income newcomers, to strive for heterogeneous neighborhoods, to welcome citizens regardless of race, creed or color — is to invite financial disaster. If the town fathers are to be faithful to their economic trust, they must practice discrimination. Having forsworn association with the metropolis, which might possess the variety of land uses to hold the injurious effects of the property tax to a minimum, there is now no stopping point. Ethically, segregation may be intolerable, but from the individual perspective of any given suburb, the continued splintering of the metropolitan region is now a financial necessity.

The upshot of this inquiry into the implications of property taxation in suburbia is that, so far as the question of financial adequacy is concerned, the answer is, "It all depends." Some suburbs have ample resources to meet the demands of modern government; others are obviously inadequately equipped to stand on their own. As long as the property tax is the bulwark of their defense, the capacity of the suburbs to survive breaks down into at least two different issues, with a broad twilight zone in between. The answers to these questions require a study of the strategy of two types of suburbs as they go about resolving their quite different financial problems.

For the suburbs blessed with natural advantages, where big mansions are in existence and Levittowns have not appeared, the strategy of "high value" dictates a constant surveillance of the changing metropolitan scene to make sure no unwelcome intruders are admitted. A whole series of tactics are usually employed: the judicious use of regulatory powers, special requirements and restrictions demanded of builders, discrimination in taxation and in the quality of services extended to particular neighborhoods, selective annexations, imaginative employment of eminent domain, are all standard weapons in the battle. Collectively, they attest to the strength of will and stubbornness of suburban officials and citizens in preserving their land values and their communities.

The most spectacular weapon, of course, is the use of regulatory powers — zoning and subdivision control — for here the potency of the value-differentiation policy is most clearly seen. Henry Fagin has documented for the New York region the extent to which suburbs will go to preserve high values and exclude low ones. Among his investigations there appears the case of the New Jersey township which imposed an informal building permit moratorium "until 'the law' finally caught up with it"; the instance of the suburb which prevented mass development by requiring that each house differ in certain design characteristics from five of its neighbors; the town which set a five-acre minimum lot size; and the New Jersey borough which owns one third of the land in its jurisdiction and sells lots at the rate of a dozen a year to purchasers of its own choosing. Throughout the cases he studied, Fagin found a consistent policy, in towns which were financially able to support a growing population, to resist new residents and inexpensive construction. His extreme instance was the town which cheapened the existing school program while advocating, as an alternative, policies to encourage birth control.

In more detail, Charles Harr has reviewed the type of zoning program, popularized by the Wayne Township, New Jersey, case. Here, not only did the suburb establish a minimum house size, but it required a larger living space for those houses without an attached garage than for those with such an appendage, on the dubious rationale that the proper care of the automobile affected the health and safety of the family. Acting to halt suburban expansion, Wayne established stringent zoning regulations and set the minimum price of new residences above that of older comparable buildings. In the end, the New Jersey Supreme Court upheld the township, and neither Wayne nor New Jersey is unique. Around San Francisco, St. Louis, and Boston, and in almost every metropolitan area, zoning restrictions have come into effect which can only be designed to require high-cost construction or none at all.

Coincidentally with zoning regulations, communities frequently use a second tactic: they establish, as part of the building regulations or as prerequisite to construction permits, a series of requirements for builders — supplemental taxes, fees, land dedications for schools, parks, donations of facilities. These requirements often serve good purposes, but they also direct special discrimination against lower-value homes, for the charges are almost always passed on to the buyer, and sometimes they serve outright to prohibit development.

A third device — employed in low-value as well as high-value communities — is the creation of special districts within parts of a suburb to offset the financial drain of lower-value houses where they occur. The supplemental taxes which these districts impose result in a higher total tax burden than the suburb could otherwise legally levy and allow a discriminatory tax burden to be imposed on lower-income residents. So the consultants from the University of Pennsylvania could blandly assure the supervisors of Middletown Township that permitting a Levittown within their borders would not lead to financial difficulties; the "three expensive services" of street lighting, fire hydrants and refuse collection, the consultants suggested, "can be financed through special district taxes or assessments, paid for by residents of the Levittown area only." The greater the proliferation of districts, the greater the probability of taxing similar property values at different rates.

Discrimination may also take place in the provision of services, to help assure that tax returns cover costs and to penalize — if they cannot exclude — lower income residents in the more expensive parts of suburbia. Suburban governments commonly differentiate today in the type of fire-fighting facilities and police services required in certain areas, and, significantly enough, these differences do not correlate with need but rather with taxable value. In the words of one commentator, "Them what has taxable value gets," and exclusive residential streets are usually better cleaned and repaired, high-pressure fire systems first installed there, and the neighboring school newer and better staffed. It is only in the slum areas of the large cities, where high expenditures are required to maintain law and order and overcome the hazards of congestion, that per capita expenditures are likely to be higher than in the better parts of the better suburbs.

These weapons — zoning, building requirements, tax and service differentiation — are part of every planning kit, and, as tools, there is nothing reprehensible about them. It is also clearly legitimate for every community to shape its land-use pattern, to use foresight, to prevent blight and to develop as its citizens desire. The ethical issue, if there is one, is not the propriety of these stratagems, but rather the extreme forms which they may take. Ethics aside, a factual evaluation of the policies of well-to-do municipalities in terms of their capacity to protect their own seems to lead to one conclusion: given the reluctance of the courts to intervene and the number of methods available to suburban officials for the practice of discrimination, the high-value suburbs can remain high-value if they wish. In their response to the welfare state, they can do more than survive; they can flourish.

While the exclusive residential suburb, and perhaps the well-planned industrial enclave, can take care of themselves, relatively few suburbs can succeed in enticing only expensive real estate inside their borders. The bleak fact remains that most new suburban construction is of an inexpensive character and that, despite unparalleled prosperity and all the innovations in residential financing, private or public, suburban property values are declining relative to the central city. Moreover, some suburbs incorporate only after the developers' bulldozers have come and gone, leaving a pent-up demand for municipal services that the property tax could not finance if every home in town were worth fifty thousand dollars. In other cases, the political bulwarks against invasion prove weak, and even in settled communities zoning standards crumble and hundred-foot frontages are authorized. Finally, there are limits, legal and moral, to the extent of segregation that is permissible. The courts may ultimately strike down the most outrageous regulations and restrictions. Here and there, community ethics forbid the self-imposition of a ghetto philosophy. The new migrants are settling somewhere in suburbia, and as they do, municipal costs rise, property values become depressed and financial adversity becomes the rule, not the exception.

For the unwanted, kept out of the exclusive suburbs, a policy of value differentiation will not help, for they cannot zone themselves away. New strategies and tactics are required, both within the local finance system and from outside. One common method is to dispense with all but the most rudimentary of public services, and sometimes even with those. John Scott reports on Whyte's suburban Park Forest that the salvation of its government is that its citizens are fortunately unaware of the array of services its big city neighbors offer. "It is an interesting fact," he writes, "that if you have an honest police department and one that takes good care of lost kids, you can get a lot of credit for giving a high level of police service when, in fact, you may actually not be giving as good police service as at least is potentially possible within the police force of a large city."

The taint of poorer services and amateurism, regardless of the financial effort the new suburbanite is willing to make, spreads beyond the maintenance of law and order. Sewer systems are frequently not available even when the density of population clearly requires them, and often there are neither storm sewers nor water distribution systems. Streets may not be paved, street signs and lights not available. Fire protection is almost always provided by volunteer departments, and though the firemen may be enthusiastic, they are not likely to be as competent or efficient as professionals.

Even for the schools, the public function suburbanites treasure most fondly and for which they will spend most willingly, compromises are made. The desire to escape big city schools, to secure for their children the advantages of better teachers, newer buildings, smaller classes and higher instructional standards, becomes ultimately self-defeating. Precisely because the school is the heart of the community and its independence consequently most jealously guarded, the pooling of its financial support among jurisdictions is generally a last, desperate resort. Suburbanites frequently prefer overcrowding, inexperienced teachers, double sessions, and the deterioration of standards rather than to relinquish their personal supervision, however ineffective, over their schools. So, while the *New York Times'* survey of contemporary metropolitan problems could find public school systems in expensive suburbs that epitomized the suburban ideal, it found two other types as well: one in the mass development suburb in which the schools had been overwhelmed by the influx of new residents, and the other in the older suburb in which the new residents were not a majority and their demands for better education were ignored by the old-timers who wanted above all to keep the tax rate down.

Yet even the poorer suburbs cannot push the quality of public services below the minimum for urban life, and where the suburban government has municipal powers and effective representation in the state legislature, a second tactic for self-survival is frequently employed. Every effort is made to broaden the local tax base by whatever means are available. Rarely can the suburbs impose lucrative new levies on income or general sales, or establish municipal businesses. But they can, in company with rich suburbs, require subdividers to finance streets, curbs, gutters, sewers and street lights, and they can join other municipalities in imposing a whole series of clumsy and expensive nuisance taxes.

The discovery and exploitation of these new sources of revenue vary from state to state according to legislative authorization, but it does not, in the last analysis, bail the suburbs out. Despite increased yield from these revenues, the new funds come nowhere near to "replacing" the property tax; they merely slow down the rise in property tax rates which follows the increased demand for public services. The new revenues are, moreover, typically available only to municipalities. Suburban counties and school districts must rely far more on the property tax than do other units of local government, while financial pressures may be heaviest on them.

Given the limited jurisdictions suburbia imposes upon itself, no single municipality can go far in developing a balanced tax system. For all their valiant efforts — the rows and rows of parking meters installed, the special licenses invented, the hidden charges inserted in the sale prices of "immoral" luxuries — suburban governments do little more than add nuisance burdens to the total tax bill. If the array of special taxes they have devised in the last decade were applied vigorously and enforced rigorously, the whole system of local nonproperty taxation would fall of its own weight. And it would fall because, given the intense financial competition among metropolitan jurisdictions, any suburb moving too far out of line would experience economic decline and abandonment. It would deserve to fall, for when the crazy-quilt of extra levies came to replace the property tax, it would be even more regressive than that tax has proven.

By striving to emulate the manners of the exclusive suburbs, then, the poorer jurisdictions push their analogy to the grassroots image to an extreme they may not desire: they recreate, for their governments at any rate, the conditions of frontier scarcity and poverty, the struggle for community existence that characterized the new settlements on a new continent. Left to themselves — as suburban municipalities were in Florida after the boom and bust of the twenties, and throughout the nation in the early years of the depression — these suburbs move inexorably to bankruptcy. Fractured urban government can recreate social and political conditions of small town life, but in a fundamental sense the reformers were right in emphasizing the economic base for community existence. No government is an island, if that island cannot have the means for its basic self-support.

Norton E. Long

WHO MAKES DECISIONS IN METROPOLITAN AREAS?

The peculiarity of "the metropolitan problem" is that it is characteristically felt to be a problem requiring a governmental solution for which there is no readily available appropriate governmental machinery. This means that there is no structured decision-making process that has been developed for dealing with this order of problem. The lack of such a structured process means further that there is little institutional support for decision-makers envisioning their primary role as representing a "metropolitan public interest" rather than the interest of their particular group, organization or local government. The most likely role to be called into play in a territory without common political loyalty and institutions is that of the special interest ambassador.

The term, metropolitan problem, almost seems to assume that there is a metropolitan common interest, and the assumption that there is a metropolitan common interest leads easily to the notion that there is a metropolitan community. Many earnest souls have thought that the European problems should follow this same logic, to say nothing of the even more ambitious World Federalists. Common problems may create a

Reprinted from Norton E. Long, *The Polity*, copyright © 1962 by Rand McNally & Company, Chicago, pp. 156–164, with the permission of the author and the publisher.

community among those who share them. However, much history, especially where people have become accustomed to living under different governments, with different values and resources, underscores the painful fact that common problems may do little more than produce common quarrels.

What this adds up to is that the term decision in our title may be optimistic. One makes a decision in a business, a government, a conference of ambassadors, maybe even sometimes at the summit, but these are structured decision-making institutions. What is characteristic of metropolitan areas is the lack of overall decision-making institutions. This does not mean that there are not institutions with power in metropolitan areas. It does mean that there are not institutions with sufficient power and overall responsibility to make decisions settling metropolitan issues and solving metropolitan problems. As a consequence, it is rare that we can speak of who makes metropolitan decisions. What we can speak about is who makes decisions that have a significant effect on metropolitan problems.

Characteristically, metropolitan issues do not relate to problems that are solved by decisions in the sense we would use that term in a business or governmental organization, and naturally so, since the metropolitan area is not organized so as to be capable of making decisions. What does happen is that issues and problems have a career and over time processes of interaction develop through which interested and powerful parties exercise influence over the outcome.

We might then concern ourselves with who makes decisions that influence the processes by which metropolitan problems and issues get handled. As in a business, one hates to admit that the concern just drifts along by guess and by god, so we are reluctant to admit that this is the way that a metropolitan area runs. This is especially true if one has little faith in an unseen hand guiding the selfish interests of the particular groups and local governments to an unintended but beneficent metropolitan result. Yet in large measure, the metropolitan area is a kind of natural governmental ecology in which institutions, groups and governments have developed a system of largely unintended cooperation through which things get done and the area considered as a system functions. The owls and the field mice, the oaks and the acorns, the flora and fauna of the woodlot have worked out over time a most effective system of unintended cooperation that, barring catastrophe, preserves and maintains a systemic balance, though one that evolves over time.

By and large, we accept a similar system of unintended cooperation for running our economy. The complex task of supplying the city of Philadelphia occurs without any central planning machinery. The fact is we are used to a largely unplanned economy producing functional results. It's a little difficult for us to accept this of an unplanned polity, but to a considerable degree this is just what happens in a metropolitan area. To be sure, the analogy to the economy may be closer to oligopoly than free market competition. What we have is a number of institutions, public and private, sharing a common territory, making demands on each other, cooperating, hindering, damaging and helping in an interdependent set of relations with no overall government exercising control.

The relationships among the governments, government departments, Federal, State and Local, businesses, associations, newspapers, and the myriad groups whose activities intersect and interact have grown up over time. They have a history, they have created habits and customs, use and want, ways that are accepted for handling problems that arise. The metropolitan area as a system for handling common problems is a going concern. The rather considerable problems of very large populations living under great diversity of governments have been managed.

If we look at the who, who make decisions in the metropolitan areas, we will be most interested in the actors, individual and institutional, that play the major roles in the process by which the metropolitan system handles the issues that confront it. We can best appreciate these actors if we see them as dealing with metropolitan problems from the limited point of view of a particular institutional base. This particular institutional base determines the point of view of the actor and how he scores his own success or failure. Much of the blame that is heaped on the heads of actors in the metropolitan scene for their lack of a sense of overall responsibility stems from the failure to recognize the constraints of their institutional reality. It is idle to blame a downtown store for behaving like a downtown store or the Port of New York Authority for behaving like the rubber-based, toll-fed, revenue-bond undertaking that it is. There are very few actors whose particular institutionalized interests parallel in any complete way the metropolitan area. Just as there are almost no institutions, private or public, whose interests and organization cover the metropolitan territory, so there are few, if any, whose interests extend to any considerable number of the problems of the metropolitan area.

By and large, actors and institutions in the metropolitan area, civic ritual apart, are confined in their interests to particular areas and particular problems. Highways, schools, sewer and water, housing, parks and recreation, these problems have their peculiar clientele just as the diseases that afflict the human body have their special funds. Thus, in the highway area you may have a Port of New York Authority, a Bob Moses and the Triborough Bridge Authority, a New York City Transit Authority, Commuter Railways and Buses, a two or more state governments and their assorted departments, a variety of political communities, businesses, trade associations, civic organizations, newspapers, all involved. Quite probably, the issues in the transportation field will be agitated with little effective concern for overall problems of coordination and none whatever for the implication of highway resource allocation for other claimants in the metropolitan area.

If we were to make a typology of the key actors in the typical metropolitan area, it might run as follows. First, we would have the metropolitan dailies. In almost all cases, they would exhibit a commitment to the preservation of downtown real estate, a consequent concern for mass transit, extending frequently to the advocacy of subsidy, a belief in planning and a disposition to favor some form of metropolitan integration. These newspapers are in a position to agitate the issues they favor, reward with publicity the politicians and civic leaders who agree with them and by appropriate news selection determine to a large extent what most people will be thinking are the hot issues. Rarely, except in a place like Miami, can the metropolitan press carry a general proposal for governmental change. On piecemeal bond issues and administrative matters, however, it can do much. Beginning to enter the field as a competitor in some areas are television and radio. Just how the structure of their interests will differ from that of the metropolitan press is not clear.

Frequently opposing the metropolitan dailies and following a particularist line is the community press. Usually, they support the interests of small business threatened by planning and the parochialism of suburban city governments.

Of equal importance with the media are, of course, the public officials concerned with the production of public services that cut across political boundaries or require resources that must be allocated among a number of claimants. These officials run the gamut from village to state and nation. They embrace such disparate undertakings as schools, watersheds, airports and a host of other things. Quite often it is the service departments of the governments badgered by their clientele that press the metropolitan issues with still other government officials in their budgetary capacity playing the role of reluctant Solomons.

Downtown stores, real estate interests concerned with central city property values, commuter railways, central city banks, central city and even other politicians concerned with the implications of the worsening of the central city tax base frequently make common cause with the press, university professors, the foundations and the civic leaders in a crusade to save downtown. A subsidy at the expense of the highway user for mass transit, a massive urban renewal program, a new layer of metropolitan government, at the very least, a metropolitan planning agency, all or some combination of these, comprise a set of symbolic and frequently more than symbolic acts by which a multitude of parties with the most varied concerns express their feeling about the dynamic changes that are transforming urban America.

However, these overall actions have all too often bogged down in the quagmire of divisive local interests and electoral conservatism. Given the circumstances of local public life it is usually easy to mount a campaign of metropolitan reform. The electoral consultation which our home rule tradition insists on forces such proposals to run the gauntlet of the antagonism of suburban voters to the central city, vested interests of all kinds in the status quo, central city ethnic and minority groups who fear any dilution of their achieved central city power and a host of public officials and employees who may fear the unsettling of their empires and jobs. Certainly, high among the list of the who that make metropolitan decisions, if no more than negatively, are the varied active electorates called into play by referenda and the officials who have a stake in the existing system.

The revolutionaries who wish to overturn the status quo are most often university professors, foundations, Leagues of Women Voters, Chambers of Commerce, civic leader businessmen especially those with a stake in downtown, those with a concern in the planning of major metropolitan highways and utilities, suburban residents, officials and real estate promoters needing sewer and water facilities, the media people seeking a cause and the intellectuals of local government who follow the thinking of *Fortune*, The National Municipal League and "the authorities."

The attempts at revolution have mobilized financial support from elements of the business community such as Civic Progress, Inc., in St. Louis, and the Cleveland Development Foundation. They have usually enjoyed the support of the metropolitan dailies, the League of Women Voters, the professors and most of the do-gooders. The opposition the campaigns have mobilized, especially where general metropolitan integration has been sought, has been sufficient to insure defeat at the polls. These defeats have usually been as much due to the political ineptitude and lack of energy of the proponents of change as to the power of the opposition.

It must be remembered that the existing metropolitan areas are going concerns — going systems — as systems we can expect them to react vigorously to attempts to seriously alter them. If the existing system of local government could be easily changed it would be intolerably unstable. If no powerful interests were vested in the status quo, the existing order would have so little allegiance it could scarcely run, much less endure. Some such situation obtained in Miami, the one successful case of metropolitan integration and a case where change won by an eyelash and the decision could have gone either way.

If we turn from overall decisions such as those that are embodied in researching county charters, studying metropolitan regions, writing new local constitutions and campaigning to the piecemeal decisions that are by their sheer cumulative weight determining the future of the metropolitan areas, a different order of actions emerged. Clearly among the most significant decisions affecting our metropolitan areas are those which determine the importation of cheap rural labor from the South, Puerto Rico and Mexico, without any provision for adequately housing it in standard housing. The demand for labor insures no equivalent demand for standard housing; it is in fact a demand for slums. Given the desire of the average low income rural immigrant to the city for television, the automobile and the other gadgets of the affluent society, plus his habitation to a very low housing standard in his place of origin, it is not surprising that expensive standard housing should be low on his list of priorities.[1] Doubtless, we could force urban immigrants to buy housing rather than other consumer goods by outlawing substandard housing. We probably won't and this is a key decision in metropolitan areas. The central city has a vested interest in slums as do those employers of cheap labor and those sellers of consumer goods which compete with housing for the slum dwellers' dollar.

Another key decision made by real estate people, bankers, building and loans, suburban neighborhoods and the rest, is whether the new minorities, Negroes, Puerto Ricans and Mexicans, but especially Negroes, will be able to follow the earlier ethnics into the melting pot of middle-class America or whether the color bar will prevent assimilation. This decision which will be made by a myriad of individual decisions will determine whether or not we create our own version of Algeria in our larger cities with an alienated group of second-class citizens led by an unassimilated, rejected but educated elite.

The decisions by our businesses on the location of industry, of manufacturing, retail trade and office buildings will over time critically determine the fate of downtown, the relation of residence and place of work and the future of our system of metropolitan transportation. While we may talk bravely of a pattern of land use control and a massive rehabilitation of the central city, the odds are probably with Professor Raymond Vernon of Harvard that our public expenditures and our controls are unlikely to be sufficiently massive or powerful to offset the natural locational forces. This seems the more likely if dozens of communities scramble to beef up their tax base in a competition for industry to meet mounting municipal costs. With the property tax still a major reliance of central city and suburbs, the struggle for tax base will conflict with and in all probability override the efforts at a general plan of metropolitan land use.

While it is unpopular to say it, one of the crucial decisions in the metropolitan areas will relate to the preservation of the middle-class

---

[1] I wish to credit Anthony Downs of the University of Chicago with the forceful development of this point.

values of American culture. Despite all its clumsiness the separate but not watertight compartments of the suburban communities prevent the flooding of schools and neighborhoods by an undigestible mass of immigrants of a different culture. In all probability, despite an uneasy conscience, there will be efforts by middle-class neighborhoods to preserve the political dikes that protect their values. However unsatisfactory, and it is clearly unsatisfactory, the present system of social absenteeism in the massive change in the central city has probably rendered impossible a desirable balance between the social classes. The recolonization of the central city by disenchanted suburbanites is probably little more than the utopia of the builders of luxury high rise apartments.

We can confidently expect that as the incomes of the mass of central city residents rise they will make the same key metropolitan decisions that the earlier middle-class ethnics made — to cross the tracks into suburbia.

Since the positions of power in our society can be expected to fight for survival, it can be expected that the vested interests in downtown should fight as hard for the preservation of outmoded central city land values as the embattled farmers have to preserve an outgrown pattern of agriculture. When one looks at the vested stake in central city real estate it is hard to imagine that the fight to achieve public subsidies to resist its obsolescence will be less than that put up by agriculture. Certainly, there might seem to be a greater appeal for spending the massive sums that now go into subsidizing an unproductive agriculture on the maintenance of our obsolescing central city plant. The sentimental appeal that persuades us to save the family farm can and has been raised to save "downtown." As yet the appeal goes no further than the appeal for urban renewal, and the subsidization of commuter railways and mass transit. If this does not work, we can expect the ante will be raised rather than the end abandoned.

An older generation accustomed to what Mumford has called the paleotechnic city, the city of steam and mass transit, can be frightened by a specter, the specter of the city of the automobile, Los Angeles. Lord Marple, the British Minister of Transport, said recently, "I saw Los Angeles, the city of the future, a fate we must avoid." Perhaps one day we will cease to regard Los Angeles as a monstrosity and accept the technological obsolescence of the older city. Our agricultural experience indicates the old will die hard.

One last decision, the greatest, I think, in our lifetime and the one nobody made but that has changed everything. In 1929 the shape of the American income was a pyramid with a broad base of the bulk of society close to the means of subsistence living at a family income of below $2,000. In the twenty-five years that *Business Week* once said remade America, 1929 to 1954, the income structure changed from a pyramid to a diamond — America had become a middle-class country. Even in 1929, the middle-class values led to a family centered suburban standard of life. This has been the dynamic. As the lower half of the present diamond of our income structure shrinks with the growth in its income we can expect the new middle classes to continue the trek and the pressure of their movement to continue to tax the public sector of our local economies.

Beyond the dynamic of the growth of the new middle class is the growing market orientation of industry and the new pattern of settlement of business in the metropolitan areas. How the community earns its living will, as always, be a vital determinant of the structure of metropolitan areas.

Ours, however, is an affluent society and the increasing desire to consume public goods will press constantly on our governments. Thus, the rush to the week-end especially with the four-day work week may mean that the peak loads for play will outweigh the peak loads for work on our highways.

The decisions then that may be most important in our metropolitan areas are economic, piecemeal, harmonized if at all by market forces. This is not to say we could not generate enough political power to make effective public metropolitan decision-making possible; it is to express a doubt that we will, in more than a piecemeal way, substitute government action for the forces of the economy. I suspect that as long as the existing system functions even tolerably well, we will tinker with it getting rid of the worst annoyances but putting up with what we know rather than venturing on untried seas. Should Miami and other areas provide an attractive imitable lesson, however, we can expect new civic fashions to spread. The unresolved problem of local government remains the desire for sharply increased amounts of public goods but at the same time stable or decreased taxes, the desire for the fruits of planning and control and the desire for the energy and enterprise of unregimented economic individualism.

Perhaps it is our successful capacity to live with and entertain these contradictory desires that is the genius of our tradition. As an Englishman once told an exasperated French colleague, "England is governed by parliament, not logic."

Jameson W. Doig

REGIONAL POLITICS AND "BUSINESSLIKE EFFICIENCY": THE PORT OF NEW YORK AUTHORITY

For some observers of urban politics, the specialized public authority is the most advanced form of government, in which long-range planning and efficiency have replaced the short-term compromises and corruption found elsewhere in political life. To others, the public authority or special district is among the least satisfactory forms of government, for it insulates an area of public action from the process through which policy decisions should be made — public debate on conflicting goals and priorities, with decisions on policies and funding made by officials directly responsible to the voter. A third perspective focuses not on determining the goodness or harmfulness of the authority mechanism, but rather on exploring the resources and strategies which the authority uses in achieving both its professed "public interest" objectives and the goal of keeping the organization itself alive and healthy.

The efforts of the Port of New York Authority to define and help in solving the urban transportation problem during the past half-century provide some evidence relating to all three perspectives. At the very least, an observer may appreciate the dedication and acumen with which one of America's preeminent governments identifies and pursues its highest goals.

Established in 1921 by interstate compact, the Port Authority was charged with developing the "terminal, transportation and other facilities of commerce" in the New York-New Jersey region. The compact gave the Port Authority broad responsibility in the Port District, a bistate area extending about 20 miles in radius from the Statue of Liberty; its capacity to carry out these duties was limited, however, by its inability to levy taxes or assessments or to issue orders binding upon private or other public agencies.

The Port Authority was at first expected to devote its main energies to rail and harbor freight distribution in the region. However, it found the

Adapted by the author for this volume from *Metropolitan Transportation Politics and the New York Region* (New York: Columbia University Press, 1966), pp. 28–37, 217–20 and *passim*.

railroads unwilling to cooperate in the establishment of joint yards, joint rights of way, or other plans to rationalize the rail system; and little progress was made toward carrying out the original program. In the late 1920's, the Port Authority turned to vehicular facilities. By 1931, three bridges between New Jersey and Staten Island were open for traffic, as well as the George Washington Bridge, connecting New Jersey and Manhattan. In 1931, the Authority also acquired the Holland Tunnel, built by another interstate agency. This network of toll bridges and tunnels was highly successful financially, and the Authority was able to branch out. In 1932 a freight terminal was opened in Manhattan, in 1944 a grain terminal was acquired, in 1947 the Port Authority leased Newark, Idlewild (Kennedy), and LaGuardia airports, and between 1948 and 1951 it took over administration of Port Newark and of Teterboro Airport and began operating two truck terminals and a bus terminal.[1]

Passenger rail operations were not entirely neglected during these decades. Between 1928 and 1931, the Port Authority joined with other groups in the region in a study of the passenger problem, an effort abandoned because of traffic decline during the depression. In 1937 the Port Authority submitted a report recommending that a trans-Hudson rail tunnel be constructed; and in 1949, at the request of New Jersey Governor Alfred E. Driscoll, the Port Authority completed a study of a proposed rail line between Newark Airport and the waterfront.

Although the Port Authority was willing to study the problem, it showed no interest in expanding its own responsibilities to include rail passenger service. In its 1937 report, the Authority estimated that the proposed project might run a yearly deficit as high as $5.3 million. The report concluded that the Authority itself could not undertake the project, since lack of taxing power limited it to "self-liquidating projects." The 1949 plan carried an estimated annual deficit of $1.2 million, and again the Authority declared its inability to take on such a deficit operation.

As the vehicular projects, wealth, and diversity of operations of the Port Authority increased, criticism of its "neglect" of rail transit also grew. Commuter associations and the railroads were joined by the

---

[1] For a detailed study of the Authority's early development, see Erwin A. Bard, *The Port of New York Authority* (New York: Columbia University Press, 1941). Other important sources of information on the Authority are Wallace S. Sayre and Herbert Kaufman, *Governing New York City* (New York: Russell Sage Foundation, 1960), Chap. 9; Herbert Kaufman, "Gotham in the Air Age," in Harold Stein, ed., *Public Administration and Policy Development: A Case Book* (New York: Harcourt, Brace, 1952), pp. 143–97; and U.S. House of Representatives, Committee on the Judiciary, *Port of New York Authority, Hearings before Subcommittee No. 5*, 86th Cong., 2d Sess. (1960). On public authorities and other independent specialized governments, see John C. Bollens, *Special District Governments in the United States* (Berkeley: University of California Press, 1957).

Regional Plan Association, the *Newark News*, and other regional spokesmen in urging the Port Authority to reconsider involving itself in rail transit. By 1950, as the need for some public action to stem the rail decline became more apparent, the governors of New York and New Jersey also began to show some interest in the Port Authority's changing its position.

In response to these criticisms and queries, the Port Authority took a firm stand, a position which it was able to maintain until 1959–60. The Port Authority argued, first, that it was "completely unable to purchase or otherwise assume deficit financing of rail transit operations." Any passenger rail facilities, the Port Authority asserted, would operate at substantial deficits, and an integrated transit system in the New York-New Jersey area would probably involve annual losses of $35 million to $40 million. Since the Authority was required to support its program entirely on its own income, such a deficit operation would make it impossible for the Port Authority to sell revenue bonds for new facilities and would force contraction of its entire program. "Any implication that the Port Authority was even considering the financing of rail transit," its officials maintained, would "seriously impair" its credit structure. The Authority also opposed any plan that would provide tax resources to meet Port Authority deficits, for such a step would subject it to "political influence," thus destroying the "sound business" principles on which it operated.

"The only long range solution" to the transit problem, the Port Authority argued, was the creation of an interstate public corporation, with power to "make up deficits out of taxes apportioned equitably among the communities which depend upon rail service."[2]

The position taken by the Port Authority was in part unassailable. It could not expand and perhaps not even survive if required to assume a continuing rail deficit so large that other income could not offset it. But some of its arguments were open to debate. Might it not be able to assume limited responsibilities in the rail field, either directly or by allocating some of its surplus bridge and tunnel revenues to a separate organization? Also, was it preferable as a matter of regional policy to create a separate and perhaps competing agency for rail, rather than integrating both rail and road under one authority, supported by its own revenues and taxes?

In maintaining its position, the Port Authority was not limited to the logic of its arguments. As it entered into a long and intensive campaign to ward off responsibility for rail passenger service, the Authority possessed a number of politically significant advantages — widespread

[2] See Austin J. Tobin, "The Work and Program of the Port of New York Authority," Feb. 10, 1953; PNYA, *Annual Report, 1952*, p. 1.

public support, a relatively large degree of formal independence in policy-making, substantial fiscal resources, and well-developed political skills. The nature of each of these advantages deserves further comment.

The Port Authority's achievements and current plans have generally been supported enthusiastically by business groups, newspapers, and other regional spokesmen; the admiration of state legislators and the two governors has been evident as well. Acclaimed during the postwar period for its "far-reaching program," for "imagination and resourcefulness, vigor and initiative," and for "great service to business and industry" while avoiding the "evils of governmental bureaucracy and governmental waste," the Port Authority has been able to count upon widespread backing for its desire to maintain its financial autonomy and its preferred range of activities.[3]

The ability of the Port Authority to determine its own policy preferences and to avoid transit projects has been greatly aided by several structural characteristics and related traditions. Whereas most state agencies are under the supervision of a single official, appointed by the governor and removable at will, the Port Authority is guided by twelve commissioners, six appointed by each governor, for overlapping six-year terms. The chairman of the board of commissioners is chosen by the members themselves, and no commissioner may be removed by the governors except for cause, after a hearing. These legal factors have substantially modified the influence that either governor can wield over Port Authority policy-making.

Still, the appointive power itself provides the governors with the means to select persons to represent their own views or a range of views that they believe should have influence upon an agency. In some public authorities the appointive power has been used in this way; the Chicago Housing Authority, for example, included in 1949 "a Jew, a Catholic, a Negro, a small businessman, a big businessman, a labor leader, and a social worker-intellectual."[4] Traditionally, commissioners of the Port Authority have been drawn from a far narrower stratum; banking and business predominate, and members of the board are frequently wealthy. In 1952, for example, two commissioners were presidents of banks in the

---

[3] Some of the praise for the Port Authority and other authorities is combined with a strong measure of dissatisfaction with the normal workings of the democratic process. As the New York *World-Telegram & Sun* editorialized, "The truth is that all too frequently men elected to office are not qualified to tangle with complicated, modern municipal management. They may be overly vote-conscious. They may be hog-tied to political bosses. They may be just plain incompetent. But whatever the reason, time after time when the politicians have gotten in a jam they have had to create an authority and call on successful businessmen to bail them out" (March 12, 1952).

[4] Martin Meyerson and Edward C. Banfield, *Politics, Planning, and the Public Interest* (New York: Free Press, 1955), p. 49.

region, six were board chairmen, presidents, or vice-presidents of business firms, and one was the publisher of a large newspaper, the Bergen *Evening Record*; the other three included a member of a major law firm, a consulting engineer, and a university professor. That year, commissioners of the Port Authority sat on the boards of directors of more than sixty corporations, including such major companies as Prudential Insurance, American Can, Remington Rand, and New Jersey Bell Telephone.

This is not to imply that business experience should disqualify one for service on the Port Authority. On the contrary, given the importance of financial criteria in its work and the complexity of management involved, it is perhaps desirable and inevitable that business competence would be sought for the Authority. Nor should one infer that the commissioners are concerned only with business criteria and values. Some have had careers outside the business community, some of the businessmen have held other public posts, appointive or elective (party service has at times been a criterion in appointment), and a few commissioners have identified themselves as much with their governors and broader regional concerns as they have with the immediate goals of the Port Authority. On balance, however, the previous experience of the board has been consistent with the conservative approach taken by the Port Authority — opposition to acting on a broblem as financially uncertain as rail transit or to any actions that might reduce the financial and administrative autonomy of the Authority.

The relationship between the commissioners and the Port Authority staff has reinforced these policies and the ability of the agency to determine its own priorities. The twelve commissioners are unpaid, each has a full-time job elsewhere, and the Port Authority's complex activities have traditionally been carried out with great skill and success. As a result, many commissioners have lacked the time and inclination to master the Authority's methods and problems; the hurdle has been especially great for those who might consider pressing for a rethinking of traditional Port Authority goals. Inevitably, the full-time staff has exerted substantial influence in the development of overall and instrumental policies.

Staff influence has been heightened by the high quality and long tenure of most top-level officials at the Authority. The executive director, Austin J. Tobin — "stocky . . . vigorous and pugnacious-looking" — is one of the nation's outstanding administrators.[5] Although less well known than some of his counterparts, Tobin fits admirably the characterization of J. Edgar Hoover and General Curtis E. LeMay:

> Both presided over major expansions of the organization while refusing to take on functions not closely related to its fundamental purpose. Both culti-

[5] Quoted from profile of Tobin, *New York Times,* July 14, 1959.

vated reputations for themselves as tough, no-nonsense, hard-driving administrators, and for their agencies as efficient, technically expert, hard-working
organizations, employing the most up-to-date devices of technology in the
single-minded pursuit of their mission.[6]

Closely allied with Tobin have been highly qualified officials in such
fields as aviation, port development, and public relations. The Port
Authority has been able to obtain officials of high competence in part
because of the agency's high reputation and in part because it offers
salaries unmatched by most public agencies. Tobin receives $70,000 a
year, a government salary exceeded only by that of the President of the
United States; seven top officials are paid more than $40,000 annually,
and thirteen others receive more than $30,000.

Many of the Port Authority's senior career officials combine ability
with long service in the agency. Tobin joined the Port Authority in 1927
as a law clerk and worked his way up through the ranks during the next
fifteen years. Several of his top aides also count their service from the
1920's and 1930's. With extended service, staff members accept and
indeed absorb the goals of the organization. When appointment to top
positions comes after many years in an agency, officials are therefore less
inclined to reassess past policy or in any way to "shake up" the
organization. So it is with the Port Authority, and the ability and
commitment to the agency of its senior officials operates to reinforce its
independent position.

Autonomy in policy-making is also a product of the Authority's
independent financial resources (from tolls, rents, and other charges) and
its independence in personnel and other administrative matters. Budgetary autonomy is especially important. As Sayre and Kaufman have
pointed out in their analysis of authorities operating in New York City,
there are several advantages here:

> First, the authorities do not have to undergo the public budget hearings be-
> fore the Board of Estimate, at which so many of the pressures on ordinary line
> agencies are brought to bear. Second, the authorities do not have to defend
> their plans and projected expenditures to budget and fiscal officers of the city or
> any other government. . . . Third, they are not exposed to deprivations of in-
> come through appropriations delays or slashes, a common means of subduing
> line agencies. Fourth, they are not limited by the detailed appropriation items
> of the regular expense budget of the city. In sum, their operating policy deci-
> sions, as these are reflected in their budgets, are made internally rather than in
> dealings with outside agencies and officials, in private rather than in public, and
> the authorities are the undisputed masters of their own operating resources.[7]

[6] Samuel P. Huntington, *The Common Defense* (New York: Columbia University Press, 1961), pp. 310–11. LeMay's organization was the Strategic Air Command, Hoover's the Federal Bureau of Investigation.

[7] Sayre and Kaufman, *Governing New York City*, pp. 330–31.

In the Port Authority, this independence is combined with impressive financial resources, based mainly on profits from increasing bridge and tunnel traffic. In 1952, Port Authority assets were just over $400 million; by 1960 they had increased to more than $1 billion, and in 1969, total assets were $2.7 billion.[8]

These characteristics give the Port Authority a degree of independence more often associated with a private corporation than with a public agency. Such a conclusion has been accepted and indeed favored by Port Authority officials. As Austin Tobin explains:

> An authority is designed to put revenue producing public facilities on their own feet and on their own responsibility; to free them from political interference, bureaucracy and red tape. . . . This test of management, the administrative standards of a well-managed private corporation, is the test that should be applied to the [Authority's] responsibilities and duties.

"The Commissioners of the Port Authority function as a Board of Directors," Tobin concluded. "My own executive office has the same normal responsibilities as those of the president of a private corporation."[9]

Outside interests can affect the policies of the Port Authority directly and effectively in several ways. The governor of either state may veto any action taken by the Port Authority, and the state legislatures may refuse to enact laws needed for new projects. Certain municipal and other controls can also be cited.[10] The Port Authority has found it necessary to develop strategies to neutralize potential opposition from these sources, and it has executed these strategies with great political skill during the postwar period.

The Authority's basic strategy has been to carry out a vigorous program directed toward its preferred goals. Vehicular, airport, and marine terminal facilities are constantly being built and improved. This policy generates widespread public approbation; it has also insured that large

---

[8] During these years, net revenues rose from $29 million (1952) to $67 million (1960) and $122 million (1969).

[9] Tobin, "The Work and Program of the Port of New York Authority." Tobin's business-oriented perspective is also reflected in his views on local government: "It is obvious that one of the primary subjects of citizen interest concerns the manner in which a municipality handles its finances. *Above all else*, the people expect their officials to give them prudent and conservative management of public funds." (Austin J. Tobin, "Public Relations and Financial Reporting in a Municipal Corporation," May 23, 1951, emphasis added.)

[10] For example, the need to obtain approval of a municipality before connecting vehicular projects with city streets, independent audit, and removal of the commissioners for cause. The first assistant to the executive director listed these and other limitations on the Port Authority — including its annual reports and information given to the press — in concluding that the PNYA is subject to adequate democratic controls. (M. E. Lukens, address, Sept. 12, 1953.)

reserves are not built up — reserves that the Authority might be asked to apply to rail transit.

Closely joined with its expansion policy has been a skillful public relations program, aimed at persuading the general public and political leaders in the region of the importance of current Port Authority activities. The director of public relations participates in policy meetings, issues a constant stream of press releases, and makes available to newspapers "reliable background information for use in determining editorial policies."[11] These publicity efforts have emphasized the achievements and "nonpolitical" nature of the Port Authority and the intimate relationships between these two factors.[12]

The Port Authority has not relied only on these indirect methods to ward off political pressures. The agency's views have been presented informally to the governors of both states and to influential members of the two legislatures. These efforts have been continuous and have been carried out by commissioners and top staff officers closely acquainted with the officials concerned. State legislators have also been given special tours of Port Authority facilities, and each new project has been presented to the legislators and to the general public with a substantial publicity buildup.[13] These strategies have been largely effective in securing political

[11] Tobin, "Public Relations and Financial Reporting." In Tobin's view, press releases and newspaper editorials could serve as adequate substitutes for the ballot box: "We look upon the press as the medium of exchange between our agency and the millions of people and thousands of businesses . . . for whom we are working in the Port District. During the past six years, the Port Authority has enjoyed approximately 1400 favorable editorials in the New York and New Jersey press. We feel we can interpret this as a vote of public confidence in our program." The effectiveness of the Port Authority's public relations program is attested to by several awards received by the agency's director of public relations — for example, the Silver Anvil of the American Public Relations Association for "the most notable public relations performance in the field of government."

[12] In addition to press relations, the PNYA uses several approaches in order to ensure the friendly attention of the region's publics. A community relations department maintains continuing contact with the municipalities from which the Authority had leased facilities and operates a speakers' bureau. Port Authority executives meet frequently with investment banking groups and other business associations to explain the Authority's work. And staff members often hold policy positions in such nongovernmental organizations as the New York Real Estate Board and the Citizens Budget Commission.

[13] The 1960 House investigation uncovered occasional examples of other relationships between the PNYA and political leaders. For several years prior to 1952, for example, the Port Authority handled part of its insurance so as to add to the income of a firm owned by an important state legislator in New York. During the period 1945 to 1952, this assemblyman introduced twenty bills favored by the PNYA; and several resolutions calling for investigation of the Port Authority died in the Ways and Means Committee, which he chaired. See U.S. House of Representatives, *Port of New York Authority, Hearings before Subcommittee No. 5*, pp. 1173–97, 1448–57.

support for Port Authority goals and independence at the state capitals; the governors' veto power has been used infrequently, and the legislatures have rarely failed to authorize new projects.[14] The comments of New York Governor Thomas E. Dewey in 1952 typify the general view of the Port Authority during the first postwar decade and suggest the success that the agency has had in maintaining public acceptance of its goals and methods:

> In its thirty-one years of service to the two States the Port Authority, without burden to the general taxpayer, has provided almost half a billion dollars' worth of terminal and transportation facilities. Through its great public works, it has set an example for the administration of public business on a sound and efficient basis.[15]

Because of these several factors, the Port Authority was able to maintain a substantial degree of independence in policy-making during the early postwar period and was largely able to decide when and where to expand its facilities. Pressure from the railroads and commuter interests for action on rail transit posed no immediate threat to the politically powerful Authority. Still, the Port Authority had to remain alert. Further rail-service deterioration could increase the size and importance of the rail coalition, and the rail group might expect to find allies for any concerted attack upon the Port Authority among those who criticized the agency for other reasons. These included the residents of the areas around Port Authority airports, who were critical of the noise and danger involved in airport operation, and local officials from towns that lost land to Port Authority projects. Also, small but vocal groups attacked its toll rates and other policies, and scholars and planners criticized the public authorities for increasing the fragmentation of metropolitan areas. Although these critics were usually isolated minorities, their political strength could increase dramatically upon occasion (as it did temporarily following a series of plane crashes near Newark Airport in 1951–52).[16] Since pressure from the rail coalition might be augmented greatly by such groups, the Port Authority was prepared to exert its

[14] During its first 25 years of operation, the PNYA's minutes had been vetoed only once, and that veto had later been withdrawn. The veto has been used about ten times since World War II, a small number in view of the dozens of important actions taken by the Port Authority's Board without gubernatorial objection during these years.

[15] Quoted in the Port Authority's *Annual Report, 1952*, frontispiece.

[16] In late 1951 and early 1952, three planes crashed in the vicinity of Newark Airport, bringing the PNYA under attack and causing the airport to be closed temporarily. During this period, the agency was vigorously attacked by a number of groups; it was called a "totalitarian government" by one Newark public official and a "Mafia organization" by a New Jersey congressman. In spite of intense criticism in a few local areas, the Port Authority was able to muster widespread support for its work and emerged unscathed. See Paul Tillett and Myron Weiner, *The Closing of Newark Airport* (University, Ala.: University of Alabama Press, 1955).

considerable resources to avoid being chosen as a "solution," and if possible to help locate an alternative approach that would leave it unfettered by rail transit. . . .

The Port Authority's efforts were successful for many years, but by the early 1960's the Authority had abandoned its traditional position and agreed to devote a portion of its income to rail facilities. Even this apparent failure was in reality a success. The Authority combined its change of policy with safeguards that would make further encroachment on its independence more difficult, and with bistate agreement that it could construct a 110-story monument to the Authority and its works.

The conflicts and negotiations leading to these changes illustrate the political skill and other resources of this powerful regional enterprise. They can be summarized in a series of stages beginning in the early 1950's.

TOWARD A COORDINATED TRANSPORTATION POLICY. The first step was the creation of a series of state agencies to review the regional transportation problem, culminating in the bistate Metropolitan Rapid Transit Commission in 1954. The MRTC was to study transit needs in the New York-New Jersey region and "recommend . . . possible measures for meeting such needs." In its early meetings, the Commission drew up study plans which would result in a general transportation plan for the region, including highways, bridges, and tunnels, as well as rail services. Some MRTC members argued publicly that the Port Authority's vehicular facilities and plans, and its past inaction in the rail field, should be closely scrutinized.

TURNING A THREAT TO THE PORT AUTHORITY'S SERVICE. The creation and early actions of the MRTC directly threatened the port agency. The Commission statements and studies might increase the pressure for Authority action in the rail field, while preparing the way for closer external control over its bridge and tunnel activities. On the other hand, if the MRTC studies concluded that the Port Authority should not take on any rail transit duties, and that a separate, tax-supported agency should assume these responsibilities, the independence of the Authority would be strengthened. The Authority had to remove the threat and use the opportunity, and its staff acted with considerable skill to achieve this goal.

First, because the states had authorized very little money for the MRTC's studies, the Port Authority realized that it might be able to offer additional funds while obtaining some influence in shaping the Commission's work. After intensive negotiations, the Authority agreed to provide $500,000 or more for the studies, in return for joint policy control. The MRTC would also have to agree not to use the study funds to develop a general plan for rail and road facilities in the region, and it would have to accept without further study the Authority's position that it could not undertake any deficit operations. With the states unwilling to provide the needed funds from hard-pressed budgets, and no other alternatives available, the MRTC reluctantly accepted the conditional offer.[17]

The next step was to legitimize the studies and protect the Authority's public image. In early 1955, the two agencies announced that an agreement had been reached and emphasized the "comprehensive" nature of the proposed rail studies, and the large amount of funds to be devoted to the effort. In return, they were rewarded with congratulations from state officials (who were glad to be relieved of further pressure to finance the studies) and from the region's leading newspapers. *The New York Times* thought the step represented a "highly constructive turn in Port Authority thinking," and New Jersey's *Bergen Evening Record* thanked the Authority for its "courageous decision," noting that here was "a study that starts without preconceptions or prejudices. . . ."[18]

Next, in a series of complicated maneuvers initiated by the Port Authority staff and the Governor of New Jersey, several of the MRTC members most critical of the Authority were forced to resign and were replaced with men willing to accept the conditions of the joint agreement.

Finally, while the studies were carried out in 1955–57, Port Authority staff members were assigned to follow them closely, challenging any approach or conclusion that might suggest the possibility of a self-supporting transit plan (i.e., a transit system which could be operated by the Authority).[19] The port agency then receded into the background while the MRTC announced the results of "its" studies: A bistate Transit District should be created to construct a new rail system between New Jersey and New York City, and to meet passenger service deficits (of $9 million a year) on railroads operating in the bistate area. Costs would be met through increased local taxes in the region. The report did not mention the Port Authority as a possible contributor or operator of rail

[17] The problem of interstate competition within the region was an important factor in the lack of state support for the MRTC. Some state officials were suspicious of the regional jurisdiction of the Commission, which might result in funds from one state being used to conduct studies of primary benefit to the other state.

[18] *New York Times*, January 14, 1955; *Bergen Evening Record*, January 15, 1955.

[19] For example, staff members skilled in traffic analysis and general persuasion challenged the conclusion of one prominent consultant that future traffic on a new rail loop might be great enough to make that section of the rail system self-supporting, and they finally convinced the firm to eliminate any discussion of this possibility from his report.

services, or discuss the issue of coordinated planning of rail and road facilities.[20]

THE LIMITS OF INFLUENCE. When the District plan was presented in 1958 for approval by the states, limitations on the Port Authority's capabilities became apparent. In New York State, support by the Authority, New York City business leaders, and the railroads overcame opposition by New York's mayor; the District bill, with its implication of local tax support for regional rail service, was approved by both houses of the legislature and the Governor soon after it was introduced. And in New Jersey's senate, the bill was also approved, with Port Authority influence helping to provide the final vote needed for passage.[21] In the New Jersey assembly, however, local opposition to the District and to relieving the Port Authority of all responsibility for rail transit was too strong. An alternative proposal, directing the Authority itself to "develop, improve and coordinate" rail passenger facilities in the region, was introduced. After several months of hearings and public debate, both proposals died in the assembly in early 1959.

THE PORT AUTHORITY "SUCCUMBS." With the Transit District defeated, and with rail passenger service continuing to deteriorate, the governors of the two states were under increasing pressure in 1959 to meet rail problems — both directly, through the use of state funds and powers, and by persuading the Authority to allocate some of its wealth to rail service. The first breach in the Authority walls was made by Nelson A. Rockefeller, who in his 1968 gubernatorial campaign had stressed the need for state action in this field. Soon after taking office in January, 1959, Rockefeller and his aides began negotiations with the Authority to convince it to reverse its traditional position. An initial plan would have required the Authority to use its own credit to buy new commuter cars to be leased to the railroads. The Authority resisted, and obtained the support of the investment community and of New Jersey's Governor Robert B. Meyner (whose approval would be needed to force the Authority to undertake the program).

20 The MRTC proposals were publicized in two stages. A preliminary report, released in May 1957, recommended a District to construct a $345 million transit loop and to meet operating deficits on the region's railroads. The final report of January 1958 proposed that initial legislation be limited to creation of a District, which would request specific measures after further study. The final report also supported the view that the District should expect to construct a new rail loop, and to use local tax resources to meet these costs and current railroad deficits.

21 One commissioner of the Port Authority was a Democratic county chairman in New Jersey, and the state senator from that county was persuaded to reverse his opposition and vote for the District bill (thereby providing the 11th vote, with 11 needed for approval).

The final result was a compromise, reluctantly supported by the Port Authority, that would require the agency to purchase and lease commuter cars, with state guarantees provided for the commuter-car bonds. The Authority now had a continuing responsibility in the rail field, but its own toll-generated funds were still inviolate.[22]

In 1960 New Jersey state officials also proposed a plan that would require the Authority to use its own moneys in the rail field — to buy railroad cars and ferries and to lease them to the railroads. No state guarantees were included, and there were no restrictions on the possibility of further, expanding use of Authority funds. Although it had successfully resisted a similar plan in New York a year earlier, the port agency was unusually vulnerable at this point. Increasing criticism was directed at the Authority for its inaction as rail service deteriorated. Its proposal in late 1959 to construct a new jetport in suburban Morris County had generated intense wrath in northern New Jersey and in the state legislature. In early 1960 a Congressional committee initiated an investigation of the past actions, plans, and alleged malpractices of the Authority.[23]

Confronting attacks from several quarters, the Port Authority decided that there was more to be gained by negotiating with New Jersey officials than by rigid adherence to its traditional position. If negotiations could produce a highly limited role for the Authority in the rail field, this would forestall greater pressures on the agency in this area and improve its general public image. Several months of intensive negotiations between the Authority staff and state officials followed, and in early 1961 an agreement was reached: the Port Authority would purchase the Hudson and Manhattan Railroad (a small but heavily used commuter line operating between New Jersey and Manhattan), and it might later assume other rail duties. However, the total annual deficit from its rail operations could not exceed 10 per cent of the Authority's General Reserve Fund, and projections indicated that the H&M deficit would absorb most if not all of this amount. New Jersey officials involved in the negotiations agreed that an absolute contractual limitation of this sort was needed, or the Authority could not sell bonds for the H&M project or other programs. "It gets down to how badly we need the H&M," declared a state spokesman. "Do we want it on the investors' terms or not at all?"[24]

[22] The commuter car program was approved by the two states in April and May 1959. New York State also approved several other measures to assist the railroads at that time.

[23] See, for example, New Jersey Commission to Study the Financial Structure and Operations of the Port of New York Authority, "Public Hearing" (Trenton: September 27, 1960); U.S. House of Representatives, Port of New York Authority, Hearings. . . .

[24] Dwight R. G. Palmer, State Commissioner of Highways, in a public statement,

Meanwhile, Manhattan business interests and the Port Authority had joined forces in urging that the agency be authorized to construct a massive World Trade Center, at a cost of $350 million or more, in lower Manhattan. There was some question whether New Jersey would approve Authority construction of a vast complex of buildings of particular benefit to New York. Therefore, in a final round of negotiations, New Jersey found its rail plan blocked by New York State until New Jersey authorized the Center. In the spring of 1962 the Port Authority was given permission to acquire and operate the H&M railroad, and to build a "great new" World Trade Center with "twin towers of gleaming metal, soaring 110 stories" — an edifice just high enough to supplant the Empire State Building as the tallest building in the world.[25] The Authority found its plans widely acclaimed, and its public position, which had sunk to a low point in 1960, rebounded strongly by 1962. Also, while accepting limited rail responsibilities, the Port Authority continued to expand its road facilities and maintained its position that close coordination of all rail and highway planning and financing in the region would not be beneficial.[26]

Several years later, as the Port Authority approached its fiftieth anniversary, it was under renewed attack for failing to contribute more adequately to rail transportation, and for allocating funds instead to a "monstrous real-estate venture" (the Trade Center). One prominent critic characterized it as a "rigidly conservative money machine harnessed to serve . . . the private visions of an astonishingly narrow, relentlessly opportunistic management," while the newly elected Governor of New Jersey criticized the Authority for its failure to develop an integrated system of rail and road transportation.[27] In 1970 and early 1971, as rail deficits and traffic congestion in the New York region increased, the Port Authority found itself under mounting pressure from both state governors and from local officials to use its surpluses for rail transit projects. The 1962

January 26, 1961. The authorizing legislation includes the 10 per cent limitation as a statutory covenant with the Port Authority's bondholders. Thus the PNYA cannot be required to undertake further deficit-producing rail operations even if both states agree that it should do so.

[25] The quotations are from PNYA, *Annual Report, 1963*, p. 41. The H&M was renamed PATH, for the subsidiary that operates the system (the Port Authority Trans-Hudson Corporation).

[26] On the Authority's attitude toward coordination, see Austin J. Tobin, address before the Regional Plan Association, October 5, 1960; PNYA, *Metropolitan Transportation* — *1980* (New York: 1963), pp. 299–304 and *passim*.

[27] See Theodore W. Kheel (labor mediator and adviser to New York's mayor on transit problems), "How the Port Authority Is Strangling New York," *New York* (November 19, 1969), pp. 45–50; and the interview with present Governor William Cahill during his pre-election campaign, reported in *New York Times*, October 20, 1969.

REGIONAL POLITICS AND "BUSINESSLIKE EFFICIENCY" 125

contractual limitation, incorporated into Authority bonds in the intervening years, now became an important factor in protecting the agency from
major rail projects.[28] With this safeguard, and with its net operating
revenues at record heights, several new projects announced or underway,
the character of the Board and staff largely unchanged, and staunch
supporters well placed among business and political leaders, the Port
Authority managers looked forward with confidence to a second fifty years
of "imaginative and resourceful" activity, using their funds "prudently
and conservatively" in the service of the region and of the Port Authority
itself.[29]

[28] The Port Authority did agree in February 1971 to study the feasibility of a new
rail line from Newark Airport to Newark and New York City, another line from
Kennedy Airport to Manhattan, and a new rail tunnel between New Jersey and
Manhattan. At the same time, Austin Tobin reaffirmed the Authority's opposition
to undertaking any deficit rail operation unless it were limited enough to be consistent with the 1962 restriction. Any change in that covenant, he argued, would
be illegal (as a violation of the obligation of contracts clause of the U.S. Constitution), and would halt the ability of the Authority to sell bonds or carry out future
projects of any kind. See New York Times, May 9, 1970; February 12, 14, 25,
March 5, 6, 1971.

[29] To summarize the Port Authority's position more specifically: Its assets
at the end of 1969 were $2.7 billion (six times the level of 1952), and its net
operating revenues in 1969 were $122 million (four times the 1952 figure). Its facil-
ities in mid-1970 include six interstate bridges and tunnels, two bus terminals, six
airports, ten facilities for trucks, international shipping and other commercial activities, and one rail system. Major projects underway or envisioned in 1970 include a
$200 million redevelopment at Newark Airport, $350 million in construction projects at Kennedy Airport, an $80 million addition to the mid-Manhattan bus termi-
nal, and two new terminals for PATH. The PNYA staff was still headed by Austin
Tobin, and many of his senior aides were drawn from those who held high posts
twenty years earlier. Many of the Port Authority commissioners were different, but
the background of the 1970 Board was very similar to the Boards of the early 1950's:
in 1970, seven commissioners were bankers, stockbrokers, or leaders in other business enterprises; four were lawyers with important corporate connections; and the
12th was the chairman of another public authority in the New York region — the
Metropolitan Transportation Authority.

CENTRALIZATION AND DECENTRALIZATION IN THE CITY

3

As in the metropolis, the dispersion of power along territorial and functional lines typifies politics in the American city. The pattern of fragmentation in the central city also reflects its size and heterogeneity. In most cases, the city is the only big government in the metropolis. Its institutional arrangements are more complex than those of the suburbs. Often its fiscal and professional resources exceed those of the remaining political units of the metropolis combined. The average city provides a far wider range of public services than the surrounding suburban jurisdictions. Police, education, welfare, health, sanitation, and transportation services in cities produce greater bureaucratization and unionization of public employees than in any other sector of the metropolitan political economy. Moreover, politics in the city are more partisan and professional than in the suburbs. Ethnic, racial, class, and sectional conflict is more common in a city political system with its diverse groups and highly differentiated neighborhoods than in the small-scale, relatively homogeneous political arenas of suburbia.

Since the central city is, by definition, a single political jurisdiction, territorial decentralization is less significant in the city than in the metropolitan area where it is the cardinal fact of political life. Nonetheless, neighborhood and other territorial interests frequently play an important role in dispersing power within the city, especially where strong local party organizations have survived and municipal councils are elected from districts. In such systems, neighborhoods, acting through their political leaders or elected representatives, often can veto city actions they oppose. In almost every city, pressures from the neighborhoods for special consideration of their problems and interests temper the natural centralizing tendencies of the bureaucracies and professionals. Reinforcing this grass roots demand for territorial attention has been the spatial separation of social and economic groups within the city, whose ethnic, racial, and class concerns define neighborhood interests. Issues often are expressed in territorial terms, such as the insistence of lower middle-class and blue-collar whites on preserving the neighborhood school and the demand for community control of schools, police, and other local public services in the black ghettos.

Functional fragmentation, on the other hand, usually is more advanced in the central city than in the metropolitan area, due to the size and the scale of city services. Complex governments are more likely to become functionally decentralized than smaller ones that provide a limited range of services whose integration and control are relatively simple. In the city, government has become increasingly specialized as new functions have been added and existing ones expanded. With complexity and specialization have come departmentalization, bureaucracy, civil service, professionalism, and unionization. Each of these developments has increased the influence of municipal service workers over the activities of their agencies. Police commissioners and patrolmen, school superintendents and teachers, health officers and librarians, traffic engineers and street sweepers — all seek autonomy from the "political" institutions of the city, meaning primarily the elected mayor and council. Their slogans are familiar — "keep the politicians out of the schools," "no interference from City Hall," "there is no Democratic or Republican way of paving a street."

Facilitating this universal quest for functional autonomy has been a distaste of most city dwellers for "politics" and the concomitant appeal of a "businesslike" approach to the tasks of local government. In their campaigns to make local government more honest and economical, municipal reformers capitalized on these sentiments, as well as periodic public outrage at the excesses of the political machines. Almost always, blueprints for a more efficient city government entailed fragmentation along functional lines through the creation of independent boards and agencies and the introduction of merit systems for public employees. Independence also appeals to the clientele of a city agency, since it strengthens the influence of those groups closest to the agency vis à vis the influence of other components of the political system, both official and unofficial. In addition, autonomy often is promoted by federal and state programs for housing, health, and education, since professionals at the higher levels seek close functional links with their counterparts in the city.

Not only are political power and public resources dispersed in the city, but both are inadequate to the massive problems that confront the typical city. The city may be larger and have more capability than any other unit in the metropolitan area. Its mayor may be the most visible and influential political figure in the metropolis, commanding the remnants of an ethnic political machine, substantial backing in the business community, and solid support in the black ghetto. Yet, as Scott Greer points out in his analysis of the political systems of the larger cities, the city's size and resources, its mayor and his sources of support, its increasingly professional bureaucracies, are no guarantee that the challenges of urban growth and change will be met effectively. Instead, Greer sees a disappearing economic elite, a sluggish bureaucracy, and a stagnant party system combining to produce an inertial "machine of the incumbents" that cannot check the flight of the middle class and industry to the suburbs, halt the decay of neighborhoods, or meet the demands of the increasingly militant ghettos.

Some mayors, perhaps most, accept the *immobilisme* of the fragmented city political system. As Greer puts it, they "reign but do not rule." A few, like Lindsay in New York and White in Boston, attempt to redirect the energies of the system, engaging in often frustrating struggles with those who want to preserve the status quo. That vigor, commitment, and ambition in City Hall do not guarantee success is made clear in Frederick Wirt's appraisal of San Francisco and its "politics of hyperpluralism." San Francisco is a classic example of municipal fragmentation. Designed to prevent corruption rather than to facilitate strong government, the city charter scatters authority among scores of agencies, establishes a plethora of elected posts, necessitates frequent direct public participation in decision making through the referendum, and weakens the role of political parties with nonpartisan elections in which a plurality is sufficient for victory. As in many cities, ethnic, territorial, and bureaucratic interests merge in San Francisco, reinforcing the functional autonomy of the major city agencies and heightening conflict between the descendants of the earlier immigrants who control the bureaucracies and the more recent arrivals who want jobs and influence. Usually, such a system is responsive to those who have a vested interest in its operations, but it does not respond effectively to the needs of its diverse constituents.

One way for a city government to overcome its fragmentation and inertia is to find a man who can get things done. A few such men have helped to build almost every American city, but none has rivaled Robert Moses of New York in the scope of his operations, his accomplishments, and his political influence. A succession of mayors and governors commissioned Moses as their master builder, permitting him to fill the vacuum created by the dispersion and complexity of the political system of the nation's largest city. But as Jeanne Lowe's account of Moses' stewardship of the urban renewal program in New York indicates, men who get things done often exact a heavy price for their accomplishments, especially from those who always have paid most and received least in the American city.

Urban renewal destroys more homes in poor neighborhoods than are replaced by public housing and other government programs for low-income families. Expressways in cities are routed through black ghettos and other low-income areas. Schools, health care, refuse collection, and public transportation services typically are of lower quality in the poorer sections of the city than in the middle- and upper-income areas. Public welfare, police, and other public services with great impact on the most recent arrivals in the city tend to be unresponsive to their needs and interests. These are some of the consequences of powerlessness. The masses of urban poor lack political influence as well as economic resources. Compared with other groups in the city, the poor have few leaders, are poorly organized, and vote infrequently. Until recently, the poor were politically invisible, people whose interests did not need to be considered. Even the political machine, whose influence was built on the support of the Irish, Polish, Italian, and other immigrants who crowded into the city, failed to employ its control over city government to benefit those whose votes kept it in power. To be sure, the machine provided employment and a route of social mobility for some, and an assist in becoming part of an alien society for most of its constituency. But the typical boss was interested in the acquisition of wealth, not its redistribution. Rare indeed was the machine-controlled city government that forced landlords to lower exorbitant rents, sought to improve the wretched living conditions of the immigrants, or devoted its energies to providing adequate public services for the urban poor.

All problems of powerlessness are intensified for the blacks who have moved to the inner areas of American cities in increasing numbers during the twentieth century. Blacks are the victims of a tradition of political separation that formally excluded them from politics in many cities and diluted their voting influence in others through the use of racial gerrymandering, intimidation, and fraud. Most blacks came to the cities when the need for unskilled workers was declining, and when the city bureaucracies, the construction trades, and other traditional sources of employment for urban newcomers were controlled by the descendants of the earlier immigrants. In most cities, political machines also were declining. Where the machines survived, they typically subordinated black interests to those of the groups that dominated the organization. Limited opportunity —

combined with the inadequate education provided by segregated city schools and the occupational immobility caused by the increasing distance between suburban jobs and ghetto residences — has increased the number of poor among blacks in comparison with other groups of city residents. White racism has erected more formidable barriers to the quest of blacks for better homes, quality education, good jobs, and social justice than were encountered by any of the earlier arrivals in the city.

Given these circumstances — especially considering the steadily expanding impact of public welfare, urban renewal, and other government programs on the poor — no one should be very surprised by the demands for black power that have emanated from the ghettos during the past few years. Nor, warn Frances Fox Piven and Richard A. Cloward, should anyone be very optimistic about fulfilling these demands. In their view, the outlook for black control is limited by the dispersion of power in the city and the strength this fragmentation provides other groups, especially those who control the public bureaucracies. Even when a black is elected mayor, as in Cleveland, Gary, and Newark, black power is diluted by the financial weaknesses and jurisdictional limitations of the city. As a result, under black or white control, the city must depend on the metropolis, the state, and the federal government. In all these arenas white home owners and businessmen with interests to protect in the city are far more powerful than the urban blacks.

Another route to power for blacks and other disadvantaged groups in the city is community control over such public activities as education, police, welfare, housing, and health services. Considering the impediments to citywide control and the concentration of blacks within certain sections of the city, this approach has substantial attractions for those who seek to alter the status quo. As Joseph Featherstone indicates, the campaigns for community control over the schools have been fueled by the ineffectiveness of the traditional centralized educational system in the black ghetto and other low-income city neighborhoods. For some, the black demand for community control is no more than a city counterpart to political decentralization in the suburbs, where responsive local public service agencies and neighborhood control over the schools, police, and land use are the rule rather than the exception. For others, particularly the professionals who manage the major urban public services and the rank-and-file who provide them, community control poses a serious threat to professional standards, political influence, and economic security, as well as to the very notion of a city with city-wide institutions and services.

Scott Greer

THE MACHINE OF THE INCUMBENTS

Continual increase in scale has had four major consequences for the problems of urban government and their solution. It has produced an increasing bureaucratization of governmental and other functions: it has led to rapid organizational mergers in private enterprise; it has radically changed the general character of the urban population; and it has resulted in a massive multiplication of the population and therefore of the size of the organizational tools of urban government. Let us consider each of these in relation to its implications for the classic big city machine.

The bureaucratization of governmental services affected the machine in two separate ways. First, with the Great Depression of the 1930's it became apparent that all Americans were part of a nationwide economic system, and when that system failed the problem of unemployment and poverty was a nationwide problem. As a consequence, what had been charity became the work of the Department of Health, Education and Welfare, and vast programs were administered through the nationwide bureaucracies of government. Second, the management of local governmental enterprises became increasingly professionalized; the reformers were successful in convincing the people (and later the politicians) that such services as the city provided were better handled by civil servants, selected and trained through nonpolitical methods to do their jobs without favoritism or political counsel. These two changes struck deep at the roots of politics as a simple exchange system. The goods which the precinct captain once traded for votes were disbursed by a federal agency staffed by civil servants. The decisions about street layouts, hospital construction, zoning, and planning, once so profitably controlled by politicians, were increasingly made by professional public personnel — planners, hospital administrators, traffic engineers. At the same time voting became better organized, and mechanized, with a bureaucracy (subject to review) in charge of the tallies. Quality control made fraud difficult and dangerous. Both at the lowest and highest levels the exchange system of the machine was mortally damaged.

The rapid and continuous process of organizational merger had other

Reprinted from *Governing the Metropolis* (New York: Wiley, 1962), pp. 65–81, by permission of the author and John Wiley & Sons, Inc.

effects upon the urban polity. The drawing of major enterprise into national organizations and the further bureaucratization of the corporation, as it separated ownership from management, resulted in a class of professional managers whose first duty was to the nationwide, or international, corporate network. The most powerful economic figure in town was no longer the owner of the major industry; he was a manager. Consequently, the economic dominants (as they are sometimes called in the literature on the power elite) became increasingly withdrawn from concern with the local community. Schulze has documented the steps by which Ypsilanti, Michigan, moved from a classical power elite structure to one in which the branch plant managers were interested in the local community only on rare occasions. Rather than wishing to run the show, they only wanted a veto on certain kinds of government acts. Otherwise, they did not wish to be involved.[1]

The result of corporate merger has been the freeing of economic organizations from dependence upon, and hence interest in, particular cities. This has combined with the increasing geographical mobility of the managerial elite; as they move upward in the corporate hierarchy they move around the country. They become identified with one community only when they have ceased to be occupationally mobile. (One longitudinal study indicated that, even in Red Wing, Minnesota, a town of ten thousand, the personnel change among those nominated as civic leaders was more than 60 per cent in the relatively short period of six years.)[2] Turnover of leadership makes effective organization (the compromising of interests, the assignment of tasks, the integrating of action) extremely difficult. Furthermore, we must remember that the business leadership in a city of any size is apt to be divisible on more issues than those on which it is unitable. (A recent study by Scoble, for example, shows a very low rate of consensus among the dominant leaders in a New England town of less than fifteen thousand persons.)[3] It requires *more* work to achieve coordination when there is high turnover, yet there are fewer people committed to achieving it. In short, the changing nature of exclusive, membership organizations has greatly weakened their machinery for controlling the political decisions of the city. And such change is of particular importance in the metropolis, the headquarters city of the corporation.

Meanwhile, the population of the metropolis has been chang-

[1] Robert O. Schulze, "The Bifurcation of Power in a Satellite City," in Morris Janowitz, editor, Community Political Systems, Glencoe, Ill.: The Free Press of Glencoe, Inc., 1961.

[2] Donald W. Olmstead, "Organizational Leadership and Social Structure in a Small City," American Sociological Review, Vol. 19, pp. 273–281.

[3] Harry Scoble, "Leadership Hierarchies and Political Issues in a New England Town," Community Political Systems, Morris Janowitz, editor, Glencoe, Ill.: The Free Press of Glencoe, Inc., 1961.

ing. . . . Social rank has on the average moved upwards; the illiterate, unskilled workman of foreign birth is a vanishing breed. Even in the central city education, occupation, and real income have risen to once-unimaginable levels in the past sixty years. At the same time, the children and grandchildren of the foreign born are socialized from the beginning to the American urban milieu. As a result of these changes in combination the definition of the vote has changed; it is no longer simply an expression of ethnic solidarity, but rather a more complex decision, based on a variety of interests. The children of the immigrants live in a different city from that of their parents and have different techniques for managing their urban environment. Their toleration for fraud shrinks as they become more informed and committed to American civic virtues. Their vote is not for sale.

An indirect effect of increasing size, but an important one, is the suburban-central city dichotomy. With increasing population and static boundary lines, the population of the metropolis is almost equally divided between central city and suburbs. . . . Those who remain in the central city are predominantly ethnic and working class social types. In 1950, according to Philip Hauser, "Los Angeles was the only city among the five largest in the United States in which the native white population of native parentage was greater than half, and even there it was only 55 per cent.[4] These populations are the ones most likely to prefer the Democratic party in national elections; when there is a partisan organization of local elections (and this is true of all but one of our very large cities) the working class and the ethnic voters go Democratic. A direct consequence is the collapse of the Republican Party in the political arena of the central city. One by one, Republican strongholds are giving way to Democratic majorities, as the nordic white Protestant middle class makes its way to the suburbs. Today, in many of our great cities, two or three Republican council men represent the "two party system" among a host of Democratic officials. As the process of segregation by polity continues, the central city will become, in fact if not in theory, a one-party state.

Finally, we have to consider the increase in the size of urban concentrations. In 1900 two American metropolitan areas had a population of a million or more; in 1960, there were nineteen complexes this large. The sheer aggregation of population had two major effects upon the control system of the central city. First, and not to be overlooked, was the sheer increase in the size of the problems that had to be handled within the rounds of urban housekeeping, and the consequent size of the organizations which handled them. The City of New York, for example, employs 50,000 persons in its educational system, 26,000 in its police

[4] Hauser, *Population Perspectives*, New Brunswick, N.J.: Rutgers University Press, 1960, p. 125.

department, and 13,000 in its fire department.[5] The sheer aggregation of numbers and budget results in the proliferation of organizational centers with a degree of autonomy and, hence, power. The number and strength of leadership groups are multiplied with increasing population.

The total effect of these changes has been the destruction of the old-time political machine, and with it the power elite. Increase in scale has destroyed the basis for the political machine *as an exchange system*; in the urban wards of Stackton it is as hard to recruit precinct workers as in the small-town Republican strongholds of Illinois. Whyte reports the visible attrition of the Democratic machine in Boston during the 1930's, while Reichley discusses the steady weakening of Republican power in Philadelphia during the same period.[6] The ability of the political boss to control his "Hessians" and through them the vote of the people, may have been over-rated in the past: it is very easy to over-rate it today.

The collapse of the exchange system has, in turn, destroyed the ability of the power elite to call the tune. Businessmen have never had a preponderant influence, at the polls, on the city population as a whole. They have relied upon the machine as a mechanism for translating money into political power. By bribing the politicians and by contributing to campaign chests, business interests assured themselves a strong voice in the political decisions of the central city. Even with the Republican Party's power fading away they could still exert leverage upon the Democratic machine, for the machine was primarily a nonideological exchange system. With its weakening, however, the businessman had literally no way of reaching the voters.

The result is a drastic separation of numbers and wealth in the contemporary metropolis. Businessmen, resident in the suburbs, have great stakes in the central city polity. That polity, however, is controlled by a set of politicians who have a declining need for the businessman, and who are elected by the votes of the ethnic and working class constituencies of the center. Such a separation of numbers and wealth is not, of course, contrary to the democratic dogma. It is, however, an anomaly to those who still consider the businessman as the first class citizen and his interests as paramount for the community.

It is also anomalous to those who explain American government

---

[5] Wallace S. Sayre and Herbert Kaufman, *Governing New York*, New York: The Russell Sage Foundation, 1960.

[6] The political machine in Stackton is described and analyzed by Peter H. Rossi and Phillips Cutright in "The Impact of Party Organization in an Industrial Setting," in Morris Janowitz, editor, *Community Political Systems*, Glencoe, Ill.: The Free Press of Glencoe, Inc., 1961. For the Philadelphia case see James Reichley, *The Art of Government*, New York: The Fund for the Republic, 1959. William Foote Whyte presents a study, in depth, of the changing relations of the machine to the ethnic neighborhood he studied in Boston, in *Streetcorner Society*, Chicago: University of Chicago Press, 1943.

through the theory of the two-party system, with its assumptions of organized control and competition for power. The anomaly leads us to ask: How, then, does the government of today's central city operate? How is it that order is maintained and essential tasks are performed?

The disappearance of party competition in the general elections of the central city does not destroy party organization. Instead it changes the basis of organization: the old-style exchange system is replaced by a new order. Before discussing the new state of things, however, it is important to note the cause and consequences of one-party government for the dominant Democratic organization.

The central city electorate, with its predisposition to vote Democratic, is (like the Southern Democrats) basically a captive electorate. Whoever is designated Democrat on the ballot will usually get a majority of the votes. One might jump to the conclusion that such one-party government could mean only a sort of totalitarianism. Instead, it seems to result in general loosening of the control mechanism; as V. O. Key demonstrates for the one-party system in the South, the very basis for much of the party's control is weakened by the disappearance of the opposition party.[7] The reduction of threat in the general election eliminates the need for party discipline and ferocious esprit de corps for, no matter what happens, the Democratic Party will take most of the elective offices.

Under these circumstances, however, the Republican minority is rapidly demoralized. Political organization is postulated upon occasional victory; moral victories are sustaining only when there is some eventual possibility of non-moral, tangible victory. In the central city, however, Republican votes continue to decline despite all efforts made by the Republican Parties. As this occurs, the Republican Party's leadership and its elected local officials in cities like St. Louis and Chicago begin to resemble Republicans of the South. They are either lonely idealists, whose words are purely symbolic since they lack power to implement them, or else a sort of auxiliary of the dominant Democrats. (Chicago's delegation to the State legislature in Springfield includes the "sanitary Republicans," Republican legislators whose chief source of income is office in the Democratic-controlled Chicago Sanitary District.) Such officials may even vote with the Democrats and against their fellow Republicans on crucial issues. Thus even if the Republicans had a powerful issue, it is doubtful that the existing leadership could mobilize a campaign to exploit it. They stand not so much for an alternative governance as for the existing distribution of electoral strength in the central city; in fact, they depend upon it for their working conditions.

The Democratic monopoly of victory in the general election, however, means that the primary election becomes the major arena for gaining

7 V. O. Key, *Southern Politics*, New York: Alfred A. Knopf, 1949.

office. And at the primary level the party organization is considerably weakened, for nomination to office (tantamount to election) becomes an apple of discord thrown among the Democratic ranks. In some cities the party cannot officially designate a slate in the primary; even when it can, its decisions are basically divisive. There are many deserving party men, and little to prevent one from running from his district. If he has been an effective leader at the block and precinct level, he may very well win, for the mobilization of friends and neighbors can easily produce strong opposition to the organization's designated candidate. Since the candidates do not need actual logistic support in the general election (the simple party designation will usually suffice), the field is clear for "mavericks" to compete.

Yet the party organization can usually control most of the offices in the primary election. The reason for this is clear enough; the ordinary voter usually does not know or care enough about the primary to vote. Thus the organization, though it may control only a small percentage of the potential vote, can nevertheless swing the margin of victory to its candidate. This organizational level is considerably augmented in many cities by the organization's control of the electoral machinery. Efforts range from differential requirements for certification as a candidate, to the ignoring of irregularities in the campaign and the voting (though the latter practices are becoming increasingly dangerous ...). We may surmise also that much of the power of the organization results from a simple misapprehension of its effective force by potential dissidents. The machine *was* all-powerful for many years in some of our cities; those interested in politics are differentially exposed to the organization. They may fear official disapproval, not just in the immediate election, but in the future. Even if the party machine's power is now a myth, myths may long outlive their factual base and have consequences.

Thus the organization maintains a continuing control, though not an ironclad one, over the distribution of offices. However, with the disappearance of effective opposition it no longer needs the money of the businessman to win its campaigns. Being able to win the general election in any event, the power relations between politician and business leader have shifted radically. The politician is clearly in the more advantageous position: he has the trading cards.

There have also been radical changes within the dominant party's organization. With the weakening of the machine, the power relation between the nonelective party Boss and the elected officials reverses. First the elected mayor develops a considerable autonomy from the machine; standing above all other elected figures in the metropolis, his role is visible and his words are news. From the rostrum of office he tends to dominate the mass media, and through the media develops a powerful electoral attraction of his own. Then party ceases to be a differentiating label in the one-party central city; the major differentiator becomes incumbency. Those who are in office become *de facto* rulers of the party, for the party needs them more than they need its cohorts. They dispense the patronage and make the decisions.

Thus the central city mayor assumes a major if not dominating role in the *dramatis personae* of local politics. Other stellar roles include the head of the county government and perhaps the president of the council or board of aldermen. They also are familiar figures in the news, for they are elected officials with city-wide constituencies in image if not in fact. Along with them rise the managers of the great governmental bureaucracies, school superintendents, engineers, police commissioners, and the like. Such men, elected or appointed, stand for the expertise of their office, the legitimacy of the tasks which their bureaucracy performs, and the logistics of money and men. The dominant figures in central city politics tend to be the dominant officials of government; they constitute a "machine of the incumbents." No matter how they reached office in the first place, once there they are formidable forces.

The central city mayor can, indeed, become an enemy of his party's organization. Concerned with the entire city, he is sensitive to opinion in the middle class, familistic, outer wards of the city; his political score in the general elections depends upon his ability to carry these "good government" and "newpaper" wards. He responds to the criticism of the daily press and the statements of public leaders representing various interests: welfare, hospital, education, and the like. Though these interests cannot defeat him at the polls, he nevertheless engages in implicit bargaining with them, anticipating the effects of his words and actions on the newspapers, civic leaders, and hence, the outer wards. At the same time the central city mayor is the dominant public official for the entire metropolitan area. Insofar as there is a metropolitan community, he is its highest elected official. (In St. Louis, suburbanites and central city voters alike accorded the Mayor of the City more trust and confidence than all other leaders combined, and their reasons rested upon his office, his expertise, and his character as a civic notable.) As representative of more than the laundry list of special interests in the area, he stands for the general welfare. Businessmen, no longer his employers, return as influentials insofar as they are virtual representatives of many values and aspects of the metropolis.

In fact, the central city mayor tends to believe that good government is good politics. But in the process of pursuing good government he may destroy much of the effectiveness of the Democratic organization.[8] The

8 Banfield discusses the destructive effect of the "good government mayor" at some length in *Political Influence*, New York: The Free Press of Glencoe, Inc. 1961.

separation of the offices of precinct captain for the party and precinct captain of police may be good governmental administration: it may also be very demoralizing for the political actors who had counted upon the promotion to police captain as a possible reward. Nevertheless, the metropolitan mayor is free to continue his swing towards good government, for the machine cannot control him. And he may look beyond the central city, to position in the state government, or the federal government in Washington, where his "good government" policies may count heavily. Furthermore, he is, ironically, strengthened at home by his symbolic separation from the machine. He can have his cake and eat it too. Meanwhile the old-style political machine is further weakened; the rewards of political work disappear right and left. As one consequence, the persons who can be recruited for the hard and tedious work at the block level change in character; the ranks of party workers become disproportionately composed of those who have few alternatives for social distinction and mobility. The over-all picture is one in which old-style machine politics fades away before the new order, the machine of the incumbents.

To repeat the argument: The continual segregation of population by governmental boundaries means an increasing domination of the central city vote by the poor, the ethnics, and therefore the Democratic party label. This, in turn, relaxes the tensions of conflict at a party level, leading to a one-party state. To be sure, the process has gone further in some cities than others; it is still possible for the Republicans to win a battle occasionally if their wards are numerous and the Democrats make a series of catastrophic mistakes.

This will become rarer as the proportion of working class ethnics increases. It is also true that, in West Coast cities like Los Angeles, Republicans may rule under the guise of nonpartisanship. It is likely, however, that such cities, never having known a machine, have simply skipped a stage and landed directly in the future — the one party or non-party polity ruled by the machine of the incumbents.

One-party government, in fact, approaches very closely the condition of non-partisan government. The weakening of the party organization's hold on the incumbents softens the impact of those who wish to translate wealth and social power garnered in other fields into pressure on the policy of the city. The incumbents are freed from many pressures; however, it is a "freedom from," rather than a freedom to accomplish new and radical enterprises. This is because power becomes basically fractionated and dispersed. The elected officials, the heads of the great bureaucracies, state and federal levels of government, private capital, and the party organization, each hold certain resources necessary for massive action. To these must be added the governmental divisions of the metropolis. Multiple municipalities, counties, and special districts are vested with the legitimate power to perform certain tasks and to refuse to cooperate in others.

Banfield's description of Chicago emphasizes the continual deadlocking of these forces. In *Political Influence* he notes that the political head (usually the mayor) will ratify almost any proposal on which principal parties can agree. He thus escapes criticism from newspapers, civic leaders, and the like. However, he hesitates to force compromise because of the cost in goodwill, support, public image, or other intangibles of influence. He can usually afford to wait indefinitely for decisions to emerge: what usually emerges is stalemate. Of the six major issues Banfield studied (all of the major public issues for a two-year period), two were resolved, one was abandoned by its protagonists, and the remainder were simply tabled. Thus half the major public issues remained in limbo. This is hardly evidence of a tightly knit ruling clique. Instead, Banfield sees the power elite as essentially part of "The Mythology of Influence."

> The notion that "top leaders" run the city is certainly not supported by the facts of the controversies described in this book. On the contrary, in these cases the richest men of Chicago are conspicuous by their absence. Lesser business figures appear, but they do not act concertedly: some of them are on every side of every issue. The most influential people are the managers of large organizations the maintenance of which is at stake, a few "civic leaders" whose judgment, negotiating skill, and disinterestedness are unusual and, above all, the chief elected officials. Businessmen exert influence (to the extent that they exercise it at all) not so much because they are rich or in a position to make threats and promises as, in the words of one of them, "by main force of being right."[9]

To be sure, Banfield thinks that if all the wealth were organized in a permanent organization, it could exert great influence on the polity. This is not likely to come about, however, for three reasons: (1) there are fundamental conflicts of interest among private organizations, (2) the required communication would be great enough to cut seriously into the time necessary for private interest, and (3) any formal organization would rapidly become immobilized by its own commitments and organizational structure.

The overriding power of the mayor is also a logical possibility in Banfield's interpretation. He dismisses it in these words.

> To be sure, his power is great enough, thanks to the machine and to his ability to make the trades the planners deplore, so that he can exercise wide discretion in almost any matter. But being able to exercise wide discretion in almost any matter does not mean that he can exercise it in *all* matters. With

9 *Ibid.*, p. 288.

respect to any one or two, or any few, moves, he is free. But if he wishes to stay in the game and to win, most of his moves, like most of the moves of the "civic leaders" and the businessmen in *their* games, must be determined by the exigencies of the game itself. Like them, he must act as the game requires or else get out of it.[10]

Thus Banfield's picture of Chicago is one that underlines the stability of the order, its underlying resistance to change, and the recalcitrant nature of government as a tool for major control and planning.

Sayre and Kaufman come to similar conclusions with respect to the greatest city in the country, New York City. Much as they love it, they report that its government is essentially static and conservative. The council is hamstrung, the mayor has responsibilities far beyond his power, and the Board of Estimate (made up of borough presidents and some central city officials) has usurped effective power. The result is a city government which has no legislative process, no strong executive, no party division visible to the public: one which is, in short, neither democratically responsible nor capable of a strong polity. Neither innovation nor planning can come about except in piecemeal response to the maintenance needs of the great city bureaucracies whose managers are as important in New York as in Banfield's Chicago.[11] For the Mayor of New York to function as leader and responsible head of the government he must be a political genius. When any social role requires such a rare person to operate it, we can judge it poorly designed for a world dominated by the "fairly bright."

The mayors of our great cities, symbols and symbolic leaders of the metropolitan community, reign but do not rule. They are brokers, conciliators, who reconcile the people to what they get from their government. They legitimatize the *fait accompli* on the rare occasions when the necessary resources for action result from transitory coalitions among the major contending organizations. For the rest, they preside over routine caretaker governments. And from one point of view, this is what the situation may seem to demand. The pioneer work of building the plant and establishing an order for the central city is long since complete: the population explosion will not rock its foundations, for a vast apparatus is in existence, and new growth will largely settle outside the center, in suburbia. The great bureaucracies which provide necessary governmental goods and services are already in being: they pursue the organizational destiny of expansion, increasing professionalization and multiplying the career opportunities for civil servants. All this they can do within the precedents established in the past and legitimatized through use.

[10] *Ibid.*, pp. 302–303.
[11] Sayre and Kaufman, *op. cit.*, Chapter XVII.

There is, however, no organization capable of mounting a major offensive for innovation. The central city's polity is passive and adaptive before the continuing results of increase in scale; only catastrophe seems capable of creating the opportunity for new development. Meanwhile, the trends continue; the suburban move of industry is added to the differentiation of central city and suburban populations, the increasingly obsolete neighborhoods, and the increasing proportion of colored populations who suffer most from economic depression and expect the most action from their city government. Taken all together these trends result in a rapid drift of the city away from its older status of centrality and totality. Faced with such changes, most people who consider the central city's destiny agree that massive counteraction, planning and construction, and governmental change are necessary. Such counteraction is difficult to imagine within the governmental structure of our great cities as they operate today.

Frederick M. Wirt

THE POLITICS OF HYPERPLURALISM

Because, as Alexander Hamilton noted, men are not angels, government is needed; but from the beginning the makers of American charters have been almost obsessed by fears of too much government. The Platonic method of controlling arbitrary power — by recruiting only moral men — has found limited use in our history. It is Aristotle who informs the American political tradition: the division of power so that no one gets too much — power is set against power, ambition against ambition

Reprinted from "Alioto and the Politics of Hyperpluralism," by Frederick M. Wirt, TRANS-action, Vol. 7, No. 6 (April 1970), pp. 46–55, with the permission of the author and TRANS-action. Copyright © April, 1970 by TRANS-action, Inc., New Brunswick, New Jersey.

and interest against interest. The hope is that in this way, "Nobody gets everything, nobody gets nothing, everybody gets something."

Few American cities have embraced this traditional principle more enthusiastically than San Francisco. Here the politics of public decision-making proceeds in a context of such fragmentation of power that the traditional principle has come to its logical end — powerlessness. . . .

Political decisions are our focus, those having a public impact and those most often in the domain of government. Decisions that arise out of private organizations also have public consequences, of course, and hence they too are a part of the pool of political decisions. When the Transamerica Corporation decides to erect a gigantic skyscraper in downtown San Francisco, it will have immense effect on many city dwellers. Although I won't discuss this sort of decision here, one has to keep in mind that this world of private decision-makers exists and that it is made up of both a Big Establishment and a Small Establishment. The distinction is not merely the amounts of money available to each. The Big E is peopled by financial and industrial capitalists and managers whose interests run far beyond the Bay to the nation and the world. The Small E centers on the group whose financial interests extend only to the Bay Area, and particularly the city itself.

The Big E pays little attention to San Francisco politics or its government, while many in the Small E do so with perseverance and fascination. Both have material interests at stake in local government, of course, but the Big E's are long-run, while the Small E's are short-run. Both cooperate on cultural, civic and generally nonpolitical matters. And in the last analysis, one can safely suppose that it is this constellation of private interests that makes many if not most of the decisions that allocate values in this community and that therefore affect most people most enduringly. Government, however, often has to deal with many of the problems that arise as the result of these private decisions. Local government may have little to do with the origins of such problems; it may not help in the takeoff, but only in the flight — and often only when cries of "Mayday! Mayday!" fill the air.

Barking Party Politics

For anyone accustomed to the frenetic party politics of such big American cities as Chicago, Detroit, New York and Boston, the party politics of California cities must seem mysterious, if only because of their absence. Like the dog in the Sherlock Holmes story, they are important because they do *not* bark. One finds traces of their presence in party leader titles and in announcements of committee meetings. But such spoor lead to nothing at all.

The evanescent nature of California parties arises from the state's distinctive political culture. Its central feature is a distrust of politics and politicians and a magical belief that if you give something a different name, you can change its essential quality — like the Victorians calling chicken breast "white meat." But the abolition of political parties didn't make politicians and politics vanish. They only shifted their field of operations into what Eugene C. Lee has described in *The Politics of Nonpartisanship* as a "politics of acquaintance" in which one's political loyalties and values are shaped by friends and neighbors, or by specific interests close to one's heart or pocketbook.

Such is the politics of the city of San Francisco today, although it was not always so. Before World War II, the Irish totally dominated Democratic politics; but in the post–World War II period their dominance began to loosen. Both parties now reveal a high degree of factionalism, and it is not uncommon to see interparty coalitions on behalf of specific candidates or issues. . . .

This fragmentation is well illustrated in the 1967 election of the dominant political figure of San Francisco today, Mayor Joseph Alioto. First of all, the basic rule of the game in such races is that victory is by plurality — highest takes all. This plurality system clearly militates against coalitions, which would be needed if a runoff election were required to achieve a majority winner. Fragmentation is thereby enhanced. Thus in the 1967 contest there were three candidates: Alioto; Jack Morrison, Democratic member of the Board of Supervisors (the legislative body under city-county consolidation); and Harold Dobbs, the Republican. All of this, remember, was formally nonpartisan.

The 1967 Mayoralty Race

Alioto's victory that fall was deliberately built on the support of a number of factions. When the rising Democratic leader, State Senator Eugene McAteer, died in the spring of 1967 on the verge of certain election as mayor, portions of his following gravitated to various places. Some of his chief lieutenants are said to have suggested a Small E member as candidate, but he declined and endorsed Alioto, who at that point was little known publicly, despite solid duty on the school board and a legal career in anti-monopoly law that had made him a multimillionaire.

Alioto thereupon inherited much of McAteer's organization, which included both traditional conservative Democrats and some CDC [California Democratic Council] members. But the main CDC support was and still is behind Congressman Phillip Burton who supported Supervisor Jack Morrison against Alioto. Organized labor, in this town where labor is very important politically, swung from the CDC to back

Dependent Children) gets only $1,800 a year. The Public Housing Act of 1937 proclaimed the goal of providing decent housing for the poor; today there are about 10 million substandard dwelling units in the country, for only 600,000 units of public housing have been constructed. Our national policy of full employment, enunciated by legislation in 1946, has proved to be meaningless rhetoric.

Worse yet, manifestly egalitarian measures have been turned against the poor. Federal agricultural subsidies, established to aid all farmers, actually helped to bankrupt small ones and enrich large ones. The Housing Act of 1949 asserted the right of every American to "a decent and standard dwelling unit," but initiated the Urban Renewal Program that destroyed 350,000 low-rental housing units in the course of reclaiming slum neighborhoods for commercial facilities and better-off residents. Several hundred thousand more low-rental homes were demolished during the same period by public works and federal highway construction — programs also put forward under the banner of improving the urban environment. Indeed, these programs "for the community as a whole" have succeeded in destroying more low-rental units than government has constructed since the Public Housing Act was passed.

Finally, what concessions the unorganized poor did get actually inhibited their capacity for political action. This is especially true of public welfare and public housing programs in which benefits are made conditional on compliant behavior by recipients. The poor, dealt with as supplicants by functionaries who can evict them or cut off their checks at will, are rendered more helpless in exchange for the benefits they receive.

New proclamations about action to help the poor are now being made, and new programs discussed. But what reason is there to suppose that these measures will not also be tokenistic, or turned to serve the interests of other groups, or designed to intimidate the recipients still more? For the simple truth is that governmental action has not worked for the unorganized poor and is not likely to work for them in the future unless they become a political force in initiating and shaping it.

If the history of past programs is not fully convincing, consider the major proposal now being advanced to ease violence in the cities — namely, that public subsidies be used to spur investments by national corporations in ghetto housing and employment. This plan is being promoted by alliances of corporation executives and political leaders, with representatives of organized labor and civil rights bringing up the flank.

The corporate interest in these proposals reflects more than a response to the promise of subsidized profit-making. Violence in the cities results in the wholesale destruction of property. And the spreading disorder, threatening to pit racial groups against each other in armed conflict, undermines the civic stability on which large-scale enterprise depends.

Moreover, corporate enterprise can now take a benevolent stance toward blacks because it no longer has a major stake in domestic racism. At an earlier stage of production, racism helped to depress the cost of labor by ensuring a supply of cheap black workers as well as a supply of scabs to inhibit union organizing among whites. But labor costs are now a less important factor in profits, and union organization has turned out to be an advantage in stabilizing and regulating the work force. Racism is no longer an economic asset; by threatening social stability, it has become a liability.

Corporate investments will result in quick improvements in the ghetto. But what pressure will there be for continuing and expanding investments once order is restored? Other markets are more profitable, and national political leaders can derive greater political advantage by turning subsidies to larger or more influential groups — such as suburbanites. Furthermore, if national corporations absorb the subsidies for programs ranging from manpower training to redevelopment, no black enterprise will emerge. The ghetto will merely become a subsidized market to be exploited by white enterprise; once again, it will be weakened by a coalition acting in its name. There is, in short, good reason for poor blacks to beware of corporate representatives bearing tax-deductible gifts.

How, then, are the black poor to develop greater political influence? Some observers point to the fact that the growing concentration of blacks in the central cities is making them a substantial electoral force. Earlier groups of the poor, it is noted, exploited the resources and powers of municipal government to aid their rise in the economic order; why not blacks as well? The parallel is far from exact, as we shall show. For the moment, however, let us assume that the black community is not weaker than earlier ethnic communities, and that city government is as important in the federal system as it once was.

First, as majorities in the cities, or even as large voting blocs, blacks would have the means to prevent the recurrent incursions on the ghetto by urban renewal, highway construction, and public works programs. At the same time, funds now being spent on others could be directed to improving ghetto services and facilities. Municipal power might also be used to force private enterprise and unions to admit Negroes. Public officials have numerous sources of leverage: they fix budget allocations for services and projects, approve private construction plans, and decide whether to pass on requests for state and federal grants. Each of these decisions is an occasion to exact concessions from other groups. Employers who want city contracts can be induced to hire and promote blacks. Similarly, unions can be opened to Negroes by blocking approvals for new construction or by threatening to reform archaic building codes on which their jobs partly depend.

These powers also offer a way for blacks to gain access to the more desirable neighborhoods now occupied by the white working and middle classes. Black government can override resistance to public housing in white areas and enforce bans on discrimination in the rental and sale of housing. Where public officials are elected on a precinct basis, the spread of blacks would entrench their political control by assuring majorities in each district.

Acquiring access to white institutions is one way to advance; developing black institutional relationships to the society is another and more important way. Separatist institutional development will not take place quickly, but in the long run its effects could be profound, for nothing about the Negro community is more conspicuous than the absence of its own institutions. In part, this condition is a heritage of slavery and of laws passed in the wake of Reconstruction which prohibited free assembly and the formation of associations among Negroes. The traditional isolation of most blacks in rural and feudalistic settings has also inhibited the formation of institutions, especially of a kind that would be viable in the city.

The need for communal institutions is one of the major themes of black power advocates. And municipal control could be the key. Where else is the money to come from to foster such a development? The black poor are very poor, indeed, and they confront an economy dominated by large-scale corporations, in which the would-be entrepreneur has far less likelihood of success than in the more open economy of the past. Nor can much be expected of efforts to unionize blacks, for many of them, if they work at all, are in occupations too marginal and dispersed to be organized effectively (e.g., domestic service). Moreover, the black middle classes will not lead a separatist development; they have been absorbed into white institutions and cannot be enticed back unless substantial occupational rewards are available. To overcome these obstacles, blacks need the resources controlled by municipal officials — contracts for all manner of projects and services to nurture new enterprises, as well as the leverage over white economic interests to induce them to deal with black enterprises. In these ways urban power might in time enable the black community to develop the infrastructure which has served other groups so well, especially black economic enterprise and black labor unions to organize the workers in the resulting jobs.

Finally, greater black influence in national politics depends on strong local organization capable of promoting electoral participation and assuring discipline. To build organization, black leaders need the platform of municipal office to articulate black interests and the resources of public office to reward their followers. For all these reasons, many now see the city as the hope for the Negro.

But the prospects for black urban power, as we have just defined them, rest on the erroneous assumption that American politics are formed by voting numbers alone. The conventions of electoral politics are regularly subverted in many ways. Those already holding power will not yield the spoils of office quickly or easily to new majorities. Even when official representation is achieved, responsiveness by government requires a constituency capable of watching over and pressuring officials. To be sure, blacks will assume nominal power in the cities because of the sheer weight of their numbers; but compared to earlier groups, blacks have few organizational ropes to keep rein on their leaders. Black officials will find themselves confronted by a variety of well-organized white groups — such as unions of public employees — who have the power to obstruct the business of government. They will be pressed to defer to these white interests, and an unorganized black constituency will give them the slack to do it. Although it may be too soon to draw conclusions, the first statements and appointments of Cleveland's newly elected black mayor suggest just such conciliation of whites.

Moreover, local government has been greatly weakened since the heyday of the ethnic urban machine. Localities now collect a mere seven per cent of tax revenues, while the federal government collects two-thirds. This fiscal weakness underlies the great vulnerability of local government to national centralized power, reflected both in the schemes for intervention by national corporations discussed earlier, and in new encroachments by the federal government under the guise of metropolitan planning.

The national government is using its multitude of existing programs for localities to form a new system of metropolitan-wide bureaucracies. This new level of government will impose federal policies on localities in the course of channeling grants-in-aid to them.

The need for metro administration is commonly justified on the ground that the concentration of people in sprawling urban areas has produced a host of problems — transportation, water supply, pollution control — which transcend narrow municipal boundaries. The solution of these problems is said to require programs planned and implemented on a metropolitan basis. For some problems, perhaps so; however, many urban problems remain unsolved, not for lack of area-wide planning, but for lack of political will. That communities do not apply for federal funds to build public housing needs no explanation beyond local reluctance to house the poor and black. Nevertheless, metro bureaucracies are emerging, and they will supersede the cities just as blacks come to power.

Whose interests will the federal metro agencies reflect? It takes no special acumen to see the answer. Their policies will be formed in deference to the inner-city and suburban whites who are an overwhelming majority in the metro region. Thus programs for the inner city will be designed to protect and ease the ethnic working classes, the residual middle class, and corporate groups with heavy property investments in the core. And there will be suburban services and facilities to meet the needs of decentralizing industry and white residents, whose electoral power now exceeds that of inner-city populations. Judging from the past, programs for blacks will be designed to treat their presumed deficiencies — to engender "good work habits and incentives," strengthen family life, improve mental health.

If the black middle class has so far benefited from technological change, it will prosper even more from the corporate-metro solutions to the urban crisis. To smooth the path of intervention, the black middle class will be absorbed into white corporate and metropolitan agencies. It should not be surprising, therefore, that these new approaches are already being hailed by Negro elites. The rationale given is that they will further integration — metropolitanism is said to be the way to breach the wall between ghetto and suburb in housing and education, and corporate programs the way to promote economic integration. But as metropolitan administrations take control, they are not likely to promote the dispersal of blacks to white neighborhoods in the face of resistance by an area-wide majority; meanwhile, white corporate control will be extended to the ghetto. Thus these new systems will enable whites, even as the ideal of integration is invoked, to maintain political and economic hegemony over the black masses.

The black poor, then, have few prospects for political or economic advancement. Because of the current disruptions, they will get a few concessions to restore tranquillity. But once the cities are tranquillized, what then? As we have said, the main chance for black power is in the cities, but the odds are lengthening. If there is a question to be debated, it is not whether the idea of black power is desirable; it is whether the power of this idea can prevail in the face of the continuing centralization of corporate and federal power over the city.

Joseph Featherstone

THE CRISIS OF AUTHORITY

Despite the chaos in New York City, a number of cities are gingerly moving towards some form of decentralization and local control. Worried administrators are trying to read the murky lessons of New York's disaster: it is obvious that any planning for decentralization has to include representatives of all the important political elements in a city. There should be one single plan, instead of half a dozen. Guarantees of teachers' rights have to be spelled out. And if decentralization is preceded by any experimental dry runs, such as the demonstration districts in New York, it will be necessary to delegate powers and lines of authority with a great deal of precision. Such experiments may be necessary on political grounds, but they inevitably work as lightning rods, attracting trouble, offering easy marks for sabotage to those opposing change, and exposing the fundamental issues at stake. The experience of New York with its demonstration districts resounds like a funeral bell with one practical lesson: any experimental districts ought to include some white middle-class areas, and probably should include poor and lower-middle-class whites as well. White parents have to be persuaded that they, too, can benefit from lay participation in school reform. The failure to do this in New York — to name, for example, the integrated Joan of Arc district on the upper West Side as one of the model districts — was a major error.

These and other tactical considerations must be weighed, but when all is said, there is no set of techniques for dodging the underlying dilemmas posed by the movement for community control. Lurking like carp below the surface of the school disputes are a number of shadowy issues very nearly without precedent in our history. There are intellectual issues arising out of the new communitarianism of portions of the middle class, and new challenges to the professionalism of the urban bureaucracies. There are the political issues raised by the minority revolutions. And intertwined with these are the educational issues. One of the difficulties in the school crises is that all the questions — each complex and baffling enough in its own right — fuse together, so that protagonists find

Reprinted from "Anti-city, a Crisis of Authority: The Problem Is More than Schools," *The New Republic*, Vol. 161, Nos. 8 and 9 (August 23, 30, 1969), with the permission of the author and *The New Republic*. Reprinted by permission of *The New Republic*, © 1969, Harrison-Blaine of New Jersey, Inc.

themselves forced to take sides on a whole range of complex concerns all at once. It seems to me that, under the circumstances, only ideologues and bigots can look at what is happening with undivided minds. Two concerns, both as yet badly defined, form part of the intellectual background of discussions of decentralization. The first — the widespread sympathy with demands for increased local control — is still only a mood. The second — the attack on professional monopoly of the professions — is as yet reflected in a few weak stirrings of rebellion. Both may become more important as time goes on; ultimately the constituency for community control and reform of the professions may include more than just the oppressed urban minorities.

Race and the collapse of services for the poor fire the movement for community control now, but it also draws on wider currents of feelings. Resentment at the way the cities work has been festering for 20 years. As Nathan Glazer says, the program for community control antedates the black revolution — it was drawn up by middle-class theorists like Paul and Percival Goodman and Jane Jacobs. Nor was it an exclusive concern of a few white intellectuals with a taste for anarchism. In moving out to the suburbs many people were choosing, among other things, to sacrifice certain amenities of city life for a setting in which they had some leverage on government and access to the authorities — or at the very least, choices about such matters as the educational environment in which their children were to grow up. Clearly there were many other reasons for the middle-class exodus, not least of which was the desire to escape the presence of the new black immigrants. And of all places, the suburbs illustrate the extent to which American life is organized in mass national units: their chain stores and their similarities of landscape are reminders that there will always be a limit to how much local control any of us will have in a continental, and even international, economy. But granting all this, I still think Glazer is right: one aspect of the growth of suburbia has been middle-class dissatisfaction with urban services, distrust of the vast city bureaucracies, and aversion to being administered.

This resentment of a distinctly modern condition of powerlessness is shared by portions of the population in all the advanced technological societies. It unites conservatives and radicals — like an SDS girl I spoke to who had worked with some John Birchers against an urban renewal project in South Boston. It is accentuated by the recurring incapacity of majoritarian democracies to come to terms with their ethnic and cultural diversities — an incapacity which has produced waves of separatist (and often reactionary) movements in countries like Britain, Belgium, and Canada. In America, attention has focused on the rise of black nationalism, but a similar mood of resentful communitarianism lies at the roots of the spreading white middle-class revolts against urban renewal plans, superhighways, and ABM missile sites; it is responsible for a measure of the campus unrest, as well. In distinct ways, Eugene McCarthy, George Wallace, and Robert Kennedy were able to top it in the last Presidential campaign, invoking what Richard Goodwin has called the sources of our public unhappiness. So far it remains simply a mood: it has not been able to crystallize itself into any institutional shape. The main intellectual failure of those who share it has been a reluctance to grapple with the problem that demands for participation and local control have to be squared with the fact that this is a nation of 200,000,000 people, many of whom are organized into hierarchies, bureaucracies, and unions. What is called for is the kind of intellectual enterprise that Paul and Percival Goodman began in *Communitas*, an attempt to spell out real alternatives to our present urban life. What we are getting, instead, is simply a reiteration of the dim aspirations of a troubled middle class for accountability, participation, and a politics of private expressiveness. Nonetheless these dissatisfactions with the urban order, and the call for more participation and local control, are very much in the air: even though their intellectual sources are different from those of the minority revolutions, they have contributed to the declining legitimacy of the urban institutions now under fire.

This mood informs an assault now underway against the bureaucracies and professions. In an explosive new context, the advocates of community control of the schools have revived a traditionally stormy issue in American education: whether laymen or professionals will run the schools. This may signal the slow beginning of an important shift in thinking — not just for blacks, but for the white middle class, too. In the past, radicals and reformers have tended to assume that virtue must dwell with the professionals, whose standards are usually more progressive and universal than those of their clients; local control in the South, everybody knew, spoke in the accents of parochialism and bigotry. This is a classic argument; it remains true today. Its force has been somewhat blunted in recent years, however, as it also becomes plain that large numbers of professionals — in medicine and other fields as well as education — are digging in to protect vested interests from reasonable public scrutiny and accountability. In many cases the professionals are hiding behind obsolete and self-serving credentials and licensing systems. The furor over schools has obscured how general these problems are becoming. In the midst of the Albany legislative sessions on school decentralization, for example, there were a number of skirmishes over hospitals — particularly Harlem Hospital — that raised similar issues. Both hospitals and schools are failing the poor, and lack of money is only part of the problem. In both, the professionals have a natural stake in keeping themselves in charge and the public out — although there are indications that a number of disgusted doctors may end up crossing over to the ranks of a community control movement.

Reform of structures that have simply grown up over the years is clearly long overdue, although this may not be the most opportune moment for a sensible debate. Many children of the affluent are talking as though they wanted to repudiate all professional standards. A few teachers, doctors, lawyers, and others are seriously working to define a new professionalism — one that would serve clients instead of the profession. Up to now, their influence hasn't been great.

Intolerable schools and collapsing health services give the revolt of the urban minorities more of a focus than middle-class longings for participation; but while it is more specific, it shares many of the same battle cries and poses, with one great exception, similar challenges to the professionals. The exception, of course, is race. A new black community consciousness is stirring; and we are witnessing an ambitious attempt to organize the black ghettoes into a political force around issues like community control of schools.

To take the measure of all these stirrings is far from easy. As with the middle-class left, a good deal of black revolutionary rhetoric barely masks a profound despair; and politics too often becomes a matter of inflammatory gestures, rather than programs. And for all the organizing that is going on, blacks in the cities are still dismayingly weak as a political force. The needles turn in the old, old grooves: people don't vote, leadership in the "community" is divided and greedy, few organizations are capable of surmounting the grinding factionalism. As a political fact, it is wise to remember, black power is still a slogan: real power in the ghetto remains the same as ever, an occasional veto power over the white armies of occupation.

Nevertheless there are signs of a change, particularly in the aftermath of the various community action programs of the war on poverty. In many ways these programs were a bust, provoking long, senseless quarrels among the poor over bones devoid of any meat. In the absence of massive employment and income programs, bitter fights over participation seem rarely to have been worth the candle. But veterans of the poverty programs have been trained to organize; and they emerged from the whole futile process with a conviction that there are plenty of things wrong with the institutions serving ghettoes besides lack of funds. The community action programs didn't produce a revolution, as their hysterical enemies charged; they didn't alter the feelings of the poor about being powerless, as sentimental advocates hoped. They have, perhaps, established an important precedent in the ghetto: successful programs to help the poor probably can no longer be run without the active participation of representatives of the poor. This includes schools.

In the course of a curiously ambivalent assessment of the community action programs, Daniel P. Moynihan pointed out that one of their principal results has been the creation of a new black leadership at a time when minorities are struggling for more power in city politics. Discrimination and the decline of opportunities for unskilled work in the inner-city cores have made blacks more dependent on public institutions than earlier immigrants. At the same time, civil service reform and the professionalization and upgrading of municipal services have denied many entry into the sorts of jobs that were once available through patronage to the old-time ethnic political machines. In a sense, as Moynihan says, the poverty programs have been a substitute for Tammany, a political apprenticeship. Much of the drive for community control of schools in New York has come from people trained to hold meetings, write proposals, operate mimeograph machines, and make trouble for bureaucrats by the various community action programs of the war on poverty. There is no cause to romanticize this process of political development or to exaggerate its progress. Harlem has its full share of the oldest politics of all — jiggery-pokery and corruption. It is too early to say with any confidence that the new leadership emerging will in fact be an improvement on the old. What is clear is that the school crises have joined this new ghetto leadership to another new group, black professionals, ambitious and eager to reform the schools.

There are different priorities in this alliance: for some, schools come second — they are merely a focus for organizing a community. For others — for most of the professionals, and, one suspects, for most thoughtful and active parents — reforming the schools is the main task.

If the new forces in the ghetto succeed they will in the end have to make a settlement with a society that is increasingly meritocratic and committed to more and more "objective" criteria in advancing people to better jobs. Perhaps they will be able to link up with a general reform aimed at loosening up rigid professional structures, making qualifications for jobs rest on performance, rather than credentials. Right now this seems a long way off. The experience of earlier groups with the bureaucracies suggests the need for some perspective: once you break in fully, the walls can help protect you, too, a consideration that will not escape the attention of black professionals as they start defining their roles in community-controlled institutions. The push to organize the ghettoes poses questions that time may answer, but which now look close to insoluble. The rhetoric of the organizers masks a basically conservative aim: many argue that the way to join up with a society that has excluded blacks up to now is to organize as a group. But conservative or not, this tactic exposes the uncomfortable truth that life in America, for all our universalistic pretensions, is organized on the basis of competing racial and ethnic groups. Ethnic identities persist in voting patterns and ways of living: they are vital realities, not a survival from the past. Earlier groups, it must be said, did not usually manage to break in to established institutions, which is what blacks are attempting: the more common pattern was to create their own, on the margins of society — political machines, the crime syndicates, and the Catholic Church being prime examples.

There are no other levers of power within reach: blacks have no money, and in most cities they don't have anything like a majority of votes. They have two perennial weapons of the underdog: the appeal to the universal values — equality, justice — America says it lives by, and the threat of disruption. The first has produced some gains, but is not likely to carry them very much farther, and the second is wearing dangerously thin. So they have to organize, knowing as they do that any effort to organize along racial lines will cut them off from white allies. Many admit the risks involved, that community control will always be something of a sham without massive national jobs, income, and housing programs. An administrator in one of the New York demonstration districts thought about this and conceded: "The reason why we're picking on the schools is that everything else has failed."

Sooner or later discussions of these matters come round to the need for national political coalitions, for which there would seem to be no realistic immediate prospects. The decentralization crisis is in part a reflection of this political failure. Behind the struggle for community control of the ghettoes lies the somber truth about America in 1969: here, as St. Paul says, we have no continuing city, only groups pursuing self-interest to the edge of self-destruction.

Community control of the schools spells deep trouble; many of the criticisms levelled at it strike me as quite sound in theory. There are always going to be sharp limits as to how much one can accomplish simply by staging elections in unorganized communities. Community control will not mean more money for public education — indeed, one danger is that it could signal further withdrawals of white support from ghetto institutions. It raises risks of confrontations between hysterical whites and black extremists; as in New York it can provoke a conservative and racist backlash. And it always has to be remembered that it does not necessarily mean any change either in teaching or in learning.

Finally, however, such reservations are beside the point. The school system is shaking to pieces. There is a crisis of authority, and there has to be a political settlement. The opponents of the movement for community control have said — correctly — that it is a threat to order because it discredits many existing institutions. It does this for the good reason that they aren't representing the interests of ghetto residents. In that sense it is revolutionary, although we should remember that most trade unions, including the UFT, used to operate on the far side of the law, and that peace usually comes about when organized groups know that they have enough strength to come to terms, but not enough to destroy each other.

The opponents of community control have been unwilling to admit how much authority has ebbed away from institutions in the ghettoes. They have been unable to pose any political or educational alternatives. Legitimacy can only be restored by a redistribution of power. The unanswered question in New York City, and elsewhere, is the extent to which any redistribution of power has to be along ethnic and racial lines. Peace of sorts can come to the schools and other ghetto institutions. How much better they will then be is another matter. Less bureaucracy will be an improvement, as will more parent participation and local accountability, but there is no evidence that any of these reforms will necessarily improve children's learning. The movement for community control is a political phenomenon. It has been the focus of debates on education because there seems no way of moving schools in any direction unless the political dilemmas are first resolved. Educationally speaking, it is not a program, but simply a response to what are believed to be the failures of integration and compensatory education. Actually, integration, like Christianity, has rarely been attempted in any intelligent way. (A notable exception is Berkeley, California.) Its failure in places like New York was political: not enough people wanted it. The same thing is true of compensatory education: no dramatic, expensive attempt has been made anywhere to make schools for black and poor children *better* than schools for the middle class. This, too, has been a political matter: few people are willing to spend that kind of money. (For one thing it might be better spent on jobs and income programs.) While it is true, however, that the final returns are not yet in on integration and compensatory programs, it would be foolish to ignore the depth of our political failures. For some time to come, it will be chimerical to hold out promises of either integration or adequate compensatory programs in most districts of a city like New York.

Throughout the discussions of education, little has been said about parents' involvement, aside from a number of misleading claims on this score from the ranks of those supporting community control. Yet some of the most promising schools in our cities have been on a scale sufficiently small to make participation work. The experience of small privately financed "community" schools and storefronts has confirmed what some of the better preschool and Head Start programs have discovered: that apart from political considerations, there are sound educational arguments for active parent involvement in schools for younger children — because what parents do and say is more important to the lives of small children than anything a teacher does.

Some thoughtful people in the ghettoes say that these private ventures, at present financed by string and chewing gum, point towards a day when public education as we know it will be dead in our cities, a victim of its inability to resolve its besetting dilemmas. Despairing activists in the community-control movement are saying that they have given up on the public schools, although nobody has any idea of how sources of public money could be tapped to feed private ghetto schools. Over the next few years there may be some experimenting with public tuition grants to groups of parents interested in setting up their own schools. Like decentralization and community control, this will be sold as a sovereign remedy, guaranteed to cure every ill that man or horse is heir to. Again, some skepticism will be in order: the poor have not traditionally fared well at the mercies of the free market. One look at the fraudulent schools supposedly teaching computer programming to ghetto residents should convince anybody of the limits of free enterprise. Still, the crisis may push us that way, and if it does we may have to change some of our historic ideas about education. As David Cohen puts it, the state might come to be seen as the regulator of the schools, rather than the agency that actually operates them. There have been glimmerings of this notion throughout the decentralization controversy in New York: all the different community-control proposals tacitly assumed new responsibilities for state education authorities — regulating such matters as civil liberties and the teaching of bigotry, maintaining standards, and overseeing the distribution of state and federal aid according to equitable formulas.

There is plenty of educational experimenting left to be done, and out of all the present turmoil there may emerge schools that are diverse, and better than those we have. One of the few clear lessons in this whole muddled business, however, is that the schools mirror the society. Its political failures have generated a crisis that schools alone can never solve. At long last, we are learning that the schools won't be able to pick up the marbles for the rest of the social order.

SUBURBIA AND THE
POLITICS OF ACCOMMODATION
4

Suburbia's political system differs from that of the central city. Instead of a single large government, suburbia has many small ones, most with fewer than 25,000 residents. In place of professionalized politics, there is nonpartisanship and amateur government. A city manager and a part-time unpaid council take the place of specialized bureaucracies and an elected mayor earning $20,000 or more a year. In comparison with the city, the fiscal, personnel, and political resources of the average suburb are meager. In fact, its most important political resource is its independent existence. Autonomy provides suburbanites with a substantial degree of local control over the vital parameters of community life. It also protects them against absorption by the city or a larger suburb, or inclusion in a regional arrangement which threatens unequal costs and benefits. Political activity in these small communities tends to be focused on local issues, particularly tax levels, maintenance of property values, and the schools, which usually have their own independent political system, complete with a nonpartisan school board, a professional superintendent, and autonomous taxing power. As Herbert Gans emphasizes in his discussion of political life in a mass-produced, lower middle-class development, local government in the suburbs usually heeds the interests of its relatively homogeneous constituency.

Autonomy also fosters differentiation among suburbs, which in turn encourages the proliferation of suburban governments and homogeneity within communities. Social, ethnic, and income differences among suburbs are as important as those between the city and suburbia. Whereas the many sections of the city are amalgamated in a heterogeneous political system, neighborhood differences in social status, income, and property values are institutionalized in suburbia through the creation of numerous independent municipalities. As Robert C. Wood points out (see p. 241–246), the key elements in the politics of differentiation are the zoning and building codes and the tax and service policies of the autonomous suburb. The larger the metropolitan area, the greater the splintering of suburbia, and the wider the range between the rich suburb and the poor one. Special purpose suburbs also become more common. They are created to provide their industrial and commercial constituents with a favorable local governmental climate in general and low taxes in particular. The process of differentiation combines with the forces of growth and change to produce, particularly in the larger metropolitan areas, great variations in size and homogeneity of suburbs. As suburbs age, they tend to become more heterogeneous, especially if they are relatively extensive in their territorial scope. Some of the older suburbs nearest to the central city have acquired many of the city's problems — deteriorating housing, segregated schools, rising welfare expenses, and racial conflict.

The spread of geographic autonomy through the creation of general purpose suburban governments promotes functional autonomy. Special districts are created to supply services such as water supply or sewage disposal, whose provision is beyond the capabilities of the multiplying suburban municipalities. These unifunctional devices also are employed within a suburb to ensure that only those directly benefited — for instance, the residents of a housing development requiring that septic tanks be replaced with a community sewage disposal system — pay for public improvements. Like their giant cousins serving the entire metropolis, the small special districts that dot the metropolitan landscape usually are unifunctional, revenue-financed, and politically independent. As indicated in the account of the San Francisco Bay Area's experience by Stanley Scott and John Corzine, small unifunctional districts raise many of the same political, fiscal, and planning issues associated with metropolitan authorities.

Interlocal cooperation is an even more common response than special districts to the challenge of providing public goods and services in the decentralized metropolis. Cooperation ranges from ad hoc informal agreements to detailed contractual arrangements. Among the more widely used devices are sharing of facilities, granting of extraterritorial jurisdiction, and contracting for services supplied by another community. Since interjurisdictional agreements are made in response to individual problems, the agreements are often unifunctional rather than multipurpose. For the same reason, their growth is haphazard, following no general plan. However, as demonstrated by

Thomas R. Dye and his colleagues, the pattern of interlocal cooperation is influenced by differences among the units of the fragmented
metropolis. Their findings indicate that intermunicipal agreements in
the Philadelphia area are more likely to occur when communities
resemble each other socially and economically. Thus, the politics of
interlocal cooperation reflects the politics of differentiation.

Counties also help suburbs to adjust to urban growth and change.
In the 130-odd single county metropolitan areas, county government
is a natural candidate for tasks which are beyond the jurisdictional
or fiscal capabilities of the municipalities. Even when they do not
encompass the entire metropolitan area, counties retain jurisdictional advantages over the basic units of local government that lead
them deeper into metropolitan development. Almost everywhere, the
county provides urban services in the unicorporated areas where
there is no other local government. However, onrushing suburban
development strains the county courthouse. Under the pressures of
urban change, the leaderless, part-time, decentralized, and rurally
oriented political and administrative machinery of the county gives
way to elected or appointed executives and professional administrators and technicians.

Urban county government is more highly developed in California
than anywhere else in the United States; and so is the role of the
county in assisting suburbs to cope with the pressures for increased
public service. Richard M. Cion shows that Los Angeles County's
Lakewood Plan is an ingenious contracting scheme in which the
county provides individual municipalities with almost every conceivable local service, from police protection to weed abatement. By participating in the plan, the community reaps the prime benefit of independence — control over land use — without having to pay the usual
costs of autonomy, since the diseconomies of small size are avoided
through the purchase of prepackaged services from the large and
relatively efficient government of Los Angeles County. Because it
successfully meets the service needs of the residents of a growing
segment of the metropolis, the Lakewood Plan fosters continued proliferation and differentiation.

The fragmented, small-scale suburban political system uses these
devices, as well as growing state and federal involvement, to accommodate itself successfully to the steadily rising pressures for more
public goods and services. The system of accommodation has shortcomings, as the readings in this chapter indicate. It encourages proliferation and differentiation, diffuses responsibility, weakens the representative processes, handles some kinds of problems far more
effectively than others, and lacks any commitment to the general

welfare. Nonetheless, the system of accommodation works sufficiently well to foreclose more extensive approaches to the provision of public services in suburbia. Since it preserves the autonomy of the individual suburban jurisdiction, most suburbanites see it as a successful system.

But local autonomy is preserved at a price. The principal feature of the politics of accommodation is the growth of functional autonomy. Increased use of special districts, assistance programs, and other devices shifts control over broad areas of public policy from local officials and the electorate to relatively autonomous agencies responsible for particular functions of government. More and more key decisions affecting local and regional development are made by intermunicipal sewer agencies, county park districts, metropolitan water authorities, state highway departments — all independently financed agencies responsible for one function and insulated from the local political process.

Diminished local control is an ironic development since the desire to maintain the political and fiscal integrity of the community underlies the system of accommodation. Functional autonomy only partially diminishes local control, however, since it rarely threatens directly the most critical of all local political concerns, the regulation of land use. In addition, the system of accommodation is highly flexible because most relationships are voluntary. Ordinarily, there is no way to compel a unit of government to participate in an interlocal agreement, a special district, or a county or state program. The units of the metropolis can avoid involvements that do not promise benefits commensurate with costs. Thus, communities can choose to accommodate by "going it alone" or failing to act. Unilateralism maintains local control, but usually at the price of higher taxes and sometimes lower levels of service. A policy of inaction almost always hurts the residents of the abnegating community, and sometimes also their neighbors downstream or downwind who cannot escape the consequences of untreated sewage or polluted air.

Two sharply contrasting views of the politics of accommodation and its implications for metropolitan development complete the chapter. Evaluating the decentralized political system largely in terms of its ability to provide public goods and services efficiently, Vincent Ostrom, Charles M. Tiebout, and Robert Warren view the "polycentric" metropolis and its processes of accommodation with equanimity. Underlying their analysis is the model of the competitive economic marketplace. They applaud the Lakewood Plan for developing "quasi-market" conditions and achieving an admirable degree of flexibility and responsiveness in the provision of public services.

Ostrom and his colleagues conclude by arguing that the process of accommodation has provided most metropolitan areas with "a very rich and intricate 'framework' for negotiating, adjudicating, and deciding questions that affect their diverse interests."

Robert C. Wood grants that the process of accommodation can meet the service needs of most residents of the decentralized metropolis. By so doing, the many modes of adjustment create the essential conditions for the survival of the fragmented political system. But Wood deplores the system's exclusive concern with services; and doubts that the polycentric metropolis can thrive since a prolongation of the institutional status quo means more unplanned growth, widening social and economic disparities, and a continued lack of concern for the general welfare of the metropolitan area. The incomplete political system of the accommodating metropolis, he concludes, is both undemocratic and unequal to the challenges imposed by rapid social change and a complex economy.

Herbert J. Gans

THE DECISION-MAKING PROCESS
IN LEVITTOWN

Just as decision-makers constantly seek certainty in a political system marked by uncertainty, so they attempt to avoid decisions in a governmental system which requires decisions. Government is organized toward bureaucratic routine; it aims to carry out municipal services entrusted to it in such a way that appointed officials will hold their posts

From *The Levittowners* (New York: Pantheon, 1967), pp. 333–339. Copyright © 1967 by Herbert J. Gans. Reprinted by permission of the author and Pantheon Books, a division of Random House, Inc. Retitled by the editor.

and elected ones will be re-elected, and that criticism and conflict are minimized between elections. The ideal is a situation in which precedent can rule and no new decisions are needed.

But new problems arise and decisions must be made. Broadly speaking, the decision-making process is ruled by four criteria. *First*, government is normally passive; it waits for issues to come to its attention. In Levittown, the decision-makers initiated action only on internal governmental expansion necessary for the smooth functioning of the bureaucratic apparatus; on state or federal statutory requirements; on issues which required little effort, cost, or structural change and resulted in favorable publicity; on matters which benefited Levittown as a whole in the continuing competition with other communities; and when they had no choice but to act. For example, the Township Committee initiated a polio vaccination program without citizens' asking for it, because it was easy to do and earned political goodwill, and the school board raised school budgets because the increasing number of students left it no other alternative.

Second, government avoids or postpones decisions that cannot be resolved without conflict or that expose the gap between the actual and the performing government. The Township Committee tried to bring ordinances out of the caucus to the public meeting only when unanimity had been achieved. *Third*, government gravitates toward decisions with immediate payoffs, avoiding those which produce mainly long-run effects. Government is reluctant to establish new precedents or set into motion irreversible policies that may restrict its flexibility in the future. For this reason, if no other, long-range planning and the formulation of permanent "policy statements" are discouraged. Of course government does plan, but principally for goals of its own choosing — for example, the staging of performances and the adaptation of decisions to future election campaigns. It also sets policy (albeit unwritten) when government agencies develop working routines. But long-range plans that require higher current expenditures to produce a result 5 or 10 years later (for example, to forestall future school overcrowding) are only implemented if outside funds are available or if community pressures give the decision-makers no other choice. By and large, however, planning and explicit policies are advocated by voters whose demands are being ignored in current decisions and unwritten policy, their hope being that these demands can be included in long-range plans.

Fourth, the decision-making process is structured so that, whenever possible, every elected official is free — or feels he is free — to reach the decision dictated by his conscience and by his desire to benefit the community. Whether or not he is ever really free is debatable, but the feeling of being so allows him to claim that he is not required to pay attention to citizen pressure, to include his own values in his decision, and to identify these as the public interest. Feeling free to vote "according to his conscience" allows him to make decisions that will please his reference groups and the constituents from whom he gets the most votes.

The application of these criteria resulted in decisions which: (1) maintained Levittown's governmental bureaucracy and municipal services up to voter expectation; (2) aided the party in power; (3) benefitted large or otherwise influential voter blocs and satisfied interest groups that were either in constant contact with the government, could apply pressure on it, or had campaign funds to contribute (or withhold); (4) represented pet projects or vested interests of individual decision-makers.

Obviously, the decision-makers used their decisions to improve their own and their parties' election chances. Although citizens' requests were few, they carried out those easily satisfied and those from large or visible voter blocs. Demands from the Catholic leadership group always received attention because the Catholic population was large, and the Democrats tried to satisfy requests from the Jewish community because it was well organized and therefore assumed to be a cohesive voter bloc. Unorganized residents were similarly favored if their demands were modest, considered desirable by the decision-makers, and not likely to arouse opposition from more powerful voters or interest groups.

But most decisions, other than housekeeping ones, were made for the interest groups closest to government. At the time of my study, the most demanding one was the Levitt organization, which needed frequent approval of its building program and made demands and suggestions on a wide variety of issues. In fact, the builder was consulted so often that for all practical purposes he was a member of the actual government. In addition, most decision-makers accepted the builder's claim that what was good for him was also good for the township. For example, Levitt was able to persuade the Utilities Authority not to link competing small shopping centers to the water and sewer lines he had built until he turned the lines over to the township. In the early years, the decision-makers even checked with the builder on decisions in which he had no interest. Lacking staff aid of their own, respecting the know-how of Levitt executives, wanting to make sure the firm would not oppose their final decision, and believing that Levitt had the right to be consulted on everything, they sought his advice on a wide variety of topics.

Paying close attention to the builder was also dictated by political considerations. Not only could he exert power at all levels of government, but many Levittowners were favorably inclined toward him, so that political incentives for opposing him were few. Working class residents were grateful for the opportunity to buy a suburban house they could not have afforded otherwise, and middle class residents, though less grateful, went along with his demands as long as they meant lower taxes or affected yet unbuilt neighborhoods. Only the cosmopolitans opposed him, for, being able and willing to look further into the future, they could see that Levittown could not solve its tax problems so long as he continued building, thus minimizing their chance to obtain schools and other municipal services that met their upper middle class standards.

The other major interest group was made up of businessmen who had bought land in Levittown and wanted to build stores and shopping centers. Here, too, the municipal government was generally eager to please. Wanting more taxables in the township, it welcomed the arrival of new businesses — so much so that Planning Board meetings were sometimes set to accommodate the schedules of applicants for licenses and zoning changes.

Finally, the decision-makers supported each others' pet projects; protected the vested interests, political domains, and private businesses each had staked out; and went along with colleagues' personal grudges. Even when beset by internal strife, the decision-making bodies always united to defend members against attack from citizens. For example, school board members allowed a colleague to continue his advocacy of municipal recreation although the school system wanted to retain control of recreation facilities; and the Township Committee did not interfere with one committeeman's personal vendetta against another leading politician, even though it was politically ruinous.

Nevertheless, the model that best describes decision-making in Levittown is "political benefit–cost accounting," for, generally speaking, the decision-makers tried to evaluate the costs and benefits of any decision for their own and their party's political future. Of course, they did not apply such a model systematically, but acted intuitively. Sometimes they had too little information about even the obvious costs and benefits of their decisions, and rarely were they aware of the subtler and long-range ones. Lacking sufficiently detailed feedback, they did not know which voters might be affected by a specific issue and how they would react. Moreover, the personal values of the decision-makers and their conceptions of the public interest were added to the mix, so that often decisions only approximated those suggested by the model.

The Responsiveness of the Decision-making Process

Although Levittown's public decisions were made by a handful of elected officials, responding principally to demands and pressures from a small number of citizens and interest groups, many decisions were remarkably responsive to the rest of the citizenry, particularly the lower middle class majority. While I could not compare residents' attitudes with decision-maker actions on every decision, the data I have support the hypothesis of responsiveness. The random sample was asked for its views on seven major issues, and in all but two the majority of respondents supported the governmental decision. For example, 89 per cent favored (or had no opinion on) the desirability of a city manager, 56 per cent were concerned about rising taxes, and 73 per cent went along with changing the name of the township from Willingboro to Levittown. On the question of doctors purchasing homes for office use, 36 per cent were in favor, 15 per cent had no opinion, and 49 per cent were opposed — suggesting why the final decision of government was a compromise that restricted two nonresident doctors to a house. Likewise, an almost even split between those for, against, and undecided about racial integration suggests why the township government and both political parties refused to get involved in the issue.

Decisions and citizens' attitudes diverged on liquor, and Levittowners' opposition to the Township Committee's approval of a wet community contributed to the incumbent committeeman's defeat at the next election. The reduction of the kindergarten entry age, which the school board rejected, was favored by a slight majority, but most had no opinion, and the divergence can be attributed to the school board's minimal contact with its constituents at the time of decision. A 1964 survey of attitudes on school policy among a much larger sample showed that the residents usually favored the status quo or had no opinion, thus producing convergence with school board decisions. For example, 29 per cent wanted smaller elementary school classes, 18 per cent wanted larger ones, but 53 per cent preferred no change or had no opinion. Likewise, 30 per cent favored higher expenditures for education; 16 per cent, lower ones; but 54 per cent wanted no change or expressed no opinion. No wonder the school board felt it had a mandate for a policy of minimal change. These data cannot *prove* decision-makers' responsiveness, for the surveys were conducted after the decisions were made, did not limit themselves to voters actually concerned about the issue, and did not measure the intensity of their concern. Perhaps the best illustration of the overall responsiveness to the majority is that whenever the decision-makers went against majority opinion, they promptly lost the next election. Only Levitt usually received what he wanted, but when his demands were opposed by the residents, they voted out the decision-makers who went along with him.

The pattern of responsiveness can be traced back to the election system. The selection of candidates assured officeholders who were representative of the large mass of voters, and their handling of issues reflected the vagueness and confusion which the voters themselves felt. Moreover, both parties agreed substantially on basic assumptions. Both came out for low taxes, a minimal role for government, and decisions that would favor the majority whenever possible; both opposed the demands and political styles of working class people and upper middle class cosmopolitans. Of course, the fit between candidates and community was hardly perfect, and most of the time Levittowners felt they were choosing the lesser of two evil ones. They grumbled about politics, but they were not dissatisfied enough to act and did not support minority factions or independent slates. After all, decision-makers rarely had significant impact on the really important aspects of their lives; they could not solve the community's central problem, taxes, and they were not expected to solve the financial, job, family, and child-rearing problems of individual Levittowners.

But if the decision-makers were responsive when the majority demanded it, they were anything but responsive to other than the powerful minorities. The election's diffuse and general feedback apprised the politicians of the majority opinions, but it did not inform them of minority demands. Nor were the performing and actual governments attuned to these demands, for the performance was structured to assure the majority that all was well, and the caucus and parties sought decisions that would attract the majority at the next election. Moreover, the decision-makers could not represent minorities either. A Township Committee of three men (and later of five and even a school board of nine made it impossible to elect minority representatives to the actual government, and since decision-makers sought unanimity before passing ordinances, there was little room for the consideration of powerless minority opinion. Even when decisions were reached by majority vote, the decision-making body and the issue itself had to be structured so as to create a dichotomous (or at best trichotomous) set of alternatives: for, against, or a compromise that would swing enough opposition votes. As a result, even the school board usually split into only two factions, and when more existed, these had to combine to affect a board decision. Consequently, the decision-makers could deal responsively with issues favored by a large mass of voters or an influential minority, but not with those of significance to a number of less influential ones. Since minorities were more frequent petitioners for action than the majority, the decision-makers were often unpopular with small groups of residents, which only encouraged them to generate yet more support from the majority and to restrict feedback from minorities even further. In effect, then, the government could not be responsive to the pluralism of the community.

Sometimes the decision-makers did not even have to be responsive, for if they had the power to act and could not be held responsible for their actions by the voters, or if the large mass of voters did not care, they were free to do as they pleased. For example, they could sometimes give business contracts to their friends, rezone unbuilt portions of the community to benefit the builder or other businessmen, and draft ordinances to fit the requests of an influential petitioner — and without evoking much protest. Levittown's government was more representative than most, for it lacked appointed positions of great power or "rotten borough" election districts which would enable an individual decision-maker to act without concern for the voters. Perhaps the main obstacle to responsiveness, whether to majority or minority, was the decision-makers' willingness to support their colleagues' individual interests and personal biases, for citizen protest had to be sizeable before their group solidarity weakened.

Stanley Scott and John Corzine

SPECIAL DISTRICTS IN THE SAN FRANCISCO BAY AREA

There are nearly five hundred special districts in the nine-county Bay Area, excluding school districts, multi-county districts, irrigation districts, and a number of others whose functions are not urban in character. Each of these districts normally performs only one municipal-type function in the area it serves. The few types of districts that are empowered to provide a range of services as the need arises, such as the community services districts, have not done so for the most part, but have remained de facto single-purpose districts.

Reprinted from *Special Districts in the San Francisco Bay Area: Some Problems and Issues*, pp. 1–11, 13–14, 16–18, with the permission of the authors and the Institute of Governmental Studies.

Normally, two or more special districts are found in any unincorporated area having urban service needs. Fire protection districts, highway lighting districts, sanitary and county sanitation districts, county service areas, and sewer and sewer maintenance districts, are the most numerous types in the Bay Area. Hospital districts, fire protection districts, municipal water districts, county water districts, flood control and water conservation districts, and sanitary districts, in that order, reported the largest expenditure during fiscal year 1960–61.

Approximately half of the districts in the Bay Area are governed directly by the county boards of supervisors. These entities are, in effect, special taxing areas, through which the county government can raise funds to finance services within the districts. Such county-controlled districts are not a primary concern of this report. The other half of the districts are autonomous units, being governed by their own local boards. Most of these boards are directly elected (193). A minority of the districts (41) have appointed or ex-officio boards.

The special districts treated in this study have been established primarily to provide municipal-type services in urban communities that do not have a municipal government. Thus, one would expect districts to occur: (1) in areas with a moderate degree of urbanization, and (2) in areas outside the boundaries of existing cities. In fact, they are found most often on the fringes of incorporated areas, and within some of the newer and smaller cities.

There is a rough correlation between a county's unincorporated urban population and the number of special districts. San Francisco, consisting solely of incorporated territory has no special districts of the kinds considered here. Los Angeles County, which has the largest urban unincorporated population in the state also ranks first in the number of special districts. Sacramento County ranks second on both scores, and Contra Costa County fifth. Alameda County, with most of its urbanized area now incorporated, has comparatively few districts.

Superficially the chronicle of special districts in the Bay Area reads like a success story. Under district auspices many services are being supplied to important suburban communities that would otherwise have annexed to cities or incorporated separately. To be sure, the use of special districts in place of city government may be advantageous in some communities that are lightly urbanized, are growing slowly, and need only one or two services. But the proliferation of districts, and their retention even after the communities served have clearly matured into urban status, have raised many questions and resulted in a number of serious criticisms of autonomous local districts. These problems and issues are reviewed in the following sections.

Low Political Visibility

Special district elections are scheduled according to statute. The election date varies, depending on the type of district. Fire protection districts, for example, hold their elections annually on the first Tuesday of April; sanitary districts, biennially, on the second Tuesday in September in even numbered years; county water districts, biennially, on the fourth Tuesday in March every second year after the district's formation; and public utility districts on the first Tuseday in May every second year after formation. The elections are seldom given wide publicity; the local papers may or may not carry the returns. Unless a controversy has arisen in a district, the voters are not likely to be aware of the identity of either the incumbent directors or the opposing candidates, if any.

The result is very low voter participation. A recent sample revealed a median turnout at special district elections to be 27 per cent, significantly lower than for either county elections (67 per cent), or city elections (45 per cent).[1] The turnout for special district elections is also normally much lower than the participation level in statewide primary or general elections. These averaged 63.8 per cent and 80.7 per cent, respectively, for the 1950–60 period. . . .

Low participation is, however, only part of the story of limited voter interest and awareness. District elections are often canceled because there are no contests, and the county board of supervisors simply re-appoints the unopposed incumbents. For example, 62 sanitary district and 121 fire protection district directors' elections were canceled during 1956–62, far more than were held. A survey of fire protection districts in Alameda County failed to find evidence that a single election had been held in any of the county's fire protection districts during the period 1955–62. The following comment by the secretary of the Tiburon Fire Protection District in Marin County dramatizes the infrequency of elections:

> In the last 13 years there have been only two elections in this district . . .
> only one commissioner is on this board because he was elected by the people.
> The remainder have been appointed or reappointed by the board of super-
> visors because nobody cared enough to contest their chairs.[2]

One reason for voter apathy and lack of concern is that citizens are not informed about or interested in district activities. Even if they were, the

---

[1] Don Koepp, "Nonpartisan Elections in the San Francisco Bay Area," *Public Affairs Report*, Vol. III, No. 4, Bureau of Public Administration, University of California, Berkeley (August, 1962), p. 3.

[2] *San Rafael Independent Journal*, September 19, 1962.

sheer number of districts and the frequency of elections make impossible demands upon the voters' time and attention. A sanitary district representative commented: "I know of two areas where there are five overlapping districts. They haven't had an election for eight or ten years because of the enormous trouble involved."[3] Still other reasons for low voter interest have been suggested:

> The distribution of the range of turnout into two distinct groups, that of county governments, unified school districts, and city governments, and that of elementary, special, high school and junior college districts, suggests that turnout may be related to a sense of community identification or, at least, community visibility. In those elections where definite and familiar geographical boundaries exist, as in counties, cities, and school districts having boundaries coterminous with cities, turnout is higher than in elections for those units having boundaries which are diffuse, overlapping, or unknown to the voter, i.e., *the single-purpose districts*, the small elementary school districts, and the larger but overlapping high school and junior college districts. [Emphasis supplied][4]

An extreme example of lack of district "visibility," or in this case, even of self-awareness, concerns the Brentwood Recreation and Park District in Contra Costa County. Under a recent law the three types of recreation districts were given until July 1, 1962 to reorganize according to new provisions of the Government Code, otherwise they would be dissolved automatically. The Brentwood district, whose only facility is a one square-block park in the City of Brentwood, failed to reorganize. As reported in a news story ". . . the district's five directors were stunned when it was accidentally discovered the district had ceased to exist seven months ago."[5] This raised some difficult problems regarding ownership and disposition of the park. It was necessary to pass emergency legislation at the 1963 session to permit recreation of the district, thus affording Brentwood a way out of its dilemma.

Low Fiscal Visibility

With few exceptions, the autonomous special districts have their taxes collected by the county. The districts submit a budget to the county government, which levies the necessary tax rate to raise the amount required. The county's role is ministerial: The board of supervisors has no

---

[3] California. Assembly Interim Committee on Municipal and County Government, Hearings on Special Districts — Sewers, Sacramento, California, September 1958 (mimeo) Statement by Eugene K. Storgis, Counsel, Stege Sanitary District, p. 32.

[4] Koepp, *op. cit.*, p. 3.

[5] "Seen the Park District? Brentwood Can't Find It," *Oakland Tribune*, February 12, 1963.

effective power to review and adjust tax requests submitted by the autonomous districts. Because the tax bill comes from the county, however, most voters assume that the county is in some way finally responsible for district tax levies. This partially explains the lack of awareness of the average taxpayer regarding the financial operations of districts. The phenomenon is analogous to the low political visibility just described. Since interest is minimal, special district budget deliberations are not observed. As with district elections, little or no publicity is given to the actions of the district boards. When citizens are upset over the activities of a district their normal response is to direct their complaints either to the county board of supervisors or to a municipal jurisdiction which they consider responsible.

Because of the large number of districts, all counties except San Francisco find it necessary to figure different tax rates for a huge array of tax code areas:

> San Mateo County, for example, has well over 400 different code areas for taxing purposes with approximately 75 special districts performing 8 to 12 different functions. The county taxpayer, when presented with his bill, often has very little realization that the Board of Supervisors is responsible for less than a third of his total tax rate and yet his ire and admonitions to do something about these growing tax bills are directed at the Board of Supervisors — not, it should be noted, against the various district boards about whom he knows very little, if anything.[6]

Most Bay Area counties publish a compilation of the tax rates assessed in the county, broken down by code areas. Sometimes this is sent out with the annual tax statement. Contra Costa County, in appreciation of the fact that many homeowners never see their tax bills — because they are handled by the financial institutions holding the mortgages — sends out a tax breakdown with veterans' exemption slips as well as with tax bills. Marin County includes this information in its final budget; San Mateo and Alameda send out single sheet charts; and San Mateo and Santa Clara counties compile separate books of tax rates and property valuations which they make available to taxpayers. Each of these efforts represents an attempt to inform the taxpayer of the maze of jurisdictions and tax rates that make up his total property tax bill.

The unincorporated community of Lafayette in Contra Costa County provides a good example of the variety of property tax rates levied on the average suburban home.

[6] California. Assembly Interim Committee on Municipal and County Government, Transcript of Hearing, Sacramento, California, January 17, 1962 (mimeo) Statement by E. Robert Stallings, County Manager, San Mateo County, p. 52.

1963–64 PROPERTY TAX RATES, LAFAYETTE
(UNINCORPORATED AREA IN CONTRA COSTA COUNTY)

1. County tax rate	$2.345
2. Flood Control and Water Conservation District	.020
a. Flood control zone 3B	.180
3. County service area, library	.075
4. Contra Costa County Water Agency	no tax
5. Lafayette Fire Protection District	1.008
6. Mosquito Abatement District	.025
7. Central Contra Costra Costa Sanitary District	.570
8. Alamo-Lafayette Cemetery District	.028
9. East Bay Municipal Utility District	.200
10. San Francisco Bay Area Rapid Transit District	.084
11. Bay Area Air Pollution Control District	.010
12. Lafayette Elementary School District	3.177
13. Acalanes High School District	2.371
14. Contra Costa Junior College District	.416
15. County schools service fund for children who are severely retarded mentally	.003
16. Education of handicapped children	.001
Total	$10.513

County taxes amount to only $2.345 of the $10.513 total rate — or about 20 per cent.

Adverse Effect on Local Governmental Structure

Districts have sometimes been employed strictly as transitional devices to provide essential services during the early stages of urbanization. This appears to be an appropriate role for them, at least in situations where annexation is not feasible. Too often, however, districts have been created when they were not really needed, or have been retained as permanent entities in the face of continued growth and the resulting need for more effective local government.

Despite the need for general-purpose local government in urban areas, overly permissive special district legislation has made it possible for important portions of the metropolitan area to urbanize and develop without ever having to incorporate as a municipality or annex to an adjacent city. Districts have, in fact, sometimes been the primary *obstacle* to municipal incorporation or annexation. Sanitary districts and fire protection districts, especially, have sometimes prevented or hindered municipalities from extending their boundaries logically. Such districts, actively operating on the outskirts of a city, will often resist annexation or incorporation movements which threaten their existence. Once an area has its water, sewer and fire problems solved, it is likely to ignore the less obvious advantages of annexing to a nearby municipality. Thus a city may be faced with unplanned commercial and residential development on its borders which it can neither control nor annex. . . .

Sanitary districts, fire protection districts, water districts and park and recreation districts may hamper the efforts of local government to achieve coordinated planning. For example, independent special districts may be formed to provide sewers and water in an isolated area, making possible premature housing development inconsistent with county and city general planning. In Contra Costa County, fire districts have proven an effective obstacle to county plans for consolidation of fire protection facilities.[7] Other examples of districts which have in some manner or other resisted annexation and thus have probably affected adversely the development of a more rational governmental structure include the Agnew Sanitary District, now dissolved, which resisted absorption by the City of Santa Clara; the Tennyson Fire Protection District, whose original territory has been almost wholly absorbed by the City of Hayward, the East Vallejo Fire Protection District, which levies a $1.00 tax rate to contract with the City of Vallejo for fire protection, and the Cupertino Sanitary District in Santa Clara County. These are only a few examples; city and county officials in the Bay Area could name many more.

A specific case of the adverse effect of special districts on local governmental arrangements is provided by the complicated situation involving the City of Walnut Creek, the City of Pleasant Hill, and the Pleasant Hill Recreation and Park District, all in Contra Costa County. At one time certain groups in the then unincorporated community of Pleasant Hill — which is encompassed by the Pleasant Hill Recreation and Park District — wished to annex *in toto* to the nearby City of Walnut Creek. Step by step annexation was suggested by Walnut Creek officials, but was rejected by Pleasant Hill. Walnut Creek then agreed to annex the whole area, but the annexation election failed. Directors of the recreation and park district were active in the fight against annexation. If the annexation had succeeded, the district's functions would presumably have been taken over by the city recreation department.

The recreation and park district's directors then actively promoted the idea of incorporating Pleasant Hill. Subsequently Pleasant Hill was incorporated. The new city did not choose to attempt a withdrawal, although a study made before the incorporation of Pleasant Hill suggested that, after incorporation, the Pleasant Hill Recreation and Park District should be dissolved and its functions assumed by the city. The

---

[7] This comment should not imply that fire district consolidation is necessarily more desirable than other organizational approaches. Some municipal officials in Contra Costa County believe the cities should assume fire protection as a municipal function, and should serve their unincorporated fringe areas under contract. In any event, the existing fire districts would probably oppose this suggestion as vigorously as they do district consolidation.

reasons advanced were that recreation and park maintenance is a normal city function, and that significant savings would accrue from consolidating of maintenance, administration and overhead.[8]

Potential resistance from the recreation and park district was an important reason why the City of Pleasant Hill did not attempt to take over the district's functions. There may have been another factor: Many municipalities, especially new or newly expanded cities, do not necessarily wish to dissolve the special districts serving them. By retaining several districts, a city can maintain a low property tax rate and pride itself on its thriftiness. Such frugality is usually an illusion, however, because the total tax rate includes the district levies.

The Pleasant Hill situation is further complicated by a small area lying within the Pleasant Hill Recreation and Park District, and containing some twenty or thirty householders, that has been annexed by Walnut Creek. The residents are faced with double taxation — by the district and by the city — for recreation services. (The district's rate is approximately $0.50). The people involved and the officials of Walnut Creek have appealed to the district's board, to no avail. The board states that withdrawal would work a financial hardship on the rest of the district.[9] The City of Walnut Creek argues the area is not a substantive portion of the district, and that the homeowners joined the city with the intention of taking advantage of the municipal recreation program.

Repeated attempts have been made to amend the law, which does not allow for automatic withdrawal upon annexation. It leaves to the district board the decision whether or not to allow an area to withdraw. Liberalizing amendments were defeated in both the 1961 and 1963 sessions of the legislature, primarily due to the influence of the recreation and park district's association lobby.

There is still another complicating factor. Walnut Creek and Pleasant Hill both have their eyes on unincorporated area lying between the two cities. The existence of the recreation and park district, and its policy against giving up territory even when annexed to a city, tends to favor Pleasant Hill by militating against annexation to Walnut Creek. This is because areas going into Walnut Creek would be exposing themselves to double taxation along with the troubled householders mentioned above. The situation has led Pleasant Hill city interests to oppose liberalization of the district law.

In a nearby area an aggressive sanitary district almost succeeded in stifling the growth of the City of Concord in 1954 by attempting to annex land all around the city. The district was already operating to the

[8] Public Affairs Research Inc., *Pleasant Hill Government Study* (August, 1958) p. 28.

[9] "Recreation District Fights Annex Bill," *Oakland Tribune*, May 8, 1963.

south and west of Concord, and it was proposing annexations to the east. This situation not only enabled developers outside the city to bargain with the city council about development standards in the additions by threatening to join the sanitary district, but also it threatened to stop the city's growth. The city won a major annexation election despite vigorous opposition by the sanitary district. If the city had not won the election, it is conceivable that Concord might now have little more than 12,000 residents, instead of the current 56,000. Walnut Creek is included in this same sanitary district, and had a 1962 population of only 10,000, although the surrounding unincorporated territory comprises an area and population hardly less than that of Concord. . . .

Ease of Creation and Difficulty of Dissolution

Districts have a good deal of appeal as the "easy way out" for communities in need of a specific service. The creation of a district is often believed to be a less expensive way of obtaining service than incorporation as a municipality or annexation to an existing city. Thus there is a good deal less resistance to the creation of a special district than to municipal incorporation or annexation. Also, the legal provisions for district formation are often less strict and easier to comply with than are municipal incorporation or annexation requirements.

Furthermore, it is much simpler to create a new district than to dissolve an old one. The legal requirements for formation are often easily met — especially in the absence of significant community opposition. People interested in acquiring a service have only to hire an attorney or appeal to the county for help in setting up a special district.

Once a district is in existence, however, vested interest groups grow up around it, having a stake in its perpetuation. Employees and members of the board of directors often oppose district dissolution, consolidation, or annexation by a city. On a larger scale, many types of districts and/or district employees are organized into statewide associations. These groups usually oppose any state legislation that would curtail their members' activities. Further, extraordinary majorities are often required in dissolution elections, whereas formation is usually accomplished by a simple majority vote, or sometimes merely by a petition signed by a minority of landowners. And there are still a few instances of districts with no statutory provision for dissolution.

Following are a few examples of marginal districts that cling to life. The East Vallejo Fire Protection District, remnant of a much larger district that once almost surrounded the City of Vallejo, receives fire protection services from the city under contract. The district remains in existence for the sole purpose of levying a tax of approximately $1 per $100 of assessed valuation to pay for the contracted fire protection. A somewhat similar case is presented by the Tennyson Fire Protection District in Alameda County. Most of the area previously served by the district has been annexed to and is served by the City of Hayward. The district continues to resist annexation, despite the logic of such action, as indicated by the fact that the district's only remaining fire station is actually within the city.

In Contra Costa County six county water districts were recently dissolved whose functions had been taken over by East Bay MUD years before. After these districts had the bonds retired there was no reason for their continued existence. Yet it took a great deal of encouragement and energy on the part of the county before the districts were finally liquidated.

Use of Districts by Developers

Although municipal-type districts were originally intended to provide the residents of an unincorporated urban community with limited public services, in recent years they have sometimes been employed in totally unpopulated areas. Thus a land developer may utilize such districts to facilitate the creation of a new residential community on a tract of raw land. The result is a public agency that is, in fact, an individual or a private company "wearing another hat" and thereby assuming the privileges and advantages of governmental status. Unquestionably this practice has facilitated development, but it has also often left the public interest without adequate protection. . . .

The Estero Municipal Improvement District in San Mateo County, and the Embarcadero Improvement District in Santa Barbara County were created in 1960 by special legislative acts. Each law established an independent special district in a designated area for the purpose of financing utility installation, other public improvements, and municipal-type services in connection with land development.

Each district was to be governed by a three-man board elected by owners of land in the district, who were given one vote per $1.00 of assessed valuation of land owned. These provisions made certain that the owners (developers) would select the districts' governing bodies during the period of development. The districts were also empowered to issue tax-exempt general obligation bonds on a two-thirds vote by land owners, who were again given one vote per $1.00 assessed valuation owned. Again, this provision meant that the developers could approve the issuance of governmental general obligation bonds.

Ninety-five per cent of the property within the Estero district is owned by T. Jack Foster and Sons. The real estate development firm is reputed to have paid $12.9 million for its property, which consists of 2,606 acres of marshy land in San Francisco Bay. Shortly after the Estero district was created, it authorized $55 million in general obligation bonds. These funds will be used to fill and reclaim land, lay streets and provide utilities. Plans call for a community of some 35,000 people when "Foster City" is fully developed.

> Seated in offices shared by the Foster firm and the Estero District, the developers and district officers predict Foster City will be worth $550 million when completed about eight years from now. As the district's land-filling operations proceed, the Foster firm intends to sell most of the lots to builders who, in turn, will put up and sell houses. The bonded debt of the district will be a first lien on the home owners' properties.[10]

The Estero project has the approval of the San Mateo County manager and the board of supervisors. Up to this point it appears to be a well-run enterprise. However, the Assembly interim committee pointed out that nothing in its organization, except the integrity of the developer, and safeguards which he has voluntarily employed, prevent an occurrence similar to that which took place in the Embarcadero project.

The aim of the Embarcadero Municipal Improvement District was to transform 1,320 acres of ranch land into a community. The two developers and their private secretary comprised the board of directors. Operating through the district, the developers authorized the issuance of $8,874,000 of general obligation bonds, and in January, 1961 sold $1,207,000 as a first issue.

Later, when a Los Angeles mortgage firm that had helped finance the enterprise failed, the state investigated, and a Los Angeles County grand jury indicted the developers on 35 counts of grand theft, misuse of public funds, and conspiracy. As it turned out, the developers had misappropriated private development funds and had also obtained district bond money through a false statement when improvements were purchased by the district. The developers were convicted of over 30 counts of grand theft and violations of the corporation code.[11]

The following statement was made by Marshall S. Mayer of the investment frauds unit in the Attorney General's Office:

> The Embarcadero District illustrates the major weaknesses of special laws which are designed to permit land promoters to create public agencies to aid in the development of subdivision land. When laws are tailormade for this purpose, when they omit basic governmental safeguards, such as prohibition

[10] Norman C. Miller, "Tax-Free Enterprise: Land Developers Form Districts with Right to Sell Bonds," *Wall Street Journal* (Pacific Coast Edition), March 14, 1962, pp. 1, 9. See also Sidney P. Allen, "A New Kingdom for San Mateo," *San Francisco Chronicle*, Nov. 6, 1962, p. 44.

[11] California. Assembly Interim Committee on Municipal and County Government, *Committee Report on the Uses of Special Assessment Procedures and Independent Special Districts to Aid Land Development*. (1963), p. 34.

against self-dealing, separation of governmental powers, and when they provide
no audit controls by independent bodies, the likelihood of abuse corresponds
directly to the opportunity for abuse. The Embarcadero District sadly reflects
this truism.[12]

District Diseconomies and Financial Problems

Because of their relatively small scale, the operations of many special
districts are subject to unavoidable diseconomies. One example is the
sewer or water systems sometimes constructed by small districts in rapidly growing areas. These limited facilities may soon be outmoded or
out-grown, whereupon costly replacements may be necessary. Or several
different jurisdictions, each attempting to deal with portions of a larger
watershed, may build separate sewer and collector systems that are not
only inadequate, but are in the long run more expensive than a unified
system would have been.

Fire districts provide one of the best examples of built-in diseconomies
in district operations. The following comment refers to conditions in
Sacramento County, but it can also be applied to many situations in the
Bay Area:

Arbitrary political boundaries and limited size and assessment valuation mili-
tate against efficient and effective provision of services. An example of this can
be seen in the fact that in the unincorporated area there are 26 fire districts.
Location of fire stations, for instance, is often determined on the basis of service
within the political boundaries of the district, with little or no attention given
to service to other areas adjacent to the district, but located in other fire districts. No possibility for automatic distribution of equipment between districts
exists so that in districts where rapid urbanization is taking place rural-type
equipment becomes surplus, rather than being shifted to the rural areas of another district. Such logical distribution would be possible if there were a coun-
trywide fire department.[13]

A Contra Costa County official recently commented in similar fashion
on fire district diseconomies in the central Contra Costa area. There are
surplus fire stations, he contended, in several of the county's fire districts,
a condition that is caused by the multiplicity of fire-fighting jurisdictions.[14] Many of these problems could be remedied, of course, by
fire district consolidation or by their annexation, where appropriate, to
cities providing fire protection. This possibility has been explored and is
currently being pressed by the Contra Costa Taxpayers Association. At

---

[12] *Ibid.*
[13] Letter from Mr. Fred Christensen, Information Officer, Sacramento County,
September 19, 1962.
[14] *Lafayette Sun,* July 12, 1963.

least one example of successful consolidation has taken place in Marin County, where the Homestead Valley Fire District and the Tamalpais Valley Fire District joined in 1962 and reduced the tax rate for the 1962–63 fiscal year, besides providing better service.

An entirely different problem is posed by the heavy reliance of most districts on the property tax. This limitation on revenue sources is compounded by the fact that many districts are located in suburban areas with little or no industry and only modest commercial development. In such areas the district property tax burden may fall rather heavily on the homeowner.

Municipal governments have a more diversified tax structure than special districts, being able to obtain revenues from a variety of sources. The sales and use tax alone amounted to nearly 19 per cent of total city revenues (statewide) in 1961–62. The sales tax, together with such other non-property tax sources as licenses and permits (6.3 per cent), fines and penalties (3.6 per cent), and franchise taxes (1.1 per cent), yielded nearly 30 per cent of all California municipal revenue in 1961–62. The property tax provided only a little over 37 per cent of total city revenues. As the State Controller has pointed out, 1961–62 municipal sales and use tax receipts alone represented a property tax rate equivalent of $0.91 per $100 of assessed valuation. The combination of sales tax receipts and the other non-property sources mentioned above produced revenue equivalent to a property tax rate of approximately $1.60 per $100 assessed valuation. Considering that the statewide average municipal property tax rate is less than $2.00 and the median only $1.35, the importance of non-property tax sources to city government is clear. In addition to the non-property tax revenues, city governments also obtain 14.51 per cent of their revenue from subventions from other governments, a source that is not normally available to special districts. These figures illustrate quite effectively the weaknesses of the special district as a means of raising revenue to support municipal-type services in unincorporated areas.

The question of *balancing* service costs is an unsolved problem in areas served by special districts. Cities can weigh the costs of their different services against one another. They cannot afford to let the cost of one service, such as fire protection, throw the whole city budget out of line, leading to neglect of other city functions. But, relying on special districts, an area may have highly developed fire protection and primitive police protection in the same community. There is also likely to be little or no coordination or communication among the local governmental agencies serving the same area. In fact, the district apparatus, by its nature, leads to competition for the tax dollar, and this fragmented government can be expensive.

Another question, that of the efficiency and public responsibility of independent special districts, has never been thoroughly investigated.

Charges of inefficiency and irresponsibility are sometimes heard.[15] This is not to imply that all or even a sizable fraction of special districts are not well run. But the very lack of public knowledge about districts makes it difficult to assess the quality of their operations.

[15] Cf. Tiburon Fire Commission, Open Letter to the Grand Jury (Jan. 4, 1962). This regards the condition of the Tiburon Fire Protection District as of May 1959 when a new board of commissioners took over. A record of poor management existed for the previous two years, including inflated prices paid for land, unaccounted for expenditures by the fire chief, and district debts exceeding the budget. A county water district in Contra Costa County — now dissolved — had enough money left over after its bonds were retired to pay the secretary of the district $15 a month from bank interest, without touching the capital. The other members of the district's board did not realize this — thinking the district had been dissolved automatically years before.

Thomas R. Dye, Charles S. Liebman,
Oliver P. Williams, and Harold Herman

DIFFERENTIATION AND COOPERATION
IN A METROPOLITAN AREA

A distinguishing characteristic of metropolitan areas is areal specialization, or differentiation among spatially defined subpopulations with respect to class or status, life style, and economic function. To sociologists the relationship between specialization and urbanization is a commonplace. Their analysis has commonly centered on isolating the types of specialization and their discrete effects. Ecologists have described functionally

"Differentiation and Cooperation in a Metropolitan Area" by Thomas R. Dye, Charles S. Liebman, Oliver P. Williams, and Harold Herman, reprinted from *Midwest Journal of Political Science*, Vol. 7, No. 2 (May 1963), pp. 145–155, by permission of the Wayne State University Press. Copyright 1963 by Wayne State University Press.

differentiated zones and sectors and have even identified specific behavioral patterns associated with the residents of particular areas. To the political scientist, one of the most interesting attributes of metropolitan areas is the fact that urban specialization very often coincides with political boundaries. Not only has the familiar bedroom community become incorporated as a political entity, but within metropolitan regions one can also find industrial enclaves, recreational resorts, commercial centers, intellectual retreats, racial and ethnic ghettoes, company towns, and religious colonies which correspond roughly with local political units.

A central hypothesis of this paper . . . is that social and economic differentiation among communities in a metropolitan area is associated with differing local governmental policies. Local governmental decisions in a metropolitan area are made at hundreds of decision centers, each set in a separate social and economic environment, each responding to different types of interests, and each struggling to maintain a separate existence. As a result of these differing conditions, local governments can be expected to select differing policy alternatives designed to cope with specific interests within their constituencies.

Yet because of the interdependency of urban communities, some interests express themselves through demands for integrative or cooperative actions among local governments. Frequently it is suggested that certain services can be administered more economically and planned more intelligently when handled on an area-wide basis, or at least on a multi-jurisdictional basis. These arguments are often encountered with regard to schools, water supply, police protection, waste disposal, libraries, and street maintenance. Cooperative responses of local communities to jointly felt pressures of urbanization are not uncommon. The popular forms of cooperative responses among urban communities include the interjurisdictional agreement and joint authorities.

Students of political integration at the international level have suggested that policy consensus is the basis of viable political integration. If this same proposition is operative at the intermunicipal level and if the pattern of local policy choices is associated with social and economic differences among municipalities, then one should be able to observe the effect of urban differentiation on integrative arrangements in a metropolitan area. In short, it is our hypothesis that intermunicipal cooperation in a metropolitan area is a function of social and economic distance. Intermunicipal cooperation will tend to occur more frequently among communities which are similar in character and less frequently among highly differentiated communities. In this paper we shall attempt to set forth this hypothesis about the effect of urban differentiation on patterns of intermunicipal cooperation in an operational manner and to test it with reference to characteristics of local governments within the Philadelphia metropolitan area.

There are 238 municipalities covering the Pennsylvania sector of the Philadelphia metropolitan area. Although they range in size and density from the core city of Philadelphia with nearly two million persons to sparsely populated rural townships with less than 300 inhabitants, each of these local governments has substantially the same legal powers with which to structure its internal life and to cope with social and economic diversity. Recognizing that specialization and differentiation increase with urbanization, a distinction was made between the urban and semi-rural portions of the metropolitan area. The definition of urban as opposed to semi-rural was established at 500 persons per square mile, a figure chosen to approximate the state of urbanization of an area when urban services are generally initiated by the local government. According to this classification there were 90 urban and 135 semi-rural municipalities composing the study's sample; 12 communities were dropped from analysis because of large institutional populations which interfered with social and economic measurement.

In addition to the development of satisfactory measures of social, life style, and economic diversities, several other conditions were required for the hypothesis to be tested: (1) To have a cooperative arrangement, the potential cooperators must have or want to have the same service. (If one community has a police force and another neither has nor wants one, there is no basis for a cooperative operation of a police radio transmitter); (2) For a particular service, some municipalities must have selected a cooperative approach and others rejected it. (There must be a basis for comparing cooperating and non-cooperating communities); (3) While not absolutely essential, local governments must generally be contiguous for cooperation to be feasible. Thus in the analysis which follows, only the relationships between contiguous municipalities are subject to examination.

For the purposes of this paper, urban differentiation was operationally defined by three indices; these indices were selected for their relevance to decisions involving one or more of the most common types of interjurisdictional agreements. They are "social rank," market value per capita, and party voting.

1. "Social rank." This is an adaptation of an objective measure of community social status developed by sociologists Eshref Shevky and Wendell Bell which gives equivalent weight to occupational and educational attributes of a community's population. The occupational factor is the per cent of employed males in professional, managerial, and sales occupations. The educational factor is the per cent of persons over 25 years old with one or more years of college education. The percentages for each factor are first standardized in a range from 0 to 100 which assigns a zero score to the community with the lowest per cent in the college age or status occupational class and 100 to the highest com-

munity. Once the two standard scores are computed, they can be averaged. Thus every local unit is assigned a social rank score.

2. *Market value per capita.* A measure of community wealth which indicates the kind of financial resources which a municipality would bring to a cooperative enterprise.

3. *Party vote.* Partisan officials are the negotiators of cooperative arrangements. The percent Republican of the total vote for Governor in 1950 was used to identify the general partisan orientation of each community.

Cooperation is defined here as the joint financing of a service facility which is operated administratively as a single system. A cooperative arrangement may take the form of a contract, a joint authority, or a joint board. Non-cooperation is defined as the lack of any cooperative arrangement between contiguous municipalities which provide similar services. In the study area there are numerous cooperative arrangements for particular services. These arrangements represent local choices and are not imposed by higher legal authorities. The principal functional areas of cooperation are schools, sewers, police radio, libraries, water and solid waste disposal. Only in the first three areas is there a large enough number of cases to accommodate statistical analysis. Fortunately, these three functional areas represent three distinctly different kinds of local policies. Schools are an expression of the life style of a community but sewers and police radio systems are not. Both schools and sewers represent large financial commitments but police radio systems do not.

With 238 municipalities in the study area, there are 28,203 possible pairs of municipalities and therefore that same number of possible intermunicipal relationships. But if our analysis of intermunicipal relationships is limited to geographically contiguous municipalities, this figure is reduced to 534, the total number of pairs of contiguous municipalities.[1] This reduction was accomplished by inspecting a map of the area. Using the density classification, there were 198 pairs in the urban area, 294 in the rural, and 42 pairs comprised of one urban and one rural municipality.

Since each of the 534 pairs consists of two municipalities and each municipality is described by three measures of urban differentiation, it was possible to identify quantitatively the social and economic distance involved in each pair of municipalities along three separate indices. The absolute difference in index scores between paired municipalities constituted the measures of social and economic distance; three measures of social and economic distance were available for each pair, namely, social

---

[1] There were 66 pairs of contiguous municipalities which were eliminated because each involved at least one of the 12 municipalities with high institutional populations.

rank, per capita market value, and party voting. The smaller the difference in any index for a pair of communities, the more similar the communities in that pair are to each other, and the less social and economic distance exists between them. The larger the differences in index scores between two municipalities in a pair, the more dissimilar these municipalities are said to be. The central hypothesis of this paper can now be stated in operational terms. *If intermunicipal cooperation in a metropolitan area is a function of social and economic distance between communities, the mean of the differences in index values will be smaller for cooperating than for non-cooperating pairs of municipalities.*

TABLE I. SCHOOLS

Mean Differences Among Pairs of Cooperating and Non-Cooperating Municipalities

	Urban			Rural-urban			Semi-rural		
	Cooperating	Non-cooperating	Total	Cooperating	Non-cooperating	Total	Cooperating	Non-cooperating	Total
1 Social rank	10.4	16.9	16.0c	8.6	14.1	12.8b	7.3	7.8	7.5
2 Market value per capita	$1,131	$1,467	$1,424	$1,685	$1,437	$1,515	$957	$994	$974
3 Percentage Republican	9.0	11.5	11.2a	7.1	10.2	9.2a	8.0	8.8	8.4
Number of pairs	26	172	198	13	29	42	162	132	294

a Differences between cooperating and non-cooperating pairs of municipalities are significant at the .10 level of significance.
b Differences between cooperating and non-cooperating pairs of municipalities are significant at the .05 level of significance.
c Differences between cooperating and non-cooperating pairs of municipalities are significant at the .01 level of significance.

Table I presents the data on school arrangements. For the hypothesis to be borne out, the mean of the differences for cooperating pairs must always be less than for non-cooperating ones. Table I indicates that this is the case to the greatest extent in the urban area, is barely corroborated in the semi-rural one, and only partially so in the rural-urban — the area comprised of those mixed pairs of rural and urban municipalities.

The major incentive for cooperative school arrangements is the pooling of resources in constructing high schools. Both from a capital financing and a curricular standpoint, small municipalities have greater difficulty building high schools independently. As the number of pairs in the various categories of Table I indicate, the total incidence of agreement is greater in the semi-rural than the urban areas (urban 26 and semi-rural 162). This difference however, cannot be explained merely by the differences in size of urban and semi-rural municipalities. According to current Pennsylvania state policy, school districts should have at least 5,000 pupils. This means that ideally most municipalities with under 25,000 persons should be parties to joint arrangements. According to this standard only 12 urban and one semi-rural municipality are large enough to have independent systems. In fact there are many more than twelve urban municipalities with independent systems, but none in the semi-rural area. Indeed many urban municipalities which are quite small maintain their independence through *ad hoc* tuition arrangements with various neighboring governmental units.

Our hypothesis suggests that the more extensive use of cooperative school arrangements in the semi-rural area is a function, in part, of the lesser social distance among pairs there than is found in the urban area. Note that in the "Total" column the mean of the differences is larger for each index value for the urban area. Urban specialization tends to create sharp social breaks which follow municipal boundaries. Thus the intermunicipal social distances influence not only the pattern of cooperation, but also its extent. Only 26 out of 198 urban pairs had agreements, while, 162 out of 294 rural ones did. The urban-rural pairs lie in between with 13 out of 29 cooperating. The 26 urban pairs which did cooperate were atypical for the sample area. The mean difference in social rank for the entire urban area is 16.0, but only 10.4 for the cooperating communities. A similar pattern holds for the other three variables although not always at a high level of significance.

In the urban-rural area the mean differences in market value per capita between cooperating and non-cooperating pairs is in the opposite direction of that expected. Since none of the differences in market value per capita in any of the three sample areas is at a .10 level of significance, the difference in the urban-rural area might have arisen solely due to chance. It may also be a function of the market value index which does not always coincide with the year in which an agreement took place; variances of as much as ten years between index and agreement year are included.[2] Most communities do not experience rapid demographic changes. However, along the fringes of the urban area the most rapid shifts take place. Fringe area industrialization and large housing developments are the most common form which these changes take. It is likely that some disparities in market value per capita have taken place subsequent to the development of joint school systems. The hypothesis is

[2] Methodologically, data for indices of agreeing pairs should be gathered at the time agreements occur. Aside from nonavailability of data in all years, there is a problem of selecting the proper year for an index of non-cooperating pairs.

supported even in this changing area with regard to social rank and the related variable, party voting. Either populations channeling into fringe areas are not upsetting the social balance of agreeing pairs, or changes in social composition occur at a slower rate than any of our other indexes. Our observation is that both these propositions are true.

TABLE II. SEWER AGREEMENTS

MEAN DIFFERENCES AMONG PAIRS OF COOPERATING AND
NON-COOPERATING MUNICIPALITIES[a]

	Total			Delaware River outlet			Other outlets		
	Cooperating	Non-cooperating	Total	Cooperating	Non-cooperating	Total	Cooperating	Non-cooperating	Total
1 Social rank	15.9	15.3	15.6	17.4	11.9	16.1	11.2	18.0	15.0
2 Market value per capita	$1,223	$1,829	$1,440[b]	$1,278	$2,194	$1,506[b]	$1,057	$1,537	$1,324
3 Percentage Republican	10.5	11.4	10.8	11.2	10.3	10.8	8.5	12.3	10.6
Number of pairs	113	63	176	85	28	113	28	35	63

[a] Differences between cooperating and non-cooperating pairs of municipalities are significant at the .01 level of significance.
[b] Differences between cooperating and non-cooperating pairs of municipalities are significant at the .05 level of significance.

In the semi-rural area the differences in means are all in the expected direction but at less than a .10 level of significance. Additional applications of the social rank concept to the Philadelphia metropolitan area suggest an explanation for this apparent difference between urban and semi-rural behavior. We suspect that social rank is not as determinative an influence in the public policies of semi-rural areas as in urban areas, where the closeness, size and more frequent interactions of populations evoke greater consciousness of differences in community social status.

Education is one of the more vital policy areas through which local communities may express particular cultural and social styles of living. Another service, which is essential for urban living, but which has very little to do with life style, is the disposal of sewage. The analysis was repeated for sewage disposal agreements. One of the conditions for analysis was that both potential parties to an agreement must provide the service in question; thus only sewered communities are included in the sample. The condition confined the sample to the contiguously urbanized area around the core city. A review of the first portion of Table II under the heading "Total" indicates that there is little difference between agreeing and non-agreeing pairs with respect to social rank and party vote. There are significant differences with respect to community wealth. The conclusion might be drawn that municipalities do not mind negotiating with neighbors of differing social rank and party over matters of as little social significance as sewage, but are concerned about their neighbors' wealth because the maintenance and future expansion of the joint system will be influenced by the tax situation of the members. However, as the remaining portions of the Table show, this is only partially true.

The municipalities along the Delaware River are old industrial locations. They frequently have substantial tax bases, but low social ranking populations. As one goes up the tributary streams from the River, the social rank rises. Since sewage "runs down hill," the low status communities have had a monopoly of the access points for sewer trunks to the river. For the higher status upstream communities to solve their problems, they must deal with the lower status downstream communities. Table II lists all sewered communities with systems emptying directly into the Delaware River from the Delaware-Pennsylvania state boundary to Bensalem Township, which represents the strip of prewar river front development. These are labeled "Delaware River Outlet."

These pairs of municipalities with sewer agreements have higher mean social rank difference (though not significantly higher) than the pairs of municipalities without sewer agreements. However, with regard to taxable wealth (market value per capita) the agreeing municipalities in the Delaware River Outlet sample have a significantly smaller mean difference than the pairs of municipalities without sewer agreements. Joint sewer systems are rarely financed by uniform tax rates applying to all participating municipalities. Rather the shares to be paid by each municipality are worked out at the time of the agreement. Nevertheless, as was indicated above, the economic well-being of cooperating munici-palities is a matter of vital concern to the partners. High status municipalities in the Delaware River Outlet sample had no choice but to negotiate agreements with low status communities, but it would appear that they sought to cooperate with those low status communities that were high in taxable resources.

The differences in party voting between agreeing and non-agreeing pairs in the Delaware River Outlet sample are similar to the social rank pattern. This is not surprising since there is a .703 coefficient of correlation between social rank of each municipality and the percent Republican in the election used for the party affiliation index.

The remainder of the sewered communities not in the Delaware River Outlet sample are shown in Table II under the heading "Other Outlets."

These municipalities are located further up the stream from the Delaware River and along the Schuylkill and its tributaries. In these areas, municipalities frequently have a range of choice in deciding which other communities, if any, they will join in building sewerage systems. Here there is no solidly built-up riparian industrial strip monopolizing river access.

Agreements among these communities occur between those of similar status (social rank). It is interesting that although the agreeing communities also resemble each other more closely than do the non-agreeing communities with respect to taxable wealth, the difference between agreeing and non-agreeing communities is not statistically significant, even at the .10 level. It would appear that where a range of choice does exist, status is a more important determinant of agreement than are taxable resources.

Party voting again shows the same pattern as social rank. The question may be raised whether it is social rank or the party affiliation of the negotiators which influences the pattern of cooperative arrangements. The data indicate that social rank is the more important variable. In both school and sewer agreements, whenever there are significant differences between agreeing and non-agreeing municipalities with respect to social rank, there are also significant differences (up to the .10 level) with respect to party voting. But in each instance, differences in social rank are greater (they are at a higher level of statistical significance) than are differences in party voting.

School and sewerage systems have entirely differing social and cultural connotations, but both involve expensive capital facilities. Thus in each case the formation of cooperative systems means at least protracted negotiations among the leadership representing the communities, though perhaps little general public involvement in the case of sewer systems. The formation of a cooperative police radio network involves very modest financial contributions from participating municipalities, is of concern primarily to police technicians, and is a subject which generally should involve the general public very little.

TABLE III. POLICE RADIO AGREEMENTS

MEAN DIFFERENCES AMONG COOPERATING AND
NON-COOPERATING MUNICIPALITIES[a]

	Cooperating	Non-cooperating	Total
1 Social rank	14.2	17.1	15.9
2 Market value per capita	$1,645	$1,304	$1,445
3 Percentage Republican	11.3	11.5	11.4
Number of pairs	80	114	194

[a] None of the differences was significant at the .10 level.

Here the pattern of cooperation indicates no preference for similar municipalities among cooperating pairs. Table III gives the results for all pairs which have police radios. Only pairs from the urban area are thereby included. For this rather minor service, social and economic distances apparently do not control the pattern of cooperation.

The interjurisdictional agreement and the joint authority are the most popular forms of metropolitan political integration at the present time. Operations performed with data on these forms of integration in the Philadelphia Metropolitan Area tend to support the hypothesis that intermunicipal cooperation is a function of social and economic distance. Areal specialization appears to be an important obstacle to cooperative relations among urban communities. It was observed that cooperative arrangements are more frequent in the relatively undifferentiated semi-rural sectors of the metropolitan area and less frequent in the highly differentiated urban sectors. It was also observed that what cooperation did occur among the urbanized communities of the metropolitan area tended to occur among communities which were socially and economically similar rather than dissimilar. In addition, our findings indicate that social distance is a more important determinant of cooperation than is economic distance.[3]

These findings suggest that social and economic differentiation among urban communities may be fundamental to the whole question of metropolitan government. The highly differentiated character of metropolitan communities may operate to maintain our present "fragmented" structure of local government and to inhibit the growth of intergovernmental cooperation. Of course social science at least since Durkheim has been acutely aware that interdependence is a concomitant of specialization and that our interdependent system must be organized in some manner. The demand for effective organization of metropolitan areas is likely to continue. But because of the highly differentiated character of urban communities, integrative demands are likely to be accommodated through patterns of cooperation which least conflict with the divisive effects of differentiation.

[3] For a discussion of changes in social and economic variables affecting interjurisdictional cooperation, see the authors' "Social Status, Tax Resources and Metropolitan Cooperation," *National Tax Journal*, XVI (March 1963): 56–62.

Richard M. Cion

ACCOMMODATION PAR EXCELLENCE:
THE LAKEWOOD PLAN

The City of Lakewood, California, presents a perfect example of instant suburbia. In 1950, what is now Lakewood was primarily bean fields. During the next four years, developers transformed the land into a community of 50,000. Its growth was typical of post-war expansion throughout the country. In a pattern repeated over and over, suburbia moved outward, turning farmland into development tracts and crossroads into shopping centers. In Lakewood the bean fields disappeared, on Long Island the potato fields, and outside of Chicago the corn fields; but everywhere the result was the same: new homes appeared to house a predominantly young population. In this sense, Lakewood was a typical community. However, the political conditions in Los Angeles County stimulated a unique response: the contract plan.

Under the plan, cities contract with the County of Los Angeles for a wide range of municipal services (see Figure 1). For example, a city may purchase police protection by reimbursing the County for its costs in providing a patrol car on continuous duty with attendant backup services; or the city may purchase the services of more than one car if it so desires. Thus, the city is given some control over service quality through its power to determine how many units of a given service it will buy. The plan is distinguished from other systems of interlocal agreements by its comprehensiveness; participating cities enter the arrangement with the intention of securing all or most of their municipal services through contracting. The County acts as a clearing house, supplying specified services as they are demanded in the quantities requested by the cities.

At its inception, the Lakewood Plan represented the convergence of three conflicting forces. On the one hand, the older cities in Los Angeles County opposed what they called subsidization of the built-up unincorporated areas by the County's board of supervisors. As in most areas, the Board had been paying for the services rendered to unincorporated areas out of the County's general fund. Simultaneously, the board of supervisors and the County bureaucrats were anxious lest incorporation of large segments of unincorporated territory reduce the size and quality of the

Reprinted by permission of the author.

SERVICES PROVIDED TO CITIES BY THE COUNTY OF LOS ANGELES / JULY 1, 1964

CONTRACTS AND RESOLUTIONS

* Resolution Pursuant To General Services Agreement
1 By Contract

Source: Los Angeles County, Tabulation of Services Provided by the County of Los Angeles to Cities July 1, 1964.

225

County's service establishment. And finally, the unincorporated communities themselves desired control over their own territory. They sought the ability to guarantee the character of their population and the directions growth would take within their boundaries. The Lakewood Plan accommodated all of these various interests. Through incorporation, it gave the unincorporated communities the control they desired. At the same time, it removed the threat that incorporation posed to the County bureaucracy by retaining County services in the areas already using them. And by providing for the incorporation of built-up unincorporated communities, the plan cut the substance out of the older communities' complaints about subsidization; no longer could the League of California Cities complain that its members were bearing the financial burden of rendering services to people living in those communities.

In terms of popular acceptance, the Lakewood Plan is a success. Its clientele regard it with a euphoric mixture of contentment and admiration. One County official says the plan "is a partnership of cities and the County to provide joint services at the least cost while both agencies retain the power of self-determination and home rule."[1] This attitude is echoed by officials and citizens of the twenty-nine cities which depend on contracting for provision of virtually all of their municipal services. Yet, satisfied though its subscribers may be, the Lakewood Plan raises a number of troublesome issues. Plan communities must pay a high price for control over their own destinies. While contracting does provide them with decent services, it also restricts their freedom of action, severely limits the alternatives open to their leaders in many fields, forces them to bargain with the County for changes in policy, and compels them to operate within the rather narrow constraints of the contract plan.

Under the contract arrangement, no unit is capable of acting independently for long; each is tied to the others by the workings of the plan. All of the relevant interests give up a significant measure of independence in return for what they perceive as the values to be derived from participation. Ultimately, the only considerations of importance in the policy making process become those connected with preservation of the system. System-maintenance criteria replace other, more appropriate standards in determining governmental action.

Because the system satisfies their major goals, metropolitan actors do not perceive the sacrifices which they make in order to obtain the benefits of participation. And these sacrifices are real and considerable. Contract cities give up control over their service functions. Consider the case of a County sewer maintenance district coextensive with three newly incorpo-

[1] Arthur G. Will, *Lakewood Revisited: Six Years of Contract Services.* A paper presented to the First Annual Municipal Seminar of the California Contract Cities. Palm Springs, California. April 29, 1960, p. 1.

rated contract cities. Unless the three city councils agree on policy matters, one or more of them will be frustrated. In practice, the governing body of the district will tend to ignore the councils and set policy for itself. Or consider the case of the sheriff's department. Every contract relevant to law enforcement contains a "sheriff supreme" clause. In essence, the clause provides that in the event of conflict between a city's views on law enforcement policy and the sheriff's, the sheriff has the final word. The plan is replete with such instances in which cities have no formal opportunity to achieve control over their services while remaining within its framework. And because withdrawal is always expensive and often impossible the cities are forced to remain within that framework.

In some cases, the system does not even let a city find out what its problems are, or permit it to do anything about them if it knows what they are. For example, there is uniform dissatisfaction with the sheriff's system of reporting on police activities to cities. Several city managers have noted that they are unable to determine the extent of their juvenile problem. Moreover, as the contracts are presently drawn, a city could not hire additional juvenile officers if it wanted to. Under the contract plan, a city is unable to initiate or pursue a program directed at some particular problem in which it is especially interested. In part this is an administrative failure and in part it is a flaw inherent in the system. Communications could be improved; indeed steps are being taken to make the sheriff's reporting system more satisfactory. However, as long as law enforcement services are sold on a patrol-car-package basis, there will be no way for a city to attack specific problems — it will be able to hire only the prescribed package of services and will not be able to obtain greater numbers of specialized officers.

Finally, while contract cities have nominal control over service levels, they are unable to establish independent service policy. Only the willingness of the County departments to negotiate disputes and to alter established policy has preserved a measure of local control. As a case in point, in 1958 the sheriff's department agreed to abandon a long-standing prohibition against the use of one-man cars. Until that time it had been the sheriff's practice never to send a man out alone in a patrol car. Several contract cities felt that the sheriff was being unnecessarily conservative and that his policy was increasing the cost of police protection unreasonably. There followed a lengthy debate which ended in a compromise. The sheriff adopted the use of one-man cars during the day shift; the cities were satisfied. Thus a workable settlement was reached after each side had a chance to present its own position and to assess the importance of the issue to the other. The whole incident illustrates the willingness of County departments to negotiate when necessary.

But the statement that County departments are willing to negotiate, and if possible to accommodate the demands of the cities is not identical with the statement that the cities have control over service policies. Quite the contrary, the long and tortuous bargaining behind the sheriff's acceptance of one-man cars did not constitute an exercise of home rule. The city councils involved did not change service policy, rather they used political pressure to induce the sheriff to change policy. There is a vast difference between a city council adopting a resolution to the effect that procedures will be altered in the future and the same council voting to engage in negotiations with the County over future policy.

Cities are willing to give up immediate control over policy because they have to; for most plan cities, the economy of participation was a necessary prerequisite of incorporation. The contract city subscribes to the plan in order to preserve its independent existence and to protect itself from outside encroachment by undesirable groups. Through application of the land-use controls which become available to it upon incorporation, the contract city is able to insure the continuing homogeneity of its residents. Complete control over service policy is the price it must pay for the benefit of incorporation.

When asked about the shortcomings of the plan, contract-city officials observe that they can cancel any agreement upon sixty days' notice. This right, they assert, insures the city's ultimate control. As long as the County's commitment to the arrangement remains strong, and there is no reason why it should not, then the city's right of withdrawal will guarantee its strong position in the bargaining process. However, experience has shown that it is not always easy for a city to cancel a contract when it wishes. In 1958, the newly formed City of Norwalk revised its police service policy. The city administrator, E. Frederick Bien, felt that the sheriff's services were expensive and unresponsive. A resolution to form a municipal police department was proposed and eventually defeated by a three-two vote of the Norwalk council. Interestingly, the decisive vote was cast by the measure's author. According to one councilman, the sheriff applied strong pressure to the group to reject the resolution, a view supported by other knowledgeable observers. In this case, the sheriff used his powerful position in County politics to prevent a city from exercising its formal right of withdrawal from the plan.

One point emerges clearly — a city cannot always withdraw from the contract system if it wants to. Its actions are not internally controlled; rather they are subject to outside political influence, particularly from actors in the County government whose interests lie in the continuation of the status quo. The city's great power in the negotiation process is largely a myth. Moreover, the myth is preserved by County officials for purposes of public relations. As one high-ranking County official observed, if the cities felt they had no control, new cities would fail to subscribe to the plan and the County's interest in its expansion would not be served.

Thus, the cities' drive for independence paradoxically results in a gross restriction of their freedom of action in all fields save one. While left with the ability to control their own land-use patterns, Lakewood Plan communities are unable to set independent policy in other areas. This is the price they pay for the ability to retain their particular character in the face of the rapid growth of the metropolitan area.

City interests are not the only ones subordinated to the maintenance values surrounding the plan. The County's commitment to the arrangement derives from the fact that contracting assures the continued growth of its service departments. However, by supporting the Lakewood Plan, County officials place serious limits on their freedom of action. While the County does have a position of strength relative to contract cities, it would be impractical to use pressure every time a city made a request. Frequent use of pressure would arouse city resistance and would discourage new cities from employing the arrangement. Therefore, County policy is to work whenever possible within the framework of the plan.

This decision implies that the County is ever ready to negotiate its differences with a city and, if necessary, to yield ground in the face of determined requests. It further implies that the County will make all of its resource allocation decisions with contract services in mind. For example, when establishing a new district library, the board of supervisors is likely to put it in a contract city if possible. When constructing a fire station or other facility, it must consider the stability of its contracts with cities in the area. Hence, the County must work under a certain amount of uncertainty; there is always the possibility, however remote, that contracts will be cancelled. In order to minimize the possibility, the board of supervisors tends to be very solicitous of contract cities.

Government in Los Angeles is then carried out by means of a dialogue between the cities and the County. Neither is free to pursue its own interest, yet neither is explicitly aware of the limitations placed upon it. The result is what Roscoe Martin calls a "fluid federalism."[2] All participants work to further their own interests within the rather rigorously defined constraints of the contract plan. The fluid quality derives from the fact that the constitution is continually subject to change by negotiation. But by subscribing to the system, the participants agree to work within its limitations; each must curb its own potential in order that the system as a whole will work, and each does so.

[2] Roscoe C. Martin, *Metropolis in Transition: Local Government Adaptation to Changing Urban Needs*, Washington, D.C.: Housing and Home Finance Agency, 1963, p. 23.

In the process, limits are placed not only on city and County interests, but also on the interests of the metropolitan area as a whole. A significant result of the Lakewood Plan has been to stimulate the creation of thirty-one new cities in Los Angeles County. That in itself would be enough to discourage any hope of voluntary cooperation for the solution of regional problems. Moreover, if the character of these new communities is considered, it is immediately apparent that voluntary regional consent on any significant matter is most unlikely. For example, the City of Industry is a bizarrely shaped industrial center. Following the outline of the Union Pacific and Southern Pacific Railroad yards, Industry is a tax shelter for factories and warehouses. In order to meet the minimum population requirement for incorporation (500), the city counted the inmates of an insane asylum. A court challenge to the legality of this procedure was halted before a decision was reached when the plaintiff declared himself no longer interested by virtue of the fact that he had moved out of the area (and into a house somewhat more luxurious than the one which he had occupied at the beginning of the suit). Obviously, Industry is not interested in any scheme which would mean sharing its huge tax potential with the rest of the County.

Industry is neither an extreme nor an unusual case. The cities of Commerce and Santa Fe Springs are similarly composed. Dairy Valley is an agricultural enclave whose population is composed principally of cows. Other cities have their own peculiarities. Rolling Hills is a city without public streets; they are all owned by a private corporation. Hidden Hills is literally a walled city; its residents can close the gates and refuse to let anyone in.

But the proliferation of special interest cities, each an additional veto in the unit-veto system of regional government, is not the only result of the plan. A desperate need in the metropolis is planning for the future — planning for orderly development, for judicious use of resources, and for regional facilities. Each time a new city is launched, the ability of the County's planning organ, the Regional Planning Commission, to meet the challenges or urbanization effectively is further vitiated. Instead, the County, through the Lakewood Plan is forced to implement a variety of local land-use plans, each a design which stresses protectivism, preservation of particularistic values, and ignorance of regional needs. Although the Regional Planning Commission continues to construct master plans for the entire County, it is increasingly powerless to implement them.

Another of the plan's significant products is the subtle alteration it works on the role of County bureaucrats and officials. In most metropolitan areas, if there is a strong central government like a county, the officers of that unit generally have good reason to support area-wide government. Big government is in their interest; they are likely to be the recipients of whatever new powers arise out of metropolitan reform. But the Lakewood Plan has rechannelled County imperialism. Instead of supporting the formation of regional government, the County is committed to the status quo. Because the plan provides a means of insuring the County's position, the bureaucrats' natural tendency to seek widening of their power through a more general government is aborted. They live contentedly within the framework of the Lakewood Plan, their power already secure, their reason for seeking metro gone.

Far from strengthening the impetus toward regionalism, the Lakewood Plan actually vitiates it. By creating new and more aggressive enclaves of particularism in the County, each one protected by the home rule provisions of the state constitution, by strengthening the desire for status quo on the part of county officials, and by making the Regional Planning Commission totally ineffective, the plan builds the first line of resistance against metropolitan approaches to metropolitan problems. Moreover, the plan itself does not attempt to solve these problems. Planning, water supply, transportation, sewage, education, segregation — they are all beyond its scope. In so far as it eliminates the need for more local departments, the plan alleviates some of the duplication of functions which typically wastes metropolitan resources. But it avoids the hard problems. As a system of interlocal agreements, it cannot extend itself to regionalism; it is limited by the extent of consensual patterns among its subscribers.

It is interesting to note that the political system which emerges in Los Angeles County resembles politics in New York City as pictured by Sayre and Kaufman: "a loose-knit and multicentered network in which decisions are reached by ceaseless bargaining among the major categories of participants in each center, and in which the centers are partially but strikingly isolated from one another."[3] Thus, the nation's largest city, New York, and its most diffuse metropolis, Los Angeles, have developed curiously similar distributions of influence out of vastly different environments and institutional arrangements. In both areas, and indeed in all polycentric systems, three characteristics are consistently exhibited: First, by definition, there are many relevant actors, each invested with an independent base of power. Second, government is conducted by negotiation; no one actor is powerful enough to control policy alone, and no group of actors is motivated to unite on a large range of issues. And third, no actor is able to freely and completely pursue his own interest. The only interest which is fully served is that of the system itself; all others are subordinated to it.

[3] Wallace S. Sayre and Herbert Kaufman, *Governing New York City; Politics in the Metropolis*, New York: Russell Sage Foundation, 1960, p. 716.

Vincent Ostrom, Charles M. Tiebout, and Robert Warren

IN DEFENSE OF THE POLYCENTRIC METROPOLIS

Allusions to the "problem of metropolitan government" are often made in characterizing the difficulties supposed to arise because a metropolitan region is a legal non-entity. From this point of view, the people of a metropolitan region have no general instrumentality of government available to deal directly with the range of problems which they share in common. Rather there is a multiplicity of federal and state governmental agencies, counties, cities, and special districts that govern within a metropolitan region.

This view assumes that the multiplicity of political units in a metropolitan area is essentially a pathological phenomenon. The diagnosis asserts that there are too many governments and not enough government. The symptoms are described as "duplication of functions" and "overlapping jurisdictions." Autonomous units of government, acting in their own behalf, are considered incapable of resolving the diverse problems of the wider metropolitan community. The political topography of the metropolis is called a "crazy-quilt pattern" and its organization is said to be an "organized chaos." The prescription is reorganization into larger units — to provide "a general metropolitan framework" for gathering up the various functions of government. A political system with a single dominant center for making decisions is viewed as the ideal model for the organization of metropolitan government. "Gargantua" is one name for it.[1]

Reprinted by permission of the authors and The American Political Science Association from *The American Political Science Review*, Vol. LV (December 1961), pp. 831–842.

[1] The term is taken from Robert C. Wood, "The New Metropolis: Green Belts, Grass Roots or Gargantua," *The American Political Science Review*, Vol. LII (March, 1958), pp. 108–122. Wood defines gargantua as "the invention of a single metropolitan government or at least the establishment of a regional superstructure which points in that direction." We do not argue the case for big units *vs.* small units as Wood does in his discussion of gargantua *vs.* grass roots. Rather, we argue that various scales of organization may be appropriate for difficult public services in a metropolitan area.

The assumption that each unit of local government acts independently without regard for other public interests in the metropolitan community has only a limited validity. The traditional pattern of government in a metropolitan area with its multiplicity of political jurisdictions may more appropriately be conceived as a "polycentric political system."[2] "Polycentric" connotes many centers of decision-making which are formally independent of each other. Whether they actually function independently, or instead constitute an interdependent system of relations, is an empirical question in particular cases. To the extent that they take each other into account in competitive relationships, enter into various contractual and cooperative undertakings or have recourse to central mechanisms to resolve conflicts, the various political jurisdictions in a metropolitan area may function in a coherent manner with consistent and predictable patterns of interacting behavior. To the extent that this is so, they may be said to function as a "system." . . .

No a priori judgment can be made about the adequacy of a polycentric system of government as against the single jurisdiction. The multiplicity of interests in various public goods sought by people in a metropolitan region can only be handled in the context of many different levels of organization. The polycentric system is confronted with the problem of realizing the needs of wider community interests or publics beyond the functional or territorial bounds of each of the formal entities within the broader metropolitan region. The single jurisdiction, in turn, confronts the problem of recognizing and organizing the various subsidiary sets of interests within the big system. It is doubtful that sub-optimization in gargantua is any easier to accomplish than supra-optimization in a polycentric political system.

The performance of a polycentric political system can only be understood and evaluated by reference to the patterns of cooperation, competition and conflict that may exist among its various units. Cooperative arrangements pose no difficulty when joint activities produce a greater return to all parties concerned, if the appropriate set of public interests are adequately represented among the negotiators. A contractual arrangement will suffice. As a result, this discussion of the behavior of a polycentric political system will focus upon the more difficult problems of

---

[2] We use this term for want of a better one. An alternative term might be "multinucleated political system." We do not use "pluralism" because it has been preempted as a broader term referring to society generally and not a political system in particular.

Polycentric political systems are not limited to the field of metropolitan government. The concept is equally applicable to regional administration of water resources, regional administration of international affairs, and to a variety of other situations.

competition, of conflict and its resolution. If a polycentric political system can resolve conflict and maintain competition within appropriate bounds it can be a viable arrangement for dealing with a variety of public problems in a metropolitan area.

Competition[3]

Where the provision of public goods and services has been successfully internalized within a public jurisdiction, there are no substantial spill-over effects, by definition. In such circumstances there need be no detrimental consequences from competition in the municipal services economy. Patterns of competition among producers of public services in a metropolitan area, just as among firms in the market, may produce substantial benefits by inducing self-regulating tendencies with pressure for the most efficient solution in the operation of the whole system.

Variety in service levels among various independent local government agencies within a larger metropolitan community may give rise to a quasi-market choice for local residents in permitting them to select the particular community in the metropolitan area that most closely approximates the public service levels they desire. Public service agencies then may be forced to compete over the service levels offered in relation to the taxes charged. Such competition, however, would only be appropriate for those public goods which are adequately internalized within the boundaries of a given political jurisdiction.

Conditions amenable to competition normally exist among local units of government where a number of units are located in close proximity to each other and where information about each other's performance is publicly available. Information can lead to comparison and comparison can lead to pressure for performances to approximate the operations of the more efficient units. Where more than one public jurisdiction is capable of rendering service in a single area, further competitive tendencies may develop. Contractual arrangements among public jurisdictions for the provision of specific public services have long provided a competitive alternative to each jurisdiction which might otherwise produce its own services.

The separation of the *provision* of public goods and services from their *production* opens up the greatest possibility of redefining economic functions in a public service economy. Public control can be maintained

---

[3] This analysis is confined to competition between units of government and makes no reference to competitive forces within a unit of government. Competition among pressure groups, factions and political parties is a fundamental feature of the democratic political process, but is not within the primary focus of this paper and its concern with the polycentric system.

in relation to performance criteria in the provision of services, while allowing an increasing amount of competition to develop among the agencies that produce them.

With the incorporation of the City of Lakewood in 1954, Los Angeles County, for example, expanded its system of contracting for the production of municipal services to a point approaching quasi-market conditions. Newly incorporated cities, operating under the so-called Lakewood Plan, contract with the county or other appropriate agencies to produce the general range of municipal services needed in the local community.

Each city contracts for municipal services for the city as a whole. Services beyond the general level of performance by county administration in unincorporated areas are subject to negotiation for most service functions. Each city also has the option of producing municipal services for itself. Private contractors too have undertaken such services as street sweeping, engineering, street maintenance and repair and related public works. Some contracts have been negotiated with neighboring cities. As the number of vendors increases, competition brings pressures toward greater responsiveness and efficiency.

By separating the production from the provision of public goods it may be possible to differentiate, unitize and measure the production while continuing to provide undifferentiated public goods to the citizen-consumer. Thus Los Angeles County has, under the Lakewood Plan, unitized the production of police services into packages, each consisting of a police-car-on-continuous-patrol with associated auxiliary services. A price is placed on this police-car-on-continuous-patrol package, and a municipality may contract for police service on that basis. Within the local community, police service is still provided as a public good for the community as a whole.

Problems of scale arising from possible conflicts between criteria of production and criteria of political representation may be effectively resolved in this way. Efficient scales or organization for the production of different public goods may be quite independent of the scales required to recognize appropriate publics for their consumption of public goods and services. But competition among vendors may allow the most efficient organization to be utilized in the production, while an entirely different community of interest and scale of organization controls the provision of services in a local community.

The separation of production from provision may also have the consequence of turning local governments into the equivalents of associations of consumers. While Sidney and Beatrice Webb viewed local governments as associations of consumers, the dominance of production criteria in American municipal administration has largely led to the subordination of consumer interests.[4] However, cities organized to provide the local citizenry with public services produced by other agencies may be expected to give stronger representation to consumer interests. Among the so-called Lakewood Plan cities in Los Angeles County, for example, the local chief administrative officer has increasingly become a spokesman or bargainer for local consumer interests.

In this role, the chief administrative-officer is similar to a buyer in a large corporation. Recognizing that the greater the number of vendors of public services, the greater the competition, the local chief administrative officer may seek to expand the number of his potential suppliers. As competition increases, vendors become more sensitive to the consumer demands he negotiates.

The production of public goods under the contract system in Los Angeles County has also placed considerable pressure upon the county administration to become more responsive to demands of the public service clientele organized through their local cities. Important changes in operating procedures and organizational arrangements have been introduced into the county's administration of police protection, fire protection, library services, street maintenance, building inspection and engineering services in order to increase efficiency and responsiveness.

Under these circumstances, a polycentric political system can be viable in supplying a variety of public goods with many different scales of organization and in providing optimal arrangements for the production and consumption of public goods. With the development of quasi-market conditions in production, much of the flexibility and responsiveness of market organization can be realized in the public service economy.

Several difficulties in the regulation of a competitive public service economy can be anticipated. Economic pricing and cost allocation are dependent upon the development of effective measurement of municipal services. Since the preferred states of affairs in a community cannot be converted to a single scale of values such as dollar profits in a private enterprise, it may be more difficult to sustain an objective competitive relationship in a public service economy. Although costs of contract services from different vendors of a public good may be the same, objective standards for determining the value of the benefits are needed, and may be hard to come by; otherwise the latitude of discretion available to the negotiators may limit the competitive vitality of the system and shift the competition to side-payoffs.

Without careful control of cost allocations and pricing arrangements, funds from non-competitive welfare functions might be used to subsidize the more competitive service areas. In Los Angeles County, close scrutiny

[4] Sidney and Beatrice Webb, *English Local Government: Statutory Authorities for Special Purposes* (London: Longmans, Green and Co., 1922), pp. 437 ff.

of cost accounting practices and pricing policies by the grand jury has helped to prevent funds from being so transferred.

Any long-term reliance upon quasi-market mechanisms in the production of public goods and services no doubt will require more of such careful scrutiny, control and regulation than has been applied toward maintaining the competitive structure of the private market economy. The measurement of cost and output performance may become an essential public function of the state in the administration of metropolitan affairs if continued reliance is placed primarily upon a polycentric system in the government of metropolitan areas.

Reliance upon outside vendors to produce public services may also reduce the degree of local political control exercised. The employee is subject to the control of the vendor and not directly to the control of the municipality. In contrast to the more immediate lines of responsibility and communication between local municipal employees and city officials, reliance upon vendors to provide municipal services may also restrict the quality and quantity of information about community affairs that are provided to the city's decision-makers. This constraint on information might reduce the degree of their control over public affairs.

This discussion merely indicates some of the considerations to be examined in an analysis of the effects of competitive arrangements in providing public services. As long as the particular contracting agencies encompass the appropriate set of public interests no absolute impediment to their use need exist. With appropriate public control, competitive arrangements may afford great flexibility in taking advantage of some of the economies of scale for the production of public services in a metropolitan area, while, at the same time, allowing substantial diversity in their provision for the more immediate communities, based upon political responsibility within local patterns of community identification.

Conflict and Conflict Resolution

More difficult problems for a polycentric political system are created when the provision of public goods cannot be confined to the boundaries of the existing units of government. These situations involving serious spill-over effects are apt to provoke conflict between the various units in the system. Arrangements must be available for the resolution of such conflicts if a polycentric political system is to solve its problems. Otherwise, competition and conflict are apt to become acute.

No community, on its own initiative, has much incentive to assume the full costs of controlling adverse consequences which are shared by a wider public. The competitive disadvantage of enforcing pollution abatement regulations, for example, against individuals and firms within a single community, when competitors in neighboring communities are not required to bear such costs, leads each community to excuse its failure to act by the failure of other similarly situated communities to act. In a polycentric system this is especially serious where many of the public "goods" involve the costly abatement of public nuisances.

Concerted action by the various units of government in a metropolitan area is easier to organize when costs and benefits are fairly uniformly distributed throughout the area. By way of example, this has been done under contractual agreements for mutual aid to assure the mobilization of greater fire-fighting capability in case of serious conflagrations. The random and unpredictable nature of such fires causes them to be treated as a uniform risk that might occur to any community in the larger metropolitan area.

Similar considerations apply to efforts to control mosquito infestations or air pollution. Leagues of cities, chambers of commerce and other civic associations have frequently become the agencies for negotiating legislative proposals for the creation of mosquito abatement districts, air pollution control districts and the like.

More difficult problems for the polycentric political system arise when the benefits and the costs are not uniformly distributed. Communities may differ in their perception of the benefits they receive from the provision of a common public good. In turn, a community may be unwilling to "pay its fair share" for providing that good simply because its demands for provision are less than in neighboring communities. These situations call for effective governmental mechanisms which can internalize the problem. If necessary, sanctions must be available for the enforcement of decisions.

The conflicting claims of municipal water supply systems pumping water from the same underground basins in Southern California, for example, have uniformly been resolved by recourse to legal actions in the state courts. The courts have thereby become the primary authorities for resolving conflicts among water supply agencies in Southern California; and their decisions have come to provide many of the basic policies of water administration in the Southern California metropolitan region. The state's judiciary has played a comparable role in conflicts among other local government agencies in such diverse fields as public health, incorporation and annexation proceedings, law enforcement and urban planning.

The heavy reliance upon courts for the resolution of conflicts among local units of government unquestionably reflects an effort to minimize the risks of external control by a superior decision-maker. Court decisions are taken on a case-by-case basis. The adversaries usually define the issues and consequently limit the areas of judicial discretion. This method also minimizes the degree of control exercised following a judgment. California courts, in particular, have accepted the basic doctrines of home rule and are thus favorably disposed to the interests of local units of government in dealing with problems of municipal affairs.

The example of municipal water administration may be pursued further to illustrate other decision-making arrangements and their consequences which bear upon the resolution of conflict in a polycentric political system.[5]

While litigation may be an appropriate means for resolving conflicts over a given supply of water, local water administrators in Southern California have long recognized that law suits never produced any additional water. Organization for the importation of new water supplies was recognized as the only means for solving the long-term problem.

Los Angeles built the first major aqueduct to import water into the area on its own initiative. This water supply was used to force adjoining areas to annex or consolidate to the City of Los Angeles if they wished to gain access to the new supply. The condition for the provision of water required adjoining areas to sacrifice their identities as separate political communities. To get that one public good they were forced to give up other public goods. This provoked sufficient opposition to block any new developments which were not based upon consent and cooperation. The mechanisms for the resolution of subsequent conflicts were required to take on new forms.

The importation of Colorado River water was later undertaken by a coalition of communities in Southern California formed through the agency of the southern section of the League of California Cities. The League afforded a neutral ground for the negotiation of the common interests of the City of Los Angeles and the other cities in the metropolitan area which shared common water problems. After satisfactory arrangements had been negotiated, including provision for the formation of a new metropolitan water district and endorsement of the Boulder Canyon project, a Boulder Dam Association was formed to realize these objectives. In due course a new agency, the Metropolitan Water District of Southern California was formed; and the Colorado River aqueduct was constructed and put into operation by this new district.

More recently, the Southern California Water Coordinating Conference, meeting under the auspices of the Los Angeles Chamber of Commerce, has been the agency for negotiating regional interests in the development of the California Water Program. The Metropolitan Water District was not able to represent areas in Southern California which did not belong to that district; and the rise of a variety of special municipal water districts precluded the League of California Cities, which represents

<hr>

[5] For further detail see: Vincent Ostrom, *Water and Politics* (Los Angeles: Haynes Foundation, 1953), esp. chs. 3, 6 and 7.

cities only, from again serving as the agency for the negotiation of metropolitan interests in municipal water supply.

These illustrations suggest that a variety of informal arrangements may be available for negotiating basic policies among local government agencies in a metropolitan area. Such arrangements are vital in negotiating common interests among them. The larger public is taken into account in an informally constituted political community. These arrangements work effectively only so long as substantial unanimity can be reached, for formal implementation of such decisions must be ratified by each of the appropriate official agencies, including the state government when changes in state law or administrative policies are involved.

Higher levels of government may also be invoked in seeking the resolution of conflict among local governments in metropolitan areas. Again recourse is sought to a more inclusive political community. Under these circumstances, conflict tends to centralize decision-making and control. The danger is that the more inclusive political community will not give appropriate recognition to the particular public interests at issue and tends to inject a variety of other interests into settlements of local controversies.

Appeal to central authorities runs the risk of placing greater control over local metropolitan affairs in agencies such as the state legislature, while at the same time reducing the capability of local governments for dealing with their problems in the local context. Sensitivity over the maintenance of local control may produce great pressure for the subordination of differences while conflicting parties seek a common position approximating unanimity. A substantial investment in informal negotiating and decision-making arrangements can be justified from the perspective of the local authorities if such arrangements can prevent the loss of local autonomy to higher levels of government.

Ironically but logically, this effort to avoid recourse to conflict and the consequent centralization of decision-making tends also to reduce the local autonomy or degree of independence exercised by the local governing boards. Pressure for agreement on a common approach to some metropolitan problem limits the choices available to any particular local government. However, this range of choice may still be greater than that which would result from a settlement by a central authority. Negotiation among independent agencies allows the use of a veto against any unacceptable position. Agreement must be negotiated within the limits of the various veto positions if the alternative of recourse to an external authority at a higher level of political jurisdiction is to be avoided.

To minimize the costs of conflict to their power positions, administrators of local government agencies in metropolitan areas have tended to develop an extensive system of communication about each other's experience and to negotiate standards of performance applicable to various types of public services. Professional administrative standards may, thus, operate to constrain the variety of experience in local government agencies. Information about areas of difference and of potential conflict tend to be repressed under these circumstances. The negotiations about common problems through informal agencies are apt to be conducted in secrecy, and careful control may be developed over sensitive information.

These pressures to avoid the costs of conflict and seek agreement about metropolitan problems reflect the importance to local governments of resolving general public problems by negotiation at the local level in a metropolitan community. To the extent that these pressures are effective, the patterns of local government in a metropolitan area can only be understood by attention to the variety of formal and informal arrangements that may exist for settling area-wide problems.

Contrary to the frequent assertion about the lack of a "metropolitan framework" for dealing with metropolitan problems, most metropolitan areas have a very rich and intricate "framework" for negotiating, adjudicating and deciding questions that affect their diverse public interests. . . .

Robert C. Wood

METROPOLIS AGAINST ITSELF

What emerges from [a] review of the accomplishments and failures of metropolitan governments is not a prediction of catastrophe or of governmental bankruptcy. The governments have attended to the minimum needs of their citizens well enough to prevent any fundamental breakdown. Indeed, the whole history of metropolitan reform, or more

Reprinted from *Metropolis Against Itself* (New York: Committee for Economic Development, 1959), pp. 39–44, with the permission of the author and the Committee for Economic Development.

properly, the failure of reform movements, reveals that the regions' population have not become dissatisfied with the existing conditions to the point of supporting major reorganizations.

What does emerge is the conclusion that metropolitan governments which retain allegiance to autonomy and diversity can discharge effectively only one major responsibility — the provision of minimum urban services and facilities. The efforts required to sustain an adequate volume of public investment for ordinary service activities, and the complicated arrangements necessary to provide minimum standards throughout the metropolitan areas, preclude any real possibility of developing coordinated regional services or perfecting institutions for regional policy-making. The present pattern of metropolitan government can keep house; it cannot make and carry out plans for any substantial remodeling or new construction.

This state of affairs, it should be pointed out, does not necessarily commit the metropolitan governments to continued operations at a subsistence level, nor to growing inequities and disparities. As the process of economic growth goes on, it seems reasonable to expect that the pressures on even the most hard pressed jurisdiction will lighten. If the diffusion of commercial establishments continues, for example, their activities will locate where their customers are most closely congregated and their markets largest. Thus, they will bring tax resources in excess of service demands to the residential suburban municipalities most urgently in need of revenue. Similarly, industrial plants, in their search for elbow room, are likely to be attracted to the newest municipalities where the rate of population growth is fastest, and the get-going costs of community development most severe. As these migrations continue, more municipalities will receive the "windfalls" of shopping centers, amusement areas, medical buildings, and industrial parks, and tax revenues will be augmented accordingly.

Even the central city need not necessarily despair at the course of present economic trends. A substantial proportion of the growing service industry still needs to locate in the core — for example, advertising agencies, banks, law firms, and consultants. So do the home offices where communication, "the knowledge of the industry," gossip of the trade and face-to-face confrontations are prerequisites for doing business. So does the growing category of specialized and unstandardized manufacturing processes. Small firms which offer intermediate component products to a number of industries, which require unstandardized inputs or produce unstandardized products, and which maintain irregular schedules, find external economies downtown which few suburbs can supply.

The implication for the central city is, of course, that the businesses so engaged are relatively insensitive to tax changes. Existing levies can be increased, new taxes on earnings and incomes imposed, and the firms will still "stay put." The advantages of communication, proximity to client and competitor, fractional use of transportation facilities, rented space, a larger labor market, and close inventory control, outweigh the tax penalties involved. Thus, the city may be able to obtain substantially higher revenues to meet the challenge of obsolescence than it — or its businesses — have formerly supposed.[1]

These trends of economic growth are not the only evidence indicating that the present pattern of governments can continue to endure against mounting pressures and avoid making a serious attack on regional problems. There is, after all, a firm ideological basis for the belief that "keeping house" is all a local government *should* do. The traditional American theory of local government holds that a municipality is "nothing but a bundle of services," that administrative problems and service problems and tax problems are the only problems at the local level. The old saw runs that "there is no Republican or Democratic way to pave a street," and this doctrine persists despite the ideological content of housing and renewal programs, health activities and zoning ordinances. So long as this doctrine exists, few citizens will seriously look to their local governments to tackle the renewal problem, the transportation crisis, the urban sprawl in a thoroughgoing manner.

Even if the public comes to demand these more positive programs, it is unlikely to be willing to pay the price for a thoroughgoing reorganization and reform. Linked to the "bundle of services" philosophy is the even stronger conviction that the government closest to home governs best. Autonomy is valued for the democratic benefits it bestows: the opportunity for direct popular participation, the chance to know public officials personally, and the fact that local issues are concrete and understandable. City services combined with grass-roots governments have a persuasive appeal in the modern metropolitan region — and the values of this union are not likely to be rapidly abandoned.

Indeed, the grass roots appeal is so persuasive that the very inequities created by the present pattern of government have their defenders. The existence of a number of little governments in a single area, it is sometimes argued, provides each citizen with an array of alternatives in ways of living and in levels of public services. Thus Professors Banfield and Grodzins see the modern metropolitan region as allowing "spheres of free choice for individuals and community groups"; "wide options to be exclusive and expressive." They believe a large number of governments is desirable because "the consumer is in the position to know what

---

[1] For a more extended examination of these trends, see the author's "The New Metropolis: Green Belts, Grass Roots or Gargantua?" *American Political Science Review*, LII:1 (March, 1958).

combination of goods and services — trees and sidewalks as against food and clothing, for example — will give him the greatest satisfaction.[2]

Yet, if the present system of metropolitan government can be supported by economic trends and defended philosophically, it still produces by-products which must be recognized and which, in the long run, may be unpalatable. A single-minded fixation on the service concept of government, an insistence on the preservation of political autonomy and multiplicity, mean, first of all, that it is impossible to have a vision of what the metropolitan regions might become. When each jurisdiction goes on its separate way, urban sprawl continues, with its companions of spreading blight, cheap commercial developments along major highways, inadequate parks, congested schools, mediocre administration, smog, traffic jams, recurrent crises in mass transportation, and the hundred and one irritations of undirected growth. The "gray belt" which Raymond Vernon has so graphically described continues to expand, and the municipalities caught directly in its path are left to grapple with its consequences, one by one. In place of a coordinated attack on the less attractive by-products of urbanization, each jurisdiction tries to avoid the conditions it regards as unpalatable, to protect its own, and to let its neighbors fend for themselves. When local government disclaims responsibility for the regional environment, the capacity to realize the potential of that environment is irrevocably lost.

Second, it must be recognized that under the present system, not all the citizens of the region — nor even the majority — can exercise the freedom of choice which the multiplicity of jurisdictions may offer. Though bright islands of residential suburbs exist, there is a high price on their homes, and for many people there are no real alternatives except the backwaters of the city and the suburban-development house on the quarter-acre lot. Even the individual who can choose his home where he wishes may be disillusioned. Once settled, he has to accept his tastes as frozen, or resign himself to the ineffective position of the minority group — or move each time his values and opinions change.

A third consequence of the present state of affairs is that, as local governments disclaim any responsibility for regional services and for policy-making, this responsibility moves upstairs. The Federal government comes to exercise predominant influence over certain decisions — as it does today in redevelopment and highway construction. The State government calls the tune in recreation and public health, and in some ways, even in education. Or the "non-political" authorities arrive at some sort of compromise agreement, at the lowest common denominator, of what the shape and future of the region should be. The local

---

2 Edward C. Banfield and Morton Grodzins, *Housing Policy and the Government of Metropolitan Areas*, special report prepared for ACTION, 1956.

governments of the region, by refusing to make policy, by attending strictly to the business of providing services, by defending local autonomy in the legal sense, forfeit the real authority to control and direct their own affairs.

Finally, so long as the present system of government exists, the regional economic system itself functions less effectively. Lacking a mechanism for regional policy-making, the metropolitan political system is unable to use planning, zoning, redevelopment, and transportation programs to assist the processes of production and distribution. Instead, as Kirk R. Petshek has pointed out, since the governments cannot take into account the new facts of regional economic life, they make these processes less efficient. Their mistakes in investment and regulatory programs, their competitive attitude toward their neighbors, mean extra costs for private business.[3] Thus when redevelopment authorities do not assign space to appropriate economic uses, when the transportation system fails to provide easy access to work or bypasses sub-areas otherwise suitable for development, when water is not available at attractive industrial sites, the economy assumes additional burdens. Public investments and decisions made at the wrong time, in the wrong place, and in the wrong way, serve, in Petshek's words, to "counteract the trend or 'mainstream' of development," and thus are "completely ineffectual, or act in such a way that the whole economic structure is rendered less efficient." At a time when rapidity of growth seems a critical factor in national survival, this tendency of government to work at cross purposes to the economic system may well be the most serious consequence of all.

If these consequences seem undesirable, and if their deficiencies appear to outweigh the advantages of diversity and insularity, then quite obviously a new and different philosophy of government is in order. The requirements of policy-making will have to take precedence over the requirements of simply maintaining some semblance of organized community existence. The carefully devised structure to permit a tolerable flow of public investment will have to give way to a structure which has the authority to make decisions about the region's transportation network, its broad pattern of land use, its common recreational facilities, the renewal of its obsolete sections, the contamination of its air and streams, and the preservation of nature's amenities. The system of representation — of individual citizens looking directly to one small government or to no government at all — will have to be replaced by a system which uses parties, pressure groups, professional politicians and executives and legislators elected on a regional basis — in short, by a modern democratic system. . . .

[3] Kirk R. Petshek, *Address* to the NAHRO Research Meeting on Urban Renewal and the Changing Urban Structure, May 15, 1958.

But this can happen only if the residents of the metropolitan area change their concept of local government and are prepared to accept a philosophy of positive and coordinate action in place of a "business as usual" and essentially competitive philosophy. Not until such a change in attitudes and convictions occurs can local governments adapt to the metropolitan age and grapple seriously with the problems of metropolitan growth. The customary criticisms that the present structure is administratively inefficient, financially inequitable, poorly organized, and unnecessarily expensive, are not sufficient to bring about this change in outlook. Only a recognition of the new responsibilities of local government will go to the heart of the difficulty: the fact that big governments and policy-minded governments are essential companions of big and complex economic systems.

Throughout this century, people have debated the question of whether or not the American political system could countenance an unbridled laissez-faire economy — whether it did not have to intervene by selective measures to redress the balance of competition, at times to preserve it, and at times to guide it. But in the modern metropolitan region, the question is reversed. The issue is whether or not a modern economic system, requiring positive stimulation and selective aid and direction by public authority, can tolerate an unbridled laissez-faire profusion of governments which systematically avoid any responsibility for these matters.

THE POLITICS
OF METROPOLITAN REFORM
5

Snarled traffic, polluted water, overtaxed educational systems, spreading slums, racial conflict — these and numerous other problems inevitably accompany urban growth and change. More and more people living in rapidly expanding metropolitan areas generate seemingly insatiable demands for more water, schools, highways, parks, and a score of other public facilities and services. Traffic congestion, water shortages, and overcrowded schools result primarily from the inability of hard-pressed local governments to keep up with growing demand. The unwillingness or inability of local taxpayers to foot the bill underlies deficiencies such as nonexistent or inadequate facilities for sewage treatment and for recreation. Another category of problems arises from the changing pattern of urban development: the decline of public transportation, ineffective ghetto schools, and the deterioration of older neighborhoods. Every one of these problems requires public action — the selection of policy alternatives, the raising of funds, and the implementation of plans. The fragmentation of the political system limits the ability of metropolitan governments to deal with most of these problems.

Prior to the sixties, metropolitan experts in the universities, planning groups, and civic associations agreed almost unanimously that the decentralized political system was the basic cause of many urban inadequacies and a critical hindrance to the solution of all the problems associated with growth and change. The metropolis, argued the metropolitan reformers, was a socioeconomic community lacking an inclusive set of political institutions. Problems arising from the social and economic interaction of the metropolis failed to respect the political boundaries that artificially divided the metropolitan community. Thus, almost every urban problem was a metropolitan problem that could not be effectively resolved by the fragmented political system, with its fiscal inequities and lack of comprehensive planning. The inadequacy of the structure of government, then, was the metropolitan problem. In local government textbooks, metropolitan surveys, and planning and civic bulletins, area-wide government was steadfastly promoted as the sure cure for the many ills of the metropolis.

By focusing on the structure of government, the metropolitan reformers carried on the tradition of municipal reform. Since their origins during the heyday of the boss and the machine, the forces of good government have sought to overcome the corruption, inefficiency, and excessive partisanship of city government through structural overhaul. In their quest for a political system that would serve the public interest — defined, of course, in terms of their own interests in economic and efficient government — the middle-class reformers promoted nonpartisanship, the city manager plan, the merit system, and many other reforms in the structure of local government. As urban development spread beyond the boundaries of the city, professors, planners, and civic leaders shifted their frame of reference, but not their basic approach. Economy, efficiency, and a "rational" government structure responsive to the general interests of the entire community remained the fundamental goals of reform. In dealing with the metropolis as in its efforts to improve the city, the good government alliance has been convinced that its values represent the general community interest. Remove the impediments to the expression of the public interest by reorganizing the fragmented political system, runs the reform argument, and the metropolis will be governed in the interest of the whole rather than in the conflicting interests of its many parts.

A typical example of the work of the metropolitan reformers is provided by the 1962 report of the Citizens Advisory Committee of the Washington legislature's Joint Committee on Urban Area Government. True to the reform tradition, the authors emphasize the interdependence of the metropolitan community, the inadequacies and inequities inherent in the fragmented political system, and the need for major structural changes to equip local governments to meet the challenges of metropolitan development.

Efforts to establish metropolitan governments have been a natural outgrowth of the research and preachings of the reformers. In the hundred-odd metropolitan areas where campaigns for area-wide government have been launched, the civic associations, planning agencies, and universities have provided most of the shock troops. Widespread support usually has come from the "big mules" of the central city: the bankers, merchants, downtown property owners, utility operators, and newspaper publishers, who hope metropolitan reform can save the central business district. Completing the membership in the reform camp are various metropolitan have-nots such as central city Republicans, suburban liberals, and ambitious young lawyers seeking publicity and political opportunities.

This alliance initiates the ritual of the campaign for metropolitan government. The metropolitan specialists, often supported by one or more of the foundations, solemnly catalog the units of government, evaluate services, compare costs and benefits, unearth inequities, and pinpoint a long list of deficiencies which can be corrected only by comprehensive planning and coordinated action. To no one's surprise, the expert survey produces a blueprint for the future featuring some sort of area-wide government. Most common have been proposals for the transformation of the county into a metropolitan government as in Miami (Dade County), Nashville (Davidson County), and Cleveland (Cuyahoga County). Alternatives are the creation of a metropolitan federation with delegated powers following the Toronto prototype or the establishment of a multipurpse metropolitan district as proposed in St. Louis and Seattle. After the survey comes the constitutional convention, a body whose name, composition, selection, and powers vary from state to state. The task of this consituent assembly is to settle on an official plan for metropolitan government. More often than not, the plan closely resembles that of the survey experts. Now the pace of the campaign quickens. Those somewhat incongruous revolutionaries, the middle class reformers and the downtown businessmen, go forth to convince the metropolis of the need for fundamental change in the political system. Almost always, the campaign ends on election day in a shattering defeat for the plans and dreams of the metropolitan reformers.

The readings in this chapter provide some answers to questions that arise from the sad history of metropolitan government. Why have more than a hundred attempts to overhaul the governmental structure of the metropolis produced so few successes that they can be counted on the fingers of one hand? Given the dismal record of metropolitan reform, how does one account for the creation of area-wide government in a few major metropolitan areas during the past two decades?

After examining the campaigns for regional government in St. Louis, Cleveland, and Miami, Scott Greer concludes that the reformers' problems arise in part from the difficulty they experience in applying the traditional themes of municipal reform to the metropolis. Most proposals either add a new layer of government as in the St. Louis District Plan or expand existing units, as was the case with Cuyahoga and Dade Counties. Units of government, elected posi-

tions, or political jobs are rarely eliminated. As a result, the municipal reformers have sallied forth onto the treacherous terrain of
metropolitan politics without their most effective weapon — the cry
of "throw the rascals out." Other good government themes such as
economy and efficiency and the need for "streamlined modern" government to ensure a bigger and better future metropolis lack the
political appeal of what Greer calls the "purification rites," particularly when the issues are complex, the savings to the local taxpayer
are obscure, and the benefits of change are dimly perceived.

Suburbia has been notoriously inhospitable to proposals for metropolitan government, and with good reason, argues Charles R. Adrian.
As he indicates, the tenets of "metropology" are an expression of the
interests of the downtown business leaders and the urban professionals — the planners, administrators, engineers, and other functional specialists. The "folklore," he contends, is largely irrelevant to
the values and interests of the average urban dweller, particularly in
the suburbs. Adrian sees the suburbanite as far more concerned with
his access to local government and its representativeness than with
efficiency and economy. Instead of comprehensive planning and
coordinated programs, he wants to maintain his control over the
local environment. Fearing unequal costs and benefits and a dilution
of his influence in a larger polity, he rejects the notion of a metropolitan community and proposals to provide it with an area-wide government.

The fact that suburbia usually votes against metropolitan government does not mean that the politics of revolution can be explained
as a simple city-suburban dichotomy. The metropolitan status quo
has a powerful appeal for many of the participants in the pluralist
politics of the central city. Politicians have no desire to see their
constituencies altered or their jobs disappear. Ward, labor, and
minority group leaders are understandably reluctant to see their
influence diluted by the creation of an area-wide government dominated by middle-class voters. Civil servants fear for their seniority,
pensions, and bureaucratic folkways. Even the pro-metro façade
among the city's economic interests proves to be fragile as businessmen with city contracts, favored positions, and other ties to the
status quo enlist in the growing ranks of the opposition. In a
fictional case study that reflects the experience of a number of
metropolitan areas, Paul Ylvisaker portrays a city in the throes of an
unsuccessful campaign for area-wide government.

Since 1957, these formidable obstacles to the creation of a metropolitan government have been overcome in Miami, Nashville, Jacksonville, and Indianapolis. None of these is among the most complex
metropolitan areas. Miami, the largest of the four, was the 25th rank-

ing metropolis in 1970, with a population of 1.26 million (up from 934,000 in 1960). Three of the four are in the South, where city-suburban differences traditionally have not been as pronounced as in the older urban areas of the Northeast and Midwest. In each case, special circumstances accounted for the success of the metropolitan reformers.

Miami, as Edward Sofen makes clear, is atypical in its politics, its economy, and its pattern of development. In the unorganized no-party politics of Miami, few of the countervailing forces that normally check the metropolitan reformers were present. Local political leaders were weak, political organizations nonexistent. Rapid population growth and turnover left few citizens with strong attachments to their communities. Elements that normally oppose meropolitan government such as organized labor and minority groups are politically ineffectual in Miami. Operating in this power vacuum, the standard alliance of downtown businessmen, civic leaders, central city newspapers, and public administration specialists carried the day. But even in Miami they barely mustered a majority, as only 51 per cent of the 87,000 voters (about one-quarter of the Dade County electorate) who went to the polls on May 21, 1957, voted for the metropolitan charter.

Conflict between politicians rather than its absence as in Miami was the critical factor in the creation of the Nashville-Davidson County metropolitan government in 1962. Four years earlier an area-wide government proposal had been defeated in a lackluster campaign despite the support of the central city mayor and the leading county politician. In 1962 the mayor and the county leader, long-time factional rivals, took contrary positions on a new metro proposal. With the mayor and his faction leading the opposition and the county organization supporting metro, far more political activity on the part of professional politicians resulted than normally occurs in campaigns for metropolitan government. Equally important, smoldering resentment in the suburbs over a series of aggressive annexations by Nashville brought the reformer's best weapon — the "purification rites" — into play. A vote for metro became a vote against Mayor Ben West and his city hall machine.

As in Nashville and Davidson County, the consolidation of Jacksonville and Duval County was facilitated by the absence of incorporated suburban municipalities, which reduced the number of vested interests in the status quo. The experience of Nashville and Jacksonville suggests that medium-size metropolitan areas outside the most heavily settled urban belts, which have relatively simple jurisdictional systems and which are encompassed by a single county, provide the best opportunities for metropolitan reformers. Using these criteria, reformers would not choose Indianapolis as a particularly good prospect for metropolitan government. Although the metropolitan area lies within Marion County, it is twice the size of Nashville or Jacksonville and more complex politically than Nashville, Jacksonville, or Miami. However, an unprecedented action of the Indiana legislature upset these calculations. Using the fundamental powers that a state government possesses over its local governments, the legislature ordered the consolidation of Indianapolis with Marion County with no provision for a popular referendum on the question.

Too few metropolitan governments have been in operation for too short a time to make any comprehensive assessment possible. In Miami, Metropolitan Dade County has streamlined an outmoded administrative structure, developed an area-wide plan and enforced uniform subdivision requirements, implemented county-wide traffic enforcement, and taken the first steps toward regional action in housing and transportation. But internal conflicts, inadequate tax resources, weak leadership, and repeated attempts by opponents to strip Metropolitan Dade County of its powers have limited the accomplishments of the nation's largest area-wide political jurisdiction. The experience in Nashville has been more encouraging. In his appraisal of Metro's first few years, Daniel Grant concludes that many of the expectations of the supporters of metropolitan government have been fulfilled and few of the fears of its opponents have materialized. In Grant's view, blacks have not been adversely affected by metropolitan government in Nashville. Nonetheless, black opposition to the development of area-wide government remains widespread in urban America. As Piven and Cloward point out (see pages 173–181), the attractiveness of metropolitan government has increased in areas in which suburbanites and central city businessmen perceive Metro as a means of depriving central city blacks of control of City Hall. In both Jacksonville and Indianapolis, the desire to dilute black political strength in an area-wide government contributed to the successful recent efforts to consolidate city and county.

Citizens Advisory Committee,
Joint Committee on Urban Area Government,
Legislature of the State of Washington

TOO MANY GOVERNMENTS

Local government in Washington was designed for a simpler day when people were fewer and the line between city and county was clear. It has grown by patchwork additions of cities and special purpose districts and is now a crazy quilt of overlapping jurisdictions, costly in higher taxes to the homeowner and businessman alike.

Most of the governmental units, like most of the people, are in the metropolitan areas. In King County there are now over 200 units, more than any other county in the United States except one. At least fifteen local units have been added in the last three years, and proceedings are now pending for the creation of three more small cities and a special purpose district. Similarly, in 1959, Spokane County had 135 units; Yakima, 119; Pierce and Snohomish, each 93; and Clark County, 44.

The profusion of "little governments" is well illustrated by the Highline School District, south of Seattle, whose 100,000 residents are governed, taxed, or served by King County, the school district, the Port of Seattle, four small cities (Kent, Tukwila, Des Moines and Normandy Park), eight sewer districts, eleven water districts, six fire districts, a library district, a road district, a drainage district and the County Housing Authority — thirty-six local governments, with over one hundred elected officials.

The suburbs east of Lake Washington show a similar patchwork of cities and special districts, with, for example, two islands of unincorporated territory inside the city of Bellevue, and twenty-six units of local government having jurisdiction over part or all of the Bellevue School District.

The Tacoma metropolitan area is following the same pattern, with Pierce County, 11 cities, and 57 districts electing 299 officials in the urbanized area.

The Spokane area adds townships to county, cities and districts, and

Reprinted by permission from *City and Suburb — Community or Chaos* (Report of Citizens Advisory Committee of the Joint Commitee on Urban Area Government), June 1962, pp. 4–9.

has special problems from the 43 domestic water suppliers of suburban Spokane.

A large urban area is more than the sum of its separate parts. It is a complex system for production, recreation, education, worship, play and rest. All its people share a common interest in the efficiency, order and livability of the whole. A dust producing manufacturing plant can be located in an industrial zone of one city adjacent to residences in the next. Poor streets in one area can shift traffic to another community ill prepared or situated for the load. Wastes from one community can pollute the waters or air of another. Residents of a densely populated area without parks can overcrowd the playgrounds and picnic spots of neighboring communities. Small sewage treatment plants side by side can unnecessarily raise everyone's costs. There is in economic and social fact a metropolitan community, but in government there is none.

Such fragmentation is sapping the strength of local government. No citizen, no matter how civic minded, can inform himself of the affairs of a dozen or more local governments. No voter can keep track of the performance of 50 or more local elected officials. Citizens have lost control of their local affairs when they are unable to place responsibility for faulty decisions or inaction.

Nor is this divided government responsive, for it cannot respond to major problems which ignore its boundary lines. Time, energy, and money are being wasted in mounting traffic congestion; water and air pollution grow; downtowns are in trouble, older neighborhoods blighted, and social problems rise. Each of the hundreds of local officials of the metropolitan area is alert to see that no action to remedy these ills falls too heavily on his jurisdiction; none is responsible to see that there *is* action. Frustrated by local inertia and confusion, the citizen turns increasingly to state and federal programs for urban needs.

Fragmentation damages the financial as well as the political health of local government. Traditionally it was assumed that a family lived, worked, shopped, and sent its children to school within the boundaries of one unit of local government. But such is rarely the case today, when, for example, a man living in Lynnwood may drive through Seattle to and from work at a plant in south King County, while his family shops in Everett. Property taxes on the family's house are paid to the city of Lynnwood and to Snohomish County, while the street, police and other costs of rush hour traffic are borne by the city of Seattle. The plant, moreover, pays property taxes neither to the city, county, nor school district which serves the employee's family, nor to the city whose facilities bring its worker to his job. Fragmentation of the metropolitan areas separates benefits and burdens in ways which are often basically unfair.

In general, it is the central cities which suffer most to provide extra streets, police protection, parks, libraries and other facilities for expanded daytime populations of suburban residents they cannot tax. There is, moreover, in our local property tax system a built-in inequity between city and county residents. City residents tax their property to pay for their police, parks, garbage dumps and other services; they are taxed again by the county partly to furnish some of these urban services for the residents of unincorporated areas. In King County, where property within the city of Seattle constitutes two-thirds of the county's assessed valuation, and property within all cities and towns constitutes four-fifths, city and town property owners are paying 80 cents of every dollar spent by the county on local urban services for tens of thousands of county residents. In 1962, this will amount to a subsidy of about $2,300,000 from Seattle property, about $2,775,000 from all the cities taken together. Ironically, elderly and low-income property owners struggling to rehabilitate their property in Seattle's Yesler-Atlantic urban renewal area are subsidizing residents of expensive suburban communities.

A similar inequity appears to exist in other populous counties where the county general fund supports police protection, local parks, garbage dumps and other urban services for densely settled unincorporated areas. In Pierce County, city of Tacoma property is 54% of the total assessed valuation, and property within all cities and towns represents 63.4%; in Spokane County, corresponding figures for the city of Spokane and all cities are 62.8% and 65%, respectively. In these counties, as in King, city property owners pay most of the cost of the local urban services received by county residents from the county general fund.

To function, an urban community must move people and goods quickly and economically between areas for work, recreation and rest. Transportation is everybody's problem — the downtown merchant wants easier movement for his shoppers and places for them to park; city residents are taxed to pay for wide arterials used to capacity only twice a day; the manufacturer suffers higher costs from late employees, delayed raw materials, slow deliveries, and valuable land tied up in parking lots; the distributor needs extra salesmen to serve the urban area. Suburban residents spend precious hours meant for children and gardens in autos and buses on congested highways and bridges, wasting the gain of shorter working hours on longer travel time. For many, commuting is a twice daily ordeal through a miles-long alley of used car lots, junk yards, service stations and billboards. To all of us, inadequate transportation means higher costs of what we buy.

For years transportation in our metropolitan areas has meant more and more automobiles, more and still more highways, fewer and still fewer riders on public buses, longer and longer commuting times. We have only to look at Los Angeles to see the futility of sole reliance on the automobile-highway answer. There, over two billion dollars have been spent on freeways, and the automobile has consumed two-thirds of the downtown land for highways, streets, and parking facilities — without ending congestion.

The peak hours are the critical times, the times which overtax facilities, pocketbooks, nerves and patience. There is growing agreement that we must supplement the automobile with improved mass transportation, growing recognition that capital facilities of such a system will require tax support from the whole "commuter shed," growing realization that other alternatives are still more costly.

It is now too late to design mass transit facilities into Seattle's 175 million dollar central freeway or the 30 million dollar Evergreen Point Bridge, but this lack of coordination should not be allowed to continue. We cannot afford more single purpose structures when multiple needs must be met. About half a billion dollars will be spent by the state, county, and cities in King County in the next decade on highways and bridges, many of which are presently being designed. They must be planned and coordinated for the requirements of a mass transit system as well as private automobiles. There is, however, no unit of government presently making such plans, none coordinating state and local activities into a balanced urban transportation system.

Of all the problems of the metropolitan area, none is more urgent than the acquisition of parks and recreation sites and the preservation of other open land. In the words of a recent editorial, we are witnessing a "voracious gulping of the land," an urban sprawl so rapid that if present suburban land use patterns continue, the more than one million additional people expected in King County by the end of this century could fill it from Puget Sound to the foothills of the Cascades.

Recreational use of land is growing even faster than population, for we have more leisure time each year, more opportunity to enjoy walking, boating, sports and family outings. For parks and waterfront, however, we are living largely on the generosity of our parents and grandparents. Seattle's 315,312 people of 1920 had 2,209 acres of parks, about 144 persons per park acre; its 558,000 people of 1960 had only 2,646 park acres, or 211 persons per acre. In the suburbs where population has boomed since World War II, local park acquisition has not kept pace with population growth. King County's recent purchase of Marymoor Farm adds its first new large park to serve the entire area in many years. Public support of this purchase shows the rising awareness of open space needs.

The Spokane and Tacoma urban areas must also act now to preserve parks, waterfront, and other accessible open land for the thousands of new residents coming each year. The city of Spokane has many large parks, almost all acquired half a century ago, but there are already few sites of ten acres or more left in the fast growing valley to the east. In the Tacoma suburbs, too, concern over parks is rising. But action is slow in coming, and action cannot be delayed. Each piece of land is unique; once developed, it is lost to the general public. Indeed, experience shows that park land must be acquired beyond the developed areas, for land prices rise quickly once subdivision begins nearby.

Washington's large urban communities are peculiarly blessed with forests, lakes, and mountain views. But woodlands can be cut, lakes shut off from public access, views blocked. The first resident of a hillside may enjoy watching the construction of a house in the valley below, but he is shocked as woods and farms change to rooftops, wires, and television antennae. The fisherman is not concerned over the first summer house along his favorite stream, but is confused and angry when a solid row of houses blocks him from the banks. Our grandparents looked ahead to keep green space, beaches and beauty for us, but our vision has been short in recent times. We are taking our landscape for granted; its beauty is being mined, not tended.

Like transportation and open land, the provision of clean water, the disposal of wastes, and the preservation of clean air are tasks increasingly difficult for each local unit to perform. Seattle's water lines and Seattle Metro's sewage disposal plan demonstrate, however, the effectiveness and economy of metropolitan-wide systems. Both have anticipated the needs of an entire urban area; both demonstrate that metropolitan problems can be solved when attacked comprehensively, and with the courage to plan for decades ahead.

Seattle brings pure mountain water from the Cascades at low cost to about 735,000 people of the metropolitan area, serving not only its residents, but selling wholesale water to thirty water districts and municipalities as well. Present projects, when fully developed, will guarantee mountain water for a future metropolitan population of more than two million. In contrast, the city of Tacoma brings its water from the Green River watershed of the Cascades but does not supply the needs of its suburbs. The nearby community of University Place suffers from inadequate water supply and distribution. A metropolitan-wide system would benefit Tacoma and its suburbs alike.

There is a natural water supply under most of the Spokane metropolitan area which is easily reached by wells. As a result, there are forty-three domestic water distributors in suburban Spokane. Many of these districts, co-ops, and companies are doing an excellent job within their areas, but duplication of facilities, differing pipe sizes and pressures, and no means for systematic interconnection are shortcomings paid for by suburban residents in increased costs, sometimes inadequate service, and higher fire insurance rates.

Sewage disposal presents a still gloomier story in which the structural defects of fragmented local government are sharply exposed. In King County, before establishment of the Municipality of Metropolitan

Seattle, raw sewage was being discharged into the Duwamish River, Elliott Bay and Puget Sound at about sixty places, and ten to fifteen million gallons of treated and untreated wastes went into Lake Washington every day. Effluent from thousands of malfunctioning septic tanks was rising to ground surface and, in some areas, flowing in open ditches. Health agencies necessarily stopped construction in some areas, while elsewhere citizens invested millions of dollars in septic tanks which became more inadequate each day.

Within the metropolitan areas, not a single foot of salt water shoreline, and very little fresh water, was safe for recreational use. Lake Washington was degraded and rapidly approaching permanent impairment from algal growth. In brief, water resources were being ruined, health dangers created, orderly growth stunted, millions of dollars wasted, but even after years of discussion, the nineteen cities and twenty-two sewer districts of the Lake Washington watershed could not agree on any joint solution. Fragmented government could not act.

Only state enabling legislation for a metropolitan-wide unit and the voters' establishment of the Municipality of Metropolitan Seattle saved this appalling situation. Since its formation in 1958, Seattle Metro has planned and is now constructing a trunk sewer and treatment system for the entire Lake Washington watershed, a system which will end pollution in the watershed over the next ten years, most of it in the next five. The Metro trunk lines will also permit cities and districts throughout the area to develop orderly and economical sewer systems during the next 75 to 100 years.

Danger signals are growing now in the Spokane metropolitan area where more than 200,000 people literally live on top of their water supply. Blessed by nature with a giant underground river of clean water flowing slowly from the Idaho border beneath valley and city until it empties into the Spokane River, the metropolitan community may spoil this magnificent asset by pollution. The 181,000 people of the city of Spokane discharge wastes through sewers and treatment plant to a spot downstream on the Spokane River. The 46,500 residents of the Valley, however, have only septic tanks draining through gravel and boulders toward the water below. New people arrive every day, new septic tanks are built, and the concentration of effluent in the earth increases. Health authorities have repeatedly warned citizens and local officials that action should begin now, for once pollution is discovered, it will be too late. The water, if contaminated, will not be pure again for years.

Here, also, fragmented government poses barriers to action. The city of Spokane has no jurisdiction in the Valley; neither county nor township has authority to build sewers; and a proper answer might require action by the entire metropolitan community. Everyone's water supply is threatened, but "everyone" has no government to act.

Tacoma has sewers and treatment plants adequate to handle its own problems of sewage disposal, but problems are accumulating in the suburbs. The drainage area around Lake Steilacoom and that of Clover Creek are reaching an acute state in which not even treated sewage can be safely added. The Lakewood area has problems ahead. There is a clear need for a comprehensive sewage system in the Tacoma area, but there is no unit of government authorized to construct or finance such a system.

Wastes of the urban community not buried in the earth or discharged into the waters are thrown into the air. Tons of material go up daily from thousands of smokestacks, chimneys, exhaust pipes and incinerators. Serious health, agricultural, economic and nuisance effects results — a heavy burden of respiratory ills, dirty buildings, expensive air purification systems, crop damage and cleaning bills.

Air pollution grows with population, and public patience is already growing short. In December 1961, 1,323 residents of Tacoma and Pierce County petitioned the Governor to put a stop to air pollution from a smelter in the city of Ruston, surrounded by Tacoma. Angry housewives of South Seattle forced an end to city burning of refuse at the South Park dump. On February 1, 1962, air pollution made front page headlines in Seattle, for air and sunlight conditions brought serious smog to the Puget Sound region and a new record of air pollution. Smog is rare in western Washington, but the stable air and abundant sunlight of the Spokane area lend themselves to its formation.

That a serious problem exists is clear. Equally clear is the inadequacy of present efforts to manage the problem. Seattle and Tacoma have modest pollution control ordinances, but air does not respect city boundaries. Pollution control districts were authorized by the Legislature some years ago, but none has been established to date. No authority exists, moreover, for applying controls within any jurisdiction which does not voluntarily agree.

Blight in cities, inadequate services in the suburbs, jammed highways, polluted water and air — these are warning signals of sickness in our urban communities. The cure for these ills lies, in the first instance, in major changes in the finances, structure, and powers of local government. Also essential are an informed and active citizenry and good men in office, but they are not enough, for the present structure defeats the efforts of citizens and officials alike. Good men with poor tools work hard to produce little; good men with good tools accomplish much for all.

Scott Greer

THE MORALITY PLAYS
OF METROPOLITAN REFORM

... Movements aimed at achieving overall metropolitan government ... are efforts to make revolutions, bloodless to be sure, but far
from pacific and rational. Each plan proposes a radical change in the
division of power, rewards, and labor in the governance of the metropolis.
Each proposes basic changes in the structure of control and in the process
by which controllers are recruited. They are minor in the sense that they
are proposed within the broad framework of constitutional, democratic,
local government. (Each of them assumes a referendum.) Furthermore,
they are minor insofar as they are local and segmental, referring only to a
part of a local polity, which is, in turn, extremely dependent on the state
and federal government levels.

Some people, however, take them very seriously indeed and have
elaborate arguments supporting their involvement as well as the particular
positions they take upon the issues. We wish, first, to look at these
arguments in terms of certain broad norms of government,
understandable to a wide array of political actors in the society. We have
called these complexes "morality plays," for they are typically dramatic in
tone, self-contained in aims, and archetypal in form; they represent
vocabularies with which men may converse about common interests or
disputes. ...

The morality plays of American civic life ... seldom transcend the
formally governmental. Their emphasis is, again and again, upon the
structure of government: the integration of different municipalities, the
structural change of country governments, improved public personnel
policies, and so forth. Rarely do we see a morality play that attempts to
unite the enormous engines of private corporate enterprise (and *their*
policies) to those of the public enterprise. Urban renewal is such a play.
In short, the common culture of metropolitan reform, the morality plays
that allow the actors to organize and speak to the citizens, can be seen as
a set of blinders. They reveal certain aspects of the metropolitan area at
the cost of suppressing many others.

Reprinted from *Metropolitics* (New York: John Wiley, 1963), pp. 1–4, 6–10,
13–18, by permission of the author and John Wiley & Sons, Inc.

. . . The inherited morality plays of American civic life may be seen as a conservative tradition of radical reform, conservative in the procedures used in change but radical in the consequences expected. In these dramas, innovators struggle to apply new definitions of broad norms to the specific machinations and actions of their local governments. Out of the conflict between their notions of what should be, derived from these sacred rubrics, they criticize what is. Struggling to change the cities, these innovators emphasize the form of the charters — the constitutions of the cities. (As Adrian has remarked of the National Municipal League: "In its 'model' charters and laws, its booklets and pamphlets, it made available to local groups ammunition that included all of the most recently developed reform favorites.")[1] They frequently go to the voters with their innovations, because of the broader norms of the democratic system.

The movement to improve local government in America has typically dealt with administration and representation. It has aimed at the exclusion of ordinary business interests from the motivations of political officials, at the broadening of the electorate so that the public interest may be represented, at the increased coordination and efficiency possible with professionalism and centralization of local government. Urban home rule, the city manager system, the nonpartisan election (or proportional representation), election at large, the "strong executive," have been some of the specific aims of the movement.

To be sure, not all of these formulas are now in favor with all urban reformers. The general approach has permeated downwards, however, through many strata of the opinionated. We may imagine the public for local government to be a pyramid, with the technical innovators at the top, then the congeries of educated, middle-class men of good will (and ladies, particularly those in The League of Women Voters), the lawyers with vested interests in the subject, and finally the interested citizens. In general, change at the peak of the pyramid does not affect the lower echelons for many years. Thus the technical innovators are bound to the inherited vocabulary because of its utility in communicating with their publics. . . .

Anselm Strauss has recently documented the ideological resistance of Americans to their urbanization. He shows us clearly the resistance of many kinds of people to the living conditions of a great city.[2] Americans have not easily accepted the concentration of poverty and blight typical of the center city as their ecological home. The "city beautiful"

---

[1] Charles R. Adrian, *Governing Urban America*, New York: The McGraw-Hill Book Company, 1955, page 60.
[2] Anselm Strauss, *Images of the American City*, Glencoe, Ill.: The Free Press, 1961.

movement of the past, the urban renewal program today, indicate support for a movement to transform the earthly city into the Heavenly City. Equally long-standing and just as impressive has been the struggle to reform the politics of the central city — to take government away from those who regard it as a business, a hunting license for a peculiar kind of game, and turn it into a process as responsible as our idealized memory of the New England townships, as efficient as our stereotypes of the corporate headquarters.[3]

The key arena has been government. The earlier battles for civic reform concentrated on the problems of the central city, for the city's boundaries included reformers and reformees, just as its powers were the key powers for corruption, achievement, change, or stasis. However, the governmental boundaries have shifted greatly with the continuous growth of the city and the outward move of the middle class. Those who care about urban reform are usually suburban in their residence. Robert Wood has noted the congruence of the socially homogeneous, small-scale suburban community with the dream of the "republic in miniature."[4] Though Americans have, willy-nilly, become a preponderantly urban people, they have refused to accept an image of the megalopolis as their true home. Instead, they have endeavored to transform the conditions of the great city into "garden towns" — and have, in the suburbs, come close to achieving their aims. The American middle class, in trying to make itself at home in the urban area, has solved many problems by developing suburban neighborhoods separated from the central city by governmental walls.

But other problems have been created in the process. We need not review the consequences of the suburban hegira for the polity of the urban area as a whole; they have been discussed many times by knowledgeable observers.[5] Let us say in summary that the consequence of governmental proliferation at the municipal level has been to aggravate problems of providing public services, determining equity, and planning for the future. Furthermore, the proliferation of municipalities has prevented development of a polity that might face these problems in any systematic or effective way. These considerations are at the roots of what has been called, in a phrase, "the metropolitan problem." Middle-class persons who were usually those most concerned with governmental reform in the older city solved their personal problems by removing to suburbia. In the process they were also achieving the political dismember-

[3] Adrian, op. cit.
[4] Robert C. Wood, Suburbia, Its People and Their Politics, Boston: Houghton-Mifflin, 1959.
[5] For a recent example see Exploring the Metropolitan Community, ed. John Bollens, Berkeley and Los Angeles: University of California Press, 1961.

ment of the social city. The ghosts of old pieties return to haunt some consciences in suburbia.

These ghosts all speak for an image of the city as a unity. And indeed, there is a plausibility in the notion that our contemporary metropolitan areas, despite their hundreds of governments, are still unitary. They represent one local labor market, one housing market, one transport and communication system: they are interdependent in many ways. But in one major way they are different from the city of the past: their governmental boundaries do not include all of the interdependent, problem-generating population. Thus the morality plays that defined the civic problems of the past are still usable: they are simply shifted to a larger stage — the sprawling urban complex which crosses political boundaries of many cities and counties. But now a first condition for resolving the older conflicts in old ways becomes the integration of local government. Seen not as an end in itself, but as a means to older ends, metropolitan government comes to represent a "one best way" to solve many traditional urban problems.

Definitions of these traditional urban problems may be usefully grouped around three kinds of morality plays. Each is as old as urban reform and as American as apple pie. The first is the Purification Ritual, or "Throw the rascals out!" The second might be called the drama of "Capitalist Realism," in which rational men strive to modernize "horse-and-buggy" government. The third is that of fertility and the future: "Progress or Decay! Our City Must Choose!" Each of these plays has a basic cast — heroes, villains, and innocent bystanders. Each has an end in view and a demon in view. Each script assumes the sacrosanctness of the reform and the efficacy of the means to achieve it: all imply that political validation is the one key for opening the way to the Heavenly City.

Purification Rites. In his study of the history of British town planning, William Ashworth attributes public concern for slum clearance, civic beautification, and planning to one major source: middle-class anxiety over disease and crime in the slums.[6] A great deal of the American middle class's concern for local government has been connected with anxieties aroused by evils that threaten their person and pocketbook: the corruption of political office holders, the judges who "sell their eyes," the working relationship between police and criminals known as "the fix."

A typical morality play of Purification begins with indictment of the villains, politicians who have used politics as a business. *The Shame of the Cities* was written by Lincoln Steffens in 1904, but in the late 1950's a national magazine devoted an issue to "The Shame of New York"; the

[6] William Ashworth, *The Genesis of Modern British Town Planning,* London: Routledge and Kegan Paul, 1954.

villains remain the same: party politicians, elected officials, policemen, judges. The heroes are typically reform candidates (or officials) playing the role of "Mr. District Attorney." The demon in view is the threat that "the gangsters will take over the city," that public morality will collapse, that safety of person and property will go by the board. The end in view is the elimination of the corrupt from public office — "surgery" — and their replacement with the upright. These themes recur ad infinitum in American civic dramatics. Through time, the major change has been the belief that the political system as a whole is evil, and thus we have the efforts to invent a bureaucracy which will be self-correcting and which will eliminate the corrupt, even as it rewards the just.

Capitalist Realism. The effort to create a self-correcting system is closely allied to the effort to modernize local government. Here the civic demons appear as statistics. The statistics show waste and inefficiency. They show overlapping jurisdictions, confusion of responsibility, and lack of responsibility. They show incompetent men in important offices, competent men bypassed in the decision-making process. The drama has its roots in the speed of change in American society at large, contrasted with the slow pace of governmental change. It is a theme from Dickens or Galsworthy: government remains in chancery, while great problems wait outside the courtroom.

The villains are those who oppose progress, for whatever reason. Their commitment to the status quo gives rise to various imputations of dishonesty, malfeasance, or simple stupidity. And the heroes are technicians who are experts in government, businessmen who want to see government run at least as well as the business corporation. From the early efforts to get rid of bicameral legislatures in the cities to the most recent efforts to introduce performance budgets and "scientific personnel management," the drama has been that of mechanical revision, resisted tooth and nail by those who benefit from the status quo. It is the attack of the twentieth century on ox-cart government.

The beast in view is the possibility of astronomical costs for little gain, increasingly inadequate services, or breakdowns in such important jobs as police protection and sewerage. The increasing tax bill and the declining service payoff are the bogeys. The aim seems to be to "take garbage collection out of politics" and to turn government into the large-scale public business it should be. Triumph is the achievement of rationality: a perfected bureaucracy operated by professionally trained managers and judged as a business concern.

Fertility and the Future. There is a civic patriotism as old as the planting of new cities, a commitment to hallowed ground. In America, where cities sprang up from the prairie and proliferated with the spread of the railroad, every crossroad hamlet has aspired to be the "Chicago of

Wyoming," the "Metropolis of the Permian basin." The great plains and the deserts are littered with the bones of would-be metropolitan communities.[7]

Such cities were efforts to get rich quick. Their pioneers were entrepreneurs, and their slogan was "Boost, don't knock!" Their fortunes were measured by the increase in population, carloadings, and bank accounts. New building, any new building, was a sign of prosperity for all. This civic drama has always assumed a biological metaphor with growth as the good and decay as the horrible alternative. And growth is a result of massing what exists so that more may exist in the future. (Witness the outcry in Chicago when the Bureau of the Census decided to treat the Indiana portion of that metropolitan area as a separate unit.) "Boosterism" reflects a synthesis of the economic man's wish to improve his market and the civic patriot's identification with his city as home.

The heroes of such a drama are the "forward-looking, aggressive civic leaders," who want to make this city "the greatest center of paper-box manufacturing in the country." They act by organizing, building, advertising, allowing more room for growth (and hence, presumably, room at the top). The villains are those who have an unassailable position in the status quo, who resist change. Like the politician who prefers to lose an election rather than to lose control of his party, they would rather see the city remain stable. Every large city has its mythology about the "five families who own this town and don't want to see it change." But the beast in view is the spectacle of the town declining, losing ground in national rank orders. The fear is that of a shrinking market and a backward, physically unpleasant scene for living. . . .

These morality plays each influenced the definition of the metropolitan government as it was presented to the citizens in St. Louis, Cleveland, and Miami. The conservative tradition of reform in local affairs set the limits within which the plans were drafted, and within which their salient characteristics were defended.

In these three cities those who drafted the new charters envisaged a federal system in which existing units of government would be preserved. The new metropolitan government was seen as a vehicle to achieve what could not be done with the existing fragmented system. The radical nature of the departure was minimized, for the new plans did not attack *existing* governments so much as the existing "metropolitan system" of government. The morality of Purification was, in general, ignored. Nobody fighting for the plans could exploit the old slogan "Throw the rascals out!" The drafters of the plans seemed to assume that all were

[7] For a fascinating local history of such a would-be city see Wallace Stegner's *Wolf Willow*.

victims of the historical lag between government and the growing urban area.

The reasons for omitting the Purification Ritual have been as follows. First, in St. Louis and Cuyahoga, there was genuine belief in the integrity of existing governments *within their limits*. The long-term effort to tame municipal politics through professional management and civil service had been relatively successful in these cities. In Dade County there had been some extreme dissatisfaction with the government of Miami.[8] The belief in the integrity of existing government combined, in St. Louis and Cleveland, with a desire to neutralize the political parties, since it was thought that they might defeat any charter that threatened their organization and patronage systems. The campaigns deliberately avoided antagonizing the party chieftains. At most the supporters of the plans said "we will give you administration by experts, under elected officials responsible to the voters."

The metropolitan movement is, then, squarely in the tradition of capitalist realism. The organizational merging of the multifarious local governments for areawide services, the emphasis on metropolitan area planning and zoning, the predominance of appointed rather than elected heads for the great bureaucracies, all point to the image of technical efficiency as a goal. The Dade County plan even went so far as to specify an appointed county manager for the metropolitan area, and in both St. Louis and Cuyahoga County the issue of an elected versus an appointed head was the source of ideological conflict from study commission to voter. The vision of a new, bright, freshly painted and efficient government was presented to the voters. As a minor theme, in each area the increased "home rule" which would accrue to the metropolitan county or district was noted. This was most important in Dade County, which had been largely dominated from the state capital in Tallahassee. In St. Louis and Cleveland a large degree of home rule already existed and the theme was not very important in these campaigns.

The Fertility Ritual was a major element in each city. In St. Louis particularly, the consciousness of "decay" and the desire to continue a supposed "renaissance" was a crucial part of the campaign. In Miami, the dependence upon tourism and retirement and the assumed relationship between these economic assets and local services is given credit by one observer for almost all of the interest manifested in Metro by the business community and the civic leaders.[9] In one of the major pieces of

---

[8] "People really believed the hair-raising stories that you heard about the police sitting around with their feet on the tables, reading the scratch sheets with direct wires to the books." (*Interview Protocol* with a major executive in the mass media.) The Kefauver Committee supplied some evidence for such beliefs.

[9] Reinhold P. Wolff, *Miami Metro*, Coral Gables, Fla.: Bureau of Business and Economic Research, 1960.

campaign literature distributed by supporters of the St. Louis District Plan, economic development occupies the center of the stage.

All surveys . . . show that our area is losing out to Kansas City, Chicago, Memphis, Dallas, and other places in attracting wealth-producing industry and commerce . . . By voting for the District Plan, we can start to return to our rightful place — as the major Mid-American district between the Atlantic and the Pacific.[10]

And how was this to be achieved? We quote from the same leaflet:

The District Plan will give us a chance to plan for the entire city-country area — not just one part at a time — so that industry, commerce, and residential developments can be located where they belong without destroying property values. It will set up a means for private and public groups to work together — to plan and assemble industrial parks — away from residential areas — to offer new industry at cost. And by eliminating some of our other problems, such as the traffic mess, we'll have a chance to compete successfully for new business, and thousands of new jobs, which helps *everyone*.[11]

In short, the metropolitan government was a new means to old ends — economic prosperity, a better market for the individual, and a better city for the average resident.

These movements for metropolitan government relied heavily on two of the traditional morality plays of American civic life. Each emphasized the need to modernize local government through job analysis, coordination, and realignment of boundaries. Each offered improved services to the citizens as a reason for doing so. Each promised improvement in the local economy and, therefore, the value of the city as a place in which to work and to live.

If the public is accustomed to a given morality in the rhetoric of reform, that morality's absence will be quickly noted. The decision *not* to attack incumbent officials and existing governments for their incompetence and inability weakened the hands of the crusaders. Mounting an offensive which did in fact threaten many alignments and jobs (each plan took important powers away from municipal officials, and the Cuyahoga plan even dispensed with Civil Service safeguards), the plans provoked hostility from key members of the establishment without providing any ammunition to return their fire.

The head of a major department in the city of Cleveland gleefully related the advantage he had in fighting against the Cuyahoga County Charter.

I'd say to them, "Say — what's wrong with the present situation? You got a good government. What's wrong? Show me?" I'd get right down to specifics — "what's been done wrong?"

[10] "Some Plain Answers to Questions about the Greater St. Louis City-County District Plan," St. Louis: City-County Partnership Committee, 1959.
[11] *Ibid.*

Bypassing the elected representatives of the status quo thus pulled a key member out of the morality plays' structure. It left the elected officials blameless and free to attack the new plan from the rostrum of public office. (This made logical sense, however, if it was only the lack of a *single* system that was at fault.) As we shall see, this decision had important consequences for the campaigns in St. Louis and Cleveland.

The elimination of the Purification Ritual also affected the plausibility of the efficiency engineering approach. The decision to leave all municipalities in existence made the plans extremely vulnerable to those who felt that the existence of a multitude of governments was a handicap in attaining good governance. The first reason given by Mayor Tucker in his first speech opposing the District Plan hinged on this belief.

> The proposed metropolitan District Plan does not eliminate one existing area government — with the exception of its absorption of the metropolitan sewer district.
>
> The 99 country municipalities, the 21 fire districts, the separate City and County, and all the rest remain. Each of them is unimpaired in its present tax-levying authority.[12]

In St. Louis, the District Plan suffered from this further debility — it really added an additional government to the ones in existence. Though the other two plans escaped this through using existing county governments as bases for the metropolitan district, each was vulnerable to the attacks of purists who wished to see radical surgery on the governmental proliferation in the area.

The morality of "capitalist realism" suffered also from the tendency of the pro-Metro leaders to tell the truth. Instead of promising savings through increased efficiency, many of them tended to emphasize the *increase in services* possible through a Metro government. Again, this was less true of Dade County. There the leaders of the revolution were prone to hold out the carrot of lower taxes (though privately they believed Metro could only attack the area-wide service problems through increased taxation). In St. Louis, the protagonists tried to counter the "higher taxes" argument by showing that the plan would increase the fertility of the region and therefore its tax yield at existing rates.

The Fertility Ritual was not in basic conflict with the efficiency engineering and did not suffer from the absence of the Purificatory Rites. It did suffer, however, from its abstract and novel nature. While citizens are accustomed to hortatory slogans to "buy local," to "boost St. Louis," and the like, they are not used to the rather intricate arguments supporting metropolitan government as a source of future fertility. First, the argument moves from unknown to unknown — from land-use plan-

---

[12] Mayor Raymond F. Tucker, St. Louis: for release 7:00 P.M. Saturday, October 3, 1959.

ning to plant location — and finally to greater local prosperity, lower taxes, and better services. Second, and perhaps more important, the possibility of land-use planning depends on the *time element*. Comprehensive land-use planning has never been popular or popularly understood, for it requires a knowledge of the effects of present political acts upon consequences many years in the future. This is the dilemma of those who see most present problems as produced by past planning failures: to change present planning requires that they use, as evidence, the very complex chain of events from lack of past planning to the contretemps of today. Metropolitan government, in the context of the Fertility Rites, presents a complex *answer* to people who have never understood the *questions* — much less asked them.

In summary: the metropolitan morality play leaned heavily on two earlier plots. It omitted the most familiar of all and the one with the greatest "box office" appeal — "throw the rascals out." Omission of this theme greatly weakened the most clearly understood argument that was used — "Get rid of ox-cart government" — for it left the status quo standing. While the efficiency engineering approach and the Fertility Ritual were mutually reinforcing, the latter was largely outside the conventional realm of discourse. The chief argument shared by the rebels and the general public was that of mechanical progress aimed at greater service benefits. It was weakened by a "live and let live" philosophy with respect to the existing municipalities. It was strengthened by demand for better services. It used the older drama of boosterism, though many did not understand the plot.

Within this metropolitan morality play the protagonists of reform organized themselves and made sense of their proposal to create a revolution in urban government. They defined their roles as crusaders for a new "one best way" to achieve the Heavenly City. They defined their enemies as the protectors of separatism, in bond to the status quo (leaving, however, the "dark man" of professional politics as an ambiguous character). The cadres were developed, the struggle was joined, and eventually the voters were approached, in this vocabulary.

Charles R. Adrian

SUBURBIA AND THE FOLKLORE OF METROPOLOGY

Metropology, as the minions of Henry Luce should by now have dubbed the study of metropolitan areas, is an infantile disorder among the social sciences. Its victims are deep in the agonies that were experienced by political science a generation ago when that field was torn between those who thought that students of government should be practitioners of reforms and those who took the word "science" seriously. Related to these agonies is the fact that academic municipal reformers of some years back drew their programs largely from the goals of a segment of the business community that wanted to apply "business principles" to local government. They did not seek to expand the horizons of knowledge by empirical examination of the assumptions of the business leaders. Similarly, much metropology since 1945 has dealt with efforts to propagandize on behalf of efficiency and economy goals. In neither period of urban history — before or after 1945 — has the problem of local democracy been the central focus of the participating academics. Significantly, the municipal reformers and the students of "metropolitan area problems" also have had in common a working relationship with businessmen who are "civic leaders." Although the urban planners — members of a profession — are accustomed to working with such persons, social scientists — members of academia — have not been. This has been especially true of political scientists. The others who study metropology — the economists perhaps excepted — have only a bit more experience and probably no more acceptance by the business community.

So an alliance was formed between those who had money and believed they had problems — the business leaders — and those who craved social recognition and its pecuniary perquisites — the planners and professors. It is not surprising that this alliance produced in the years before and just after World War II "studies" and "reports" that for the most part emphasized the absence of long-range, metropolitan-wide planning, that

Reprinted from "Metropology: Folklore and Field Research" by Charles R. Adrian, *Public Administration Review*, the journal of the American Society for Public Administration, Vol. XXI, No. 2 (Summer 1961), pp. 148–153, by permission of the author and publisher.

counted the number of fire departments in an area, and deplored "unnecessary" duplications of services. A generation after Pearl Harbor had signalled the beginning of the nth urbanization movement in the United States, the shelves of city hall offices were groaning with moth-eaten and mildewed reports — reports that were not acceptable to the political decision makers because they were unacceptable to their constituents. It was not just that those who had financed and conducted the studies had sometimes mistakenly assumed that their truths were self-evident; a more serious cause of rejection centered in their almost total lack of concern with the political process and the probable ignorance of their authors of the fact that a democratic public is a "satisficing" public and not one concerned with optimum economy . . .

Many men who are regarded as "civic leaders" in America's larger cities began reaching for the panic button [in 1960]. They were joined by the municipal "pros" — city managers, chamber of commerce secretaries, mayors, and local civic-research directors. The alarm, of course, resulted from a good look 'at the 1960 census figures. These showed that an impressively large number of our metropolitan core cities had gained little or had actually lost population in the preceding decade. Former residents had retreated to the suburbs. Community newcomers of the middle classes — the now-famous "organization men" — had scarcely glanced at the central-city areas as they scurried to the suburbs looking for housing. The population losses in the huge core cities caught practically no one off guard. New York lost nearly one-quarter million people, Detroit took a 10 per cent cut, but no one was very surprised. It was in the smaller core cities — those under 200,000 population — where the shockers took place. Leaders in many of these areas thought their cities were gaining population nicely — they had local estimates to "prove" it. But dozens of Altoonas and Muskegons now find themselves in the same mold with the largest core cities — they have not gained; many have lost population. These findings need not have been unnerving to the local boosters. But they were.

The indignant cries of disbelief, the calls for immediate annexations, the demands for recounts, all stem from the fact that the 1960 census documents a trend that stomps underfoot in cruel fashion some of the dearest values of civic boosters and of some students of metropology. It is difficult for them to accept the trend as a normal part of the growth of a mobile population based on an industrial society. The folklore that many civic leaders have taken to be gospel does not permit them to accept "the trend of social and economic forces" as an explanation. Many of the leaders who formulate and guide the policies of our larger communities hold to beliefs that are based on a whole series of unrealistic assumptions about how metropolitan areas can and should be governed. Collectively, these assumptions represent the folklore that determines in large part the policy statements found in the reports of chamber of commerce committees, "citizens' committees" on metropolitan-area problems, and local government research bureaus. There were a spate of metropolitan-area studies after the results of the 1950 census became known. Now 1960 should spur defenders of the community image on to even greater efforts. They will be seeking "solutions" to the "metropolitan problem." They will call for studies, as they did after 1950, and they will expect them to rest upon the following generally accepted assumptions.

There is the belief that the core city of a metropolitan area must "expand or die" — the notion is widespread that there is no such thing as prosperous stability for a community. The idea is that central cities become socially and economically obsolescent faster if they have no expansion space within their boundaries. It assumes that the entire metropolitan area must grow and that the core city must grow at a near-equal rate — growth being measured by population. The argument is a favorite of local persons who have a financial stake in expansion — editors, chamber of commerce staff members, downtown merchants, city managers — and also serves to placate businessmen's anxieties concerning a tax base, or tax advantages to businesses beyond the municipal limits. The policy demands of this municipal application of the geo-politician's *lebensraum* theory usually take the form of plans for annexation of all of the urbanized hinterland, or of the creation of some kind of an "upper-tier" metropolitan-wide government.

The concept of growth is probably a product of our American culture which developed from the frontier where population growth was invariably associated with "progress" — progress against the Indians and forest, and in favor of Western civilization. It overlooks the fact that the real challenge in municipal policy today is to get away from the ringworm approach to urbanization — decay at the center and new growth at the periphery. It underestimates the need for finding socially useful functions for the older parts of town — as Europeans have done with considerable success in their much older cities. It represents an effort to flee social responsibility by taking over new lands rather than saving what we already have — a policy that was appropriate on the frontier, but not in a maturing America. It also represents a desire on the part of civic leaders and professionals to expand their policy controls as the area grows. These people are especially concerned about commercial development patterns. (A new suburban shopping center, particularly if it is financed from outside the area, can spell doom to central business district profits and to community fiscal control by local bankers.)

There is the belief that *efficiency and economy* are the highest political values held by the American homeowner. Leaders of metropolitan-area studies are likely to assume that efficiency of administration and economy in budgeting are the things that would be most perferred by residents — if only "politicians" didn't get in their way with selfish desires to preserve jobs and personal empires. Those who make this assumption sometimes exclaim in wonder and horror, "Why there are seventy-six different fire departments in the metropolitan area!" But to the suburbanite, who wants a voice in policies that affect his place of residence, this may spell "good" rather than "bad."

Those dedicated to efficiency and economy seem never to consider that the suburban merchant or homeowner may value other things higher — in particular, *access* to decision-making centers and *representativeness* of local government. . . . The suburban merchant wants local policies that will maximize his profits and minimize his competition. He probably sees his own suburban government as more likely to do this than would the core-city or some metropolitan government. To him, any super-government is likely to voice the values and business goals of the downtown merchants and large landowners. As a result of that feeling, the small fringe-area merchant, who frequently operates near the edge of financial disaster, is an advocate of grass-roots Jacksonianism. So is the suburban homeowner, who wants to have a hand in determining many things: service levels in the amenities provided by local government (according to what he thinks he can afford), land-use policies which he thinks will affect his property values, the kinds of neighbors he will have, and educational policies that will help determine the job and status opportunities of his children.

Efficiency and economy are probably among the suburbanites' lesser concerns — to him other things have a far higher priority. This attitude is in accord with a traditional view of Americans. We do not like to pay taxes and we do not asssociate taxes with services. Because this is the case, efficiency and economy arguments are nearly meaningless — the typical citizen probably does not see an important relationship between the way in which services are provided and the size of his own tax bill. He, rather cynically, *expects* government to be relatively inefficient. And since, to him, it is going to be inefficient come reformer or professional administrator, he wants a voice in local government. He wants to be able to reach the decision-makers when he has a problem. He has a different concept of democracy from that of the advocate of efficiency and economy who seeks deemphasis of the popular decision-making process and who has always demonstrated an anti-grass-roots prejudice. . . .

There is the belief that the public is prepared to accept area-wide planning if a politically feasible way can be found to administer it. There is no question but that long-range, integrated planning of land-use and capital developments would offer certain advantages to the residents of today's metropolitan areas. No question, either, but that the ghettoization of suburbs costs heavily in terms of depriving many persons — of lower income or lower status ethnic categories — of housing of the kind our culture considers decent. Or that restrictive suburban land-use rules drive up the price of housing unnecessarily. Or that land is often used unsystematically and wastefully when its urban development is left to profit-motivated realtors. Or that people pay many times what they might have paid for municipal capital improvements by refusing to plan ahead.... Yet suburbanites do not support area-wide planning. Indeed, they are often hostile to it. They will cooperate with planners if there is a program — perhaps a new sewage disposal plant — that can most easily be financed by joint suburban-core city action.... But basically the suburbanite, in a strife-torn world, sees his home and its local government as a refuge from conflict, as Wood neatly pointed out in his . . . *Suburbia*. A place in Vertigo Heights represents a retreat to the womb. There, in secure isolation among those who live, work, believe, and act as he does, he seeks a school plant that symbolizes his status in society and a school curriculum that meets his style of life and the expectations he has for his children. He wants his friends and neighbors to make land-use policies for him, for only they, he believes, can be trusted to mold the suburb to fit the die he and his neighbors have cast. He wants the planners to prevent the development of ethnic, class, status, or value conflicts by keeping out those who do not fit the established pattern. Effective metropolitan land-use controls, potentially, would do violence to one of the main purposes — whether for good or evil — of independent suburbs.

There is the belief that professional administration — which the core city has and a metropolitan-area government would have — is preferable to amateur administration. Preferable to whom? To many, no doubt. But the typical citizen is ambivalent in his attitude. He wants a government of friends and neighbors, but he wants one that will deliver pure water to his tap. He often prefers amateurs to professionals — as in the case of the suburban volunteer fire department which he finds far cheaper than the core city professional system designed to protect (at considerable cost) warehouses, apartment buildings, and high-rise business structures. Amateur fire fighters provide enough service to meet his demands — and a little glamour rubs off on them in the process. He is not so sure, either, about professionals in welfare, health, and even sewage disposal.

Above all, the suburbanite appears to prefer doing business with the amateur or semipro rather than with an anonymous bureaucratic professional in a city hall miles from his home or business and dedicated to professional principles and goals which he does not share or even understand.

There is the belief that a metropolitan-area super-government would save the taxpayers some money. This idea probably stems from the notion that such a government would be more efficient. In fact, however, although we could undoubtedly get a better return on our tax dollars than we do, we could not save enough money by this method to make more than a slight dent in today's huge municipal budgets. And as for economy, the prospects are dim, and for good reason. Metropolitan governments would almost certainly seek — over the long pull — to raise service levels. They would demand bigger and better streets, street lights, public health services, school plants, engineering standards in subdivision development, and the like. Furthermore, they would probably be able to raise levels at a faster rate than would be the case in a balkanized metropolitan area. This is so because citizens would probably say, "All right, we voted this thing in — now let's see it solve my sewage-disposal (storm water, street surfacing, school finance, etc.) problem!" Also, metropolitan-area government would encourage a move toward the use of more genuinely professional administrators and these men would strive toward the optimum service levels established by their particular professions, whether in public health, highways, civil engineering, or whatever. These programs would almost certainly exceed in cost any savings the professionals could accumulate through greater "efficiency." Then, too, the service levels they would be raising would be chiefly in the relatively low-density suburban areas — and the large lots of suburbia run up the cost of many services — of curb and gutter, sewers, water supply, and fire protection, for example. These demands would also raise per capita costs for the core-city property owners (unless everything were done by special assessments), for the suburban areas in most cases not only have greater needs, but have lower assessed valuation per capita than does the core city.

There is the belief that a rational distinction can be made between functions that are strictly local (suburban and core city) and those that are appropriate for area-wide super-government. Plans which seek to divide responsibilities between "lower tier" and "upper tier" (metropolitan-wide) governments nearly always conclude by making virtually all significant functions metropolitan. When this happens, the efforts being made to secure change are dissipated before they are fairly under way, for they lose nearly all of their potential support in the suburbs. There is no method by which to distinguish local and metropolitan functions that would satisfy both professional administrators and suburban citizens. An arbitrary approach is necessary and the only one that is likely to be at all successful is one that transfers to the metropolitan government only those functions that involve problems of widespread urgency throughout the area, where consensus holds that no other workable solution can be found.

There is the belief that a metropolitan area is a monolithic interest — a single community — that stands, or should stand, against the world, as do the wheat farmers or the oil producers. Civic leaders talk of a need to present "the metro point-of-view" to the legislature or Congress. But is there a metropolitan point-of-view? A metropolis is a great collection of people who, for economic and other reasons, live in close geographic proximity. They are each active in the pursuit of a livelihood, of recreation, of social activities. Each wants to pay no more of the social cost of the metropolis than he must. To him, there is a water supply problem, or a school curriculum problem, no doubt. There is a Mad River interest. But is there a Dayton "metro" interest? There is a Westchester interest. But is there a New York "metro" interest? The answer is "yes" to professional urban planners, civil and sanitary engineers, social workers but not to the typical citizen. His own concerns make his views parochial. To him, the only realistic metropolitan-area policies will be those that recognize and accept — however unwillingly — that parochialism.

There is the closely related view that a metropolitan area, if "properly" organized in a "modern" fashion, would operate smoothly and with no more conflict than, say, that in an eighteenth century New England town. There seems to be a widespread idea among civic actionists that the procrastination, name-calling, and general confusion that characterizes decision making in metropolitan areas is a result of decentralized government and is in part artificially created by job-seeking politicians. A harmonic metropolitan "public interest" is often portrayed in study reports as a reality to be striven for. Actually, however, a metropolitan area is a maze of conflicting values, goals, activities, and ethnic subcultures. The governing body of a unified metropolitan area would contain as many different pressures and cross-pressures as are found in a state legislature, and its operations probably would be no more harmonious. A "metro" government would be strife-torn and its major decisions would be produced in agony. It might encourage better coordinated policies; it would not diminish conflict.

Paul Ylvisaker

WHY MAYORS OPPOSE
METROPOLITAN GOVERNMENT

If the Good Lord and His executive angels were to engineer the change, Mayor James of Central City would resolve his doubts and come out publicly in favor of establishing an over-all government for the metropolitan area — provided, of course, that when the system was installed, he would be left in charge as metro-mayor. As an idea, "Metro" made a lot of sense; government was about the only American enterprise these days that was not organized on at least a regional and more often a national basis; and if His Honor were to continue as mayor of anything, he'd have to find some way of catching up with the more affluent citizens and taxable industries which were constantly moving just out of reach beyond his municipal boundaries.

But the trouble was, as Madison long ago discerned, the Lord's work on earth has to be done by mere mortals; instead of angels, there are only angles. Keeping a close eye on these almost guarantees that public officials and the electorate won't see or think straight — certainly, the logic of metropolitan government, being straight, can't be followed by practicing politicians, at least not headlong. The safer way is the devious route which circumscribes all the angles.

But back to the good Mayor's predicament. The idea of metropolitan government is in the air. Two years ago, all the normally otherwise-occupied notables in the area — or as that new breed of academic interventionists has been calling them, the "decision makers" — begin signing petitions, holding forums, listening to experts fetched from a distance, and in other ways acting as their wives in the League of Women Voters would have them act. These early months had been quite a honeymoon. Mayor James's natural instinct of waiting out all reforms until he saw the self-interests showing through, had helped him keep his balance and be quoted only in the most rolling of generalities. But he had begun to wonder whether politics had indeed entered a new age when at a massive luncheon assembled representatives

Reprinted from "Diversity and the Public Interest: Two Cases in Metropolitan Decision-Making" by Paul Ylvisaker, *AIP Journal*, Vol. XXVII, No. 2 (May 1961), pp. 109–113, by permission of the author and the American Institute of Planners.

of every one of the community's warring and ignoring interest groups had signed a pledge of cooperation. This alliance had so impressed a prestigious foundation that it wrote a check for more money than any of the local factfinders dreamed would be theirs to play with, "to carry out the necessary research." Necessary? Well, yes — research was one of those rituals which sufficiently cleansed the political ground for those normally above politics to walk on it; and it added a mystique which confused the old pros long enough for some new voices and fresh ideas to be heard.

But that was two years ago; now the game was again being played for keeps. The armistice of research was over; in a month, the binding question of a new form of metropolitan government was coming to a referendum vote; and there was no avoiding it, the Mayor would have to say publicly whether he was for or against. The bliss of consensus had long since dissolved. All that had held it together was undefined apprehension and ambition, each group uneasily aware that the metropolitan community had grown beyond its understanding, yet vaguely hopeful that if a new order could be established, it would be theirs to inherit. Now the fears and the ambitions had been defined; and the only common element was the familiar one of mutual suspicion and jockeying for position. Labor had been among the first to disengage. It had joined the coalition mostly because it couldn't afford the public posture of not doing so — and to keep an eye on this new political animal that just might develop into something substantial. But when meeting after meeting produced nothing immediately of use at the bargaining table, when it became apparent the coalition was too divided to forge strength out of its diversity, and as more and more of the political iceberg of metropolitan government became visible, labor's representative attended less and less frequently until sufficiently dissociated to refer openly to "Metro" as dominated by the business interests.

But "business" as a dominating monolith had long ago proved a myth. In the first place, the usual distressing number of its magnates had again displayed their amateur status in politics and public affairs. Despite their heralded record of civic participation, the coalition was their first working contact with career politicians from the ward and city committee. They were out of their element; they didn't know the names and numbers; and their radar — sensitive enough to the signals of the market — was jammed by the shower of uncertain messages which emanated from a world where the laws of social abrasion and aspiration displaced the accepted canons of efficiency and economy.

Still, more than political naïveté had stymied the business community. The truth was, it wasn't a community except tenuously and occasionally so in opposition to labor and taxes. It was split between absentee and locally owned enterprises; it was divided into big and small, into those socially registered and those not; it was bedeviled by old feuds and factions; and more relevant, it was torn between those committed to the core city and those who were accommodating very nicely to the suburban market. For example, the area's largest employment complex was entrenched in an industrial park which for a negligible cost to the companies concerned had traded local property taxes for the political hospitality of an outlying suburb; no siren call of metropolitan government could lure either the firms or the suburb from their protected enclave.

Mayor James was no stranger to this division in the business community; he had been embarrassed by it several times when "plugging the Chamber's line" only to find he had bought a factional plank — and he had exploited the same weakness on just as many occasions, dividing to conquer and even defying the local barons outright. For he knew what they and the ward politicians knew, that very few of the business leaders lived any longer in Central City; and since they no longer lived there, they couldn't vote there; and even if they could, there weren't enough of them to swing an election.

As a matter of fact, the Mayor often wondered whether the whole drive for metropolitan government wasn't basically a matter of ex-residents trying to have their cake and eat it — people who had moved to suburbia but still depended for their livelihood on white-collar jobs, businesses, and investment in central city, now trying to regain their vote and political influence by enlarging the city's boundaries. One of the Metro leaders had come dangerously close to letting the cat out of the bag by saying publicly he'd settle for a double vote for the commuter — one in the suburbs where he lived, and the other in central city where he worked. He hadn't added the reciprocal of double taxation, nor would he. Representation without taxation — what an ironic twist, mused the Mayor, of that earlier rallying cry of the American revolutionary.

Though he knew all this, Mayor James took care not to say it. On the one hand (though the reporting staff would quietly have loved him for it), he'd be clobbered by the editorial writers and publishers of Central City's newspapers who managed to be true to both halves of their schizoid selves by touting the virtues of downtown while living in the suburbs and using the press to endorse and plead what they no longer could vote for.

On the other hand, to have gone to the hustings with such candor and perhaps oversimplification would have invited extremism and demagogery. The city was tinderbox enough without touching a spark to it. Every year saw an accelerating turnover in population and a darkening of color. A decade ago he had been elected councilman from a ward with only a handful of Negroes in it; today, he was one of a handful of whites who still lived there. The rest had moved on, most of them beyond the Iron

Ring of suburbia. They lunched with him to say thanks for staying to fight their battles, and to lay out the strategy and objectives for other campaigns they hoped he would lead; then they left him to forage for his votes among the other half who lived in the city at night.

He was, he felt more and more, a man between worlds — no longer a member of the society he had grown up with, nor yet and perhaps never completely at home among the newer constituency upon whose vote his political life increasingly depended. Each campaign, each budget, each bond issue found him swinging more and more into the orbit of the newcomers and the philosophy of government which responded to their needs. Why the shift? He still wasn't sure, even though he's spent most of his term defending this growing liberality to his economy-minded friends (now supporting council manager plans in their several suburbs — "a manager is for the homogeneous," he was fond of saying to the students who visited him in City Hall, "but it takes a mayor to preside over diversity") and to the cynics of precinct and city desk. Sure, he wanted to survive: what politician, or for that matter what industrial, labor, or other leader didn't? But it wasn't only that. Not out of preference but of necessity he had come to know the minority cultures of Central City — Negroes from the rural South, Puerto Ricans, hill folk from the Appalachians, and always the steady flow of immigrants from abroad. It had taken a long time to get rid of the stereotypes through which he and his generation of well-assimilated immigrants had regarded these newest recruits to the city. Even now, lingering resentment could flicker within him when he reviewed the lengthening lists of unmarried mothers, juvenile delinquents, and relief cases with color and speech so clearly marked. The historian's reminder that it was ever thus, wasn't much comfort. It would still be his wearying job to defend these untouchables among whom he didn't belong to the well-washed to whom he did; to explain again the need for understanding to a public which lived on stereotypes and through a press which gained readership by sensationalizing the deeds it condemned; to talk the language of civil liberties to a frightened citizenry and an underpaid constabulary who lived too close to acts of violence to see where noble sentiments fit in.

But these were his city's citizens; like them or not, their welfare was his responsibility and their votes were essential to his political program and future. And like them he did — the more so as he came to see the inner logic of their own codes of conduct (he had heard even the high rate of "illegitimacy" and A.D.C. payments explained in terms no less moral than the culture of affluence), and as he penetrated the veneer of exceptional and unfamiliar behavior to see beneath it an *élan* born of adversity which had long ago been dissipated in the wealthier climate of suburbia.

They were, thought the Mayor, more attractive than some of the leaders who rose to represent them. But politics were the life blood of these people. Collectively, it was their main legitimate means of redressing the social and economic imbalance between themselves and the Haves; for an individual, it was a way of achieving in one's own lifetime the social prominence and acceptance which by the route of other callings usually took three generations to attain. Not strange that their leaders should play Robin Hood, nor that they should seem at times to be intent on turning City Hall into Sherwood Forest — may the rich and the law beware.

Among this constituency of newcomers and their political chieftains, metropolitan government was making few converts. It seemed, or easily was made to seem, a gerrymandering tactic by the same suburban element which had abandoned the central city — and their instinct for the jugular told them that if these suburbanites now wanted to resume their political ties, it must be with the hope of gaining some undisclosed advantage. Suspicious, they were jealous as well; for as their constituency grew and the older population left, they were fast becoming the majority rather than the minority. The political prospects were obvious and appealing; certainly now was not the time to dissolve their growing identity in the larger metropolitan population, nor to be led by the propaganda of increased efficiency and economy into an alliance which would divert what little resources the central city could still command to the satisfaction of suburban needs.

And the Mayor — for all he disliked the demagogery of the argument — had to admit that the prospects of the central city's gaining financially from a metropolitan system of government were pretty dim. The suburbs had reached the point where they had population enough to outvote the mother city: and they would hardly play Alphonse and Gaston with the city at the door of the public treasury. For all their wealth — more likely because of it — they were now deeper in the quicksand of financial need than the core city. In a binge of expenditures, they had built their public plant from scratch, yet their outlays were just beginning. The cost of suburban development has been vastly underestimated; trouble was, everybody had assumed the advertised price of houses was the total cost to the suburban taxpayer of his new community. Now the full bill was becoming evident; public health people, finding up to forty per cent of the suburban water supply contaminated by septic tanks, were among those who could, if asked, tell what the final tab was likely to be.

Adding central city's present and imminent charges for maintenance and renewal directly to the suburban bill via the proposed route of metropolitan government would hardly help the Mayor in his campaign for more revenue. It was tough enough prying new tax money out of city, state, and Washington, when, as now, he was under no obligation to tell

John Q. Taxpayer what all the costs of urban government amounted to.
No right-thinking man, the Mayor often thought, could avoid
concluding from this combined balance-sheet that the United States had
simply bought too much for its income — or if it managed to accumulate
enough wealth to pay the bill, it would have a hard time internationally
justifying its lavish way of life. For the country was discarding its central
cities before they were fully used or paid for, and now was buying a new
suburban plant on an instalment plan of staggering proportions.

That was where he began again to wonder whether metropolitan
governments weren't the solution — not so much of the community's
administrative problem of providing services more efficiently, but of its
problem of public morals. For the metropolis as presently organized was a
gigantic system of buckpassing, of avoiding difficult choices and
unpleasant facts, of having your cake and eating it; a system of
incomplete responsibilities which left everyone with an excuse for
inaction or a justification of acting only to the convenient extent of
self-interest; a system with opportune blinders, in which no one could be
blamed for abjuring the role of Good Samaritan and Brother's Keeper, for
the simple reason that one's neighbor or brother in need had been
gerrymandered into the other fellow's jurisdiction; a system perfectly
constructed for the Pharisee and the politician; a system he could play, as
other mayors had done before him, to his own advantage — talking about
problems, making token stabs at solving them, appointing study
commissions, blaming other jurisdictions for neglecting "their" responsibilities, and coasting with prosperity and the taxpayers' love of
postponed action to a re-election or two and then higher office, where the
whole hypocrisy could be practiced again on the clear slate of a new set
of problems and a new constituency.

The thought of higher office pulled him back to the realities of his
choice. Next year — and not again — the gubernatorial nomination might
be his if all went well, and "well" meant either a major coup of some
sort or not rocking the boat. The odds against Metro's winning at the
polls — judging from experience across the country — were more than 100
to 1; but since Sputnik, and the electorate's newly conditioned response
in favor of experiment and invention, past history was no certain guide.
Tote up the sides: For Metro — the League of Women Voters; central
city newspapers, radio and TV; the college-educated, upper-income and
commuting suburbanites; the managerial group, especially in the utilities;
and a scattering of dissident, desperate, or aspiring politicians. Against
Metro — the majority of Negroes in central city; suburban and central
city office-holders, their families, friends and relatives; suburban newspapers; the working and middle class with jobs and homes on the
same side of the city's boundaries; taxpayers' associations in the better-off
suburbs; suburban industries; and most important, those of the party who

controlled the nominations. Fill in the numbers, and it was pretty clear — the Noes had it, and only a gambling up-start would go for broke against such odds.

Damned if he supported Metro — would he be damned if he didn't? The newspapers and pundits would give him a hard time, but soon enough they'd be back in his corner — among central city candidates they had little or nothing else to turn to. There would also be disaffection and disillusion among the reform element. Many of these he'd shed no tears for — the self-interest of such do-gooders was hidden only from themselves. But he grieved genuinely when he thought of the few noble Romans he would cut the ground under by failing to endorse their campaign for Metro. These noble few were battling not for a disguised self-interest, nor for an unexamined panacea nor for the mere love of battling; they were out to stretch the mind and vision of the metropolitan community, and to give that community room and reason to grow to political maturity, finding in Metro a reform symbolic of their purpose and worthy of the effort. These people, too, had only a shallow well of opportunity to draw from; they, just as the Mayor, could risk their political equity only so many times before being pushed aside and their ideals discredited. They knew they were working against the odds, and they knew that the slim chance left to them depended on the Mayor's endorsement.

It would not be easy facing the disappointment of these noble few, less easy for the very fact they would be the most tolerant of his decision. More so than his own conscience, or whatever it was that kept echoing the categorical imperatives of his youth and his never-quieted expectancy that some day, if he were to prove his mettle and integrity, he would have to play the statesman on heroic scale even to the martyr's finish.

But was Metro this occasion? He had the courage; what came hard was the conviction.

And even if he were convinced that Metro was the public interest incarnate, and his martyrdom a way of speeding its birth, was this courage or presumption? Who was he to say that a rational order ought to be imposed on this imperfect thing called man or that a procrustean logic of the moment replace the disguised order of the evolutionary process? The present disorganization of the metropoly could hardly be blamed for the lack of solutions to all of man's problems or of resolutions of all his differences; it may, in fact, be a protection society instinctively erected against the disillusion that would follow if all institutional defects were to be corrected and man left naked to face his inherent political impotence.

And why should he feel conscience or suffer choice at all? Was "the public interest" only a theologian's invention which veiled the essential amorality of the political process — a process simply and purely of equilibrium, in which social forces out of balance strained toward equality? One could not say whether one resolution was better than another except in terms of his own interests, one could in selfishness then react, or in dispassion describe, or out of a projected abhorrence of violence help to secure an orderly and peaceful succession from one state of equilibrium to the next. Heroic acts proceeding from moral certainty were either irrelevant, or dangerous interventions inviting violent reactions.

When Mayor James lapsed that far into philosophy, he knew he had lost his way; and, by an instinct he long ago came to trust, he left off contemplating the universe and checked the specifics of the case before him, searching for the middle way out.

He found it where he should have looked at the outset, in the details of the proposal to be voted upon. It was, he saw, an attempt at compromise — a metropolitan authority for specified functions and with limited powers. As he took pen in hand, he wondered with as much amusement as he could muster what the reform element would say when they saw tomorrow's featured story.

MAYOR REJECTS METRO AS NOT ENOUGH. SAYS
NOTHING SHORT OF FULL CONSOLIDATION OF
AREA GOVERNMENT WILL PROVIDE
NEEDED SOLUTION

He knew, however, that the old hands among the politicians would smile and understand; and he turned to wondering whether Nancy, his wife, really meant it when she said she didn't want to move or whether she'd feel differently when ensconced in the Governor's mansion.

Edward Sofen

REFLECTIONS ON THE
CREATION OF MIAMI'S METRO

To explain the success of the campaign for metropolitan government in Greater Miami, it is necessary to examine the relationship of the central city to the remainder of Dade County, the socio-economic environment of Greater Miami, the people and forces who worked for the charter, and the methods that were used.

The Miami Milieu

The difference between the central city and the suburbs in Greater Miami is probably not as great as in other metropolitan areas in the nation. Dade County, because of its youth, its many homeowners, its relatively few apartment dwellers, and its unusual physical and geographical setting, is in many respects one big suburbia. Suburbanites of Dade County are not an "overspill" from the core city seeking greener pastures, but are primarily émigrés from many different sections of the United States. These newcomers have not had sufficient time to develop deep roots or, often, even firm friendships, and thus have few emotional ties to the Miami area. (It would seem that the longer the residency the greater the emotional attachment to a community.) [1]

Nevertheless, these characteristics do not vitiate the reality of the struggle between the core city and its satellites. City of Miami officials, as

Reprinted from The Miami Metropolitan Experiment (Bloomington: Indiana University Press, 1963), pp. 71–81, 83–84, 86, with the permission of the author and the publisher.

[1] A September, 1958, poll (Beiler Survey No. 12) indicated that the attitude of 433 registered voters towards the autonomy amendment, a pro-city amendment to the home rule charter, varied with the length of residence.

The statistics were as follows:

	7 months to 5 years (88 persons)	5 years to 13 years (144 persons)	13 years and longer (201 persons)
For	22.5%	23.0%	30.5%
Against	60.0	53.5	50.0
Uncertain	17.0	23.5	19.5

well as spokesmen for the city's organized business groups, have consistently maintained that central city residents have to bear the financial burden of county-wide facilities. These sentiments were dramatically asserted at a 1957 Congressional subcommittee hearing in Dade County. Robert M. Morgan, civic leader, certified public accountant, and a member of the executive board of the Miami-Dade Chamber of Commerce, blasted the various "parasite communities," which, he said, owed their very existence to the central City of Miami. Replying to a denunciation of Metro by the mayor of Miami Beach, Mr. Morgan declared that Miami Beach was about the least self-sufficient city in the nation. "We Miamians furnish them with water, we burn their garbage, we house their servants, we furnish them with roads leading to Miami Beach . . . we even carry it to the ultimate extreme, we bury their dead."[2]

Some observers contend that the charter, from its inception to its adoption, was a conspiracy of the "downtown Miami merchants." Undoubtedly, this group played one of the more important roles in the genesis of the consolidation movement, but its activities can hardly be classified as a conspiracy. Nor can the general dissatisfaction of a large number of the residents of the City of Miami be traced to the influence of the merchants. The political difficulties that plagued the city for many years might well have disillusioned even the most stouthearted. Despite — or because of — a council-manager form of government, with many nonprofessional managers over the years, the City of Miami was in constant political turmoil. Charges of corruption filled the air, and the police force was under perpetual attack for its failure to enforce the laws against gambling and other forms of vice. It was to counteract this state of affairs that the Greater Miami Crime Commission, a citizens' group, was formed in 1948.[3] At about the same time the Dade County Research Foundation was created to serve as a "watchdog" over governmental activities and to give assistance to the governments of the area whenever possible.[4]

At the very time that critics of the government of the City of Miami were strongly condemning the city council, these same critics had only the highest praise for the County Commission. The satisfaction with the

[2] U.S. Congress, House, Subcommittee of the Committee on Government Operations, *Hearings, Federal-State-Local Relations, Dade County (Florida) Metropolitan Government*, 85th Cong., 1st. sess., Nov. 21 and 22, 1957, p. 114.

[3] The Crime Commission was founded on March 31, 1948. It was approved by 250 delegates representing some 90 Dade County civic, patriotic, and business organizations at a three-day law enforcement convention at the Mayfair Theater in the City of Miami (*The Crime Commission of Greater Miami*, undated pamphlet).

[4] *Miami Herald*, Jan. 12, 1947, p. 1A. Businessmen were responsible for creating and financially supporting both the Crime Commission and the Research Foundation.

County Commission can be attributed to its unanimity of outlook, its peace and harmony, and its fairly impressive handling, at least in the public mind, of the county parks, hospital, and Port Authority. The County Commissoners, who had had long experience in their elected offices, were acting as both administrators and policy makers under a commission form of government. The existence of this dichotomy of a "good" county government and an "evil" city government, together with the desire of the city's businessmen to have the county assume the financial burdens of metropolitan functions, helps to explain the transfer to the county of the City of Miami Port Authority and Jackson Memorial Hospital. The transfer of the hospital shifted the costs of support from the city to the county. The designation of the highly respected Board of County Commissioners as the governing board of the Port Authority was seen, by the supporters of the move, as a distinct advantage to the Port Authority in its negotiations with banks. The better credit standing of the county plus the high repute in which the County Commission was held may help to explain why the airlines and the businesses dealing with the airlines preferred county to city control of the airport. Moreover, since the spokesmen for most organized business groups in the central city see Greater Miami as a single unified area, it is to be expected that the central city businessmen would favor a governmental entity that had, in fact and in law, the power to deal with the problem of airports, harbors, and seaports.

From 1945 to 1953 all plans for geographical consolidation could be traced, in part, to the efforts of the powerful business elements within the City of Miami. The 1945 plan was abortive for a number of reasons. The members of the City of Miami Commission, at the time, were of high caliber, and there appeared to be no urgency to save the city. Moreover, the strong bond that was later forged between the Dade delegates to the state legislature and the City of Miami businessmen had not as yet materialized. Even the *Miami Herald* had not at this time realized its position of power.

In the 1948 and 1953 elections,[5] a solid alliance was established between the Dade legislators and the proconsolidation elements in Dade County. Among the latter were the *Miami Herald*, the Dade County Research Foundation, the Miami Chamber of Commerce, the Junior Chamber of Commerce, and many members of the League of Women Voters. The near victory of the 1953 move to consolidate the City of Miami with the country led to the introduction, by the localists,[6] of a modified scheme of consolidation aimed at saving the cities from

---

[5] Regular elections are held in the Miami area in even-numbered years; special elections in odd-numbered years.

[6] The localists insisted upon maintaining the autonomy of the municipalities.

destruction. Even this proposal, however, was only a counteraction to the pressures from the consolidationists.[7]

The socio-political setting of Greater Miami also was conducive to the development of a metropolitan government because of a combination of characteristics peculiar to the area: the tremendous growth of population, the pervasive tourist atmosphere, the rapid population turnover, the existence of a no-party political system, the absence of relatively strong racial or religious minorities committed to the status quo, and the lack of a strong labor movement.

One student of politics has observed that for many years to come it will be difficult, if not impossible, to integrate local governments in areas where there is a two-party system.[8] Miami with its "every man for himself" type of politics has, in effect, a no-party system and, consequently, was spared the kind of struggle that might have occurred if the fate of political parties had hinged on the outcome of the move to create a new metropolitan government. By contrast, certain other metropolitan areas with more formalized party structures, such as Cuyahoga County in the Cleveland area, have reflected sharp divisions between the parties as well as within the parties on the issue of metropolitanization.[9] . . .

The opposition to recent movements to establish metropolitan governments in the United States stemmed not only from political parties but also from various pressure groups that considered themselves threatened. Minority groups which have found a *modus vivendi* in an existing government are particularly loath to change the political structure. Thus one finds that there were Negro leaders in both Cleveland and St. Louis who strongly opposed changing the existing governmental framework because of the fear that they would lose their personal influence in a larger, more rationalized government.

In Miami, Negroes constitute only 6.8 per cent of the registered voters.[10] Of those voting in the predominantly Negro precincts, an estimated 60 per cent have generally opposed the creation of a metropolitan government.[11] Although there may have been rare instances when the Negro vote on metropolitan or consolidation issues has been crucial to the outcome of certain municipal elections, this has not been the case in Dade's county elections. . . .

[7] The consolidationists espoused the abolition of the municipalities and the creation of a single government for the Greater Miami area.

[8] Edward C. Banfield, "The Politics of Metropolitan Area Organization," 1 *Midwest Journal of Political Science* 86 (May, 1957).

[9] Governmental Affairs Foundation, Inc., *Metropolitan Surveys: A Digest* (Chicago: Public Administrative Service, 1958), p. 163.

[10] Interview with Dr. Thomas J. Wood, Department of Government, University of Miami.

[11] *Ibid.*

The powerful labor unions which are found in most metropolitan areas constitute yet another political force vitally concerned with any threat to its power status. Greater Miami, however, has a relatively small number of industrial workers,[12] and although there are some 50,000 union members in the area,[13] unions have played a relatively unimportant role in Dade County politics. By contrast again, in St. Louis there are 35,000 workers in the teamsters' union alone.[14] Also, the Teamsters Local 688 is a vitally significant force in St. Louis. Labor for the most part opposed the metropolitan-oriented District Plan in St. Louis.

In a number of industrial areas throughout the nation, the businessman, or at least an important segment of the business community, has been acutely conscious of the need for the establishment of county-wide metropolitan goverment. Although prometropolitan business organizations in such cities as Boston, Cleveland, and Dayton generally were ineffectual and ill designed for political action, large sums of money were raised by business groups in conjunction with Ford Foundation and other organizational grants, to advance the metropolitan cause. In Miami, on the other hand, the business leaders allowed the Dade County Research Foundation, a business-sponsored "good government" group, to expire for want of funds.

It may be that the "countervailing power theory" of big business begetting big unions also works in reverse. In the case of Miami, the lack of countervailing organizations, in the form of cohesive labor or minority groups, meant that the business community had no real competitors in the political arena. Moreover, since the cause of "good government" groups coincided with the desires of the more powerful Miami business organizations, the latter were quite content to allow the newspapers, professional groups, university professors, and the League of Women Voters to assume the positions of catalytic leadership in civic affairs.

To these variables revolving about the amorphous power setting of Miami one must add two other factors: the lack of a real crisis situation in Miami except, perhaps, in the minds of the more knowledgeable, and

[12] In 1958 only 13 per cent of Greater Miami's nonagricultural labor force were employed by manufacturing concerns, while approximately 30 per cent of the national labor force were so employed. See University of Miami Bureau of Business and Economic Research, *Economic Almanac of Southeastern Florida, 1959* (Coral Gables: University of Miami, 1959), p. 25; United States Department of Commerce, *Statistical Abstract of the United States, 1959* (Washington, D.C.: U.S. Government Printing Office, 1959), p. 210.

[13] *Miami Herald*, Oct. 18, 1959, p. 1G.

[14] The city-wide distribution of its members and the aggressive leadership of its secretary-treasurer have made this union the most active and effective interest group in St. Louis. Once a month, assemblies of union stewards are held to discuss city problems and implement requests that have arisen toward meetings. Their actions are confined primarily to endorsements of candidates and of issues in city, state, and national elections. See Gray, *Report on Politics*, Chapter V, pp. 7–12.

the deep political apathy of most Miami citizens. From what we know of other studies, these conditions are probably typical of most metropolitan areas. The extent of the existence of citizen apathy in Miami is made clear by the following observations:

> Any testing of levels of thought and feeling in the political substructure inevitably yields new evidence of abject apathy and gross ignorance in the citizen mass. This is particularly true in dealing with the subject of local government. To find, as we did in Survey #10, that only 15% of our registered citizens could think of anything good that the county commission had done in the preceding year, or that 24% could name something blameworthy that they had done (9% named a parks concession scandal) is routine.
>
> However, somehow one expects a thing as big as Metro to make an impression. When only 32% say they have heard or read about a new county charter and had a sliver of a correct idea about it, while 13% have a quite wrong idea about it, that sinking sensation returns. It was not only in the telephone poll that 64½% said they did not know of any big change in the county government in the last couple of years. The same question had produced the identical 64½% shrugging response when asked in Survey #10.[15]

The authors of the above question concluded that those persons possessing little local political interest did not embrace a strong Metro position and, if low enough in interest, held a distinctly "neutral" position. There was also a definite correlation between high local political interest and a pro-Metro position. At first glance one might get the impression that apathy contributed to Metro's success by keeping the "neutral" and anti-Metro voter away from the polls. However, a statistical breakdown of voter turnout in the various precincts in Greater Miami refutes this. Surprisingly, it shows that there was no marked difference in voter turnout in the high socio-economic precincts, with a high degree of local political interest, and the lower socio-economic precincts with a low degree of local political interest.[16]

People, Forces, and Methods

Although the Miami environment and the political process as explained above may have created a setting conducive to the acceptance of metropolitan government, they scarcely account for the positive actions which were necessary to plan, promote, and push Metro to successful adoption. The political environment, in short, provided a favorable matrix; it did *not* provide the "catalytic action-spark." In the following pages the roles of the main actors involved in the formation of Metro will

[15] Ross C. Beiler and Thomas J. Wood, *Metropolitan Politics of Miami* (Paper delivered at the annual meeting of the Southern Political Science Association of Gatlinburg, Tenn., Nov. 7, 1958), p. 13.

[16] The information was obtained from an interview with Dr. Thomas J. Wood, professor of Government, University of Miami, December 31, 1959.

be examined and analyzed. The taxonomy of activists includes the newspapers, the business organizations, the civic groups, the Charter Board, and the professionals.

. . . The political vacuum in Miami was filled to a considerable extent by the *Miami Herald*, the influence of which in crystallizing public opinion has been recognized by friends and foes alike. The formulation of the *Herald* editorial policy is attributed by most civic leaders to Associate Editor John D. Pennekamp. Aspirants for political office eagerly seek the *Herald's* endorsement, which is extremely important in this no-party area. Some of Miami's most important businessmen, elected officials, and administrative officers meet and consult with Mr. Pennekamp on important community problems. A few of the associate editor's close contacts are characterized by their enemies as "errand boys," with Mr. Pennekamp portrayed as a puppeteer pulling the strings. . . .

A majority of the downtown City of Miami business elements constitute another faction that has consistently supported consolidation movements. The efforts of this group to win public support for Metro were centered around the activities of the Miami Chamber of Commerce. In 1955 the chamber changed its name to the Miami-Dade Chamber of Commerce and invited each of the chambers in the suburbs to appoint an associate director to the Miami-Dade board of directors.[17] The move was considered presumptuous and few chambers cooperated. It is significant that most of the local chambers of commerce, with the exception of the Miami-Dade chamber, have opposed geographical consolidation.

The Miami-Dade chamber, despite schisms within its membership, has played a significant role in all consolidation movements. The organization's support of the 1948 and 1953 drives lacked the fervor that was evident in later years, however. Despite the fact that chamber members were well represented on the [Metropolitan Miami Municipal] Board and the first and second Charter Boards, the movement for metropolitan government was never closely identified in the public mind with the Miami-Dade Chamber of Commerce.[18] The organization was considered

[17] The information was obtained from an interview with Alfred Canel, executive vice-president of the Miami-Dade Chamber of Commerce.

[18] In a late 1957 and early 1958 poll (Beiler Survey No. 10) respondents were asked what individual or group they would name as most influential in the decisions shaping the new county government. Out of 723 persons questioned (422 registered, 301 unregistered), only 5.5 per cent alluded to a category that included the Chamber of Commerce, the Junior Chamber of Commerce, neighborhood groups, clubs and fraternal organizations. The other responses were as follows:

1. No group indicated   82.0 per cent
2. Municipal (city commissioners, city officials,
   Dade League of Municipalities, police, mu-
   nicipal employee groups)   3.5

by the public to be just another "civic" group supporting metropolitan government. This was probably fortunate, for if the Metro movement had been thought to be a chamber "conspiracy" aimed at shifting taxes from the City of Miami to the county, it would undoubtedly have failed. This is not to suggest that the chamber was in reality the moving force behind Metro and that it managed successfully to disguise the fact. At most, the chamber was part of a loosely aligned group that, along with the *Miami Herald* was the Dade legislative delegation, was responsible, before appointment of the 3M Board, for initiating geographical consolidation movements — none of which succeeded. As already indicated, the initial step toward metropolitan government was a countermovement by the enemies of consolidation, who were concerned primarily with the preservation of the cities. The consolidationists joined the "localists" in support of a federal type of metropolitan government and, according to some observers, may have succeeded in leaving their consolidationist imprint on the charter.

The Dade County Research Foundation was created in 1947 primarily by business groups in the City of Miami to help bring about more economical and efficient government. The director and full-time staff of the organization was responsible for keeping its members informed of the foundation's findings and recommendations. The foundation enjoyed the respect of the community and the support of the newspapers. It reported on matters of integrity and efficiency in the operations of the City of Miami government and later of the Dade County government. John F. Willmott, first executive director of the foundation, met with opposition when he attempted to criticize the omnipotent County Commission, and in March, 1956, he thought it best to resign.[19] It was somewhat later that the *Herald* and the *News* also began to take the County Commissioners to task. . . .

Although the League of Women Voters, prior to 1957, took no official position on consolidation movements, its members individually gave strong support to such movements. The league, at the time of the charter referendum, however, officially supported the home rule charter.[20] League

---

3. County Commission and Port Authority	6.5
4. Newspapers	4.5
5. Television	1.0
6. Charter Board and other advisory boards	1.5

The response to the question on which individuals were most influential was practically nil. One would have to conclude that the "average" resident was unaware of the identity of the decision makers in the Greater Miami area.

[19] The position of executive director remained vacant until filled by Harry T. Toulmin on August 19, 1956.

[20] There were actually four separate leagues at the time — City of Miami, Miami Beach, Hialeah and Coral Gables — with a total membership of 450. The information was obtained from an interview with Mrs. John Baker, former president of the League of Women Voters of (the City of) Miami.

members were strong allies and formidable opponents. They centered their efforts on distributing pamphlets, ringing doorbells, making phone calls, holding parades, and carrying on other old-fashioned but effective means of "politicking." This group, which is most successful if it is provided with political leadership by a "nonpartisan, good government" organization, maintained such a symbiotic relationship with the Dade County Research Foundation.

The activities on behalf of consolidation by good government groups, as well as by newspapers and business groups would have come to naught without the introduction of appropriate bills by the Dade delegation in the Florida Legislature. Management of both the 1948 and 1953 consolidation bills was assumed by Dade Senator R. Bunn Gautier, who, because of his experience, his strong personality, and his political leadership might well be called the father of consolidation.[21]

Considering the role of Senator Gautier in the consolidation movement, a number of questions come to mind: Was the Senator a tool of the Miami Chamber of Commerce? Was he dictated to by the *Miami Herald*? Or was it purely fortuitous that the Senator's aims were compatible with those of the chamber and the *Herald*? The answers to all of these questions must be in the negative. It would seem that Senator Gautier at times had to rally the members of the chamber to support consolidation, rather than the reverse. Although a concord did exist between him and the *Herald*, it was hardly what one would describe as a case of follow the leader.[22] On the whole, the relationship between Senator Gautier and the consolidationist organizations evolved from interaction and a mutual concern; Senator Gautier's leadership was not merely an individual manifestation but rather a reflection of the group process at work.[23] . . .

To explain the importance of professionals in molding the charter and in gaining public support for its adoption, it is necessary to examine what might be called the "expert syndrome." Before interpreting this term, however, there should be some clarification of the different types of experts. [Public Administration Service consultant] Corcoran, in an interesting article,[24] makes a rather invidious comparison between the

[21] Mr. Gautier was a member of the Florida Legislature from 1947 through 1956. He served one term in the House and four in the Senate.

[22] The information was obtained from interviews with members of the Miami-Dade Chamber of Commerce, with representatives of the *Miami Herald*, and with R. Bunn Gautier.

[23] "It appears, then, that the group experiences and affiliations of an individual are the primary, though not the exclusive, means by which the individual knows, interprets, and reacts to the society in which he exists." David Bicknell Truman, *The Governmental Process* (New York: Alfred A. Knopf, 1951), p. 21.

[24] John D. Corcoran, "Seeking Better Government for Metropolitan Areas," 40 *Public Management* 82 (Apr., 1958).

costs and results of the PAS studies on the one hand and the "probing research" of the foundation-endowed scholars on the other. Obviously, there is need for both types of research, but it would also seem fairly evident that the PAS study was far more productive of results than the work of the scholars. The "syndrome" developed, therefore, around the "practical" expert rather than the "theoretical" expert. The practical expert's laboratory is middle-class suburbia, which has its Book-of-the-Month, its Record-of-the-Month, even its Frozen-Food-of-the-Month, and may at any moment produce its Expert-of-the-Month. The typical suburbanite, with a better than average education and fairly high socio-economic status, has escaped from the unclean realism of politics to the antiseptic atmosphere of the expert. The appeal for good government, nonpartisanship, economy, and efficiency has found a favorable response in what might be characterized as "League of Women Voters" communities. Irrational loyalties to the old and established ways of doing things have not as yet taken root in suburbia.

In Miami the image of the PAS staff as nonpartisan experts provided the symbol of good government. Public Administration Service is not only a research group but a prestige organization as well. As expert consultants analyzing the Miami area, PAS staff members were able, through their recommendations, to keep a number of issues from becoming controversial. The authority of ideas emanating from PAS influenced both the newspapers and the Charter Boards, and PAS representatives worked closely with the Advisory Committee of the 3M Board and the Executive Committee of the first Charter Board. The PAS endorsement of the charter, a sort of *Good Housekeeping* "Seal of Approval," was repeatedly emphasized by the second Charter Board in its campaign for adoption of the home rule charter.

Still another important factor in the promotion of Metro was the symbol of nonpartisanship with which the public most closely identified the Charter Board. The members of the second Charter Board, appointed by the governor at the behest of the Dade delegation, were not representative of the Greater Miami community either geographically or economically. There were 7 members from Coral Gables, 4 from the City of Miami, 3 from Miami Beach, and 1 each from Miami Springs, Miami Shores, and the unincorporated area. The members, other than those from Coral Gables and the City of Miami, did not reflect the sentiments of the voters of their communities.

A significant number of Charter Board members were men of great wealth in agriculture, business, or finance; at least 6 of the 17 members were in this category. Among the members of the board were 6 experienced officeholders, 3 attorneys, 2 educators, 1 labor leader, and 1 housewife who was a civic leader. On the basis of economic status alone, the board appears to be representative of the people of Dade County.

The board, however, was not intended to represent narrow geographic and economic interests. Nor were the board members conscious of strong identification with any specific area or group. For example, two board members — one a labor leader and the other a prominent agriculturist — were able to disregard the sharp anti-Metro feeling of their respective groups. Similarly, those members residing in Miami Beach, as well as a very intense partisan of local government from Coral Gables, joined wholeheartedly in the support of the home rule charter. . . .

Summary

Miami was able to create a metropolitan government with the very type of support that failed in other parts of the nation because of the ecological conditions earlier considered — particularly the absence of powerfully established political parties, labor organizations, and ethnic groups — and because Miamians have long been accustomed to depend on such non-party sources as the newspapers for political leadership. These factors, together with the astuteness of Dade's legislative delegation to the state legislature, the practical orientation of the 3M Board, the high caliber and independence of the Charter Board members, and the prestige of the Public Administration Service experts, were all responsible for the birth of Miami's metropolitan government.

Daniel R. Grant

THE EXPERIENCE OF NASHVILLE'S METRO

... The voters' decision on June 28, 1962, to replace Davidson County and the city of Nashville with a single metropolitan government had been preceded by more than ten years of study, recommendation, inaction, re-study, enabling legislation, charter drafting, voter rejection, re-grouping of political forces, charter re-drafting, and more intensive grass-roots campaigns both for and against metro. The form of metropolitan government adopted was basically city-county consolidation, but with a variety of features designed to meet special requirements of the state's constitution, the rural and urban areas' differing service needs, and the necessities of local political tradition. The original proposal was made in 1956 by the Nashville and Davidson County Planning Commissions, which endorsed their joint staff's study report entitled *Plan of Metropolitan Government for Nashville and Davidson County*. In 1958 the voters rejected the first consolidation charter, but four years later, after annexation moves and a controversial "green sticker" auto fee supplied fresh wind for metro sails, a slightly modified consolidation charter was adopted. The new metropolitan mayor and council were elected in November, 1962, and the new government went into effect on April 1, 1963.

What were the pre-adoption claims made for and against metropolitan government by proponents and opponents? Most of the arguments for metro may be found in the original 1956 report which, in summary, predicted that metro would:

1. Eliminate city-county bickering and buck-passing and help fix political responsibility.

2. Eliminate duplication of administrative effort and thus provide more economical government.

3. Result in greater specialization and professionalization of personnel.

4. Equalize core-city and suburban services on a "single-community" basis.

"A Comparison of Predictions and Experience with Nashville 'Metro', " by Daniel R. Grant, is reprinted from *Urban Affairs Quarterly* (September, 1965), pp. 34–54, with the permission of the author and the publisher, Sage Publications, Inc.

5. Provide a "truly progressive solution" to the universal problem to how to plan and guide urban growth in the suburban and rural fringe.

6. Eliminate city-county financial inequities.

7. Permit the financing of new suburban services on a pay-as-you-are-served basis.

8. Create a progressive-community image in the national spotlight.

With one or two exceptions, the predictions made by opponents of metro were not nearly so broad-gauged and generalized as those made by the proponents. The claims of the opponents, in summary, were that metro would:

1. Create a bigger, more centralized government which will be less responsible and less accessible to the people.

2. Increase taxes substantially.

3. Provide no benefits to rural residents, while raising their taxes.

4. Reduce the quality and quantity of services, and delay new services, in the core city area.

5. Paralyze the community in a quagmire of lawsuits by which the charter would be held unconstitutional in many parts if not in toto.

6. Result in a dilution of Negro political influence in local government decisions.

7. Remove from power the political organization of Mayor Ben West.

Before turning to the ambitious assignment of comparing predictions with actual experience, it is important to point out that the evidence presently available for such a comparison varies all the way from "conclusive" in certain cases to "totally inconclusive" in other cases. Some predictions are of such broad or abstract character that the only kind of appraisal possible is that based on the rather impressionistic opinions of "reasonable men." Other predictions may be judged correct in 1965, only to require reversal in the light of experience in subsequent years.

Predictions Made by Proponents of Metro

GREATER POLITICAL RESPONSIBILITY THROUGH ELIMINATION OF CITY-COUNTY BUCK-PASSING. In one sense this prediction has been carried out almost by definition — there is no more city-county bickering or buck-passing because the city and county have been replaced. But in the broader sense the question remains, is political responsibility for local government decisions now more easily fixed? Most informed observers in the community think so, and a survey of voters after the first year of metro reveals that, by a ratio of more than two and one-half to one, they agree that "under metro it is easier to know who to call or see when you have a problem than it was under separate city and county government."

Perhaps the most obvious manifestation of more fixed responsibility is the easier focus of public spotlight on local officials and their decisions. With only one legislative body and one chief executive, rather than two, the requirements of civic watchfulness are in one sense just one-half as great as they were before metro went into effect. The community decision-making process has been considerably simplified, particularly with respect to a single community-wide budget-making operation. School needs must be weighed alongside police, park, and health needs, and core city needs must be considered simultaneously with suburban and rural fringe needs.

Some of the most frequent buck-passing prior to the adoption of metro had to do with responsibility for providing such services as sewers, parks, libraries, fire protection, and police protection in the closely built up suburbs. While the *method* may still be confused in the minds of many, there is no doubt that the ultimate responsibility for them lies in the single metropolitan government. Obviously, plenty of opportunities still exist within metro to "pass the buck," other than between city and county, such as between mayor and council, mayor and the few residual elective officers, and mayor and independent boards. None of these cleavages seems to cut quite so deeply or affect coordinated urban development quite so seriously as did the old city-county cleavage.

ECONOMY THROUGH ELIMINATION OF DUPLICATION. The prediction of more economical government through eliminating duplication of administrative effort is probably the most common argument for all kinds of governmental consolidation proposals, and is one that can live to plague and embarrass the reformers after consolidation takes place and taxes continue to rise. Most pamphlets and speakers for metro in Nashville were especially careful to make it clear that taxes and expenditures were going up whether metro was adopted or not, and to claim only that metro economies would mean that taxes would increase *less* than without metro. During the heat of the 1962 campaign the Tennessee Taxpayers Association was pressed for prediction of actual savings by adopting a single metropolitan government. The TTA estimated probable savings of one million dollars for the year 1960–61 if consolidated government had been in effect, and said annual savings would increase to such an extent that savings during the ten-year period from 1966 to 1976 would total $18 million. The TTA was not predicting a net reduction in over-all expenditures, but rather a *lower increase* in expenditures, but this is a fine distinction that frequently fails to come through in newspaper headlines or campaign oratory.

In the opinion of this writer metro has already eliminated many duplications and has some economies to show for this, but, paradoxically, has caused increased expenditures which more than wipe out the economies. The adoption and establishment of metro set off a chain reaction of civic enthusiasm, consolidation transition studies by functional experts, recommendations which lift the horizons of citizens and officials alike, and bigger budget requests and appropriations to move in the direction of these new horizons. Thus, metro has stimulated a kind of civic revolution of rising expectations which can only result in an upward stimulus on expenditures and taxes. It is therefore possible to contend logically that metro has eliminated the wasteful duplication of street maintenance and traffic engineering equipment in city and county departments (as it has), while also reporting that metro has caused new expenditures for a great expansion of the street lighting program to light all highways out to the county boundaries. This is even more true in the case of school consolidation. Admittedly, a comparison of prediction with actual experience concerning metro economies results in an ambivalent picture.

SPECIALIZATION AND PROFESSIONALIZATION OF PERSONNEL. The claim that city-county consolidation would result in greater specialization and professionalization of personnel was based on the assumption that larger departments could and would make greater use of the principle of division of labor and that the development of career services in various departments would become increasingly common. A study is now under way to discover the early effects of metro in this general area of administration, but is not far enough along to be of assistance here. A few observations may be made, however, on the basis of general "news-paper knowledge" of the consolidation.

The task of total merger of city and county departments, agencies, boards, and commissions, undoubtedly required the greatest number of special studies and surveys by administrative, fiscal, legal, and functional experts and consultants in any comparable time period in the history of Nashville. Seventeen such studies were made between 1962 and 1965 and most of them involved the employment of professional consultant firms which made strong recommendations for greater specialization and professionalization of personnel within the new metropolitan government. Some departments are moving more slowly than others, but virtually all have felt the impact of these studies. In the case of the Fire Department a consultant from outside the state was simply employed by contract to "run the department" in 1964 and his contract was renewed for 1965. A comprehensive school survey was made by an outside group, and the consolidated school system employed a director of schools from Des Moines after a nation-wide search for the most qualified person. The metropolitan mayor created in his office the position of "fiscal-administrative officer" and moved the professionally trained head of the planning commission's research division into the new job. The police department has had the assistance of a survey team from the International Association of Chiefs of Police in trying to replace the rather unsavory image of the old city police department and county sheriff's patrol. While an opinion survey after the first year of operation indicated that voters, by a two-to-one ratio, think that "Metro has improved the Police Department," it is still too early to judge the extent of specialization and professionalization which will result. While other examples could be given if space permitted, still other agencies are not included in such a listing because they were already county-wide in jurisdiction at the time metro was adopted. In any case, early evidence indicates that actual experience is beginning to support the prediction of greater specialization and professionalization of personnel.

EQUALIZATION OF SERVICES. In contrast to many of the older metropolitan areas in the United States where suburban services are as good or even better than core-city services, Nashville's growing suburbs had been poorly served or not at all for some thirty years prior to 1960. Metro was proposed as a method of equalizing core-city and suburban services on a single-community basis. Although a great deal of "service equalization" has been going on since the inauguration of metro, much of it was initiated by two pro-metro annexations, in 1958 and 1960, totalling some 50 square miles and 87,000 people. Extension of the full complement of urban services in the annexed area was begun by the old city of Nashville and has been continued under metro. The metro charter does not provide for extension of urban services to the sizeable unannexed suburbs until they are added to the "Urban Services District" by action of the metropolitan council. According to the original plan for metro, full equalization was not to be fulfilled until it put to use one of the unique features in its design — the expandable Urban Services District.

Countywide equalization of services has already begun in the case of functions ("general services") not limited merely to the Urban Services District. The primary examples are schools and parks, for which ambitious strides have already been taken. The distinction between urban services and general services has shown some signs of becoming blurred, with several areas being sewered outside the Urban Services District, with street lighting being extended along major highways as far as the county line, and with serious discussion of the extension of fire protection throughout the entire county area. While this constitutes some variation from the original plan for two service districts, it evidences strong tendencies toward countywide service equalization in one way or another.

PLANNED DEVELOPMENT OF SUBURBAN AND RURAL FRINGE. The prediction of a "truly progressive solution" to the perplexing problem of guiding urban growth in the suburban and rural fringe is already being borne out in certain limited respects under metro, but the bulk of evidence pro or con still lies well in the future. Some of the most serious cases of unplanned, uncoordinated fringe development in pre-metro Davidson County involved illogical school location, loss of park and playground sites, and the development of housing subdivisions without sanitary sewers, curbs, gutters, street lights, or water lines of sufficient size for fire hydrants. School location fell victim to an almost ludicrous shadow boxing between the city and county school systems, with each trying to anticipate the other's strategy for annexation or new school construction. Since the county had no park system and the city had no interest in new parks outside its boundaries, tremendous areas suitable for park development were forever lost through default. The "septic tank scandal" of the suburban fringe is probably best known of all and its effects in the development of metropolitan Nashville have been told many times.

Metro has already eliminated the planning conflicts between the city and county school systems, making political boundaries irrelevant to decisions on school location anywhere within the county area. The suburban and rural vacuum in the planning of parks and playgrounds has been eliminated and several large park sites in areas outside the old city have already been acquired. The integration of the suburban and rural fringe into an area-wide sewer system is a much slower process for several reasons. Sewering suburban Nashville is an unusually slow and expensive process because of the prevalence of solid rock underlying the soil throughout the area. Furthermore, the tremendous 30-year backlog of unsewered areas diverts attention from planning and controlling the current and future spread of urbanization into the rural fringe. The job of "catching up" seems to be well in hand, even though incomplete, but it is still too early to assess metro's success or failure in the job of "keeping up" and "staying ahead" of urban development.

There is one haunting question which needs to be mentioned in any attempt to evaluate the prediction that metro would permit planned development of the ever-expanding suburban and rural fringe. What can metro do if Nashville's six projected expressway spokes hurl much of the city's new population growth out into the six adjoining counties? Is the "truly progressive solution" to last only for ten years or so, with the cutting edge of the suburban fringe then to move out far beyond the jurisdiction of metro? Such has been the experience of earlier city-county consolidations and separations. In answer, perhaps it is enough to say that metro Nashville's 553-square mile area is now one of the large municipal jurisdictions in the United States and probably comes *closer* to having sufficient geographic jurisdiction to control its fringe growth within the next few years than any other metropolitan city. Whether it will actually do this is a different question and one which cannot yet be answered.

ELIMINATION OF CITY-COUNTY FINANCIAL INEQUITIES. The two primary types of financial inequities which core city residents complained about increasingly during the nineteen-forties and -fifties were "double taxation" by the city and county while receiving certain services only from the city, and the "free ride" received by out-of-city residents who used city facilities without being taxed for them. As the complaints from the core city grew louder, some of these inequities were corrected in the nineteen-fifties by various methods: the city of Nashville transferred the health function to Davidson County, including both administrative and financial responsibility for health; the county school system was required by the state legislature to divide its local school tax revenue with the city system on the basis of pupil attendance; suburbanites were required to pay from two to three times as much for their water as core city residents; and a ten-dollar "green sticker" fee was levied on all automobiles using the city streets as often as 30 days during the year, regardless of where the user lived. The latter two became the source of much complaint by suburban and rural residents.

The record of metro is clear in this regard. All of the sources of complaint about the financial inequities mentioned above have been eliminated by metro, and most of them within the first few months of operation. Several services formerly financed entirely (or almost entirely) by city taxpayers were shifted to a countywide tax base. The primary ones are airports, parks, libraries, hospitals, urban renewal, traffic regulation, and the auditorium. The "green sticker" fee was repealed and water rates were equalized.

All of this is not to say that all complaints about taxes have been eliminated by metro, but only that the specific ones growing out of the city-county cleavage have been eliminated. As discussed below, metro has undoubtedly stimulated a new source of complaint about tax inequity — from the more distant rural taxpayers who have experienced a sizeable tax increase without sharing in some of the benefits enjoyed by the less distant suburbs. The rural residents are a very small minority, however, and the voter opinion survey revealed that in 1964 there was agreement by a ratio of not quite two to one with this statement: "The tax burden is more fairly distributed under Metro than it was before Metro was adopted."

NEW SUBURBAN SERVICES FINANCED ON A PAY-AS-YOU-ARE-SERVED BASIS. The great outcries brought on by the large 1960 annexation were aimed primarily at the likelihood that new taxes would be paid long before many of the new urban services would be received, especially in the case of sewage disposal and fire protection. Metro was sold to the suburbanites as a method of extending services systematically in "smaller bites" where services could be extended within a reasonable length of time (the charter specifies one year) after new property taxes become due. Because metro has been preoccupied with servicing the 50-square mile pre-metro annexations, no new annexations to the Urban Services District have been initiated, so this prediction has not yet been tested.

Metro took an important step in mid-1965 in the direction of easing the financial pressures connected with annexations, past as well as future, by shifting most of the cost of sewer construction and maintenance to a service charge added to the water bill. While this conceivably could have been done separately by the city and county governments without city-county consolidation, it would have been considerably more complicated and it is politically doubtful whether it would have been done. Financial aspects of the extension of fire protection outside the Urban Services District, a move pledged by Mayor Briley, are still confused as of 1965. If fire protection is extended without annexation, either the entire county area would have to be taxed for this purpose or some kind of service charge would be required. It will be difficult to make the former method comply with the principle of pay-as-you-are-served.

NATIONAL PUBLICITY FOR NASHVILLE AS A PROGRESSIVE COMMUNITY. This prediction was given considerable prominence in the original "Plan of Metropolitan Government" in 1956.

The evidence of national publicity for Nashville as a result of the new metropolitan government is abundant. Visits and inquiries from other metropolitan communities between 1962 and 1965 have been quite a burden to key metro officials and civic leaders, although a welcome burden for the most part. National magazines, as well as newspapers in other cities, have featured the "Nashville story" in their columns, and the new form of government has been in the spotlight at numerous national and regional conferences of various professional groups. The pilgrimage of political scientists to Nashville to study "metropolitics" has been impressive. In short, the publicity *has* come and gives every appearance of being on the increase.

Whether this kind of publicity will bring in new businesses and industries, however, is a question that is still not answered. No dramatic new industrial acquisitions have occurred since the adoption of metro, so that part of the prediction has not yet been borne out. It seems possible to conclude, however, that, everything else being equal, the publicity being given to metro should help Nashville in its recruitment of new industry.

Predictions Made by Opponents of Metro

CENTRALIZED GOVERNMENT LESS RESPONSIBLE AND LESS ACCESSIBLE
TO THE PEOPLE. The prediction of less responsible and less accessible
local government as a result of city-county consolidation was made by
some of the opponents of metro on the basis of the well known, rational
arguments against big government and concentration of political power.
Other opponents resorted to more sensational arguments, seeking to link
metro to "the conspiracy" by "1313" in Chicago to promote collectivism
by means of the consolidation of governmental units. The more rational
grounds for making this prediction were primarily that local legislators
would be required to represent a large number of people, that a smaller
number of departments and agencies would mean fewer access points for
citizens, and that a larger, more professional and "monolithic" bureaucracy would tend to be more aloof and impersonal in its dealings with
citizens.

It is only partly true that the metropolitan councilman must represent
more people than the pre-metro city and county legislators. Although the
councilmen in the former city of Nashville had smaller districts than the
metropolitan councilmen have, the 19 city magistrates serving on the old
county governing body were all elected at large from the entire city rather
than from single-member districts. Out-of-city magistrates were not
elected from single-member districts, either, but rather from two-member
districts, and these had for many years greatly overrepresented the rural
areas of the county. In addition, the county magistrates' term of office
was six years, rather than the four-year term for metropolitan councilmen,
and the term of the county judge, titular head of the county, was eight
years rather than the four-year term specified for the metropolitan mayor.
Thus, it could be argued with considerable logic that metro is much
closer to the stereotyped ideal of grassroots democracy than the old
county government was, but somewhat less close than the old city
government.

A much more compelling argument than the foregoing can be made in
support of metro as an ally of grassroots democracy and in refutation of
the charge that metro would result in less responsible and less accessible
government. This is based on the assumption, supported by substantial
evidence, that one of the major causes of the centralization of power and
functions from local to national government is the inability of fragmented local governments in metropolitan areas to cope with the serious
urban problems which extend well beyond the jurisdiction of the core
city. Metro was specifically designed to permit the whole Nashville
community to have a government capable of making area-wide policy
decisions, and yet a government which remains distinctly local. This

writer believes that a weighing of all of these factors in the balance leads to the conclusion that metro is providing a local government much more responsible and certainly no less accessible to the people than that provided by the former city and county.

SUBSTANTIAL INCREASE IN TAXES. At first glance it would appear that the prediction of substantially increased taxes under metro was rather quickly fulfilled when the first year's budget was adopted in June, 1963. The total property tax levy in the Urban Services District was set at $5.70, an increase of 38 cents over the pre-metro levy, and the rate for the General Services District was set at $3.70, an increase of 94 cents for those living in the unincorporated areas of the county. Metro supporters denied that the increase should be blamed on metro, citing many of the "lame duck" government's actions as cause of the increase.

Some of the causes for an increase in the property tax rate were directly related to the consolidation, however, such as the equalization of pay scales for city and county school teachers and other city and county employees, the extension of the county's free school transportation to the city area, and the general "growth psychology" engendered by the metro movement which seemed to encourage various community interest groups to press for long-desired improvements in city and county programs.

The property tax rate adopted in 1964 was the same as in 1963, but strong pressures were building up for much larger expenditures for the consolidated school system and for new services in the annexed area. Two important fiscal decisions were made in 1965 which not only provided more revenue but permitted the property tax to be reduced by 20 cents on an areawide basis (to $3.50) with an additional reduction of 20 cents in the Urban Services District (to $5.30, overall). These decisions were the placing of sewers on a service-charge basis and the adoption of a one-cent local sales tax, the latter by popular referendum in May.

HIGHER TAXES FOR RURAL RESIDENTS, WITH NO BENEFITS. A study is now underway of the impact of metro on the rural residents, including their services and taxes, but it is possible to describe preliminary appearances of the fate of this prediction. The property tax is undoubtedly higher for rural residents, having risen from $2.76 in 1962 to $3.70 in 1963 and then dropped to $3.50 in 1965. Some assessments may have been reduced and the ten-dollar "green sticker" was eliminated, but the one-cent local sales tax was added. The major tangible service increases for rural residents have been the acquisition of new parks closer to the rural areas (obviously not a high priority item with rural residents), replacement of the sheriff's patrol with a better manned, trained, and equipped metropolitan police department, installation of street lights on the main highways out to the county line, and the construction of branch libraries in suburbs closer to rural residents. These are relatively minor benefits, however, and the rural taxpayer simply shares the same fate as the suburbanite who is required for the first time to share in the "overhead costs" of the core city — financing public facilities which broadly serve the whole region.

REDUCED SERVICES IN THE CORE CITY. This prediction was made in much the same way that it is often made to discourage a core city from annexing large unserved areas. The argument is that preoccupation with the tremendous needs of the suburban areas will make core city needs seem minor by comparison and result in less attention by the consolidated government. It is a persuasive argument and can find logical support in the history of city annexations generally, but after Nashville's large 1960 annexation it lost much of its potency as an argument against metro.

Although most evidence commonly used to support or deny a prediction of this kind is subject to numerous qualifications, it should be possible to place at least a modicum of reliance on the results of an opinion survey designed to measure satisfaction and dissatisfaction with metro. In the spring of 1964 such a survey revealed that 71 per cent of the registered voters in the entire city and county area indicated satisfaction with "the way Metro has worked in its first year of operation." Surprisingly, although only 45 per cent of those in the "old city" actually voted for metro in the 1962 referendum, 80 per cent indicated satisfaction with metro in 1964. In response to the question, "what groups or persons do you think have been hurt most as a result of the adoption of Metro?" only 1 per cent mentioned residents of the old city of Nashville, compared with 20 per cent who mentioned "people who live outside the city." As a minimum, one should be able to conclude that there has been no immediate or early reduction in core city services of sufficient magnitude to cause popular dissatisfaction.

METRO AN UNCONSTITUTIONAL QUAGMIRE OF LITIGATION. Although the opponents' use of the litigation issue was considered to be last-minute desperation tactics, the 1956 report which outlined the proposed new government included a somewhat similar warning based on nineteenth-century experience with city-county consolidation. It stated:

> Constitutional obstacles and lack of legal precedent, which tend to tie up such consolidations for many years, make it imperative to prepare the way with great care and study.[1]

---

[1] *Plan of Metropolitan Government, op. cit.*, p. 19. John A. Rush has recorded many of the judicial roadblocks faced by earlier consolidation efforts in his *The City-County Consolidated* (Published by the author, Los Angeles, 1941).

If metro's record in court is any indication, then the way *was* prepared "with great care and study," for the state courts have smiled upon the new government in a remarkable fashion. Less than six weeks after the voters approved metro, a chancery court decision upheld the constitutionality of the consolidation, which had been attacked on numerous grounds, and just two months later the Supreme Court of Tennessee sustained the opinion of the lower court.

The decisions of the chancery and supreme courts were characterized by surprising speed, sympathy, and unequivocation in their support for the new metropolitan government and in the rejection of all four charges against the charter. Such other litigation as took place in the three years following the adoption of metro was predominantly favorable to metro, and most of these cases would not be classified as serious challenges to the consolidation itself. As of the middle of 1965 there was certainly no support for the prediction that metro would be either unconstitutional or a pandora's box of litigation.

DILUTION OF NEGRO POLITICAL INFLUENCE. It is commonly suggested by political scientists that core city minority groups, especially Negroes, will look upon metropolitan government proposals as schemes to dilute their voting strength in local elections, and their political influence generally. The rather compelling logic of this argument, based on the simple statistics of a steadily increasing proportion of the core city population being Negro (37.9 per cent in Nashville in 1960) and the great majority of suburban population being white, met with divided response among Nashville Negroes. One influential Negro councilman opposed metro on these grounds. But Negro leadership was carefully cultivated by metro proponents, including the filling of two of the ten charter commission posts with Negroes, and a kind of "racial gerrymandering in reverse" which virtually guaranteed the election of several Negroes to the proposed metropolitan council. As a result the "natural" tendency of Negro leaders to fear dilution of their political strength was partially offset, they divided along factional lines, and the so-called "Negro precincts" voted approximately 49 per cent for metro in 1958 and 46 per cent for metro in 1962.

To compare further the prediction with actual experience of Negroes under metro, has Negro voting strength been diluted by the adoption of metro? An analysis of all elections held since the adoption of metro finds no instance in which a candidate supported by the overwhelming majority of Negroes was defeated because of the white voters added to the local electorate by metro. Negro voting strength was, and continues to be, based on their ability to hold the balance of power between the white factions in Nashville politics, rather than on their ability to elect an official in an area-wide race by their votes alone. While it is conceivable that in a mayor's or judge's election the Negro voter's role might be less decisive because of the broadened electorate under metro, the evidence thus far indicates that when Negroes vote for a losing candidate, they have been outvoted not only in the suburbs but in the "old city" as well.

Another test of the impact of metro on Negro political influence, though admittedly an impossible one to quantify, is found in the handling of four racial controversies by the new government: (1) 1963 demonstrations for desegregation of downtown hotels and of certain "holdout" eating establishments, (2) desegregation of municipal swimming pools, (3) 1964 demonstrations for desegregation of eating places away from the downtown area, and (4) a proposal for a local public accommodations act. Little evidence of dilution of Negro influence can be found in any of these cases. On the contrary, there have been many claims that metro has been more conducive to racial harmony. Mayor Briley has said, for example, that a single metropolitan government provided a more effective framework for his committee on human relations to negotiate and conciliate without worrying about divergent city and county attitudes and actions.

While it would certainly be foolish to argue that Negro gains have been primarily a result of the adoption of metro, there is even less evidence that metro has caused a diminution of Negro political influence, or retarded Negro progress. Surveys of voter opinion toward metro, conducted by the author in 1964 and again in 1965, reveal that Negro voters express slightly greater satisfaction with "the way Metro has worked" than do white voters.

REMOVAL FROM OFFICE OF MAYOR BEN WEST AND HIS POLITICAL ORGANIZATION. The prediction that metro would serve as a device to remove from office the political organization of Mayor West was borne out in practice. Indeed, a considerable amount of the political enthusiasm generated in the second campaign for metro was the result of the political misfortunes of Mayor West and the anti-West character of the metro campaign waged by the morning newspaper, the *Nashville Tennessean*. Most observers would agree that Mayor West's vigorous opposition to metro in 1962 made it politically impossible for him to be elected first mayor of the new government in 1963, but his decision not to run was not announced until shortly before the deadline. Although Judge Briley subsequently received the endorsement of many West supporters, there was little doubt about his victory constituting an ouster of the "city machine" by the "county machine."

Even so, one could not conclude that metro was initially designed to oust the city machine, for in 1958 it was publicly endorsed by Mayor West. In any case, it should be clear from the Nashville experience that "radical reform" in local government structure is not prevented by active involvement of rival professional political leaders and, under certain circumstances, it may actually benefit from such a political clash.

Conclusions

After more than two years of experience with the new metropolitan government for Nashville and Davidson County, it is perhaps most significant that none of the predictions by metro's supporters has been proven incorrect and about half of them already give evidence of being fulfilled. In the case of the other half it is either still too early to know or the evidence is inadequate. In the case of the opponents' pre-metro predictions, two already give evidence of being incorrect, one of their predictions has been clearly fulfilled (the removal of the previous mayor from office), one other gives evidence of at least short-run fulfillment (higher taxes on rural residents without significant new benefits), and in the case of the remainder it is either too early to judge or the evidence is inadequate.

It is the opinion of this writer, based on this "early, preliminary, tentative appraisal" of such hard and soft data as now are available, that Nashville's metro is living up to most of the predictions of its supporters and is moving in the direction of proving incorrect most of the predictions of its opponents.

THE METROPOLIS
AND THE FEDERAL SYSTEM

6

In the American federal system, no metropolitan area constitutes a self-contained political system. Fiscal and jurisdictional inadequacies, the monopoly of the formal powers of government by the higher levels, and the local base of the American political system involve the polycentric metropolis in a complex web of relationships with state and federal government. From the state capital come the legal framework of the metropolitan area's local governments, money and personnel to plan and build its highway network, and funds to offset a growing proportion of the burgeoning educational expenses of its constituent units, to mention only the most important of the state's multiplying activities in the metropolis. Washington underwrites home mortgages, finances the massive federal-aid highway system, and assists local governments with urban problems ranging from air and water pollution, mass transportation, and open spaces, through poverty, public housing, and urban renewal.

Constitutional, jurisdictional, financial, and political considerations underlie the growing commitments of state and federal governments in metropolitan areas. Legal and constitutional factors are particularly important in the states. The basic units of the federal system are the states and the nation; the Constitution does not mention local government. Thus, the legal framework of the metropolitan political system is a product of the state legislature, which grants powers to municipalities and other subdivisions of the state, sets standards for incorporation and annexation, creates special districts and authorities, sanctions interlocal agreements and contract arrangements, and provides enabling legislation for metropolitan planning agencies and regional units of government. Because of the dependent legal position of the localities, state involvement in the metropolis automatically increases as local units of government proliferate and their tasks multiply.

Jurisdictional advantages also draw the states into the political arenas of the metropolis. Legal powers encompassing all or, in interstate regions, large portions of the metropolis permit the state to overcome some of the local difficulties caused by the fragmentation of the metropolitan political system. By basing aid to education on need, the state legislature can partly redress the fiscal imbalances in a suburban area composed of communities with widely disparate resources. Much of the pressure for increased state school assistance comes from the less affluent and the rapidly growing suburbs where the increasing number of children often exceeds the addition of new ratables to the tax rolls. The state's jurisdictional advantages also can provide some of the benefits of regional government. If there were no state highway department with the power to plan and build an area-wide system of arterial roadways, the metropolis would have to create a regional highway agency, perhaps at greater peril to local political and fiscal autonomy than the present system of state control. Of course, metropolitan areas pay a price to secure the benefits of the state's jurisdictional scope since state involvement dilutes urban influence in the resolution of metropolitan problems.

Another attraction of the state is its superior fiscal resources, at least compared to those of local government. In general, state income, sales, and excise taxes provide greater flexibility, equity, and growth potential than the real property tax, the chief financial prop of local government. Faced with rapidly rising demands and growing resistance to skyrocketing property taxes, mayors, councils, and school boards in the metropolis have turned with increasing frequency to the state capital for assistance, but few state exchequers have proved equal to the challenge. Demands from cities and suburbs for new and enlarged state programs have overwhelmed budget makers in every urban state. The greatest pressures for and against new programs and taxes fall upon the governor, the state official most responsive to the restive urban majority. From the moment he takes office, the governor of an urban state is caught in a crossfire between two antithetical groups, one demanding more from the state and the other opposed to increased state taxation. The fact that many voters, particularly in the metropolis, are in both camps only increases the governor's dilemma, helping to explain the high political mortality rate of urban governors in recent years.

State fiscal difficulties also have contributed to the deepening involvement of the national government in the problems of the metropolis. Constitutional and jurisdictional considerations have been much less important than money in broadening the federal government's metropolitan role. In almost every respect, the federal tax base is superior to the revenue systems of state and local government. Unlike the property levy and most state taxes, the federal income tax cannot be evaded by moving across a local or state boundary. In contrast to the receipts of state and local taxes, federal income tax revenues grow at a faster rate than the gross national product. Eyeing these mounting federal revenues, the metropolitan areas, and particularly the hard-pressed cities, have successfully lobbied for expanding federal commitments.

Of all the factors which shed light on the increased activity of the higher levels in the metropolis, none is more important than the urbanization of American politics. With urban growth has come a steady increase in the influence of cities and suburbs in the state capitals and along the banks of the Potomac. Since in more than half the states, a majority of the electorate is in metropolitan areas, a larger proportion of the nation's governors and United States Senators are responsive to urban demands. The potent role of the large urban states in the national conventions and the Electoral College has made the presidency particularly sensitive to the needs of the metropolis. Finally, the reapportionment that resulted from historic Supreme Court decisions (beginning with *Baker v. Carr* in 1962) is providing metropolitan areas with a fairer share of the seats in state legislatures and in the House of Representatives.

Growing state and federal involvement in metropolitan areas has rekindled the hopes of those who are dissatisfied with the spreading metropolis, its decentralized politics, and increasingly segregated population. They feel that the constitutional and jurisdictional powers of the states might be used to restructure the fragmented political system. State and federal aid could be made conditional upon the creation of regional instrumentalities. Growing urban investments and superior jurisdictional and fiscal capabilities could enable the higher levels to lead in developing and implementing plans that will ensure a less disruptive and costly pattern of urban development. The Council of State Governments, for example, argues that the key to solving urban problems lies with state government, resting its case for state leadership on the constitutional powers and jurisdictional advantages of the state.

In concentrating on the state's potential, however, the advocates of state leadership tend to overlook the state's past performance in the metropolis. State government is not a sleeping giant that is about to awake and revitalize the urban world. Instead, the state has played a major role in creating the sprawling, fragmented, differentiated metropolis and in developing the modes of accommodation that sustain the decentralized system. Through its powers over annexation, incorporation, and the creation of special districts, the state has facilitated geographic and functional proliferation. Few states have used their jurisdictional or fiscal capabilities to promote regional approaches to urban problems. The two most important state activities in metropolitan areas are highways and education. By concentrating on roads and ignoring public transportation, the state highway departments have contributed to urban sprawl. Because state school aid usually is skewed in favor of the suburbs, it tends to widen the educational disparity between the city and the suburbs, a gap which is a major cause in the flight of white families from the older cities.

Underlying the failure of the states to achieve their metropolitan potential are the same political forces which have doomed almost every effort to create area-wide government. As Harold Herman indicates in his analysis of state-metropolitan relations in New York, the diverse interests of the fragmented metropolis are well represented in the state legislature. Since the metropolitan area as a whole lacks spokesmen, the pressures on the governor and other state officials come from cities, suburbs, special districts, and other subregional constituencies. State action inevitably reflects and reinforces the values of these dominant interests of the metropolis. By fostering functional accommodation to the problems of urban growth and change, New York, like most states, preserves the institutional status quo, relieves the pressures for more basic changes in the system of local government, and promotes continued functional and geographic proliferation.

Traditionally, state governments have been least responsive to the needs of their older cities. Partisan conflicts and rural domination of the state legislature often resulted in state and investment policies that systematically shortchanged the cities. For many city leaders, legislative reapportionment promised an end to the years of state neglect and unfairness. But James Reichley shows that suburbs rather than cities have been the prime beneficiaries of the reapportionment of the 1960s. Reichley makes clear that although a legislature with large numbers of suburban representatives is more responsive to some urban needs than one controlled by small town and rural legislators, it also reflects the conflicting interests of city and suburb, and is particularly sensitive to the almost universal suburban desire to avoid political or fiscal involvement in city problems.

Federal activities in the metropolis have had much the same effect as those of the states. Lacking an overall national strategy for metropolitan development, federal efforts are uncoordinated and functionally autonomous. Resulting federal policy encourages urban diffusion, facilitates accommodation, and helps maintain the fragmented political system. As in the state capital, there is no consensus among the many metropolitan interests represented in Washington. My study of federal-metropolitan relations on the mass transportation issue demonstrates that the fragmentation of local interests pervades urban political behavior as much in the nation's capital as in the metropolis and the state. Differing interests, goals, and capabilities among cities, suburbs, and states produce a wide range of views and activities on a metropolitan issue contested in Washington. Like the state legislator from the metropolis, the average urban congressman rarely represents a district that encompasses the metropolitan area. Since his constituents do not view their urban problems in a regional frame of reference, neither does the congressman. Thus, my conclusions on federal-metropolitan politics parallel Herman's at the state level.

Just as the suburbs have looked to the states as their natural allies in urban intergovernmental politics, the cities have relied heavily on the federal government for help in halting the spreading slums, the flight of commerce and industry, the exodus of the middle class, the declining schools, the deterioration of transit systems, the plague of narcotics, rising unemployment, and mounting welfare burdens. Since the 1930s, Washington has been more responsive to the special needs of the cities than most of the state capitals, particularly when the Democrats control the national government. During the 1960s, the alliance between Washington and the cities produced significant increases in federal urban renewal funds, mass transportation assistance, a federally financed war on poverty aimed largely at the urban poor, and a massive program of federal aid to education that was intended to benefit cities more than suburbs. None of these new and expanded programs, however, has come close to meeting the demands of the cities' spokesmen in Washington.

In his case study of federal housing programs in "Iron City," Theodore J. Lowi reminds us that federal aid does not necessarily benefit all city dwellers. Policies made in Washington are constrained by the local interests represented in Congress and the national lobbies. In the decentralized American federal system, national programs are implemented by local officials responsive to local values, interests, and conditions. As a result, despite such lofty national goals as providing decent homes for all, ending poverty, or ensuring equal educational opportunity, federal programs usually benefit the powerful at the expense of the less influential, especially if the latter happen to be poor and black. In almost every major city, federally financed urban renewal and associated projects have increased residential segregation, reduced the housing available for low-income families, and provided more housing for middle- and upper-income groups who already had the widest range of housing opportunities in the metropolis.

Like every other component of the metropolitan political system, the federal government responds to change. Growing black militancy, the organization of low-income neighborhoods for political action (often financed initially by the federal poverty program), the election of mayors responsive to poor and black constituents, and the reaction of federal and local officials to criticism of past practices — these and other factors make it unlikely that the "Iron City" experience will be duplicated in the 1970s. But it is less clear whether the new federal policies which give greater emphasis to the interests of the disadvantaged and to the overall impact of individual projects on the community, city, and metropolis will have their intended effect. Thomas A. Morehouse's study of the urban planning requirements of the 1962 Highway Act illustrates the impediments to new policy directions posed by powerful functional alliances that cross-cut the federal system, in this case the federal and state highway agencies and their influential supporters in Congress.

Harold Herman

LIMITATIONS ON STATE ACTION:
THE VIEW FROM ALBANY

Between 1957 and 1960, New York's Joint Legislative Committee on
Metropolitan Areas Study came to the conclusion that solutions to the
problems of metropolitan areas rest eventually with local governments.
Although the committee noted the need for some state action, for the
most part, it regarded the state's role as facilitative and only occasionally
stimulative to local innovation. The legislature has signified its general
agreement with the committee's position by its actions. In effect, the state
appears to be following a course long advocated by Home Rule
enthusiasts, acting usually only upon the request of local authorities.
Leadership for metropolitan integration in New York State rests where it
probably must, at the local level.

To expect otherwise is more than unrealistic. Even though their
constituencies are larger, state political leaders are subject to the same
pressures that commit their local counterparts to continued metropolitan
governmental fragmentation. These pressures cannot be interpreted
merely in terms of self-seeking distrust on the part of politicians to any
change that threatens to upset the political systems in which their
interests are vested. All too often, this simple explanation is used to
rationalize the defeat of proposals for metropolitan reorganization,
attributing their defeat to recalcitrant politicians rather than general
unpopularity. On the contrary, political opposition to reorganization
suggests that democracy is in fact working. The divisions in community
interest that hinder local integration are accurately reflected in the state
legislature, whose members are no more nor less able to reconcile their
differences than local leaders.

But are local interests adequately represented in Albany? New York has
not been free from criticism on the grounds of legislative malapportionment. Is imbalanced rather than accurate representation of urban interests
responsible for New York's reluctance to deal squarely with the metropolitan problem?

Reprinted from *New York State and the Metropolitan Problem* (Philadelphia:
University of Pennsylvania Press, 1963), pp. 178–188, with the permission of the
author and the publisher.

317

The positions of Long Island Republican leaders with regard both to the distribution of state aid to education in 1960 and to congressional reapportionment in 1962 would indicate that, in their eyes at least, malapportionment is less a hindrance to the achievement of their objectives than the possible consequences of a Democratic majority's being seated in the legislature. They were willing to suffer some monetary loss in compromising with rural Republicans over state aid to education rather than form a coalition with the Democratic minority. In congressional apportionment, their voices have yet to be raised in demand for deserved increases in suburban representation. They seem to prefer the present security of the Republican caucus to the instability that might result from opening wide urban-rural cleavages.[1] . . .

Retaining Republican control of state policy machinery is a primary goal of upstate Republican leaders and even of some Democrats; for its alternative is Democratic control, which to many is synonomous with control of the state by New York City. This goal, in turn, is dependent upon maintaining the strength of the local roots of the Republican Party. There is then an element of self-protection in the legislature's hesitancy to tamper with local political institutions. It is operative, however, only in so far as area residents continue to believe that their limited integrative objectives are adequately being served by presently constituted political organizations. There is no evidence at this time to suggest that they feel otherwise.

Leadership is rarely expected from legislative bodies anyway. This quality is usually attributed to the Governor. Is he able to offer more positive leadership in metropolitan affairs? Those who see in the electoral basis upon which he gains office a source of strength that is denied legislators individually and collectively usually over-estimate his ability to act independently of political influence and almost always place too much emphasis on the effect of legislative malapportionment. No less a leader then Governor Rockefeller has found it extremely difficult to do anything but equivocate on metropolitan policy.

In one respect, the Governor of New York is constrained from taking too strong a position on metropolitan issues even more than are other state chief executives. The shadow of the White House, so often pointed to as a factor in his favor, tempers whatever inclination he might have to chance provoking local political leaders in both New York and the nation at large. Their support is vital to his future political ambitions, particularly in New York, where nominations for key state and federal offices are decided by convention.

[1] David R. Derge documents the preference for party- rather than constituency-oriented legislative voting in "Metropolitan and Out-State Alignments in Illinois and Missouri Legislative Delegations," *American Political Science Review*, LII, No. 4 (December, 1958), pp. 1051–1065.

In short, the state's political leaders are ill equipped to champion measures for far-reaching change in local government in the face of continuing evidence of local preference for the status quo. Consequently, they have adopted an attitude consistent with the [Joint Legislative] Committee's belief that change will occur when local pressures for uniformity of service become undeniable.

If the political branches of state government are not providing general leadership for metropolitan integration, they are at least participating significantly in the process of adapting local governmental operations to newer problems of urbanism. At times, such participation amounts to gentle prodding and persuasion. More often it takes the form of offering municipalities the opportunity to evolve their own methods of dealing with local problems. In a sense, New York is providing a type of leadership which is, if not as vigorous as that called for by the Council of State Governments and more recently by the Advisory Commission on Intergovernmental Relations, at least more realistic.[2]

The leadership called for by the council and the commission is about as operationally definable as their concepts of the metropolitan problem. Both have taken great pains to stress their practicability, yet throughout their reports lies the suggestion that a problem more deep-rooted than that which can be solved by annexation, functional transfer, and special authority is involved in metropolitan areas. But of course, they are not recommending the formation of metropolitan governments.

New York State's position is more forthright. There is no single governmental problem in metropolitan areas, but rather a number of difficulties surrounding the provision of selected public services, which existing local institutions can continue to perform with some minor adjustments. Through different reasoning, at the same time absolving itself from the responsibility for providing leadership, New York has arrived at many of the policies advocated by the proponents of more direct state leadership: the interlocal agreement, the special authority, the encouragement of expanded county activities, and most of all the sharing of state resources with local units have typified metropolitan policy in New York State.

In the development of this policy, however, New York's leaders have consistently held to a functional outlook toward metropolitan problems and their solutions. Where general legislation has been called for to permit or encourage intermunicipal cooperation, the creation of special districts, or, as the commission put it, the building of "an 'arsenal' of

[2] In a report submitted to the House Committee on Government Operations, the Advisory Commission on Intergovernmental Relations cites favorably and comes to the same general conclusions as the Council of State Governments. *Governmental Structure, Organization, and Planning in Metropolitan Areas* (Washington, D.C.: U.S. Government Printing Office, July, 1961).

remedial weapons" available to metropolitan areas, New York has preferred to deal with metropolitan problems with both geographic and functional selectivity. In one respect, it has surpassed most recommendations for dealing generally with local governments. In 1946, a per capita block grant to all local units was initiated. Critics regard this non-conditional sharing of state resources on the one hand as the best method of helping localities help themselves, on the other as the surest means of encouraging the retention of inefficient, marginal units of local government. The choice of positions is largely a matter of personal predilection. Even were techniques of measurement available, the grant's size is as yet too small to warrant drawing any conclusions.

In pursuing its functional course, the state has virtually ignored exploring annexation as a metropolitan alternative. New York's annexation laws, in addition to the usual complexity, are extremely protective to unincorporated territories. Considering the extent of fringe-area development that has taken place in highly urban New York . . . and the general opinion that annexation's usefulness is quite limited, its application to New York is highly questionable.

Again consistent with its over-all policy, New York has continued to extend the scope of its Home Rule law. Constitutional amendments in 1959 considerably broadened the range of county discretion and for the first time included urban towns within the scope of Home Rule. Village officials at this time were particularly apprehensive of the irresponsibility and isolationism that might thus have been encouraged. Their attitude reflects the changing light in which Home Rule has come to be viewed. At one time, it was held to be the answer to most, if not all, local ills. Today it is regarded with some misgivings. The Advisory Commission on Intergovernmental Relations seems to be echoing the early [New York] Tax Commissions' search for formulas delineating governmental responsibilities when it recommends

> local home rule for strictly local problems; metropolitan home rule for area-wide problems, but with the state free to legislate and otherwise act with respect to problems which transcend county boundaries and which are not soluble through interlocal cooperation.[3]

Conceivably, definition of the problem may become more difficult politically than its treatment!

Home Rule in New York has never served to prohibit the state from intervening, when it wanted to, in what are presumably matters of local "property, affairs, and government." The legislature and the courts have seen to that. Moreover, Home Rule has constantly been served up with conditions and procedural requirements that limit the freedom apparently offered.

[3] *Ibid.*, p. 20.

The County Home Rule Amendment approved by the electorate in 1959 is illustrative of the hesitant one-step-forward, two-steps-back pace that characterizes progress in New York State. The legislature had introduced the amendment in part to formalize the considerable degree of county independence operationally developed and in part to enable counties to adjust themselves to their newer metropolitan responsibilities. It offered considerable local discretion in organizing county governments, but at the same time it restored the requirement of a double-majority approval (a majority in any city and a majority in areas outside of cities) that had been dropped from the constitution by the 1938 convention. The provision requiring a triple majority for proposed transfers of functions to counties (majorities in cities, outside areas, and all units affected by the transfer) was retained in its entirety. . . .

The interplay of local preference and state policy has resulted in the state's offering and local units' choosing forms of metropolitan action least damaging to the territorial and functional integrity of local political institutions. What has been their combined effect on metropolitan integration . . . ?

The state must be credited with contributing to the process of metropolitan integration through fostering an awareness of areal need and encouraging local cooperation in tackling selected problems on a metropolitan scale. Departmental officials have been especially active in promoting awareness of the areal aspects of local activities. The legislature, in addition to making cooperative means of local action available, has at times taken further steps to stimulate their employment through the offer of grant inducements. While not always effective, their joint efforts have assisted in breaking down previous barriers to intermunicipal cooperation. Not to be overlooked is the fact that such cooperation has successfully reduced some of the problems of transportation, water supply, sewage disposal, public health, and others. Metropolitan areas are not falling apart at the seams.

Although the state is helping alleviate some of the most evident manifestations of the metropolitan problem and although it is contributing to integration, defined as a process involving the development of metropolitan consciousness, it has not assisted, primarily because it has not wanted to, integration conceived as the creation of institutional mechanisms for organizing and coordinating policy making in metropolitan areas. There is good reason to believe that state and local concentration on individual service problems is, in fact, hindering metropolitan integration thus defined.

Government is more than a provider of services; it is a political institution of social organization and control. As an integrative institution, government in metropolitan areas should perform the task of eliciting expressions of interest and reconciling differences. To a significant degree, the state itself is now performing this task in metropolitan areas, but none of the current service-oriented undertakings of the state or local governments appears to be contributing to the creation of local institutions for this purpose. The state's functional approach to metropolitan problems appears to be furthering additional metropolitan fragmentation along functional, rather than geographical, lines. Paradoxically, this is occurring at the very time that the county, partly as a result of state policy, is beginning to show a potential capacity to act as an integrative institution.

The cumulative effect of functional policies has been gradually to expand the scope of county responsibility and activity. A remodeled county government could well serve as the agency of metropolitan policy making and administration. Single counties presently include most of these portions of metropolitan areas experiencing the problems of urbanism. The county represents both the largest service unit and the largest unit of local self-government. It has gained in popular stature and respect with its increased responsibilities. The New York county enjoys an advantage in structure lacking in many other states that increases its attractiveness when compared with other proposals for metropolitan government. This traditional unit of government is already federally organized, although quite often disproportionately.

State policy does not, however, look toward the eventual employment of counties for metropolitan government. For the most part, the county has "just growed." Although the state has encouraged expansion of their activities, it has done so with no general scheme of development in mind. In the past, the state usually sought to limit county authority to unincorporated areas whenever possible. Although county-wide authority is today preferred for many functions, the change in attitude has been justified on administrative grounds, with little concern for the county as an institution for governing. The state's opinion of the role of counties in metropolitan-area government might well be summed up by Pope's couplet: "that which is best administered is best."

Functionalism adds a new dimension to metropolitan fragmentation. It poses a problem of integration perhaps more difficult than the mere proliferation of units of government. It fosters intracommunity divisions in interest and leadership, adding these to divisions already founded on jurisdictional lines.

Throughout the state, leadership in metropolitan areas has come to be associated with particular functions. To the extent that opportunities to exercise general leadership still exist in pluralistic American society, they are lessened by increasing isolation of functional responsibilities and horizontal division of these among several units of government. Even traditionally strong mayors have succumbed to the trend toward functional specialization and exclusiveness. They have seized upon urban renewal as their specialty, leaving other aspects of municipal leadership to other specialists and their interest groups.

Functional division of government has a dual impact on the citizen. It provides yet another obstacle to his understanding and participating in governmental decisions affecting him. Yet, it also offers him security, leading him to believe that there is really nothing wrong with local government (of this he needs little convincing) that a few more sewers or roads won't cure.

State and federal programs reinforce the functional-service definition of the metropolitan problem. They single out problems for treatment, holding out hopes that each successive project they encourage will bring an end to the metropolitan area's ills. One has only to read the glowing newspaper accounts of "how we solved our metropolitan problem" or "how our metropolitan area is progressing" that follow the announcement of new urban renewal, highway, or treatment-plant projects for visual evidence of their lulling effect. Functionalism thus tends to impede not only governmental integration but the development of metropolitan consciousness as well. When a problem has been solved there is little reason to continue to be concerned for the metropolitan area. Moreover, there is no evidence of a carry-over of metropolitan awareness from one specific problem to another.

Proponents of metropolitan action wage their campaigns within their respective fields of functional competence and rarely concern themselves with other problems, let alone with "the metropolitan problem." Each proposal for metropolitan action is considered on its own merits, with little apparent reliance on experience gained from other functional solutions, except where these have produced bitterness and resentment of "interference" and "domination." Metropolitan consciousness is as functionally oriented as metropolitan leadership.

Perhaps no amount of state activity can substitute for the local initiative necessary to progress toward metropolitan integration. Undoubtedly, metropolitan integration cannot occur until such time as the public is prepared to take a critical look at local government as a form of government, not merely as a dispenser of services. Can Albany hasten this day?

It can do so only by admitting that the metropolitan-area problem is political not administrative and that it involves the very nature of local government. It must discard the search for techniques of problem solving and concentrate on developing responsible and representative policy-making agencies in metropolitan areas. No number of functional jointures and agreements will ever provide a suitable governmental (and necessarily democratic) mechanism for planning and controlling the distribution of physical and human resources within a metropolitan area. Administration is not lacking in metropolitan areas; government is. There is little

indication that New York will be prepared to adopt such a change in
attitude in the foreseeable future.

A. James Reichley

THE POLITICAL CONTAINMENT
OF THE CITIES

... Under a democratic system of government — even one limited by
constitutional and economic checks, like that of the United States — the
primary source of political power is votes, which is to say, people.
Economic and moral forces certainly play a part in the American political
process, but are not consistently effective unless able to gather popular
support for the points of view they represent. The individual public
official may succumb to a bribe or rise to a moral challenge, but in the
end he will fall if his constituents are not similarly tempted or inspired.
Physical intimidation, which in most nations in the world plays a decisive
part in allocating political power, still limits Negro franchise in some
southern states, and still can turn the tide on election day in some
backwoods counties and some "controlled" city precincts. At the state
level, however, with the important exception of muffling the black voice
in the Deep South, it has had no significant effect since the demise of
Huey Long in Louisiana. Distribution of political power among regions in
most states, therefore, rises initially out of the geographical distribution
of population.

If all votes are not counted equally, of course, this rule must be
modified. Prior to the Supreme Court's series of decisions on legislative
apportionment during the early sixties, over-representation of rural
counties in many state legislatures caused serious discrimination against

A. James Reichley, "The Political Containment of the Cities," from Alan K.
Campbell, Editor, *The States and the Urban Crisis* © 1970 by The American
Assembly, Columbia University, New York, New York. Reprinted by permission of
Prentice-Hall, Inc., Englewood Cliffs, New Jersey.

urban voters and their interests. Most states gave some advantage to rural areas in their methods of apportionment, and some states, like California, Texas, and New Jersey, provided in their constitutions for one house, on the model of the United States Senate, in which representation was on the basis of area rather than of population. In addition, many states, as in the notorious case of Tennessee, which first brought the matter before the Supreme Court, simply ignored constitutional mandates for decennial reapportionment, thereby freezing representation at a period when the great majority of voters lived in small towns or on farms.

Before reapportionment, many city representatives and their sympathizers had come to believe that weighted apportionment was the *entire* cause of the relative impotence of city delegations in the legislatures. Now that the process of redrawing legislative districts on the basis of "one man-one vote" has been almost completed, spokesmen for the cities are having painful second thoughts. Some, in fact, have grown a bit nostalgic for the bad old days of domination by rural squirearchies. "At least you could buy the rural legislators!" Mayor Daley was heard to lament on a day when Chicago was faring badly at the hands of the new suburban leadership in the Illinois legislature. "The chief effect of reapportionment has been to update conservatism," according to Jesse Unruh, who in 1969 was demoted by Republican takeover of the California Assembly from speaker to minority leader. In Cleveland's embattled city hall, Mayor Carl Stokes complained recently, "One man-one vote hasn't changed a thing as far as the central city is concerned. Instead of the farmer with his conservatism and detachment, you now have the man from suburbia, who is as conservative and detached, and sometimes as hostile to the city, as the rural member."

Actually, malapportionment by the time the Supreme Court delivered its rulings was penalizing the suburbs much more than the cities. In some states, like Ohio and Texas, the practice of electing all representatives on a countywide basis in at least one house left suburbs virtually unrepresented. Table I compares representation of some major cities with that of their suburbs in the legislative house with the *least* equal representation before and after reapportionment.

Failure of reapportionment to produce city control of legislatures has left some city representatives undisturbed in their conviction that the day when cities will dictate to the states is not far off. Others, however, have felt compelled to reassess the distribution of real power, based on the size of the population groups within their states.

The Population Balance

The 1960 census, which will govern legislative apportionment in most states until 1972, showed only ten states which were not more than 50 per cent urban. Since the Census Bureau includes all persons living in towns of more than 2,500 inhabitants or in the "densely settled fringe" of urbanized areas in its "urban" category, however, this term is almost useless for purposes of political classification. Certainly residents of small towns of less than 10,000 people sense little political identity with inhabitants of major cities. Also, persons living in cities of less than 50,000 are more likely to feel antagonistic than fraternal toward such giant cities as New York, Chicago, Los Angeles, and Philadelphia, particularly if they happen to share a state with one of the super-cities. Finally, residents of the metropolitan areas outside great cities, whether technically "urban" or "rural" under the Census Bureau's definitions, are generally bound in a common "suburban" point of view.

TABLE I. COMPARISON OF POPULATION TO REPRESENTATION BEFORE AND AFTER REAPPORTIONMENT

	Percentage of state population in 1960	Percentage in House before reapportionment	Percentage in House after reapportionment
California Senate			
Los Angeles, San Francisco,			
San Diego, Oakland	26	10	25
Suburbs	39	12.5	37.5
New York Assembly			
New York City	46	43	45
Suburbs	17	11	18
Pennsylvania House			
Philadelphia, Pittsburgh	24	21	23
Suburbs	24	19	23
Illinois Senate			
Chicago	35	31	36
Suburbs	27	14	24
Texas Senate			
Houston, Dallas,			
San Antonio, Ft. Worth	27	13	32
Suburbs	9	0	0
Ohio Senate			
Cleveland, Cincinnati,			
Columbus	19	33	30
Suburbs	16	6	12
Michigan Senate			
Detroit	21	15	18
Suburbs	27	12	32

A more helpful tool for political analysis is the Census Bureau's designation of "Standard Metropolitan Statistical Areas" (SMSA) — generally, cities of more than 50,000, along with surrounding areas "socially and economically integrated with the central city." A very rough classification of political interests based on place of residence can be achieved by dividing state populations into residents of SMSA central cities, inhabitants of their surrounding suburbs, and persons living outside of the SMSAs altogether. This scheme of classification obviously creates categories which embrace multitudes of differences. There is a great distinction in point of view between residents of small cities and inhabitants of the rural countryside, both of whom are included in the third or "outstate" category. Likewise, persons living in cities with populations from 50,000 to 100,000 are operating under social structures essentially different from those which exist in the super-cities. (It may be argued that one of the root problems of the super-cities is that they provide *no* visible social structure to which the ordinary citizen can relate his behavior.) Still, the division into SMSA city dwellers, suburbanites, and outstaters provides a workable basis from which analysis can begin.

As it happens, these three groups were close to equal in the total national population in 1960. SMSA city dwellers comprised 32 per cent of the total population, suburbanites 31 per cent, and outstaters 37 per cent. Not surprisingly, as is shown in Table II this distribution was substantially different in most of the ten most populous states. (These ten states contained 54 per cent of the total population, 62 per cent of the total urban population, and 67 per cent of the total living in SMSAs. All are among the 18 states which the Census Bureau found to be more than 70 per cent urban.)

TABLE II. PERCENTAGE DISTRIBUTION OF STATE POPULATIONS
IN 1960

	SMSA cities	SMSA suburbs	Outstate
New York	58	31	11
California	34	50	16
Pennsylvania	32	48	20
Illinois	42	35	23
Ohio	35	34	31
Texas	46	17	37
Michigan	32	41	27
New Jersey	18	60	22
Massachusetts	33	51	16
Florida	24	41	35

Among the top ten states, only Ohio approximates the national distribution among the population groups. Only in New York, Texas, and Illinois, however, does the deviation from the national norm significantly favor the cities. Only New York contained an actual majority of city dwellers.

Among the other 40 states, only one, Arizona, had more than 50 per cent of its population living in cities. Only in New York and Arizona, therefore, do the cities have the potential strength to dominate state governments without help from the other two groups. In reality, cities in neither of these states have been able to gain a clear upper hand. Not only do city voters divide their support among parties and candidates in statewide elections, but also the potential city strength is split by rivalries among the cities themselves.

In Arizona, there are only two cities of significant size — Phoenix and Tucson. Phoenix by itself comprised 34 per cent of the state's population in 1960 and was more than twice the size of Tucson. Fearing total domination of the state by the metropolitan giant, Tucson has increasingly aligned itself with the rural minority. Phoenix, nevertheless, plays a powerful role in state government, and at least recently has set the tone of Arizona politics. Quarrels with the hinterland, however, do not usually come in questions of policy, since Phoenix, the home base of Senator Barry Goldwater, has remained politically quite conservative. Except for supporting a relatively generous state subsidy for education, the city has done little to promote state action on urban problems.

At the other end of the process of urbanization, the cities of New York have made important contributions to the political process which has produced what is surely the most progressive state government in the nation. Never, however, have the cities been able to exercise the dominance to which population would seem to entitle them. New York City, which in 1960 by itself contained 46 per cent of the state's population, is overwhelmingly Democratic, but during all but four years since 1939 the state has had a Republican governor. In the legislature, even after reapportionment, the cities have been unable to exercise effective control. This is partly due to the political ineptness of New York City Democrats, but results largely from the historic antagonism felt among the state's other cities toward the great metropolis. Voters in cities like Rochester, Syracuse, and Binghamton support Republican candidates in percentages unusually high for eastern cities at least partly because the Democratic party is closely identified with New York City. This situation has not left the cities powerless — Republicans since Thomas Dewey have taken care to cultivate their urban constituencies — but it has made them petitioners instead of arbiters in state government.

If cities have not become dominant in the two states where they hold actual majorities, it is not surprising that in the remaining states they have had generally tough sledding. The 22 SMSA cities of Texas, which together comprised 46 per cent of the state's population in 1960, have had difficulty acting in concert and were hampered by under-representation in the state senate prior to reapportionment. In any case, many of them, like the cities of Arizona, have usually supported conservative candidates and policies. Chicago accounted for 35 per cent of the population of Illinois, but since the state has few other sizable cities, the metropolis has had to deal for favors with the suburban and outstate blocs. In only two other states, Hawaii and Nevada — both rather special cases — did cities contain more than 40 per cent of the state's total population.

Current population trends will further weaken the position of the cities in state politics. The 1970 census will show the cities slipping well behind the other two geographic groups in population strength. For the first time in American history, more people will be found living in suburbs than in cities. Looking ahead, some projections indicate that by 1985 suburbanites will outnumber city dwellers by almost two-to-one. The effect of this swing to the suburbs has already been felt in statewide elections. Table III shows the shifting distribution of the vote in presidential elections for principal cities and their suburbs in four urban states.

Another trend in demography which will complicate the political problems of the cities is the growing percentages of Negroes in central city populations. Black majorities are projected during the seventies for such important cities as Detroit, Baltimore, Cleveland, St. Louis, and perhaps even Chicago and Philadelphia (not, however, for New York City or Los Angeles). While black governments in the cities will at last give Negroes the power base they have always lacked in American politics, it would be foolhardy not to anticipate tensions between black city halls and the predominantly white administrations in state capitols — similar, perhaps, to the antagonism that existed between Irish administrations in Boston and Yankee governments in Massachusetts during the early years of this century.

TABLE III. PERCENTAGE OF STATE VOTE CAST BY CITIES AND THEIR SUBURBS IN PRESIDENTIAL ELECTIONS

	1952	1960	1968
New York			
New York City	48	42	39
Suburbs	14	18	22
Illinois			
Chicago	41	37	31
Suburbs	19	26	30
Pennsylvania			
Philadelphia	21	18	18
Suburbs	11	14	16
Michigan			
Detroit	29	23	18
Suburbs	19	27	30

The Suburban-Outstate Coalition

The central conclusion that emerges from all of these statistics is that the cities do not now and will not in the foreseeable future have the votes to dictate means for dealing with urban problems to the states. The dream of city politicians in the fifties and early sixties that the cities might some day be able to impose their wills on the states simply will not bear the test of reality. This does not, of course, mean that the cities will have no access to power. If they are not in a majority position, neither, generally speaking, are their suburban or outstate rivals. In only four states, New Jersey, Rhode Island, Massachusetts, and California, did suburbanites in 1960 comprise more than 50 per cent of the population. In 24 largely rural states (though including Wisconsin and Indiana) outstaters held a clear majority. In the 20 remaining states, not counting New York and Arizona, some combination of city, suburban, and outstate interests is needed to form a majority. Even where suburbanites or outstaters could theoretically rule alone, divisions within their own ranks almost always force them to seek some outside support. In almost all states, some arrangement of shared power is a necessary condition for government.

Population groups can achieve power in state politics in two ways: through their representatives in the state legislature, or by affecting the results of elections for statewide offices, particularly governor. In the legislature, the city delegations were until recently forced to negotiate for favors with the outside squires who were dominant in all but a few heavily urbanized states like Massachusetts and Rhode Island. Contrary to general belief, the squires were not always unresponsive to metropolitan needs. For one thing, in the big urban states many of them were aware that they owed their positions to a kind of democratic sufferance. If they had been too outrageous in thwarting the desires of cities and suburbs, rural weighting of apportionment would not have survived for as long as it did. For another, they were often relatively enlightened men, who had made careers as lawmakers and had developed considerable knowledge of and even sympathy for urban problems.

Jesse Unruh, who worked at close quarters for many years with the squires in the California legislature, has observed that they were frequently men of independent judgment, able to continue as legislators without heavy campaign expenditures due to the very population sparsity of their districts. Since reapportionment, Unruh claims, districts are so populous that a successful candidate must either be extremely wealthy or turn to the "special interests" to fill out his campaign budget. The result has been to eliminate a breed of fairly disinterested public servants from the legislature. Mayor Daley's regret over the passing of rural legislators who could be "bought" may spring from a cruder perception of the same phenomenon — men who were willing to help the cities, if they could receive some help in return for projects which would benefit their own districts.

Nevertheless, there is no doubt that the rule of the squirearchies tended to direct state government toward essentially rural values. The things that the states have done best, as Paul Ylvisaker has pointed out, have been the things which rural constituencies could appreciate: superior highways, land grant universities, decentralized public school systems. Distinctively urban problems, though usually not wholly neglected by the squires, were inevitably regarded as being of secondary importance. Most critically of all, the outstate representatives usually practiced the rural virtue of frugality. With the encouragement of the business lobbies that were their frequent allies, they held state expenditures of all kinds, though particularly those intended for the cities, to a minimum. The fiscal straitjackets in which almost all states are still enclosed were thus formed.

The dominance of the squirearchies has now passed, because of reapportionment, in all but the most rural states, but their remaining leaders retain substantial influence. Ylvisaker, who as New Jersey's first Commissioner of Community Affairs has learned perhaps more than he wished to know of legislative behavior, has observed that the skills which the squires acquired during their years of dominance help now to preserve their effectiveness beyond their numbers. In addition, they still comprise from one-fourth to one-third of the memberships of legislatures in most urban states outside of California, New York, and lower New England. In some states, as has already occurred in Maryland, city delegations may find it possible to make common cause with the remaining squires against the rising power of the suburbs. In general, however, the outstaters will probably choose alliance with the suburbs over coalition with the cities.

Rise of the Suburbs

The suburbs, both because their interest generally lies somewhere between that of the cities and that of the outstate, and because the drift of population is so clearly in their favor, now occupy enviable positions in most urban state legislatures. After years of sometimes resentful submission to the authority of the squires, the suburbanites have at last ascended to positions of power. In Illinois, for example, in 1969 not only the governor and state attorney general, but also the president pro tem of the state senate and the majority leader and majority whip of the house of representatives were residents of suburban Cook County. Suburbanites also held key offices in the legislatures of, among other states, New York, California, Pennsylvania, Michigan, and New Jersey.

Despite the complaints of city representatives against suburban indifference and even hostility, the shift from outstate to suburban leadership has probably produced a net gain for the cities. Suburbanites, for one thing, as Moynihan has remarked, "are at least used to spending a lot of money." Resistance to state tax increases is probably not quite so strong in the suburbs as outstate. When Governor Richard Ogilvie pushed Illinois' first income tax through the legislature in 1969, he received much greater support from suburban representatives of Cook County than from their fellow Republicans downstate. Moreover, at least some of the cities' problems are shared by the suburbs. Mass transit in metropolitan areas, air and water pollution, disappearance of open space near large cities are issues to which suburban voters respond. Moreover, the very proximity of the cities, plus the fact that many suburbanites work in downtown office buildings, forces the distinctive problems of the inner cities upon the attention of suburban representatives. "We know now that a bomb that goes off in the core city affects suburbia," says New York Assembly Speaker Perry Duryea, whose home district is in suburban Suffolk County.

This does not mean that suburban representatives recognize a generally common interest with the cities, or that city-suburban coalitions are likely to appear in many state legislatures. The influence of party, for one thing, works against it. In most urban states outside the South and Southwest, city delegations are overwhelmingly Democratic and most suburban representatives are Republicans. In states with low legislative party discipline, like California, this is only marginally important. But in states with traditions of strong party discipline, like New York, Pennsylvania, and Ohio, the suburban Republicans not only view their Democratic colleagues from the cities with the normal amount of inter-party animosity, but also are strongly influenced by the conservative views of the outstate members of their party caucuses. A further conservative check on suburban Republicans in some states appears to be coming from the new breed of Republican legislators that have begun to be elected from cities like New York and Chicago. In these cities, which for many years have supported mildly progressive and hopelessly outnumbered Republican parties, Republicanism has suddenly begun to gather strength from the new conservatism of white working-class neighborhoods. Since Republican legislators elected from these neighborhoods owe their success to their ideology, they are likely to take a hard line on issues like law enforcement and welfare. Though as yet few in number, they have already somewhat conditioned the policies of Republican leaders in some legislatures.

The deeper reason for the lack of close ties between city and suburban representatives is that their interests on many issues do not really, at least in the short run, which no politician can safely ignore, coincide. The reason that the Democratic Party has so spectacularly failed to penetrate the suburbs in most states is that the Democrats are identified with the crooked politics, dirty and unsafe streets, and racial tensions of the cities, which many suburbanites have deliberately chosen to put behind them. Having reached the suburbs, they are chiefly concerned that the cities' problems shall not follow them. They are willing, within reason, to pay higher state taxes, but they insist that the state give first attention to what they regard as their primary needs. In New York in 1969, when Governor Nelson Rockefeller proposed a five per cent across-the-board cut in projected expenditures for all state programs, Perry Duryea and his fellow suburban Republicans in the legislature insisted that most of the cuts in education subsidies be restored, and that the difference be made up by doubling the slice in welfare. The legislators were undoubtedly reflecting the values of a majority of their constituents.

Actually, many outstate and suburban legislators probably go farther in providing help for the cities than is popular in their districts. Richardson Dilworth, former mayor of Philadelphia and now president of the Philadelphia Board of Education, tells of traveling to the capitol of Pennsylvania in the winter of 1969 with a group of Philadelphia businessmen in search of more state aid for the city's schools. Dilworth had threatened that the schools would close before the end of the school year if no additional funds were found. At a meeting with legislative leaders from suburban and rural areas, one of the businessmen argued, "As politicians, you cannot afford to permit the schools of the state's largest city to close for lack of money." This suggestion was greeted with laughter. "As politicians," said one legislator, "there is nothing that would do us more good than to go back and tell our voters that we wouldn't let Philadelphia have another nickel."

The cities' best hope for eventually gaining allies in the suburbs is that the present political unity of the suburban delegations will some day be broken up. The suburbs at present embrace a wide variety of economic levels and life styles. They include communities which range from cloistered rural villages to densely populated industrial slums. Their political unity, as Richard Wade has pointed out, is based almost entirely on their common fear of and opposition to the city. In time, their natural differences may begin to pull them in different directions. Close-in suburbs are increasingly experiencing problems that are similar to those faced by the inner cities. This may eventually draw them closer to the cities politically. Some movement in this direction is already occurring in the suburbs of New York. Democratic candidates now commonly win legislative contests in some districts in Nassau and Westchester Counties. The industrial towns around Detroit also send Democrats to the legislature. In the suburbs of most major Northern cities, however, the Republican phalanx remains almost unbroken. In 1969, not a single Democrat represented the districts of suburban Cook County outside

Chicago. Of the 36 legislators elected from the four suburban counties that surround Philadelphia, only two were Democrats. For the foreseeable future, such joint action between city and suburbs as takes place will occur under uneasy partisan truce rather than through intra-party collaboration. . . .

Michael N. Danielson

THE PATTERN
OF FEDERAL-METROPOLITAN POLITICS

Federal-metropolitan politics is a natural extension of the fragmented political system of the metropolis. Since the metropolitan area commonly lacks regional institutions, legal recognition, and public officials with areawide constituencies, the focus for political activity is submetropolitan or supermetropolitan. Regional issues are contested in terms of the interests of the central city, the suburbs, the authorities, and the states. From a welter of conflicting constituency interests comes a metropolitan political process in which the participants "are committed . . . to particular solutions of particular problems. What results is a competitive scramble for available resources and power. The notion that there might be common goals and resources becomes lost in the struggle."[1]

The mass transportation issue provides ample evidence of the pervasive influence of particularism on federal-metropolitan politics. When the commuter crisis first stimulated efforts to influence Washington, metropolitan actors from the New York area sought to save northern New Jersey's commuter service, safeguard New York State's tax relief

Reprinted from *Federal-Metropolitan Politics and the Commuter Crisis* (New York: Columbia University Press, 1965), pp. 183–189, with the permission of the publisher.

[1] Robert C. Wood, *Metropolis Against Itself* (New York: Committee for Economic Development, 1961), p. 32.

program, secure federal aid for the New Haven Railroad, pacify constituents in Bergen or Morris County, shield New York City from new mass transportation financial burdens, or achieve some other limited goal. Enlisting federal help for the improvement of public transportation on a comprehensive regional basis tended to be ignored, particularly by state and suburban interests, until much later.

Regional interests are represented at the federal level by various metropolitan actors, each of whom perceives regional problems in the perspective of its particular institutional base and none of whom possesses a regional mandate. Each participant brings to federal-metropolitan politics a set of values and resources which differ little from those governing its behavior in the internal politics of the metropolis. Thus, suburbia seeks federal help preoccupied with local problems, inadequately equipped for effective action beyond its borders, and fearful of proposals which threaten autonomy or unequal costs and benefits. As for the regional congressman, his position in the larger metropolitan areas resembles that of the local politician. Since his district embraces only a portion of the metropolis and his constituents rarely perceive their problems as regional, the congressman is reluctant to devote his limited resources to complex metropolitan problems. State relations with the national government on regional problems are conditioned by the pressure of mushrooming urban demands on limited state fiscal resources and the necessity of the urban governor to function in a supermetropolitan constituency in which the rural sector traditionally has been overrepresented. Dedicated to preserving the urban core, the central city comes to Washington with an areawide frame of reference and a willingness to use the region's most potent aggregate of political resources for revisionist purposes, particularly with respect to public finance.

The mass transportation issue illustrates how these differences in regional perspective and in influence at the national level interact with the traditional positions of the states, cities, and suburbs in intergovernmental relations to produce characteristic attitudes toward the involvement of the federal government in metropolitan affairs. All these factors — outlook on regional matters, capabilities in the federal arena, and orientation toward federal-metropolitan relations — combine to provide each metropolitan actor with a distinctive set of interests and goals in his Washington ventures. Different goals, such as the crisis-inspired endeavor of the New Jersey suburbanites to amend the Transportation Act, the states' efforts to save commuter service on the New Haven, or the central-city coalition's campaign to secure support for mass transportation, require distinct kinds of resources, investments, and influence. Activities in pursuit of these goals, in turn, shape the patterns of participation by the suburb, by the state, by the central city, and by the urban congressman in federal-metropolitan politics.

Since the federal government is not an important factor in suburban politics, participation in federal-metropolitan relations at the suburban grass roots tends to be sporadic, crisis-stimulated, and concerned primarily with the short-run local aspects of a problem . . . [E]ven the commuter, often cited as the most cosmopolitan of the suburbanites by virtue of his daily journey across the metropolitan landscape, usually views his transportation dilemma in a localistic and remedial perspective. In pursuing their limited objectives in Washington, suburbanites are hampered by the meager political resources afforded by their fragmented institutional base, the absence of national suburban pressure groups, and their heavy dependence on the local congressman.

Like the suburbs, most urban states have a limited and negative orientation toward federal involvement in urban affairs. The mutual interest of state and suburb in federal-metropolitan politics springs from partisan ties, as well as from a common fear of financial involvement in regional arrangements, a shared antipathy toward the city, and a mutual interest in resisting the extension of federal-city links. This last factor is particularly important since the states are extremely sensitive to the threat that direct federal aid programs pose to their role in local affairs. The behavior of New York and New Jersey illustrates clearly the typical state posture in federal-metropolitan politics: little interest in the development of long-term federal urban commitments, opposition to direct federal-local relations, and insistence that federal aid be channeled through the states.

The role of the central city in federal-metropolitan relations contrasts sharply with that of the suburbs and the states. Money, political realities, and the adverse impact of the decentralization of the metropolis on the urban core have made the central city the major force behind the involvement of the national government in urban problems. Onerous burdens have been placed on the city by the need to build expensive highways, to maintain sagging public transport systems, to replace spreading slums, to revitalize deteriorating downtowns, and to meet the burgeoning demands of an increasingly lower-class and non-white population on the local treasury. Suburban dedication to the fragmented political and fiscal system prevents the city from tapping much of the wealth of the metropolis. Help from the statehouse, where rural forces are commonly overrepresented and exchequers are chronically overburdened, is rarely adequate. As a result, argue the mayors, the cities are "the unwelcome stepchildren of the counties and the state" and "have no other choice than to journey to Washington."[2] Here the political process

---

[2] Ben West, "Federal-City Relations from the Cities' Point of View," in George Washington University, *The Federal Government and the Cities* (Washington, D.C., 1961), p. 21.

is more responsive to urban needs, here assistance can be obtained on terms favorable to the cities, and here the suburbanite can be tapped indirectly through the federal income tax.

Superior capabilities, an ability to mobilize interests from all parts of the nation, and a sustained interest in broadening the federal government's urban responsibilities make the central city the most influential participant in federal-metropolitan politics. In their efforts to enhance their alliance with Washington, city leaders can employ the many resources of the region's major unit of government, the influence of its most prominent political and economic figures, particularly the mayor, the help of the nation's great metropolitan dailies, and the efforts of the national urban lobbies. On the mass transportation issue, a combination of these assets first forged the urban-rail alliance. Then the geographical base of support was widened; as an official of the American Municipal Association noted in 1961, "Two years ago interest in federal help for commuter railroads was centered almost entirely on the eastern seaboard. But now we have west coast cities, like Los Angeles and San Francisco, and even southern cities behind us."[3] Next, the familiar central-city alliance of Democratic politicians, downtown economic interests, commuter railroad and transit operators, metropolitan newspapers, planners, professors, and regionally oriented civic groups was reproduced at the national level in support of the federal transit legislation.[4]

Suburban, state, and central-city perspectives, as well as those of the city's various districts, are reflected in the behavior of the congressional delegations from metropolitan areas. Since House districts encompass few metropolitan areas with more than half a million residents, the average urban congressman, like most other metropolitan actors, views the metropolis from a subregional institutional base and in the light of the particularist demands of his city or suburban constituents. For most congressmen, identifications with their district, party, faction, and committee far outweigh any nebulous obligations arising from the fact that they represent part of a metropolitan area. Another factor inhibiting congressional involvement in metropolitan issues is the limited capability of the average urban representative for effective action in an area of emerging federal legislative concern. Efforts in the House on the mass transportation issue highlight the restrictions imposed by committee assignments, seniority, the lower chamber's conservative leadership, party

[3] Statement of Patrick McLaughlin, *Wall Street Journal*, May 2, 1961.

[4] By 1964 the central-city forces supporting the mass transit bill had organized an Urban Passenger Transportation Association, composed of representatives of the AMA, the U.S. Conference of Mayors, the Institute of Rapid Transit, the Railway Progress Institute, and the American Transit Association; for an account of the activities of the association in attempting to steer the bill through the House of Representatives, see Newark *Sunday News*, May 24, 1964.

loyalties and rewards, personal interests and abilities, and limited staff resources. Whether in response to constituency pressures or for broader reasons, most forays on the part of the urban congressman are both nominal and ineffective.

Compared with his colleague in the House, the urban senator is more likely to bring to federal-metropolitan politics a regional outlook and an opportunity to affect the consideration of urban issues. The statewide constituency and the six-year term foster a broader perspective on the metropolis than is afforded the House member. On the other hand, the senator's Washington sphere of operations liberates him in large part from the constraints that the state institutional base imposes on the urban activities of the governor. A good example of the difference between the gubernatorial and senatorial role in federal-metropolitan politics is provided by Abraham Ribicoff of Connecticut. While governor he followed Rockefeller's lead and largely ignored the movement to develop a federal-urban mass transportation program, but after his election to the Senate in 1962 he moved to the forefront of those in Congress advocating federal assistance for metropolitan transit systems.[5] Mass transportation politics also illustrate the senator's superior capabilities for action on urban issues. Senators Case and Williams were more successful than Representatives from the New York area because they served in a smaller, less hierarchical, more liberal chamber, in which individual members have greater prestige, more committee posts, adequate staff assistance, and far greater opportunities for influence and leadership.

All these factors help explain the characteristic behavior of the various urban participants in federal-metropolitan relationships. As the many facets of the mass transportation issue emphasize, however, national forces also play a crucial role in shaping the pattern of federal-metropolitan politics. The variables affecting the outcome of federal-metropolitan interaction are national rather than local, regional, or state. The need for widespread urban support and national alliances is clear in the failure of the Transportation Act amendments compared with the success of the mass transit legislation. And because national considerations are the key to victory, leadership on federal-metropolitan issues is exercised more successfully by those urban actors who can mobilize for effective action at the national level.

The complexity of the national government and the multiplicity and magnitude of its tasks also shape federal-metropolitan relations. The federal government is hardly the monolithic entity that its critics decry.

---

[5] In fact, Ribicoff made his maiden speech in the Senate in defense of the Kennedy administration's mass transit bill.

Rather it is "a government of separated institutions sharing powers."[6] Within and among these institutions exists a dynamic pattern of conflict and consensus, competition and cooperation. Based on a national constituency, the federal executive is more responsive to urban needs than Congress is. But, as the 1961 mass transit controversy indicates, interagency conflict, budgetary constraints, and the inexorable pressures of foreign policy and national defense limit the effectiveness of the Presidency in defense of urban interests. Another critical national influence on federal-metropolitan politics is the scattering of responsibilities for parts of problems such as transportation and urban development among a host of executive agencies, independent bodies, and congressional committees. This lack of focus multiplies and entangles the channels of information and influence to federal decision makers. While widening the choice of urban claimants, this diffusion of responsibilities also invites competition, delay, and stalemate.

The result is a system in which the many pathways to the national capital attract numerous metropolitan actors, each motivated by different perspective of the urban landscape and none representing the metropolis as a whole. From a constellation of federal agencies, commissions, committees, and individuals, most seek particular remedies for the maladies of their particular fragments of the metropolis. Few of the federal participants can satisfy urban demands independently, but most can block action unilaterally. In this scramble, capabilities and influence are unequally distributed; perceptions, attitudes, interests, constituency concerns, and goals vary widely. From the interplay of these many variables comes the characteristic pattern of federal-metropolitan politics.

[6] Richard E. Neustadt, *Presidential Power* (New York: Wiley, 1960), p. 33.

Theodore J. Lowi

APARTHEID U.S.A.

The United States is over 100 years away from an official apartheid policy. Yet, after more than 20 years of serious involvement by the federal government in the "urban crisis," the social condition of American cities could be little worse if the concerned federal agencies had been staffed all those years by South African agents. A close look at the actual results of federal urban policies gives wonder how there remains any national legitimacy and why the crisis of the 1960s has not been more violent.

The crisis of the 1960s signaled the end of the era that began in the 1930s. Lyndon Johnson was the Herbert Hoover of this moment of change. As Hoover presided over the wreckage of the depression, Johnson presided over the wreckage of the New Deal. In both crises, the sincere application of established criteria began to yield unexpected, unintended and unacceptable results.

The New Deal was founded on the principle of positive government made possible — that is, acceptable to Americans — by a very special form of decentralization. Ideally, federal funds are to be passed to state and municipal administrators to deal with their problems as they see fit. The legislature is expected to set up a program without giving the administrator any guidance whatsoever for fear of intruding upon state or municipal autonomy. As K. C. Davis puts it, "Congress says, 'Here is a problem. Deal with it.'" The result we generally call enabling legislation.

The New Deal was expected to work effectively and without arbitrariness by putting the new programs in the best of all possible worlds: responsibility will be imposed upon central bureaucrats and decisions will be made miraculously in the public interest merely through the pulling and hauling of organized interests; central government expands; local influence expands as well; everybody gains. It is the providential "hidden hand" of Adam Smith applied to politics.

This neat process has been the prevailing public philosophy for the past generation. Panglossian political scientists describe it with overwhelming approval as pluralism. The Supreme Court has enshrined the essence of the New Deal in American jurisprudence as delegation of power. Most recently, political rhetoricians embrace it as creative federalism, maximum feasible participation, and countervailing power. Thanks to the work of such unlikely comrades as Lyndon Johnson, Arthur Schlesinger, J. K. Galbraith, *Fortune* and the *Wall Street Journal*, the principle of decentralization through delegation became the consensus politics that celebrated the end of the New Deal era in 1968.

What follows is a simple case study of the implementation of the two major federal urban programs in a single city. The case goes far toward explaining why the national regime in the United States is no longer taken to be legitimate by so many black people and why this sense of illegitimacy was so likely to spread eventually to whites. Legitimacy, that elusive but vital underpinning of any stable regime, is that sense of the rightness of the general political order. It is that generalized willingness to view public error or corruption as the result of bad administration. There is probably no way practicably to measure legitimacy as such, but one can usually assess roughly the extent to which a regime is less legitimate today than yesterday — just as a doctor may not say precisely what a healthy body is but can know whether it is less healthy now than before.

In this spirit, one can fairly clearly detect a decline in the legitimacy of the regime by noting the rise of instances of repression of Left and Left-sounding activities; one can also detect it by noting the increasing number of political trials and political prisoners, and, more palpably still, the increased infiltration of Left organizations by paid informers. But other indications are not limited to the Left, as for example the increasing numbers of instances of defiance of federal laws — something Southerners have been leading the country in at least since 1954. One can therefore speak of problems of national legitimacy when he begins to sense a general unwillingness to submit political disputes to recognized channels of political settlement, when he sees mediation replaced by direct action.

This case suggests the extent to which the policies of the liberal state are producing its own downfall, and along with that the failure to achieve even a modicum of social justice. Also, in its perverse way, the case illustrates the effectiveness of planning when governments do define their goals clearly and guide administrators firmly. Tragically the plan was for implementation of an evil policy, apartheid. But through the case perhaps liberals could learn a little something about how to plan for good ends.

Iron City is an urban-industrial area whose corporate boundary surrounds nearly 60,000 residents and whose true metropolitan area includes about 100,000. The history of the development plan of Iron City presents a single, well-documented case of the implementation of explicit racial goals. More than that, the nature of Iron City's official development plans and proposals upon which federal allocations were based serve to document beyond doubt the extraordinary permissiveness of federal urban policy.

Housing Policy in Iron City

The name of the city has been changed to protect the guilty. They are guilty as charged, but no more so than thousands of mayors, councilmen, planners, realtors and builders all over the country. The Iron City situation is extreme and unrepresentative, but it will soon be clear that it provides an ideal laboratory for discovering the nature and limitations of modern federal enabling legislation. Iron City is a southern city, and its development plan fostered racist goals, namely, apartheid, but in doing so its officials only stated the awful truth about the goals of land use development plans in cities all over the country.

In 1950 over 20 per cent of Iron City's population was Negro, and they did *not* live in a ghetto. There were neighborhoods of Negroes in virtually every section of town. There was a narrow strip along the river, and there were several strips in the west central and western sections in easy walking distance from the steel and textile mills. There was a largely black neighborhood in the south central section, and there was a larger concentration in the north central section, "across the tracks." (Note the shadings on the map.) There was no Harlem; the implications of the very word suggest the nonsouthern origin of systematic housing discrimination.

Iron City's has been the typical Negro residential pattern in stable, middle-size southern cities. Rather than a single Negro section, there were interwoven neighborhoods of black and white. This patchwork pattern began in the 1920s with the slow but steady immigration of Negroes from outlying areas to the growing city. Access to industry and the needs of the wealthier whites for domestic servants made "close quarters" a desired condition. For example, the Negro neighborhoods east and north of The Circle were surrounded on three sides by the wealthiest homes in Iron City. But while the residents tolerated and encouraged in many ways the proximity of the races, it could not be said that Iron City constituted an integrated community. Each neighborhood was distinctly monochromatic. There were no black-white-black-white house patterns, although there were a number of instances when several Negro families lived directly across the street from or alley-to-alley with a larger number of white families.

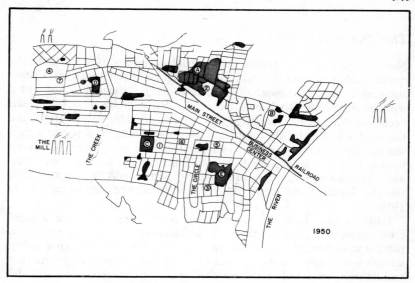

IRON CITY IN 1950

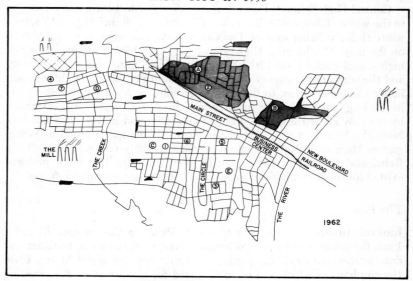

IRON CITY IN 1962

They "Knew Their Place"

Negroes seemed to accept their back-of-the-bus status and the questionable privileges they had which were unavailable to whites. Crimes committed within the race were not, as a rule, investigated or prosecuted with utmost vigor. Black bootleggers (legal sale of liquor has for years been forbidden in the county) had freer rein to cater to the blacks and the insatiably thirsty white middle class. The raising of a pig or a goat was usually allowed, in violation of public health regulations. The rents tended to run considerably lower. And merchants and newsboys were more permissive in granting or extending petty credit to Negroes. This was the dispersed and highly status-bound social situation as recently as 1950.

Early in that decade, however, most Southerners could see a racial crisis approaching, and for them the problems inherent in the residential pattern were immediately clear. In Iron City each of the major public schools was within walking distance of at least one strip of Negro housing and its complement of school-age children. The map serves to make this graphically clear.

Central High School (1 on the map) offered 9th–12th grade education to the white children who lived east of The Creek. Rebel High (4) served white children living west of The Creek, including some areas not shown on the map. Washington High School (2) taught both junior and senior high school grades (7th–12th) to Negro children from both the entire city and the surrounding county. Note the proximity of Negro neighborhoods, hence eligible children, to the white high schools. Most vulnerable to any impending court order for integration would be Central High, attended by virtually all of the children of upper-middle and middle-class families. Note also how far a good half of the Negro children commuted to Washington High and also how many of them actually crossed the paths to Rebel and Central in the course of their journey. The same problem existed for the junior high (3 and 7) and elementary schools (5, 6, and 7).

The Plan

Into this situation stepped the Iron City Planning Commission in 1951. First, the commission analyzed housing, land uses, economic facilities and deterioration. In 1952 they produced a handsome and useful Master Plan, the emphasis of which was upon the need for measures ". . . for arresting beginning blight and correcting advanced blight." On the basis of the Master Plan, a more intensive investigation was ordered toward ultimate production of a Rehabilitation Plan to guide actual implementation and financing. The result of this careful study was a professionally designed, fully illustrated, three-color, glossy paper booklet entitled *Iron City Redevelopment*. The focus of this publication was three areas, designated A, B and E on the map, in which blight had made urban redevelopment necessary.

Upon closer scrutiny, however, the plan reveals itself less a scheme for urban renewal than a script for Negro removal. All of the projects proposed in the plan are explicit on this point. The underlying intent to create a ghetto is further highlighted by the inconsistencies between the design for Area E, which had relatively few Negroes, and that for Area A, which was predominantly Negro. The latter housing was as blighted as Area E, but, curiously, the standard of blighting was not applied. There the plan called for intensification of use rather than renewal.

The plan identified Area E as:

occupied by Negroes, but the number is too few to justify provisions of proper recreational, school and social facilities. . . . The opportunity to reconstitute the area as a residential district in harmony with its surroundings was the main reason for its selection as the number one redevelopment site.

The second, Area B, was chosen because "a relatively small amount of housing — standard and substandard — exists there"; therefore it would serve "as a companion project to . . . [Area E] . . . thus affording home sites for those occupants of [Area E] who are not eligible for relocation in public housing or who, for reasons of their own, prefer single-family or duplex dwellings." Area A, as shown by the intensive survey and the maps published with the plan, contained as much dilapidated and blighted housing as Area E; but Area A was *not* designated an urban redevelopment area in the plan. Although "blighted and depreciating," it was the "center part of the area . . . growing as the focal point of Negro life." Along the main street of this area, extending into Area B, the plan proposed the building of an auditorium, a playfield and other public facilities "to serve [Iron City's] Negro community." Sites were inserted for the three Negro churches which would be removed by the redevelopment of Area E.

Before completion of *Iron City Redevelopment*, implementation projects had begun and were expanding as financing allowed. It was to be a showcase program, and enthusiasm ran high. The first steps, quite rationally, were to acquire housing for those families who were to be displaced. It was perfectly consistent with the city's view of these people that this housing would be public housing. There had been some public housing projects built under depression legislation, but the only meaningful projects were those begun in 1952 under The Housing Act of 1949. On the map the letters A, B, C and D represent the actual locations of these projects. There was never any controversy over the racial distribution of the occupants. Projects A and B were 100 per cent Negro; Projects C and D were 100 per cent white. By 1955 they were completed and occupied.

PUBLIC HOUSING PROJECTS IN IRON CITY

Project	Size (No. of units)	Percentage Negro in project	Original composition of area	Development cost
A	160	100	Negro	$1,491,000
B	224	100	Mixed	$2,491,000
C	146	0	Negro	$1,595,000
D	220	0	Negro	$2,300,000

Each public housing project was placed carefully. Project A was built in the middle of the largest Negro area. Project B was built in a sparse area, about 50 per cent Negro, but marked out in the plan as the area for future expansion of the Negro community. In the area around Project B, the plan proposed sites for the three new "colored churches" and the "colored auditorium."

Project C, an exclusively white project, was built literally on top of the Negro area around it. While it was relatively inexpensive and contained the fewest number of units, it occupied an eight-square-block area due to its design. According to the executive director of the Greater Iron City Housing Authority, it was "a rather unique design, known in the architectural trade as a crankshaft design, thus providing both front and rear courtyards." This project was cited professionally as an outstanding example of good design. And no wonder! Its maximum utilization of space, although a low-rent project, made it a combination public housing, urban renewal and Negro removal plan par excellence. Project D was also built on top of a blighted Negro neighborhood. While it was a relatively large project, it was not solely responsible for eliminating every Negro from the area, as was Project C.

Meanwhile, renewal of the central city was proceeding at a slower pace; it wasn't until 1956 that implementation projects were fully designed. Two areas, designated by the shaded areas around B and E on the map, were selected for intensive renewal. Most important was Area E, a 56-acre area relatively tightly packed with rickety frame houses, outside toilets, corn or potato plots and Negroes. In the official plan, Area E included the unconnected Negro neighborhood just north of The Circle, as well as the entire shaded area due east of The Circle. Area B was relatively sparsely populated, containing a few shacks which needed removing. In some of these shacks were white unemployables.

Within three years the two urban renewal projects were declared 100 per cent accomplished. In the official report to the Urban Renewal Administration, the results were as follows:

COMPLETED URBAN RENEWAL PROJECTS IN IRON CITY

Accomplishment	Activity	For Area E	For Area B
100%	Land acquisition, no. of parcels acquired	168	39
100%	No. of families relocated	176	24
100%	No. of structures demolished (site clearance)	236	33

In Area E every trace of Negro life was removed. As the executive director of the Greater Iron City Housing Authority put it, "In this project, all of the then existing streets were vacated and a new land use map was developed." One entirely new street was put in, several of the narrow lanes (e.g., Saint James' Alley) were covered over, and through connectors were built for a dead-end street or two.

All of Area E has now become prime property. One large supermarket, several neighborhood businesses, and two apartment complexes are operating on renewal land purchased from the authority. To serve the 95 per cent white area, an elementary school was constructed, as a consolidation of schools No. 5 and No. 6 which no longer exist. Its large playground and lighted ball field occupy most of the eastern sector of Area E. The renewal effort resulted in an equally impressive campus for the nearby junior high, No. 3. But most of the area was zoned for single family residences, and, as of 1968, the boom in construction of houses in the $25,000–$40,000 range was still in progress.

Area B now enjoys a new elementary school with a field house, lighted ball field, tennis court and playground. The city also built a swimming pool here, but it and the original municipal pool on The River were closed for several years to avoid integration of public facilities. Moreover, though redevelopment sites had been set aside in Area B for the three churches demolished in the redevelopment of Area E, each of the congregations chose locations elsewhere in the Negro community. Similarly, most of the relocating Negroes rejected Area B in favor of Area A, even though it was more densely populated and blighted. Except for the 224 units of new public housing, Area B remains underutilized. Furthermore, the major part of Area B extends north of Project B toward the mountain, where *Iron City Redevelopment* reports that although

some of the terrain is steep, much of it is gently rolling and well drained. . . .
In most southern cities there is a scarcity of vacant land located close to schools

and churches and shopping districts and served by city utilities and transportation, land that is suitable and desirable for expansion of Negro neighborhoods or creation of new ones. [Area B] is such an area.

Apparently the Negroes do not agree, and most of the area remains a graded, but raw, expanse of red southern earth on the side of the mountain. This was the one part of the plan that went wrong; this was the voluntary part, not financed by federal agencies.

Yet, as a whole, the plan was an overwhelming success. Well before the 1960 census the large Negro contingent in Area E had been reduced to 5.1 per cent of the entire census tract, and this was comprised of a few shanties behind the bottling works and the western edge of the area along The River. In Area C the removal process immediately around Central High was completed with Public Housing Project C. After 1960 some 10 per cent of the area was still nonwhite, but this was drying up still further. Removal from Area D was approaching totality. By 1964 removal from all areas west of The Creek was given further assistance by the completion of one federally supported artery running east-west through the city and the inauguration of Iron City's portion of the new north-south Interstate Highway. That brought the nonwhite proportion in the western sectors of the city down to about 3 per cent of the total population of those areas.

This is how the situation stood by the end of 1967: west of The Creek and north of Main Street (all around Area D), there remained six Negro families. When a nearby textile mill was closed down some years before, they, as employees, were given the right to buy their houses, and they have chosen to remain. West of The Creek and south of Main Street (the area including The Mill), fewer than 5 per cent of the housing units were occupied by Negroes. Virtually every one of these houses is located in isolated and sparse sections along The Creek and behind The Mill, where one can still plant a plot of sorghum, catch a catfish, and, undisturbed, let a 1948 Chevrolet corrode into dust. Closer to the center of things, east of The Creek and south of Main Street, the 1960 distribution of Negroes continues to be reduced. Every last shack is gone from Area E and the entire central section of the white city. Three small pockets remain in the western portion near Area C, and that is all that remains in all of the white city. The last remaining Negro neighborhood of any size, a group of shanties running along The River south of Main Street, was removed by the construction of a City Hall–Poli Department–YMCA complex. Area B remains completely nonwhite and underdeveloped. Area A now fills the entire triangle pointing north. It is a ghetto.

The plan enjoyed strong consensus among officials and white citizens. It enjoyed at least the acquiescence and tacit consent of the Negroes whose landlords, in any case, were white. Consensus or not, the plan would have had little chance of success without outside financial assistance. That assistance came, abundantly, from federal programs. And, most importantly, the federal personnel who allocated these funds, and still do, also had access to all the project plans, including the Master Plan and the Renewal Plan. Despite Iron City's open approach to apartheid — nothing was kept secret — federal assistance was never in question. Relative to the population of Iron City and the size of its annual public sector budget, federal aid was quite substantial — amounting to 20 per cent of the municipal budget for a few years. What we have seen here is an honest, straightforward job of federally sponsored physical and social planning. And the results were dramatic. Perhaps only New Haven, Connecticut, a city famous for its redevelopment, has had a higher per capita success ratio.

Direct federal assistance for public housing in Iron City amounted to slightly over $280,000 for the single fiscal year 1966. Each year since the completion of the four projects the city received a similar amount. This varying figure cannot be broken down among the four projects because it is computed on the basis of the "development costs" given above and granted as a lump sum. The Public Housing (recently changed to Housing Assistance) Administration of Housing and Urban Development (HUD) is authorized by law to grant *each year* to any housing authority the difference between expenses (governed by development costs) and income from public housing. Such a subsidy arrangement enabled authorities like Iron City's to borrow from private banks and to refinance through sale of relatively cheap Housing Authority bonds. What is even more significant is that, under the formula, Iron City is authorized to receive a maximum grant of nearly $305,000 per annum. It is a point of pride at the Greater Iron City Housing Authority that the full amount available under the law was never needed or requested. At a minimum estimate of $250,000 per year, federal grants to help carry the public housing have amounted to $3,000,000. And federal public housing grants are never-ending. Each year the total to Iron City goes up another $250,000 or more.

Subsidizing the Rich

Federal assistance for urban renewal, as differentiated from housing assistance, was another indispensable part of the plan. Between 1957 and 1961, by which time virtually everything but land disposition was completed, Iron City received just short of $1,600,000 from the federal government under the urban redevelopment laws. This amounts to an additional subsidy of $400,000 per annum.

The federal housing assistance was at least $300,000 for each year between 1954 or 1955 and 1957. Together with the urban renewal allotments, the total was at least $700,000 during the years of peak planning activity, 1957–1962. This money is the key to the plan's success.

But to this we must also add the resources made available through various other federal agencies. Federal highway assistance added an undetermined amount for new arteries and, incidentally, forced Negroes to move from the western edge of Iron City. The Federal Housing Authority and the Veterans Administration help to finance the lovely homes being built in Area E. It has not been possible to determine whether federal community facilities funds helped remove Negroes from The River where the new City Hall complex now stands. Nor has it been possible to determine if the local banks balked at extending FHA and VA home owner credit to Negroes seeking to build on the mountain side north of Area B. Answers would affect the meaning of the case only marginally.

Tarnished Legitimacy

First, the case bears out what many people have been saying for two decades, that slum removal meant Negro removal. But it goes further. It supports the even more severe contention that the ultimate effects of federal urban policies have been profoundly conservative or separatist, so much so as to vitiate any plans for positive programs of integration through alteration of the physical layout of cities.

Second, it supports the general thesis that a policy of delegation of powers without rule of law will ultimately come to ends profoundly different from those intended by the most libertarian and humanistic of sponsors. Moreover, it supports the unfashionable contention that some of the most cherished instruments of the liberal state may be positively evil — and that a criterion by which this evil can be predicted is the absence of public and explicit legislative standards by which to guide administrative conduct.

Third, the case of Iron City, especially the explicit nature of its racial policy, shows precisely how and why federal policy is ill equipped to govern the cities directly. The permissiveness of federal enabling legislation could do no greater harm to the social future of the cities than if harm were intended. The present disorder in the cities is explained properly by the failure of government and politics, rather than by the inferiority of Negro adjustment. The case demonstrates how national legitimacy can be tarnished to the degree that it is loaned to the cities for discretionary use and how the crisis of public authority is inevitable as long as a political process unguided by law climaxes in abuses such as those catalogued in Iron City. In sum, it helps show why liberal government based on current principles of delegation cannot achieve justice.

Every Negro in Iron City knew what was happening. Every Negro in Chicago and New York and Cleveland and Detroit knows the same about his city too. But since northern Negroes are not as docile, does that mean that federal imperium was used completely differently outside the South? True, planning authorities would never so deliberately pursue such obviously racial planning. It is also true that few social plans could be as relatively extensive or as successful as Iron City's. Nonetheless, it is undeniable that misuse of federal programs in ways indistinguishable in principle from the Iron City misuse has been widespread.

Martin Anderson, for example, estimated in 1964 that about two-thirds of all displacements resulting from urban renewal were Negro, Puerto Rican, or some other minority group. In public housing the record is even more somber. First, because the pattern is even clearer, and second, because these projects stand as ever-present symbols of the acts of discrimination by which they were created.

A study by Bernard Weissbrourd for the Center for the Study of Democratic Institutions concluded that ". . . most cities have followed a deliberate program of segregation in public housing. . . ." Until July 1967, many housing administrators followed a rule of "free choice" allowing eligible tenants to wait indefinitely for an apartment, which allowed them also to decline a vacancy on racial grounds. Still more recently it was revealed that the Chicago Housing Authority, with the full knowledge of federal agencies, cleared all proposed public housing sites with that member of the Board of Aldermen whose ward would be affected. Thus, while the whole story cannot be told from official statistics, we may conclude what every urban Negro knows — Iron City is not unique.

Separate but Equal?

According to HUD reports of 1965, only three of New York City's 69 public housing projects were officially listed as all nonwhite or all white in occupancy; but ten of Philadelphia's 40 projects were all nonwhite, and 21 of Chicago's 53, five of Detroit's 12, four of Cleveland's 14, and all of Dallas' ten projects were listed as either all nonwhite or all white. The rest of reality is hidden, because the Public Housing Administration defines an "integrated project" as one in which there are "white and more than one nonwhite, including at least one Negro family." Not only does this system of reporting make it impossible to determine the real number of truly integrated projects, it also serves to maintain local racial policies and prejudices.

The Civil Rights Act of 1965 was supposed to have put an end to such practices, but there is little evidence that it can or will improve the situation in public housing in particular or city housing in general. It was not until July of 1967 that the rule of "free choice" was replaced with a "rule of three," a plan whereby an applicant must take one of the first three available units or be dropped to the bottom of the eligible lists. All of this is undeniable testimony that the practices all along had constituted a "separate but equal" system of federally supported housing.

In June 1967, three years after the 1964 Civil Rights Act and after strenuous efforts by the Johnson Administration, two of Detroit's five segregated projects became "integrated" when one white family moved into each of two totally black projects. At the same time, at least 11 of New York's projects were classified as "integrated" when, in fact, fewer than 15 per cent of the units were occupied by families of some race other than the race of the 85 per cent majority in that project.

For 33 years the Federal Housing Authority has insured over $110 billion of mortgages to help whites escape, rather than build the city. This confession was made when the FHA instituted a *pilot* program to increase FHA support for housing finance in "economically unsound" areas. And it took the belated 1967 directive on public housing to get them to do that much. These remedial steps came five years after President Kennedy's famous "stroke of the pen" decision aimed at preventing discrimination in publicly supported housing and three years after the first applicable Civil Rights Act. Yet no such legislation or executive decisions can erase the stigma of second-class citizenship placed upon the residents of federal housing programs. Nor can more skillful administration of essentially separatist programs remove the culpability of federal participation in the American local government policy of apartheid. Rather, all of these efforts merely suggest that remedies and correctives are never going to help bad organic laws, because bad organic laws are, quite literally, congenitally defective.

Perhaps it is better to have no new public housing than to have it on the Iron City pattern and at the expense of national legitimacy. With the passing of the Housing Act of 1968 and union agreements to build modular units off-site, some will surely argue that the answers lie in the proper expansion of public housing. But unless steps are taken to prevent the duplication of the patterns reviewed here, more will hardly yield better. Other writers and officials have proposed various solutions. President Johnson suggested creating semipublic corporations to finance public low-cost housing, while Senator Charles Percy would offer incentives to private corporations. These proposals focus on the details of financing and offer further examples of the confusion shared by liberals today concerning forms of law versus essentially technocratic forms of administration for achievement of simple, ordinary justice. Regardless of the means of financing, these programs will produce no lasting social benefit without the rule of law that states unmistakably what administrators can and cannot do, what is to be forbidden, and what is to be achieved. That is the moral of the Iron City story.

Thomas A. Morehouse

ARTFUL INTERPRETATION: THE 1962 HIGHWAY ACT

The Federal-Aid Highway Act of 1962 greatly encouraged planners and students of urban development throughout the country, for it included a planning requirement which gave promise of bringing highways into harmony with the urban environment. This promise has not been fulfilled. The following discussion of what the law required and how it was interpreted by the federal Bureau of Public Roads is intended to help explain why this is so. It will attempt to show how the Bureau absorbed the 1962 requirement into the ongoing highway program in such a way as to leave the existing program structure and modes of operation intact, avoid any additional delays in highway construction schedules, satisfy the state highway departments, and yet meet the formal requirements of the law. Analysis of the planning requirement and its administration by the Bureau of Public Roads may also provide useful perspective on new planning policies initiated by the recently established Department of Transportation; and it may indicate some of the factors most likely to determine the operational meaning and actual results of such policies. . . .

Expectations and Realities

A major breakthrough in federal spending for urban highways was made with the Federal-Aid Highway Act of 1956. That act established the multibillion dollar highway trust fund, activated a massive interstate highway program, and signaled a major increase in spending for non-interstate highways as well. As a result, the federal highway program soon became the single largest and most visible public program affecting physical development of the nation's rapidly growing metropolitan areas. The sheer magnitude and visibility of the interstate program attracted the attention and concern of many land use planning advocates who saw the new highway program both as a possible threat to community planning objectives and as a potential means of shaping urban growth patterns.

Several more or less inconclusive attempts were made to establish

From "The 1962 Highway Act: A Study in Artful Interpretation," by Thomas A. Morehouse. Reprinted by permission of the author and the *Journal of the American Institute of Planners*, Vol. 35, No. 3, May 1969, pp. 160–168.

voluntary state-local transportation planning programs in the years that followed. But the planning requirement of the 1962 highway act provided the first real basis in federal law for the planners' hopes that the highway agencies might become truly effective partners in the effort to achieve better urban development:

> It is declared to be in the national interest to encourage and promote the development of tranportation systems, embracing various modes of transport in a manner that will serve the States and local communities efficiently and effectively. To accomplish this objective the Secretary . . . shall cooperate with the States as authorized in this title, in the development of long-range highway plans and programs which are properly coordinated with plans for improvements in other affected forms of transportation and which are formulated with due consideration to their probable effect on the future development of urban areas of more than fifty-thousand population. After July 1, 1965, *the Secretary shall not approve . . . any program for projects in any urban area of more than fifty-thousand population unless he finds that such projects are based on a continuing comprehensive transportation planning process carried on cooperatively by States and local communities* in conformance with the objectives stated in this section [emphasis added].[1]

The close, bilateral relationship between the federal Bureau of Public Roads and the fifty state highway agencies apparently was to be transformed into a cooperative federal-state-local arrangement for the planning not only of urban highways but transit systems as well. The total transportation system, in turn, was to be related to other elements of metropolitan growth and development. It appeared that control over highway planning and decision-making was to be shared with "outsiders," and that the character of highway planning was to undergo a significant change. Highway departments would now have to explicitly account for relationships between highways, transit, and urban land use development, and local governments were to participate in highway planning decisions. Metropolitan transportation planning programs of this character would clearly be a major innovation with profound effects on the way highway departments traditionally discharged their tasks of planning and building highways. Thus it appeared on the surface in 1962.

Today, few observers of the highway program would hold that such expectations have been realized. Indeed, disillusionment began to set in within the first few years after enactment of the planning requirement. For example, certain federal Housing and Home Finance Agency officials concluded that the planning processes being established in response to the 1962 planning requirement were essentially highway planning studies dominated by state highway departments in the traditional manner. A prominent planning consultant, highly respected by federal and state

[1] U.S., Congress, House, *Federal-Aid Highway Act of 1962*, Public Law 87–866, 87th Cong., 2d Sess., 1962, H.R. 12135, sec. 9(a).

highway officials, stated that the transportation and land use elements of planning were not at all adequately coordinated with each other in the required planning programs. An official of the Advisory Commission on Intergovernmental Relations, commenting on transportation planning programs established under the 1962 highway act, pointed to the "pervasive attitude held by many planners and others of the urban scene that little progress has been or is likely to be made toward implementation of sound transportation and comprehensive urban development plans — a feeling that something is rotten in the state of the art."[2] Federal Bureau of the Budget officials, who were directly involved in the initial stages of policy development leading to the 1962 planning requirement, concluded that the requirement was being carried out by the state highway departments in their customary manner — primarily as a technical planning problem. And the Committee for Economic Development, in a policy statement on metropolitan transportation issued three years after passage of the 1962 act, observed that "local governments usually have little control over major transportation expenditures undertaken within their jurisdiction by state highway departments using federal grants-in-aid to cover a large part of the costs."[3]

Yet, by the end of the first year after the July 1, 1965 statutory deadline, the Bureau of Public Roads was able to report that the required planning processes were "well underway" in nearly all of the 230 metropolitan areas defined by the U.S. Bureau of the Census, and that over 1,500 agreements for cooperative planning had been executed between state highway departments and local communities. Even more recently, no highway projects had yet been disapproved by the Bureau on the basis of an area's failure to meet the planning requirement.

That the law was not interpreted and carried out in such a way as to satisfy many observers of highway program activities does not, of course, mean that the federal and state highway agencies acted illegally or subverted the explicit provisions of the law. In the first place, the planning requirement is a very general and brief statement spotted with ambiguous terms and phrases: ". . . the Secretary . . . shall *cooperate* with the States . . . in the development of long range highway plans and programs which are *properly coordinated* with plans for improvements in

[2] Norman Beckman, "Politics and Administration of Plan Implementation," *Highway Research Record*, No. 102, Urban Transportation Planning Techniques and Concepts, 8 Reports Presented at the 44th Annual Meeting, Highway Research Board of the National Academy of Sciences-National Research Council (Washington, D.C., 1965), p. 1.

[3] Committee for Economic Development, *Developing Metropolitan Transportation Policies: A Guide for Local Leadership*, A Statement on National Policy by the Research and Policy Committee of the Committee for Economic Development (April 1965), p. 14.

other affected forms of transportation and which are formulated with *due consideration* to their *probable effect* on the *future development* of urban areas . . ." It was the Bureau's exclusive responsibility to interpret this and similar language of the planning provision. Further, federal highway officials were intimately involved in the writing of the law as enacted; they were quite aware of its origins within the administration and of the diversity of meanings and objectives that various participants in the policy development process initially sought to write and later to read into the law. Finally, some of the critics of federal and state performance under the 1962 planning requirement may well be applying standards of performance that are consistent with their own professional and institutional values and interests, but are based on an unrealistic assessment of the highway agencies' capabilities and program commitments.

Premises for Administrative Policy-making

Federal and state highway agencies applied two basic tests that determined acceptability of policies for administering the planning requirement. First, control over federal highway policy and program operations in the states must, to the maximum extent possible, remain with state highway departments. Second, delays in urban highway construction — particularly interstate highway construction — must be avoided or kept to a minimum. In other words, imposition of the planning requirement was not to interfere with the ongoing federal highway program. Resistance to freeway construction and consequent delays were then already becoming serious problems as the interstate program moved into the more densely populated metropolitan centers. The planning requirement could not be allowed to add to this problem; ideally, it would help smooth the way for more expeditious construction of interstate highways in the nation's metropolitan areas.

Some Bureau of Public Roads officials — those who had the major responsibility for planning policies and operations — did have a commitment to improve the urban planning base for highways and an interest in achieving increased state-local cooperation in highway planning. These officials considered it important to demonstrate that the planning requirement need not interfere with operations either of state highway departments or of the Bureau of Public Roads. Urban land use planning, for example, was in an extremely vulnerable position. If Bureau planning staff became overly zealous and were to insist on effective metropolitan land use plans as a basis for highway plans, they might succeed only in discrediting the planning function within the highway agencies and jeopardizing its future role within the federal highway program.

A long-term course of program adaptation, not radical departures in established policies and procedures, clearly appeared to be in order. The immediate task was to devise acceptable operational definitions of the key statutory terms — "cooperative," "comprehensive," and "continuing" — used in describing the required transportation planning process.

DEFINING "COOPERATIVE" PLANNING. In the first months after enactment of the planning requirement, the Bureau of Public Roads had to develop operational definitions of "cooperative" planning which would be specific enough to provide some minimum degree of guidance and direction to the state highway departments. At the same time, such definitions had to be sufficiently open-ended to allow variations within widely differing states and urban areas and to provide maximum room for maneuvering by state highway departments in their approaches to local governments. In these early stages Bureau staff worked closely with the American Association of State Highway Officials to develop acceptable solutions to this problem of administration.

Questions such as these had to be answered: Should state highway departments deal with local governments individually or through mediating agencies such as metropolitan planning bodies? Must all local governments in a metropolitan area be included in the planning arrangement? What happens if local governments refuse to cooperate? What should be the minimum amount and essential forms of local participation in transportation planning? Must local governments be represented in the planning process by elected officials, or can others such as appointed administrators, career staff officials, and citizen designees adequately represent local government interests? What levels and kinds of decision-making authority should local representatives have in transportation planning? To the state highway departments these were obviously sensitive issues. Both federal and state laws recognized the highway departments as ultimate authorities in federal highway planning and development within the states. Was the planning provision of the Federal-Aid Highway Act of 1962 to have the effect of upsetting this traditional structure of authority and responsibility?

Several policy positions responsive to these concerns were developed by the Bureau of Public Roads and the state highway agencies. First, initiative in establishing organizational arrangements for planning with local governments would remain with the highway agencies. Second, formal agreements for cooperative planning would, as a general rule, be directly between state highway departments and individual local governments — there would be no requirement for working through metropolitan planning bodies or other mediating agents of local governments in the metropolitan area. Third, to allow maximum flexibility in the form of the organizational arrangements devised, there would be no requirements that any specific numbers or types of local officials (for example, elected versus appointed) or their representatives would need to participate in the cooperative planning arrangements. Finally, the requirement for cooperation with local governments would not be interpreted to mean that any local government's refusal to cooperate would, in effect, block federal highway program operations in the metropolitan area.

The Bureau of Public Roads prepared general, open-ended regulations and guidelines incorporating the essentials of this approach. Beyond this, the Bureau limited itself to the functions of providing technical advice, training, and assistance; disseminating information about the various organizational approaches developed in different parts of the country; and concentrating on those metropolitan areas needing and requesting assistance in establishing an organizational framework and resolving technical planning problems. The Bureau would not concern itself with specific composition of the various policy, technical, and citizen advisory committees attached to the planning studies. These were considered matters most properly determined by state highway departments and local governments themselves, so long as local governments had an "appropriate voice in the transportation planning process, either through direct participation or through adequate representation."[4]

The formal device adopted to implement the requirement for cooperative planning was the memorandum of understanding, and this was to be supplemented by a transportation study prospectus covering more detailed administrative, technical, and financial arrangements for conducting the planning process. The essential function of the memorandum of understanding was to document the local government's official access to, and formal recognition of, the transportation planning process. This would be the state highway department's evidence that a "cooperative" planning process had been established. The particular manner in which local governments participated or were represented in the study was to be determined by highway departments and local governments in accordance with their own needs, preferences, and capabilities. Bureau policies in this as in other respects would be very broad and open-ended.

The state-local memorandum and the study prospectus together would outline the general purpose, procedures, and allocation of responsibilities for carrying out the established technical process of land use and traffic analysis and forecasting, and development, testing, and evaluation of transportation plans. The forms of cooperative organization thus established would be concerned primarily with the specific set of tasks defining what the highway departments considered a technically competent transportation planning process; local representatives would sit with

4 U.S. Bureau of Public Roads, Policy and Procedure Memorandum 50–9, "Urban Transportation Planning," June 21, 1967, p. 3.

state highway department officials to oversee the technical process and participate in selecting preferred plans from alternative proposals developed by the technicians; and local and metropolitan planning agencies might, if they had sufficient capability, provide land use data needed for traffic analysis and forecasting purposes. For the most part, these would be essentially ad hoc study organizations, heavily dependent on the technical capabilities of state highway departments.

As the Bureau's field offices proceeded to work with state highway departments in establishing organizational arrangements for cooperative planning, one of the early problems encountered was determining at what point local governments' lack of participation or representation would "negate" an effective planning process. In dealing with this problem, the Bureau held that while local governments or agencies might initially refuse to sign a memorandum of understanding, the planning process should nonetheless proceed on the assumption that cooperation with local governments currently withholding their cooperation might eventually be obtained. In such a case, the state highway department would need to determine, subject to concurrence by Bureau of Public Roads field offices, that the "effectiveness" of the process would not be "negated" in the interim.

At the same time, the Bureau made it clear that the state highway department was not to assume that lack of participation by local governments would necessarily negate the process either now or in the future. In the first place, this would depend on the size, functions, and authority of the community concerned. While large communities carrying on major public works programs, including local street and highway construction, and responsible for land use planning and control, might leave a significant "hole" in the planning process if they refused to cooperate, these would likely be the very communities with a greater stake in maintaining access to federal highway funds, and would therefore have greater incentive to cooperate with the highway departments. As one state highway official pointed out at a 1963 meeting of highway departments and local governments, the highway department, in determining project priorities within the state, would be "greatly influenced" by the amount of interest in planning shown by individual cities; those localities showing the greatest interest would "receive earliest attention" when it came to allocating highway funds within the state.[5]

In short, a local government's refusal to participate in cooperative planning with state highway departments was grounds neither for finding the planning process "ineffective," nor for subsequently disapproving specific highway projects that might be located in the noncooperating jurisdiction. The Bureau's interpretation of the law was that it required

[5] *Ibid.*

only that "scrupulous efforts" be made by the state highway department to obtain a local government's cooperation.

The purpose of "cooperative" planning was, of course, to provide a setting for the execution of a transportation planning process "responsive to both the programs of the state highway departments and the needs and desires of the local communities."[6] But while the programs of the state highway departments were well organized, staffed, and financed, there was little or no institutionalization of local "needs and desires" at the metropolitan level of urban transportation planning. Specifically, the community land use basis of transportation remained weak and fragmented, and the transit component of the urban transportation system was largely neglected. Representatives of local governments and agencies were absorbed into ad hoc study projects — established at the initiative of state highway departments — in which the particular program interests and needs of the highway departments predominated.

The Bureau of Public Roads' approach was thus able to accommodate both the very general statutory requirement for "cooperative planning" and the interest of the state highway departments in establishing planning arrangements which would not interfere with the technical planning processes that highway departments believed were needed to do their job competently. At the same time, the cooperative arrangements could elicit useful local contributions to the highway planning process, contributions that could be both material and symbolic. Material contributions might include planning data, assignment of technical staff, and financial support. And the symbolic contribution could be the additional legitimacy bestowed on a planning process dominated by a state highway department, but officially recognized by local governments in the metropolitan area for which plans were being made.

EXCLUSION OF PLANNING AGENCIES. These interpretations of the law provided workable definitions of "cooperative planning" relationships directly between state highway departments and local governments. A closely related problem was how to deal with existing local and metropolitan planning agencies which sought a more important function in the planning process than that of contributing data to state highway department traffic analysis and forecasting operations, or of having pro forma membership on policy or technical advisory committees. The issue was posed in some metropolitan areas where it was advocated that since the planning requirement was directed to achieving an improved local and metropolitan planning base for highway development, it followed that local and metropolitan planning agencies should at least be

---

[6] *Ibid.*

signatories to the memorandum of understanding with state highway departments. Others proposed that transportation planning study operations be located within metropolitan planning agencies, rather than in state highway departments or ad hoc study organizations under the highway departments. At the extreme, it was suggested that the metropolitan agencies might even have the authority to approve or disapprove transportation planning proposals, whatever their source.[7]

As transportation planning processes were organized in metropolitan areas, planning agencies at both local and metropolitan levels were bypassed by state highway departments which dealt directly with local governing bodies and executive officials. While local planning agencies felt that their local programs were being undercut by establishment of an areawide transportation planning program, metropolitan planning agencies resented the intrusion and competition of a transportation planning study dominated by a state highway department within "their own" metropolitan planning jurisdictions.

The Bureau's response was that the primary objective of the planning requirement was not the development of plans, but the development of *transportation systems.* The law itself stated that it was "in the national interest to encourage and promote the development of transportation systems." This was interpreted to mean that state highway departments needed to reach agreements not with local or metropolitan planning agencies, but with the "governing officials of the local communities who have authority to commit their communities to specific programs and projects. . . ."[8] Local governing officials exercised zoning, subdivision, and related control over land use development, and they authorized public works construction, including transportation improvements; these actions directly affected the "development" of transportation systems. The Bureau argued that planning agencies, on the other hand, could not commit a local government to a program for development of a transportation system. Planning agencies at both local and metropolitan levels were not only without authority to implement plans, but they were also often isolated from the legislative and executive authorities they were presumably established to serve. This was particularly true of metropoli-

---

[7] Subsequently, section 204 of the Demonstration Cities and Metropolitan Development Act of 1966 (Public Law 89–754) was to require metropolitan agency review, though not approval, of highway projects as well as other federally aided public works and land development projects. In the case of the highway program, section 204 merely formalized a process which the state highway departments already had under control as a result of the highway act of 1962.

[8] Garland E. Marple, Chief, Urban Planning Division, Bureau of Public Roads, "Urban Transportation Planning — Continuing and Comprehensive," A paper presented at the National Conference on Urban Passenger Transportation, Washington, D.C., January 29–31, 1964, p. 1.

tan planning agencies attempting to function in a metropolitan governmental vacuum.

The Bureau further pointed out that the law did not call for preparation of either a comprehensive development plan or a transportation plan; rather, it required that highway project approvals be based on a transportation planning "process." The distinction between a *plan* and a *process* was considered critical. No plans had to be completed and approved by any authorities, state or local, as a basis for highway construction projects. As interpreted by the Bureau of Public Roads, the law in this respect only required a "continuing process" in which both local and state highway department needs would be considered. Thus, while local and metropolitan planning agencies had responsibility for the preparation of land use plans, this did not mean that the transportation planning process depended on the completion of such plans or their adoption by local authorities. Nor was it required that any highway plans be consistent with land use plans, even assuming their completion and adoption by local authorities.

It was essentially through the above line of reasoning that the Bureau officially disassociated transportation planning and highway project approvals from local and metropolitan planning operations. While the planning agencies were encouraged to contribute data needed in the technical process of transportation planning, generally they were not considered to have any authority, under the terms of the 1962 planning requirement, over state highway department plans and projects.

DEFINING "COMPREHENSIVE" PLANNING. The transportation planning process was required to be "comprehensive" as well as "cooperative." According to the Bureau, a comprehensive process was one dealing on an urban areawide basis with all factors relevant to the planning of a highway system: inventories, analyses, and forecasts relating to economic and population elements of development, land use, patterns of travel demand, and all major facilities constituting an operating urban highway network. While the process would not be required to produce plans for transit improvements, predictions of future demand for public transit were to be made. The major purpose of such predictions would be to provide a more precise measure of the resultant net demand for travel by automobile. The transportation studies themselves were not to assume responsibilities for transit planning much beyond this point. Only very restricted use could be made of federal highway planning funds for transit study purposes in any case. "Comprehensive" planning was thus defined to mean full coverage of the familiar technical elements of urban traffic analysis and forecasting needed for highway network development and testing.

Accordingly, the Bureau of Public Roads concentrated on maintaining and improving technical standards for the basic traffic analysis and forecasting phases at the technical core of the highway planning process. From this base, the Bureau also required transportation studies to include investigation of land use control mechanisms and financial resources important to plan implementation, and it called for consideration of "social and community value factors."[9]

Land use controls such as zoning ordinances, subdivision regulations, building codes, and official mapping were viewed by the Bureau primarily in relation to highway planning and development needs:

> The forecasting of future land uses is subject to considerable error at best, but lacking adequate controls, "planned" development will in most instances have little chance of becoming reality. Further, land use controls are important to protect the traffic-carrying capability of, and public investment in, transportation facilities.[10]

The ambivalent nature of the highway agencies' position regarding land use planning and control as related to highway development becomes apparent here. Land use control is not the Bureau's or the state highway department's problem; it is local government's problem. Given local land use planning weaknesses, legal acceptability and technical and competence of highway planning cannot be dependent on local success in controlling land use for, as the Bureau itself concluded, "means to insure the desired type and form of community growth that are now generally available in the United States are inadequate, and enforcement of even the inadequate measures too often breaks down under economic or social pressures."[11]

The Bureau recognized that availability of "financial resources" to implement plans would influence the "selection of an urban transportation system and the programs designed to implement the system."[12] However, Bureau policies and regulations for transportation planning have not accounted for the fact that the highway trust fund assures financing of highway construction, while no comparable source exists for financing transit improvements. Nor, of course, is there any sure method of preventing this financial imbalance from biasing the planning process so that only major highway improvement proposals are given serious consideration. On one occasion, however, the Federal Highway Administrator spoke with some eloquence on this very point, acknowledging the superior "financial means and administrative processes" of state highway departments in transportation planning and development, and the relative weaknesses of transit agencies. The inevitable result was "highway-

---

[9] Bureau of Public Roads, PPM 50–9, p. 2.
[10] *Ibid.*, p. 8.
[11] U.S., Bureau of Public Roads, *Highway Planning Notes*, No. 9 (April, 1964).
[12] Bureau of Public Roads, PPM 50–9, p. 8.

oriented" construction programs, not because plans are "unbalanced," but because "the means for implementing the plans favor the highway elements."[13] In other words, transit, like land use, is not the business of highway agencies.

Finally, "social and community value factors" became a residual category deserving, as the Bureau put it, "full consideration" of highway planners: open space, park, and recreation areas are to be viewed as "important environmental factors"; "conscientious attention should be given to the preservation of historic sites and buildings"; and "care also should be exercised in selecting locations for new transportation facilities so that neighbors (sic) are not disrupted."[14] While Bureau regulations have given official recognition to these factors and encouraged their consideration as part of the planning process, adequate techniques do not exist for measuring and weighting them in the process of plan development and evaluation. The Bureau, therefore, has not been in a position to give "social and community value factors" significant weight in its own reviews of technical adequacy and legal acceptability of the metropolitan transportation planning processes required by the 1962 highway act.

DEFINING "CONTINUING" PLANNING. In addition to requiring that planning processes be cooperative and comprehensive, the law requires that they be "continuing." It is not surprising that this third statutory term should have been interpreted in such a way as to reinforce interpretations of the other two. For the Bureau, the "continuing" character of the metropolitan transportation planning process did not refer to continuities of metropolitan organizational experience and evolution, in which the state highway department and local agencies develop new institutional forms in support of metropolitan intergovernmental planning and coordination. Rather, a continuing planning process, according to the Bureau's policy, is one which provides for: "maintaining current valid data on land use, travel and transportation and related facilities by staff at State or local level to provide for updating and re-evaluating the transportation plan as conditions change from those initially analyzed and forecasted."[15]

Just as Bureau policies have permitted and even encouraged highway departments to bypass existing metropolitan planning agencies in initially organizing "cooperative" planning processes, official definitions of "continuing" planning have minimized the metropolitan institutional implica-

[13] U.S., Congress, House, Committee on Banking and Currency, *Hearings, Urban Mass Transportation Act of 1963*, on H.R. 3881, 88th Cong., 1st Sess., 1963, pp. 72–3.

[14] Bureau of Public Roads, PPM 50–9, p. 8.

[15] Ibid., p. 2.

tions of the transportation planning process in favor of its technical aspects.

Approval of Highway Projects

The critical determination made by Bureau of Public Roads officials under the 1962 planning requirement is that new highway projects in metropolitan areas are actually "based on" the cooperative, comprehensive, and continuing transportation planning process. For Bureau officials, the ultimate test of the success of their own performance in administering the planning requirement was whether they had elicited sufficient responsive action at state and local levels so as to make it unnecessary for the Bureau to disapprove — and thereby delay — highway construction projects *not* based on an acceptable planning process.

From the very beginning of deliberations on the planning requirement proposal of 1962, highway agencies and interests expressed fears that any planning requirement would obstruct and delay progress in urban highway construction programs. During the summer of 1963 — less than a year after enactment of the requirement and two years before it was to take effect — hearings were held by the Subcommittee on Roads of the House Public Works Committee to explore this very issue. Subcommittee members and testifying highway groups were particularly concerned about disputes then occurring between highway and transit planning groups in the District of Columbia, with the result that the city's highway construction program had been suspended by order of the White House pending further studies of transit and highway construction proposals. Highway interests did not want to see the new planning requirement used by any groups or agencies in Washington or elsewhere as a means of further delaying an already lagging interstate highway construction program in metropolitan areas. As the Subcommittee chairman pointed out:

> It is generally recognized that the most difficult phase of interstate highway construction will be encountered in urban areas. It is here that the program faces complexities which, unless given the most careful attention, could defeat the desirable goal of completing the entire system by 1972.[16]

One of the purposes of the hearing was therefore "to make certain that the [planning requirement] is not being interpreted in a manner that

[16] U.S., Congress, House, Committee on Public Works, *Hearings, Transportation Planning in Certain Urban Areas*, before the Subcommittee on Roads, in Section 134 of Title 23, U.S. Code, 88th Cong., 1st Sess., 1963, p. 1. The highway agencies now estimate that the system will not be completed until 1975, at the earliest.

would delay rather than expedite the completion of the Interstate and Defense Highway System. . . ."[17]

Conclusions and Future Directions

. . . The policies developed by the Bureau of Public Roads in cooperation with state highway agencies and related interests have not dealt with substantive economic, political, and social issues of urban transportation planning. They have neglected such issues as the relative levels of public investment in transit and highway facilities, the impact of highway construction on urban life and form, and the establishment of responsible metropolitan institutions for the planning and development of the urban transportation system in its entirety. The highway planning requirement is, after all, an adjunct to the federal highway program, and its interpretation and administration is the exclusive responsibility of federal and state highway agencies. These agencies, for over fifty years, have been concerned with the single purpose of building highways, and highway agency officials and staffs have developed loyalties and commitments revolving exclusively around the highway planning, engineering, and construction enterprise.

To the highway administrators and engineers, the planning requirement was not viewed merely as a force for improving planning techniques and procedures, or simply as a summons to achieve more efficient and effective highway program administration in metropolitan areas. Rather, the requirement represented a potentially disruptive innovative force, threatening established policies, procedures, commitments, and systems of decision making and program control. Accordingly, it was the responsibility of the Bureau of Public Roads to accommodate the requirement and guide its introduction into the existing system at minimum organizational and program cost.

The 1962 planning requirement was, in fact, a product of innovative forces set in motion in 1956, and demands for planning reforms, stimulated by the interstate highway construction program, continue to be pressed. The question is whether or not more effective and focused pressures for program change may yet emerge as the interstate highway system further penetrates major metropolitan centers, as highway location and design disputes become more acute, and as further delays occur in the interstate program schedule.

. . . [T]he Federal-Aid Highway Act of 1968 included an "urban impact amendment" which provides that as part of the local public hearings process, state highway departments must now consider the "social effects" of a highway location, "its impact on the environment,

[17] Ibid., p. 3.

and its consistency with the goals and objectives of such urban planning as has been promulgated by the community."[18] While this amendment adds little of substance to what was previously required by the 1962 highway act, highway departments are now legally bound to admit urban planning considerations into the hearings process and, presumably, to account for them locally as well as to the Bureau of Public Roads.

Among the more basic forces likely to influence the future course of the highway program as it operates in metropolitan areas are some which have been generated by the 1962 planning requirement itself. First, acceptance by highway officials of the principles of local participation and coordinated land use, highway, and transit planning, has led to reformulations of highway program doctrine, even though it has not led to major changes in operational policies and practices. For the first time, highway administrators began to devote significant attention to these themes in speeches, official policy statements, and congressional testimony. Incorporation of new concepts into program doctrine provides an opening — even if a narrow one — to outside interests urging changes in policies and procedures that would give some degree of concrete expression to these concepts.

Second, the law provided local governments with access to the transportation planning process through ad hoc areawide organizational arrangements. While local participation has been confined to sharing in certain administrative and technical responsibilities — rather than authority for basic program decisions — a metropolitan areawide base has nonetheless been created for a potentially more meaningful local role in the future. How much highway agencies will give depends in part on how much local governments collectively demand. It also depends on what local political, technical, and financial capacities may exist for making and enforcing their demands. In any case, a rudimentary areawide structure for "cooperative" planning and, consequently, for organized conflict and competition between local governments and state highway departments now exists in most metropolitan areas.

Third, transportation planning concepts and techniques stress the relationship between land use and travel demand patterns. This has provided entry into the transportation planning process by local and metropolitan agencies specializing in land use planning, control, and development. While most of these agencies now function more or less as data collectors for state highway departments, they are also agents of urban planning and community development values and interests that are outside the scope of competence and concern of the highway engineer-planner. If local governments demand a greater role in highway planning

---

[18] U.S., Congress, Senate, *Federal-Aid Highway Act of 1968*, Public Law 90–495, 90th Cong., 2nd Sess., 1968, sec. 24.

decisions, they will need to use these planning staffs, augment their resources, and provide an institutional setting in which planning technology might effectively serve local and metropolitan purposes defined in a functioning political process.

The fact remains, however, that metropolitan planning, urban development, and metropolitan institution-building are not principal concerns of highway agencies. Nor is it within their means or responsibility to solve the problem of transit deterioration in the nation's cities. The 1962 planning requirement, therefore, has necessarily taken operational form in accordance with the values, needs, and interests of the organizations charged with carrying it out and the environmental pressures to which they typically respond. Highway agencies and interests cannot themselves be expected to alter highway program policies and operations in any fundamental way, particularly so long as its goals are being achieved to their satisfaction and, in the urban community as a whole, there is continuing apathy and uncertainty about the directions program reform should take and the ends that should be served.

THE FUTURE METROPOLIS
7

Nothing is more certain in urban America than the prospect of growth and change. More than 80 per cent of the nation's population growth during the remaining years of the twentieth century will occur in metropolitan areas. Almost all of this increase will take place in the suburban periphery since the demographic, social, economic, technological, and political forces that created the spreading metropolis and its decentralized political system show few signs of abating. By 1985, one out of every two Americans — or 120 million of an anticipated population of 240 million — will live in the suburbs. At the same time, blacks will continue to replace whites in the older cities. Between 1970 and 1985, the black proportion of the central city population is expected to rise from one-fifth to one-third.

With most urban development expected at the outer reaches of the metropolis, the familiar political pattern of suburbanization should repeat itself countless times. The search for local control over land, taxes, and schools will promote proliferation of small-scale, autonomous governments, whereas the quest for self-sufficiency and social status can be expected to foster continued differentiation among suburban communities. Lacking adequate jurisdictional and fiscal capabilities to meet the demands for a widening range of public goods and services, the many governments of the spatially expanding metropolis can be expected to tread the well-worn path of accommodation. In order to preserve their autonomy, local governments will continue to relinquish control over numerous activities, as they create special districts, forge interlocal agreements, and seek greater state and federal involvement in the solution of their problems.

Although much of the recent political history of the metropolis probably will be reenacted, especially along the urban frontier, the

future will not reproduce the past exactly. Of growing significance
for politics in the metropolis will be the changing nature of suburbia.
As more urban dwellers acquire the means to purchase homes or
rent a suburban garden apartment, the class and ethnic base of suburbia broadens. To be sure, the politics of differentiation still makes
individual suburbs in the larger metropolitan areas relatively homogeneous, but suburbia as a whole becomes more heterogeneous.
Commercial and industrial development also is widening the spectrum of suburban politics. With apartments, shopping centers, and
industrial parks come residents with different perspectives, a new
set of economic leaders, an expanding range of issues and greater
possibilities for conflict in the formerly consensual political arenas
of suburbia. Diminished in the process is the influence of the typical
suburban home owner whose political concerns center on the protection of residential property values and the maintenance of a superior
educational system. The inner suburbs face even more traumatic
changes as low-income and nonwhite city dwellers move from the
urban core in search of better housing closer to the new suburban
industrial and commercial jobs.

   The pattern of future urban development could be very different if
more Americans valued a better-planned metropolis more highly
than they do the perceived benefits of local controls on land use,
housing, and other aspects of suburban development that foster
exclusion, differentiation, sprawl, and political fragmentation. Because most suburbanites prefer local autonomy, few of the public
decisions that help to shape the metropolis have been guided by
comprehensive strategies for regional development. Like the political
system it serves, planning in the metropolis is geographically and
functionally fragmented. However, urban public investments steadily
rise, the lack of planning, coordination, and common purpose in the
public sector becomes more costly. In an excerpt from a report prepared for the Senate Subcommittee on Intergovernmental Relations,
Charles M. Haar and his associates at the Joint Center for Urban
Studies argue that comprehensive regional planning is essential to
beneficial urban development in the future.

   Until recently, most metropolitan planning agencies had made only
a modest contribution toward the comprehensive planning and coordinated development envisaged by Haar and his associates. As with
other efforts seeking to integrate policy-making in the metropolis,
the stumbling block to effective metropolitan planning is the fragmented political system and its hypersensitivity to perceived threats
to the autonomy of its components. State legislation authorizing the
creation of metropolitan planning agencies has reflected the opposition of the dominant interests of the metropolis to coercive area-wide

planning. Typically, regional planning has been advisory, with agencies unable to compel compliance with their plans. As a consequence, the metropolitan planners rarely have fulfilled their potential for leadership and guidance. Instead, they become another faction in the already crowded metropolitan political system. Lacking power to enforce their plans and having no money of their own to implement their programs, the planners have had far less influence on regional development than the local governments that tax, spend, and zone, or the functional agencies that shape land use patterns with their highways, water lines, and other facilities.

By and large, the metropolis has ignored the periodic calls to rescue metropolitan planning from the doldrums. Washington, however, has warmed to the idea of metropolitan planning in recent years, largely because of growing unhappiness over the haphazard success of federal programs in the decentralized metropolis. Of the various federal planning requirements enacted during the 1960's, the most far-reaching are found in the Demonstration Cities and Metropolitan Development Act of 1966, which conditioned the continued flow of federal money in a large number of urban programs on the existence of a functioning metropolitan planning process. As Brian Dickinson's account of the response in Phoenix illustrates, the 1966 legislation has stimulated the organization of metropolitan councils of local officials as well as the preparation of regional plans. The new federal requirements have led to more intergovernmental cooperation, better coordination of public programs, and more influence for planners in the metropolitan political arena, but they have not significantly changed the decision-making processes of most metropolitan areas to date. As the Phoenix experience indicates, accommodation to the political values of the existing system characterizes regional ventures in the geographically and functionally fragmented metropolis, even when the areawide institutions are mandated by the federal government.

Despite the difficulties encountered by these new institutions, advocates of metropolitan government have been heartened by federal promotion of regional planning agencies and councils of local officials. For the metropolitan reformer, the next logical step is the creation of an area-wide government to guide the development of the future metropolis. The new generation of metropolitan reformers, however, have been more concerned about the problems of the inner city. Education, welfare, and housing often receive equal billing with the old standbys of transportation, sewage, and planning in the new blueprints for area-wide government. The traditional reform emphasis on centralization, economy, and efficiency tends to be tempered by a concern for nurturing small-scale institutions and ensuring the responsiveness of urban bureaucracies. The 1970 report of the Committee for Economic Development recommends two-tier metropolitan government, with powers shared by representative area-wide institutions and community-level units.

In the Committee for Economic Development's proposal, cities would virtually disappear in the future metropolis. Their functions would be parceled out to the new regional and community levels of government. Their fiscal problems would evaporate since the new units would be financed by a metropolitan tax base that would support public services on an equitable level in rich and poor communities. Other city problems would slowly but surely be dispersed over the entire metropolis as barriers to the free flow of people were removed by the new metropolitan government. While this scenario may be enacted in a few metropolitan areas, cities and their mounting problems are likely to prove hardy in almost all larger and older metropolitan complexes, and in many others as well. Governmental institutions do not wither away easily in the United States, particularly when many people have high stakes in their survival, as with institutions in the typical American city. Many suburbanites — especially the growing number in the larger areas whose work and other activities rarely take them into the city — clearly would welcome the disappearance of the city and its problems, but it is far less certain that most are ready to join with city dwellers in a new metropolitan confederation. And even if they did, how dedicated would the suburban majority in the typical metropolis be to advancing the interests of blacks and other city dwellers? Creation of area-wide government cannot guarantee a sense of regional community and concern for the general welfare of the metropolis. In fact, the existence of a formal metropolitan political arena may only intensify the political, social, and economic conflicts produced by urbanization.

Most cities, then, are likely to be with us for some time. So are their problems. Unless fundamental changes are made in urban America, argues Demetrios Caraley, slums will continue to spread, housing conditions to worsen, racial and ethnic conflicts to intensify, fiscal problems to mount, labor difficulties to increase, and public services to deteriorate. For Caraley, the basic question raised by these trends is whether the city can be governed at all. His answer is affirmative, but it is qualified by the willingness of Americans and their political institutions to redirect national energies, priorities, and resources to a concentrated attack on the problems that afflict the older and larger cities. The price of failure, argues Caraley, is likely to be "black tinderboxes," violence, political repression, and the undermining of American democracy.

Similar conclusions emerged from the Kerner Commission's 1968 report on civil disorders, which warned that "to pursue our present course will involve the continuing polarization of the American community and, ultimately, the destruction of basic democratic values." One year later, Urban America and the Urban Coalition reviewed the response of the American political system to the Commission's recommendations and concluded that there had been little basic change in the cities or the nation as a whole. Today, the situation remains the same: no massive shifts in national resources have been made; racial attitudes are hardening rather than softening; and the time bomb continues to tick in the heart of urban America.

Edward C. Banfield's viewpoint is very different from that of Caraley, the urban lobbies, and the editor of this volume. He agrees that the short-run prospects of the city are not bright, but he doubts whether government can do anything effective about urban problems. In fact, he argues, public intervention typically worsens the situation. For Banfield, the city's problems are natural consequences of the interplay of the forces of urban growth and change with inherent class differences. He concludes that the same social and economic processes that created the problems of the metropolis will decrease their future significance as the economy grows, the population ages, more people join the ranks of the middle class, and racial prejudice declines.

Charles M. Haar and Associates

THE PROMISE OF
METROPOLITAN PLANNING

City planning has come into widespread acceptance in the United States. Community plans and their related zoning ordinances, subdivision controls, and capital improvement programs influence the nature and timing of much of our urban development. The planning that is now under way is primarily planning for individual cities and towns, however, rather than planning for entire urban areas. Experience so far suggests that while much is being achieved through such planning, important opportunities are also being lost through a lack of areawide planning. Metropolitan planning is still in its infancy, but the inability of individual communities to cope with metropolitan-wide problems is becoming increasingly apparent.

In the absence of well-developed metropolitan plans, the urban patterns that are emerging today are a random collection of local plans and policies designed to meet local objectives. Yet each community, in seeking an optimum solution to its own problems, does not necessarily work in the interests of the people in the larger metropolitan area. Many suburban towns, for example, have chosen to promote the development of single-family houses on large lots as a means of forestalling costly investments in new utility systems. From their own point of view, these strategies have often been effective. But when large numbers of communities in an area limit their development in this way, the net result has often been to force a vast outward movement of people to the fringes of metropolitan areas, creating a need for new and expensive utility systems in the peripheral communities, and forcing long commuting trips to the central cities. A pattern of development that is economical for many individual suburbs can be very costly for the metropolitan area and for the Nation at large. Suburban growth since World War II has indeed required tremendous capital investment and operating expenses for new highways, schools, and utility systems. A recent study estimates that the cost of these major urban services increased by $5 billion from 1953 to

Reprinted from U.S. Congress, Senate, Committee on Government Operations, *The Effectiveness of Metropolitan Planning* (Washington, D.C.: U.S. Government Printing Office, 1964), pp. 3–8.

1957,[1] after adjustments for population growth and higher levels of service. The same study calls attention to the significant effects of urban growth costs in diverting capital investments from industry to these service facilities, and suggests that our expensive pattern of metropolitan development has slowed the rate of national economic growth.

Local planning is generally far removed from these broader regional and national concerns. A typical community plan focuses on activities that can be controlled within the local jurisdiction. The plan will specify what kinds of development are to be encouraged — types of housing, industry, and retailing — as well as the general locations and quantities of each. The location and programing of local services — parks, streets, schools, utilities — are an important part of community plans. The objectives guiding community plans are likely to include promoting a harmonious mixture of activities, supplying public services to accompany private development, and keeping the public costs of new development within local fiscal capacity.

Metropolitan planning differs both in its point of view and in the activities with which it is concerned. It focuses mainly on facilities that serve large segments of the metropolitan population: major highways, transit lines, airports, flood and pollution controls, regional water and sewerage systems, large parks, regional shopping centers, and large industrial centers. Metropolitan plans for such facilities are guided by considerations of efficiency, consistency between the location of population and the location of major service facilities, economy in the extension of utilities and services, the adequacy of transportation and other facilities to meet present and future regional demands, the reservation of sites to meet future metropolitan needs, and the overall range of development in the light of the area's total requirements for housing, jobs, recreation, and services.

METROPOLITAN PLANNING OBJECTIVES. Some of the objectives of metropolitan plans are similar to those of local plans, but with a broader geographic base. Such goals as the compatibility of specific developments with surrounding activities, the provision of adequate services, and the programing of public investments with a view to fiscal capacity are common to both community and metropolitan planning. In each case the content of the plans will differ according to whether the facilities are local or metropolitanwide in character.

Metropolitan plans, however, often seek to achieve objectives that are beyond the reach of local communities. In the Pittsburgh area, for example, high levels of unemployment have posed a special problem for some time. No single community within the region can cope effectively

---

[1] Henry B. Schechter, "Cost-Push of Urban Growth," Land Economics, XXXVII (February 1961), 18–31.

with this areawide problem, but the region at large has organized an effort to expand job opportunities. The economic study of the Pittsburgh region is a regional approach to common economic problems.[2] Its findings are intended in part to guide the physical planning of the Pittsburgh metropolitan area in order to provide appropriate sites and services to promote business and industrial expansion.

The transportation problems that beset our urban areas are also beyond the scope of individual community plans, but they have spurred metropolitan planning efforts in many parts of the country. The Penn-Jersey transportation study, Chicago area transportation study, and similar projects in Detroit, Los Angeles, Pittsburgh, Seattle, Hartford, and Milwaukee — to name only a few — have produced areawide transportation plans to cope with the problems of congestion and the need to maintain good accessibility throughout rapidly expanding urban regions.

Metropolitan planning addresses itself also to the recreational needs of urban areas. As early as the turn of the century, the Boston area's metropolitan district commission acquired land for parks according to a well-conceived plan to reserve land for future recreational use. The Regional Plan Association of New York has long been active in the same field, studying the changing needs for recreational land and open space, and drawing up proposals for continuing land acquisition and park development. State and metropolitan agencies in other parts of the country are performing the same function on an areawide basis. The new federally sponsored open-space program has already begun to strengthen these efforts; the Federal legislation calls explicitly for a metropolitan program as a prerequisite for assistance in public land acquisition.

Assuring an adequate supply of decent housing has long been a problem in America's urban areas. Numerous Federal and local programs have been aimed at maintaining a high level of new residential construction, conserving the existing stock of sound housing, and eliminating obsolete and substandard structures. Despite notable progress to date, much remains to be done in order to achieve the congressional goal of a decent home for every American family. It has become increasingly clear that continued progress will require a coordinated approach within metropolitan areas, rather than a series of unrelated housing programs within the many communities that comprise a metropolitan housing market. Tax considerations frequently lead to local housing policies intended to discourage the building of moderate-cost houses, and to promote the use of buildable land for high-value property only. When such restrictive policies cover large portions of a metropoli-

---

2 This study was begun in 1959, sponsored by the Pittsburgh Regional Planning Association, and financed by the Ford Foundation, the Regional Industrial Development Corp., and the Commonwealth of Pennsylvania. Its main purpose is to support planning and economic improvements in the Pittsburgh area.

tan area, the result may be a shortage of land for inexpensive housing and a slowdown of new building for families with moderate incomes. The urban renewal policies of separate municipalities may also work counter to the housing needs and resources of the total region. People displaced by slum clearance or rehabilitation in one community will seek other housing within a large market area that crosses local governmental boundaries. Unless relocation programs are planned on a metropolitan basis, the housing gains of the community undertaking renewal may be matched by overcrowding and housing shortages elsewhere in the region.

Metropolitan planning agencies are giving increasing attention to housing needs. The Northeastern Illinois Metropolitan Area Planning Commission is now studying the future housing needs of the Chicago region; the Regional Plan Association of New York has completed elaborate projections of housing and population distribution; and similar efforts are under way elsewhere. Federally aided "community renewal programs" in a number of large cities are also covering the metropolitan-wide housing market in their studies and projections.

Economic development, transportation, recreation, and housing are four major concerns that require a metropolitan approach for effective planning. Other illustrations can also be cited, particularly in such areas as water supply and distribution, waste disposal, flood control, and the control of air and water pollution. In large urban areas, water must often be carried from distant sources through elaborate systems of trunklines and local branches to serve residential and industrial areas. The cost of developing separate reservoirs and aqueducts for each community within an area can be enormous; the economies obtained by sharing water supply systems constitute powerful incentives for joint planning and cooperative action. For optimum use of regional water supply systems, coordination of land-use planning is also necessary. Typically, some branch lines will operate far below their technical capacity, while others will be used to full capacity. In the interest of overall economy in water supply, it is often desirable to guide new industrial and residential development to locations where there is excess water capacity, and to plan for a systematic expansion of branch lines as the region continues to grow. Metropolitan planning can make its contribution both in the advance planning of a water supply system, and in alerting local governments to the impact of their development controls upon the use and cost of the system.

The situation is similar with respect to waste disposal. Economies of scale in the operation of sewage treatment plants often promote cooperative action among local communities. Land-use controls then have an important influence on the use of the system, for the location and density of development can result either in optimum use of collector lines, or in underutilization of investments in some sewage lines and premature demands for sewer extensions.

Flood control measures, and the control of air and water pollution, also require cooperative planning by many communities if they are to be effective. In the absence of a coordinated effort, the plans of one community may be negated by the inaction of others. In the case of flood control, urbanization often creates new problems as land development removes trees, levels the contours of the ground, and covers the ground surface with structures and pavement. All these factors increase the rate of runoff of rainwater into streams and rivers, so that streambeds may no longer be able to contain the drainage resulting from a heavy rainfall. Local efforts either to restrict development in vulnerable flood plains or to enlarge river channels may be useless if neighboring communities do not take similar action. The same is true of local efforts to control stream pollution, which can be undone by the failure of upstream communities to set up corresponding controls. Local controls over air pollution are equally subject to neighboring influences; winds and air currents cross jurisdictional boundaries as freely as rainfall and rivers.

The protection of agricultural land is another problem of urbanization that local communities cannot handle on an individual basis. Prime farmland is rapidly being developed for urban purposes in many areas. Orange County, Calif., is a well-known example where new housing developments are replacing some of the most productive agricultural tracts in the country. Local governments can try to retard this process by means of special agricultural assessment policies (as in Santa Clara County, Calif.), but an effective solution requires making alternative locations elsewhere in the region equally attractive for urban development, to forestall development pressures on farmland. Diverting development to other areas depends upon building highways to provide good access, extending water and sewer lines, and zoning the land appropriately — all of which require action by many governments within the metropolitan region.[3]

In all these fields, there may be general consensus on regional objectives — a healthy economy, good transportation system, adequate water supply, suitable recreation facilities and open space, and decent housing for everyone — but local planning alone is not effective in moving toward these regional goals. First, many of them require action either by a number of local governments, or by levels of government other than the local community alone. Problems of housing, economic development,

[3] Recent studies have indicated in more detail the need for areawide planning or performance of certain functions, as for example, Advisory Commission on Intergovernmental Relations, "Performance of Urban Functions: Local and Areawide," Washington 1963, and made more specific recommendations for Federal aid. Advisory Commission on Intergovernmental Relations, "Intergovernmental Responsibilities for Water Supply and Sewage Disposal in Metropolitan Areas," Washington, D.C., 1962; "Intergovernmental Responsibilities for Mass Transportation Facilities and Services in Metropolitan Areas," Washington, D.C. 1961.

water and sewerage, pollution control, and preservation of farmland all illustrate the weakness of independent local action, and the clear advantages of joint local planning. Other areas of concern require not only interlocal cooperation but joint action by higher levels of government. Highways, for example, are typically designed and built by State highway departments, and must meet Federal standards if they are to receive Federal aid in financing. Large parks and land reserves are generally acquired and managed by State agencies or special district commissions. Effective guidance of metropolitan development almost always depends upon an intricate coordination of action by local and State governments, often involving Federal agencies as well, and upon sensitive adjustments of governmental policies to meet changing conditions of private development. Metropolitan planning can be an instrument for bringing about this kind of coordination within urban areas.

CONFLICTING INTERESTS. A second reason why local planning alone cannot achieve metropolitan objectives is the difference in point of view between local governments and the metropolitan areas at large. Although all localities in an area may see the need for regional parks, many will resist having large public parks within their own boundaries, fearing inundation of local roads by out-of-town visitors or hoping to use their open land for high-value development. New highways may be welcome — if they are just across the border in the next town. All communities may see the desirability of industrial expansion — provided that heavy industry locates in another part of the region and only research laboratories develop nearby. It will be generally conceded that moderate-cost housing is needed for workers and their families, but many local plans discourage it.

Conflicts exist in regional development, and they must be recognized. Metropolitan planning will not eliminate conflicting interests among different communities, but it will try to prevent these conflicts from interfering with the sound development of the region. Competition to attract new industry is a case in point. A metropolitan area typically has a limited amount of land that is suitable for modern industrial development, with adequate access and utilities, proper drainage and soil conditions, is priced reasonably and is available in large enough parcels. The metropolitan area at large has an interest in the best use of this land, for new jobs and increased incomes benefit the entire region directly or indirectly. Individual communities have a narrower interest in industrial development because the property tax income from a new factory goes to the community where it is located. Competition for new industry may lead to a wasteful use of industrial land: scarce in-town sites may be used for plants that could as well locate in the suburbs, so that firms later requiring central location may have nowhere to go in the region; or suburban towns may discourage certain industries from building on their vacant land because they hope for a higher tax yield from other types of firms in the future, and the region may lose a chance to strengthen its overall industrial base. A recent study of industrial renewal prospects for the Utica, N.Y., urban area[4] underlined this danger in narrowly competitive local industrial policies and urged a statesmanlike regional approach to maintain and expand employment for the entire area. Metropolitan planning can help competing localities coordinate their efforts and work for the advantages that result from economic growth anywhere in the region.

A metropolitan planning agency will speak for areawide interests when government policies are formulated and when program decisions are made. When conflicting interests are acknowledged openly, and when the regional point of view is presented clearly, it may be possible to work out agreements to resolve the conflicts in a particular situation. Localities can compromise and bargain. If the regional plan that will best promote economic growth leaves certain communities with little likelihood of industrial development for many years, regional representatives may agree to support other measures to help these communities finance local services, such as revisions in State school-aid allocations. Or the plan itself may attempt to promote the region's development in ways that will strike a balance between tax resources and service needs in each jurisdiction; thus, the community that is to obtain little industry may instead provide a location for a major shopping center, or may have its service demands limited by using its vacant land for a regional park rather than new housing.

A metropolitan planning agency will alert local governments to the regional implications of their decisions, and will work to encourage informed decision making in place of fragmented policies that plan for the region more by accident than by choice. An effective planning agency will also help to resolve conflicts between localities and the larger region, when these conflicts prejudice the development of the region. Metropolitan planning can make an important contribution in these situations of conflict merely by posing the issues and analyzing the effects of alternative courses of action. More complete information, highlighting the regional implications of local actions, will enable local decisionmakers to see beyond immediate parochial advantages and to consider alternatives more beneficial in the long run — and to justify such alternatives to their constituents.

[4] Chester Rapkin, "Industrial Renewal: Determining the Potential and Accelerating the Economy of the Utica Urban Area" (New York: New York State Division of Housing and Community Renewal and Urban Renewal Administration, U.S. Housing and Home Finance Agency, 1963).

Brian Dickinson

FEDERAL AID AND INTERGOVERNMENTAL COOPERATION: THE EXPERIENCE OF METROPOLITAN PHOENIX

Phoenix, Arizona, long a prize city of the wide-open Southwest, is now a century old. As it outgrows its cow-town image, all the problems of the older and bigger cities are rising to confound the community. Because Phoenix is a relatively new city, it has time to save itself if solutions are sought now for these problems.

A description of metropolitan Phoenix will clarify its efforts at multi-jurisdictional planning and coordination. In its climate, topography, resources, and especially in its patterns of growth, the area differs strikingly from older metropolitan regions in the East. Phoenix and its neighboring municipalities are located in the seventy-mile valley of the Salt River in south-central Arizona. The heart of the third fastest-growing metropolitan area in the nation, Phoenix is a market for cattle, cotton, citrus fruit, vegetables, and flowers, and is a financial and commercial center for the Southwest. Since World War II, it has attracted important aerospace and electronics industries. Its climate encourages winter visitors; resorts are a major industry. Thousands of retired people move to the area each year.

The region has grown extraordinarily since World War II. Phoenix itself in 1940 had a population of 65,000 in an area of 9.6 square miles. By 1950 the population had climbed to 106,000 in an area of 17 square miles. The remarkable boom came in the 1950s, when the city grew in population to 439,000 (a fourfold increase in the decade) and in area to 187 square miles (a tenfold increase). The Phoenix Planning Area, which includes the city and another 100 square miles of adjacent land, received 200,000 migrants as permanent residents from 1950 to 1968. The population of the planning area, 628,000 in 1968, is expected to reach over 1,000,000 by 1990.

The level, open ground of the Salt River Valley made it possible for Phoenix and its suburbs to grab up open land and lay out their subdivisions in a utilitarian network of streets, with no regard for plans,

This article was prepared for this volume.

future growth, or good sense. Endless strips of used-car lots trail past citrus groves in a hodgepodge of visual and economic disorder. Public transport is a joke: everyone drives, and their automobile exhausts combine with copper-smelter fallout from a hundred miles away to foul what was once the best air in the country. The population influx was so swift that it overwhelmed the subdivision and zoning regulations, and the building codes of the region. Since many open fields were not developed, 64 per cent of the land in the city of Phoenix remained vacant in 1968.

Like most metropolitan areas, downtown Phoenix has lost business to its outlying sections and to the suburbs: in the Phoenix Planning Area forty-six new shopping centers were built between 1950 and 1968. Strips of land along major arteries in Phoenix and the suburbs lie vacant, having been zoned for commercial use before the fashion turned to shopping centers. A city planning report notes: "This is a legacy for the future that will be difficult to overcome."

Metropolitan Phoenix grew too fast for any organized plan to take hold until 1969, when a plan was developed for Phoenix alone. The larger suburbs were completing individual plans at the same time. Some liaison took place among planners in the various municipalities, but it was informal. The governments in the Salt River Valley had begun cooperating in several ventures, however. From the 1930s, water and electricity production from the federal Salt River Project had been coordinated. Phoenix and its suburbs had agreed on mutual aid agreements for fire and police protection and for civil defense. Studies were conducted on solid waste disposal and pay and classification for civil service employees; both required some cooperation among the Phoenix area communities. A Phoenix-Maricopa County Traffic Coordinating Committee was formed. A Valley Area Traffic and Transportation Study (VATTS) was set up (partly in response to federal requirements); it was staffed by the state highway department. However, individual communities cooperated with VATTS researchers only after a fashion. Probably the most successful early intergovernmental cooperation was a five-city sewer system. Phoenix financed and constructed sewer lines and is being repaid by the four other member towns, depending on the amount of sewage they contribute.

These instances of coordination came about because of recognizable needs; the joint enterprises either were economical, politically sound, or both. Coordination on planning or on land use, on the other hand, moved slowly because there was no comparable feeling of need and certainly no ground swell of citizen pressure.

Although cooperation among the valley governments came on relatively noncontroversial questions, it eased the way for future areawide cooperation. Some planning is now being done, guided by a push from Washington. Section 204 of the Demonstration Cities and Metropolitan Development Act of 1966 required localities seeking federal development loans or grants to submit their applications to an "areawide agency which is designated to perform metropolitan or regional planning." This legislation was a successful carrot-and-stick approach to chaotic, undisciplined development in multijurisdictional areas. Threatened with losing grant-in-aid money, metropolitan governments rapidly organized multi-jurisdictional councils of governments and metropolitan planning agencies.

In metropolitan Phoenix, the response to Section 204 was the creation of a council of governments for areawide program coordination. The Maricopa Association of Governments included representatives from Phoenix, fourteen other communities, Maricopa County (a huge jurisdiction that adjoins the Phoenix Standard Metropolitan Statistical Area), and the Arizona Highway Department. High officials served the association: the country was represented by the chairman of its board of supervisors, and eleven of the fifteen municipalities were represented by their mayors. To comply with the federal directives, the association became incorporated in October 1967, four months after Section 204 was effective. But incorporation, as the organization's first newsletter declared, "in no way changed the basic philosophy of MAG — that of an advisory organization governed by local public officials for the purpose of providing answers to areawide problems."

A series of federal directives in 1967 and 1968 implemented Section 204. Again, communities had to comply with the directives if they wanted to continue receiving federal grant money. In the Phoenix area, the pattern has been to comply only to the extent necessary to satisfy the federal government. By the end of 1969 there still was no comprehensive metropolitan planning for the Phoenix SMSA, and little prospect of any forthcoming.

The Maricopa Association of Governments, although a chartered public corporation, has no employees. It shares the offices and staff of the private League of Arizona Cities and Towns. The League's director is the secretary of MAG; his assistant, Kenneth Driggs, is MAG's part-time coordinator.

Driggs told me that MAG has no power over its member governments, and anticipates none.[1] He said that Phoenix area communities "are basically conservative; they want to cooperate, but that's about all." There is little chance that MAG will evolve into a vehicle for metropolitan government, which seems unnecessary to him because the valley municipalities work effectively together when they need to.

Although MAG was ostensibly set up to comply with the Section 204 application review guidelines, such reviews now make up only a fraction of the organization's activities. The review, as one official explained, is "informal," and it is not particularly time-consuming or aggressive: of

[1] Interview with Kenneth Driggs, January 7, 1970.

more than one hundred federal aid applications MAG had reviewed up to May 1968, all had been returned to the applicants "without unfavorable comment." Each application is funneled to a MAG subcommittee that specializes in a subject area, and whose members are experts drawn from staffs of member communities. The policy followed whenever possible is to look over grant applications before they are presented in final form. "If we find a problem after an application is completed, we think we have failed," Driggs declared. The aim is not to assert authority but to help communities through the bureaucratic process.[2]

Besides its prescribed duty of reviewing applications for federal grants, MAG set out other responsibilities in its bylaws. It is supposed to serve as an intergovernmental forum for discussion; an agency to promote pooling of resources among municipalities for "efficiency and economy," "planning for the solution of regional problems," "facilitating interlocal agreements," and "encouraging as much intergovernmental cooperation as possible."[3] MAG regards research and coordination as its most important functions. It has incorporated the Valley Area Traffic and Transportation Study as its transportation research arm; it is conducting an areawide manpower survey with a grant from the U.S. Department of Labor; it has been coordinating implementation of the solid waste disposal study and a storm-drainage facilities study. An ambitious project in 1969 was a Criminal Justice Planning Program financed by a grant from the U.S. Department of Justice. Although these projects go well beyond MAG's initial role of reviewing federal grant applications, the association is still searching, as it has since its formation, for a useful function that does not impose on its member governments. A MAG spokesman told me: "It never has been crystal clear what our function is, how far we can go or how far we want to go." A planner in Phoenix, alluding to the federal requirement of areawide review, told me that "if Section 204 would disappear tomorrow, MAG would cease to exist."

Shortly after MAG organized, it asked the American Society of Planning Officials to outline a program of activity and to analyze the services that MAG could perform. ASPO issued its report in January 1969.[4] Its principal recommendation was that MAG should concentrate on metropolitan planning. (MAG is preparing a composite of the various local comprehensive plans, but there is no indication of what it intends to do with the composite.) Noting evidence of a "hesitancy about the

[2] By this standard, MAG's review procedures may be rated a success, although figures on the number of applications subsequently approved in Washington were not applicable.

[3] American Society of Planning Officials, *The Maricopa Association of Governments* (Chicago: The Society, 1969), p. 7.

[4] *Ibid.*

future course MAG might follow," ASPO warned the organization to make full use of its potential. It urged MAG to "become somewhat independent and aggressive as time goes on," to seek more funds, and to hire a full-time staff. In essence, the ASPO report asked the group to have goals beyond the creation of a useful dialogue and providing a more sophisticated level of grantsmanship.

At the same time, ASPO confirmed MAG's inherent weakness, by warning the association to avoid becoming involved in controversial projects, at least until it had "broadened the perspectives of elected officials." Partly with this reasoning, ASPO placed "air resources" and housing in the third priority of suggested MAG studies. Both are lively public questions in the Phoenix area. No pollution control ordinances exist, and the smog (blamed mostly on automobiles) is steadily worsening. As for housing, Phoenix voters have on three occasions in the last ten years voted down a referendum question that would have given the city its first housing code. The lack of such a code, according to V. Warner Leipprandt, Jr., the principal planner in the Phoenix Planning Department, was the main reason Phoenix' Model Cities application was rejected.[5] Moreover, building outside municipalities can be regulated only by county zoning regulations; state law bars counties from enacting building codes.

MAG has neither approved ASPO's suggested program design, nor submitted it to the Department of Housing and Urban Development. The evidence indicates that the ASPO approach makes MAG stronger than the people of Phoenix would like. The mood in the organization so far has been one of friendly cooperation, which seems to include a wish not to rock the boat by pushing for more money and staff and increased power.

Officials of the Maricopa Association of Governments persuasively defend their limited responsibility by explaining that Maricopa County already offers a political jurisdiction that can be vested with the necessary metropolitan political powers. The county is immense — an L-shaped entity 100 miles long and 140 miles wide. It includes all of metropolitan Phoenix and virtually every fringe community, plus miles of open desert and mountains in every direction. The county government of elected supervisors is powerful, and because much of its territory is unpopulated, it can devote most of its attention to the metropolitan area. The county works closely with MAG's review committees, and several county-sponsored research projects have been completed with help from local planners, using MAG as a coordinating body. MAG assumed part of the responsibility for implementing the findings of the solid waste disposal

[5] Interview with V. Warner Leipprandt, Jr., January 7, 1970.

study. A Comprehensive Health Planning Council is also among these. The county's planning department will make the composite of individual communities' comprehensive plans and is expected to expand its own planning function. Moreover, the county has taken over the administration of all antipoverty programs.

The pattern developing between MAG and Maricopa County seems likely to be one of increasing cooperation, with MAG coordinating staff services from local communities and the county financing various studies. Yet MAG still owes its allegiance to, and exists with the sufferance of, the existing local valley governments. This structure makes it unlikely that the county can acquire extensive powers to control development. The same desire for local autonomy that has kept MAG merely an advisory body will likely keep Maricopa County from taking over significant local decision-making powers. The Maricopa Association of Governments and its member jurisdictions seem to feel that MAG's research function and its job as an unofficial intermediary among localities are enough of a step for now toward regional integration. Yet such limits will not allow MAG to cope effectively with areawide problems as they intensify.

Most communities typically have refused to surrender any part of their sovereignty; Phoenix and its neighbors are no exceptions. If anything, these cities are more devoted than most of the ideal of local autonomy. Yet for truly effective coordination of development in most metropolitan areas, the various councils of governments will have to become something more than advisory bodies; they will have to gain decision-making power and leverage to implement policies. If the Phoenix example has validity for other areas, such a transfer of powers will be most unlikely unless new incentives appear. Such new incentives could come from the federal government, logically developed as extensions to the existing Section 204.

The authority of such councils of government could be augmented if they were required to formally *approve* all federal aid applications, instead of relying on their present authority to "review and comment." Yet this or any other new federal incentive is likely to intensify local governments' distrust of areawide councils. This distrust came through in a 1968 statement by Mayor B. L. Tims of Scottsdale, chairman of MAG's policy-making Regional Council. Tims said:

> In a very subtle way, the cities of Maricopa County are being hampered if not barred from making effective progress in cooperating unless they agree to surrender their right to independence in some matters — unless, in fact, they agree to establish a level of government in the urban area to which they are bound. The bait, the bribe, the incentive — to use the accepted euphemism — is money, of course.[6]

6 MAG *Regional Review*, Vol. I, No. 2 (September 1968), p. 1.

Nonetheless, Tims has remained a major force in MAG; he proclaims it a success because it is a voluntary organization:

> Cities all over the country must not be coerced out of achieving the most satisfying of all government relationships: voluntary local cooperation in the solution of local problems.[7]

The delicate task facing federal administrators of Section 204 will be to maintain the momentum already generated toward regional cooperation while avoiding the impression of coercion.

[7] *Ibid.*

Committee for Economic Development

RESHAPING GOVERNMENT IN METROPOLITAN AREAS

Today's metropolitan problems are not all permanent. Continuing change in the structure and behavior of metropolitan society will cause some problems to disappear while others will persist and be joined by problems yet unforeseen.

To meet existing metropolitan problems as well as to anticipate future ones, the United States must develop governmental institutions, instruments, and programs which are more consistent, responsive, and flexible. It must go beyond reorganizing central city and suburban government, beyond overhauling the federal and state-local fiscal system, beyond developing packages of new substantive programs. It must do all of these

Reprinted from *Reshaping Government in Metropolitan Areas* (New York: Committee for Economic Development, 1970), pp. 40–56, with permission of the Committee for Economic Development.

things and at the same time coordinate its efforts with an over-all national metropolitan policy.

Improving Governmental Machinery

Central to the solution of the nation's greatest urban problems is the creation of improved governmental machinery in metropolitan areas. Better machinery will not by itself guarantee the development and adoption of more effective substantive programs, but it is a necessary prerequisite. Nor will the reform of governmental organizations guarantee the massive supply of resources essential to solving metropolitan problems. It could, however, aid in marshalling those resources as well as contributing to their effective allocation and utilization.

Aware of the need for change, enlightened business and civic leaders in metropolitan areas have spearheaded campaigns to replace small-scale, overlapping local governments with consolidated, federated, or other forms of metropolitan government. These campaigns have stressed the fact that the economic and social interdependence of metropolitan areas has created problems which can only be solved on an area-wide basis. Such citizen efforts have produced scattered results . . .

Increasing Intergovernmental Cooperation

Advocates of area-wide government [,however,] are convinced that the changes they seek will some day materialize, if not in the fashion or at the speed they once expected. Several developments support their optimism: (1) federal assistance for the rapidly growing number of metropolitan councils of government and metropolitan regional planning agencies; (2) growing use of county home rule charters in single-county metropolitan areas; (3) adoption by many urban counties of executive-headed governments; (4) interagency — city, state, and federal — coordination through such programs as model cities; and (5) increasing intergovernmental cooperation.

Expanding intergovernmental cooperation within metropolitan areas has taken many forms, ranging from informal agreements among government officials of adjoining jurisdictions to the much more fundamental act of establishing metropolitan or nearly metropolitan-wide special districts for the performance of single functions. To date, however, intergovernmental cooperation has not reduced the number of local non-school jurisdictions in metropolitan areas. In 1962 there were 14,745 non-school governments in America's 212 metropolitan areas; in 1967, there were 15,684 in the same places, an increase of 6.4 per cent. The increase has been primarily in one-function special districts — units spawned by the inadequacies of traditional governments.

Area-Wide Government or Community Control?

Steps in the direction of area-wide government are not surprising when considered in their historical context. For nearly two centuries, American government has become increasingly centralized. Cities have expanded their boundaries by annexation. States have assumed new functions or have taken more responsibility for old ones. The national government has broadened its role in domestic affairs. Traditionally, much support for centralization has been based on the assumption that it leads to better, more responsive government and more humane social policies.

It may seem paradoxical, therefore, that today's growing support for decentralization of big city government should rest upon the same assumption. Advocates of decentralization see it as an effective means of involving members of the community in the governmental process — giving them more access to public services and more control over the government bureaucracy.

Backers of centralization, on the other hand, contend that only a larger governmental unit can achieve economies of scale and make maximum use of fiscal resources and new technologies, and for these reasons it can be more responsive to the growing needs of its citizens, the disadvantaged particularly.

It is clear from the foregoing that what is needed is a system of government that adequately recognizes *both* forces, centralization and decentralization. Such a system must permit a genuine sharing of power over functions between a larger unit and a smaller unit. It must recognize a larger unit to permit economies of scale, area-wide planning, and equities in finance. It must recognize a smaller unit to permit the exercise of local power over matters which affect the lives of local citizens.

Combining Centralization and Decentralization

All metropolitan areas are affected to a greater or lesser extent by the conflicting forces of centralization and decentralization. The interdependence of activities within metropolitan areas requires area-wide institutions for some functions or parts of functions of government. Just as clear is the need for units of government small enough to enable the recipients of government services to have voice and control over their quality and quantity.

The usual result of this conclusion is to try to divide functions, assigning some to a more general level of government and others to the local level. However, the American federal system permits a much wider choice than such a clear-cut division would imply. Federalism has, in fact, undergone continuous change and the division of responsibility among levels of government has become much less distinct. Instead of dividing functions, the practice has been that different parts of the federal system perform different aspects of the same function. Financing may be assigned to one part of this system, while administration is assigned to another. Seldom is it even this neat. Policy-making, administrative, and fiscal responsibilities for the same function may be divided in a great variety of combinations among all parts of the system. The result is a sharing of power over functions rather than a division of functions.

While the American federal system has been dividing responsibility and power among many layers of government, the gradual evolution of an American administrative doctrine has produced a set of theories and practices that tend to reduce citizen influence on many aspects of government. In part a result of the reform movement of the 1920's and 1930's, these practices were primarily designed to increase efficiency and to reduce political influence. However, concepts about separation of policy and administration, about professionalism and hierarchical control have all worked in the direction of excluding the average citizen from participation in the delivery of government services.

The kind of participation encouraged has been only at the policy-making level, where blue-ribbon citizens advisory committees are frequently employed. But below this level administrative expertise is supposed to take over. The parent of the public school child, the welfare recipient, the hospital patient, and all others whose lives are affected by government are supposed to accept as final the decisions of professional "experts." Citizens with greater political weight normally ignore these claims to expertise and effectively influence the operation of the system, be it a school system or some other public activity. Citizens with less influence — and those lacking sophistication in dealing with the political process — find it more difficult to gain access to the system.

It is in part the frustrations produced by this administrative ideology that have led to demands for decentralization and community control. For the average citizen, exerting an influence on the delivery of services is much more important than making a vague, distant impact on high-level policy deliberations.

Two Levels of Government

In principle a governmental system for America's metropolitan areas must recognize the need for both a community level and a metropolitan level of government. There are many different governmental arrangements that will meet this need. As long as legitimate demands for centralization and decentralization are met, the specific arrangements may vary to fit the economic, cultural, and political characteristics of each area. Some may require greater emphasis on consolidation of local units; others may require greater emphasis on creating units which will enhance community participation.

Therefore, in the following proposals to achieve the dual advantages of a combined community-metropolitan governmental system, we would expect variations in application. In some cases a comprehensive solution may be feasible at an early date. In other areas achievement of an effective two-level system may require several steps over a period of time.

To gain the advantages of both centralization and decentralization, we recommend as an ultimate solution a governmental system of two levels. Some functions should be assigned in their entirety to the area-wide government, others to the local level, but most will be assigned in part to each level. More important than the division of functions is the *sharing of power*. Local communities will be assigned some power over functions placed at the area-wide level of government. Further, state and federal governments must be involved in most functions. This two-level system will not provide neatness and symmetry, but effectiveness, responsiveness, and adequate resources.

In those situations where the metropolitan area is contained within one county, a reconstituted county government should be used as the basic framework for a new area-wide government. This may, but need not, include consolidation of a large dominant central city with the county government in which it is located. If there are two or more sizable cities in the county, consolidation may not be appropriate. Counties in some states already have very wide powers. An indispensable requirement is the restructuring of such counties with a suitable legislative organ, a strong chief executive, and modern management.

In cases where the metropolitan area spreads over several counties or towns, a new jurisdiction should be created which embraces all of its territory. Although a federation of existing counties and towns might be considerably easier to implement, it is clear that rapid metropolitan growth makes a stronger jurisdiction considerably more appropriate, especially for purposes of long-range planning.

Most complicated is the interstate metropolitan area. Since state government has primary responsibility for local government organization, an area-wide metropolitan government crossing state lines would require close harmony between or among the states involved. Exact uniformity of the units on both sides of the line would be impossible, but by agreement or compact the states could design a system which would mesh. Two units, one on each side of the state line, would find it far easier to work out agreements for area-wide action than the present dozens of such units. Interstate agreements have created single-function units which operate in more than one state. Similar arrangements for a multi-function unit certainly should not be beyond the ingenuity of man.

In addition to an area-wide level, modern metropolitan government should contain a community-level government system comprised of "community districts." These units might consist of existing local governments with functions readjusted to the two-level system, together with new districts in areas where no local unit exists. The new community districts should not be imposed from without, but created through local initiative by the simplest possible methods. A state boundary commission or similar body might be established to begin the process of delineating new districts. Citizen groups which seek community-district status might first make their appeal to this body if it is established.

In some cities there are areas which already possess strong community identity and these could become the new community districts. But in many cities, particularly the big cities, the sense of community is diminishing. Isolation and alienation, on the other hand, are increasing. Once the smaller political units are created — units with genuine power — a stronger sense of community is bound to emerge. In the suburbs, existing municipalities are likely to be retained as the community districts. Except in the most recently settled suburbs, these municipalities tend not only to represent "natural areas," but also to have well-developed community identities. Thus, local communities in both cities and suburbs can be guaranteed full participation within the metropolitan system.

Size and Representation

A major difficulty in establishing community districts will be determining their size. Although much of the literature on government organization places heavy emphasis on appropriate size of minor jurisdictions, the fact is there is little hard economic evidence of what the optimum size should be. Therefore, how a community perceives its identity becomes important as well as the number of people it contains.

States should establish suggested, but not mandatory, criteria to guide the actual determination of community boundaries. The states should, in addition, set down requirements which will guarantee the representativeness of the government established. Although the community districts should be allowed to determine their form of government — council, strong executive, commission, or some other form — the basic requirement of one-man, one-vote should be met.

State governments should assist the organization of community districts by enacting enabling legislation to permit the creation of a two-level form of metropolitan government and by establishing a procedure through which community districts may be created. Great flexibility as to size and governmental organization should be permitted.

The states should also prescribe guidelines for determining size and representation of the area-wide government. The practice exists in some metropolitan areas of representing community units — towns and villages — on an area-wide governing council. However, this form of representation rarely produces an area-wide point of view but rather a bargaining process through which the various smaller units try to protect their parochial interests. Therefore, we suggest that delegates to the area-wide government represent legislative districts on a one-man, one-vote basis instead of representing the community districts as such.

It is important to underline the full significance of the changes advocated here. City boundaries would become less important than they now are. There would be a boundary surrounding each metropolitan area as well as boundaries surrounding community districts within each metropolitan area.

Relating Area-Wide and Community Responsibilities

More difficult than determining community size and governmental system is establishing community administrative, fiscal, and policy responsibilities vis-à-vis the area-wide level of metropolitan government. To assist this process, states must specify criteria which will insure the following: (1) high levels of local community initiative; (2) adequate performance of all public service functions; (3) equitable distribution of the burdens and benefits of the metropolitan fiscal base; (4) satisfactory resolution of political conflicts; and (5) greater flexibility in anticipating and responding to the gamut of metropolitan problems.

If these results are to be guaranteed, some functions must be assigned entirely to the area-wide government, with the participation of local communities limited to hearings, powers of delay, and in some cases the right of veto. And, some functions must be delegated completely to the local communities. Where circumstances permit, local communities should be given the option of performing still other functions, but according to guidelines specified by the area-wide government.

State and Federal Aid

No government organization can make a major contribution to the solution of America's urban ills without adequate funding to carry out substantive programs. Such funding will require greater contributions from all parts of the governmental system.

Reorganization of government in metropolitan areas will make it possible to increase over-all fiscal resources. America's wealth is concentrated largely in its metropolitan areas and metropolitan-wide government is advocated, in part, so this resource base may be preserved and improved. The existing system of overlapping local governments results in a poor match between needs and resources and perpetuates waste, inefficiency, and confusion.

Since the community districts will vary greatly in size and resources, the bulk of their financing will be through grants-in-aid or shared taxes that come from the metropolitan level of government, the state, and the federal government. To the extent that locally raised revenues will be employed, they will be raised principally through the property tax, the only tax appropriate for a jurisdiction of the size contemplated. Fees and charges may also be employed by this local level.

Most important will be the new revenue sources available to the metropolitan-wide level. By encompassing an entire area that is economically and socially interdependent, this level will have at its disposal revenues available from sources other than the property tax. Moreover, the distortion produced by present competitive tax behavior within metropolitan areas will be substantially reduced.

Although the establishment of metropolitan-wide government will make possible a greater fiscal contribution, it will by no means eliminate the need for substantial state and federal aid. There is urgent need for a greater and more equitable state aid contribution and more attention by the states to the adequacy of their local governmental systems. The states have responsibilities for their local governmental systems. They should adapt their aid systems to the facts of metropolitanism and adjust the boundaries of local governments to fit current realities. In *A Fiscal Program for a Balanced Federalism*, we stated:

> Because of the increasing interdependence of local jurisdictions, the role of the states must grow if they are to be strong and effective partners in the federal system. The states should encourage greater cooperation and coordination among local governments in solving metropolitan problems. In many areas taxpaying ability is greatest in the suburbs but needs are greatest in the central cities. The states should do more to equalize resources available to individual local governments to combat social ills.

The powers and responsibilities of the states have been exercised sparingly, if at all. . . . [T]he . . . state aid system is designed particularly to aid suburban areas, creating far higher tax burdens in cities than in most suburban communities. The earlier bias of state legislatures for the rural areas has been translated by reapportionment into a bias in favor of suburban areas. There was a time when such rural bias was justified by the distribution of taxable resources. The wealth of the country was concentrated in the urban areas, and if minimum levels of government service were to be maintained in rural areas, aid was necessary. However, the redistribution of taxable resources within metropolitan areas between central cities and their suburbs does not justify the current suburban preference.

The states have the power to assume functions that are now performed locally, but few have assumed them. In some states, highways and welfare have become a major state responsibility, and a few municipal higher educational institutions have been taken over by the states. But there has been no major shift in functions to ease local fiscal burdens.

Although states have passed permissive legislation making interlocal cooperation possible, they have not undertaken any major overhaul of local government. This is in direct contrast to the Canadian provinces which have actually established metropolitan governments for some of their cities.

The response of the federal government to local fiscal problems has been more positive. The federal aid system, for example, through such programs as urban renewal, aid to education, and the anti-poverty program, is adjusting its assistance programs to the problems of the cities. It is possible that by giving more attention to the flow of aid the federal government will be able to help fill the gap left by the state aid system.

Both state and federal aid systems should be restructured in order to put resources where they are most needed. Equally important, state and federal aid should be used to stimulate government reorganization. The use of aid for this purpose has a precedent in its use in promoting school consolidation by the states. Therefore, we recommend that state and federal aid should be used as an incentive to promote the kind of restructured government outlined in this statement.

Restructuring central city and suburban government and revising the existing federal and state aid systems will greatly alleviate many existing metropolitan problems. However, the complexity of the problems themselves makes it doubtful that they can be solved adequately without a battery of new or modified substantive programs.

There is, at present, no lack of programs proposed to solve the nation's metropolitan problems. While many are praiseworthy, few have been designed as parts of rationally integrated packages. Consequently, they are often overlapping and flatly contradictory. When implemented in highly interdependent metropolitan areas, their consequences are often exceptionally perverse.

A reorganized local government system, therefore, can play a major role in making substantive programs relevant to the problems of metropolitan areas. Such a revised local system could give new vitality to America's traditional federalism by forcing the state and federal parts of the system to design programs which are internally consistent and genuinely responsive to the needs of its urban citizens.

Sharing Power over Functions

Despite differences from metropolitan area to metropolitan area, and from state to state, it is possible to outline some basic arrangements for sharing responsibilities for individual functions between area-wide governments and community districts. While the following breakdown of tasks must surely be modified to meet the peculiar needs of each metropolitan area, it does illustrate the kinds of division broadly necessary to insure workable two-level metropolitan government.

PLANNING. An obvious function for assignment to the area-wide government is planning. While the federal government is encouraging the establishment of metropolitan planning agencies, these units lack the power necessary to guide area-wide development effectively. Increasingly, they must be given greater control over the provision of transportation facilities, sewage disposal, water supply, and recreation areas.

Planning agencies, however, should not be given complete control over the zoning process; there must be a division of this responsibility. Community districts must have some say over zoning if they are to control their own character, but they must not allow zoning to become an institutional block against minority groups. In general, the metropolitan-wide level should be empowered to specify broad areas of industrial, commercial, and residential activity which the local communities could zone into smaller sub-areas.

Community districts, however, must have a role in the area-wide planning process which extends beyond zoning. To insure effective participation in this process, the community governments must establish their own planning agencies. These agencies should be empowered not only to develop social and physical plans for their own areas, but also to inspect and, if necessary, to delay plans designed by the area-wide government. Correspondingly, the area-wide government must be given the prerogative to veto any community plans that do not serve the interest of the entire metropolitan area — a right not possessed by the metropolitan planning agencies set up under the 1966 Housing and Urban Development Act.

TRANSPORTATION. This function must be assigned in large part to the metropolitan-wide unit because of its significance to the development of the entire area. However, the federal and state governments must assume greater responsibility for designing and financing comprehensive transportation policies. By its very nature, transportation cannot be planned solely on an intrametropolitan basis. Fortunately, in this regard, the Nixon Administration has announced its intention to develop a federal transportation policy which not only will assign priorities among modes of transportation but also will design an aid system which reflects these priorities.

Because of its importance to community development, the formulation of area-wide transportation policies must involve community participation, for metropolitan transportation systems must facilitate the journey to work, expedite the shipment of goods, and speed the flow of traffic without adversely affecting local residents. The more than 20 interstate expressway controversies now raging indicate the degree to which highway plans can upset neighborhoods and communities. Current federal regulations requiring two hearings well in advance of interstate highway land acquisitions are a meaningful step in the direction of community participation. They must be strengthened, however, by provisions mandating community involvement in the over-all highway planning process.

WATER SUPPLY AND SEWAGE DISPOSAL. By their very nature, water supply and sewage disposal, like transportation, are area-wide functions. But unlike transportation, they do not require much local participation. Any number of arrangements can be employed to provide water and sewage disposal on an area-wide basis. In the case of sewage, the area-wide government can either build and manage the entire system for itself or assign the construction and management of feeder lines, but no trunks, to the local communities.

RUBBISH AND GARBAGE COLLECTION. Unlike the sanitation functions discussed above, rubbish and garbage collection may be performed wholly at the local level. The level of service, such as frequency of pickups, can and should be left to community determination. The area-wide government's only control over this function should be one of policing — insuring that community performance meets specified limits of environmental pollution.

EDUCATION. Currently, many large city governments are weighing responses to increasingly insistent demands for greater community control over public education. These demands inevitably revolve about the conclusion that the schools — particularly those in ghetto areas — have failed.

Although community control of education has been widely discussed, the idea implies different things to different communities. In suburban communities, for example, it entails local financing. In ghetto districts it does not, for this would result in confiscatory tax rates or in the allocation of very few resources to education.

While some advocates of community control favor metropolitan or even state-wide financing of education, they often disagree sharply over what parts of the education function should be performed or controlled at the local level. In the coming months, a CED policy statement on educating the disadvantaged will discuss community responsibilities for education in poor areas.

WELFARE. Were there not changes contemplated in forms of federal and state welfare support, fiscal realities would dictate that the function at the very least be financed on a metropolitan-wide basis. However, the current discussion over welfare financing has produced strong pressures for a substantially higher proportion of financing at the federal level, which would relieve lower levels of a heavy burden.

The movement of this function to a higher level of government could also increase administrative flexibility. Therefore, in order to guarantee protection of the welfare recipients' rights, the community-level government could play an important role. Since the financing of welfare is likely to be and should be at higher levels in the system, the Department of Welfare at the community level could become the advocate of those welfare recipients who believe they are not being properly treated by the system. Such a local welfare department would also be in a better position to provide services beyond the monthly welfare check.

PUBLIC HEALTH. Like most functions of government, public health is really a group of functions, closely related but distinct in their activities. Public health is normally divided into : (1) environmental sanitation; (2) control of communicable disease (3) vital statistics; (4) maternal and child health services; (5) laboratories; and (6) health education. Environmental sanitation, communicable disease control, and statistics should be administered metropolitan-wide with state and federal governments having clear responsibilities for establishing standards, while the other activities may be handled locally and merely coordinated by the area-wide agency.

Public health offices should be located in each community with the local community government participating in the operation of these decentralized offices. In fact, health centers should be combined with those other facilities which provide non-health social services.

The provision of hospital and other medical care facilities is more complex than public health because of the mixture of public and private roles in these services. Public hospital services are now supplied by counties and cities and special hospital districts covering several municipalities. Hospital services in addition are often purchased from privately operated hospitals by local governments for indigent patients.

There is a growing demand from many citizens — although not as insistent as with education — for more community control over their hospitals. Service levels are often considered too low and, for residents of ghetto neighborhoods particularly, such services are often inaccessible.

Adequate hospital and medical care is a national problem. Area-wide governments are appropriate units for planning for the provision of such care facilities within state and national guidelines. But there must be a role in the governance of such facilities which includes places for community residents on their governing boards.

HOUSING. Related to education, welfare, and health is the provision of adequate housing. Probably no activity of government more clearly demonstrates the conflict between area-wide needs and community self-interest. Central city communities and suburban municipalities alike have bitterly opposed the placement of public housing within their boundaries.

Although housing is primarily the responsibility of private industry, to the extent that industry does not meet the needs of lower-income groups governmental subsidies are necessary. It is the public housing resulting from these subsidized programs which is opposed in many communities. The result is the concentration of such housing in ghetto areas, thereby eliminating the possible advantage of locating it in surroundings which would improve the total living environment of its residents.

Further, the location of subsidized housing in ghettos is inconsistent with the location of jobs which the residents of this housing might hold. There is obviously a need for scattered-site public housing, for rent subsidies, and for home ownership through interest-rate subsidy. Programs to provide all of these and other types of subsidized housing are on the federal statute books. All are underfunded, if funded at all.

Once the federal government puts housing policy in order and provides the necessary financing, the roles of metropolitan-wide and community governments must be fit into the system. There is a need for metropolitan-wide housing plans which include the deconcentration of subsidized housing. In fact, such metropolitan-wide plans should include the development of new towns — both inside and outside the cities — which contain populations that are balanced in terms of income and race. The type of governmental system recommended here will encourage this kind of development. At the community level, authority should be granted for participation in the planning of housing and for a role in the management of housing programs. Within large scale projects, resident participation is necessary.

Publicly subsidized renewal is probably even more related to the local community than housing. In fact, the kind of community governments recommended will provide a useful framework for urban renewal activities. Although it will be necessary for the area-wide agency to design broad outlines of urban renewal policy for the region, these area-wide plans will be in large part the sum of individual community plans.

Current model cities legislation provides the framework for the development of genuine community government incorporating not only renewal but all the other federal, state, and local programs designed to improve and reshape neighborhoods. The community districts suggested here are consistent with the original concept of model cities and seem more sound than recently announced plans to make the program applicable to the whole city.

POLICE. A two-level governmental system provides the opportunity for genuine reform of what may be the most sensitive of all public services. Parts of the police function must be area-wide — laboratories, communications systems, records systems, detective services, and inspection — if the police function is to be adequately performed. On the other hand, patrol services should probably be decentralized and under some community control.

At least one major metropolitan county — Nassau County in New York State — has demonstrated how this can be done. In that county of 1.5 million people, there is a county-wide police service covering police activities that must be area-wide. Many local communities within the county provide their own patrol services through local police departments or buy a county patrol service. The citizen of Nassau pays two police taxes — one to the county for the centralized services and another to either the village government which provides that service or to the county for district police services.

Since the citizen has his most direct and frequent contact with the patrolman, it is the patrol function which is most sensitive. Community participation in this aspect of police service will inspire greater confidence between citizen and police.

OTHER FUNCTIONS. Although other substantive functions could be covered, the basic pattern of assignment contemplated is illustrated by those already discussed. Of greatest importance is the fact that no hard lines have been drawn between functions or even parts of functions or between levels of government. The emphasis is on the *sharing of power and responsibility* and not on the assignment of entire functions to either level.

The recommendations contained in this statement recognize two preconditions for a revitalized metropolitan America — the need for jurisdictions large enough to cope with problems that pervade entire areas, and, at the same time, the need for jurisdictions small enough to allow citizens to take part — and take pride — in the process of government. Our guidelines are neither simple nor perfect. The complex pressures and counterpressures of metropolis cannot be contained by any easy, all-purpose blueprint. However, we believe that the proposals we have outlined provide the foundation upon which concerned citizens may build a better metropolitan government suited to their needs.

Demetrios Caraley

IS THE LARGE CITY
BECOMING UNGOVERNABLE?

When the question is raised about the large city becoming "ungovernable," what is really being asked is whether the gap has been sharply increasing in recent years between the performance of large city governments and the demands and expectations of their citizenry for alleviation of outstanding problems and for provision of traditional functions, including preservation of public order. Large city governments still perform some impressive feats. The sheer survival of large city governments without any major breakdowns since World War II, in the face of having to perform a constantly widening range of functions for more-demanding populations, while suffering slowly rising and in some cases declining tax bases, must be considered an achievement of the first order. Furthermore, it can be argued that with the extension of the merit system, technological advances, personnel training programs, data processing systems, and the like, urban governments are performing their housekeeping functions — e.g., fire, sanitation, water supply, street repair and lighting, and public health — with greater technical efficiency and honesty all the time.

The housekeeping functions in most large cities are, however, chronically underfinanced and understaffed and increasingly in recent years have been interrupted by strikes. Expenditures in most program areas have been rising, but so fast have employees' salaries, the cost of standard products, and the size of the population being serviced also been rising, that the extra funds seldom result in any improvement in the quality of performance. Thus what large city governments do in housekeeping matters is essentially conduct holding actions against any rapid worsening of services or deterioration of facilities. Rarely do they engage in a level of effort sufficiently intense to provide services or facilities of a quality normally expected of the federal government or of large private corporations. And as budgets become tighter, given the drain of financing poverty-related services and benefits, certain "nonessential" amenities like

Reprinted with permission of the author and publisher from *Governing the City: Challenges and Options for New York*, Proceedings of The Academy of Political Science, Vol. 29 (August 1969), pp. 206–223.

parks, zoos, museums, and libraries have in some cities had to be sharply curtailed. Strikes by municipal employees have already stopped the operation of public schools, garbage collection, transit facilities, welfare services, and hospitals in various cities, and not even police and fire departments have been free of strike threats, feigned mass illnesses, and slowdowns.

Much more serious than their underperformance of housekeeping functions is the little success large city governments have shown in ameliorating conditions of life of the poor that have come to be increasingly concentrated in urban slum ghetto areas. These poor are primarily black, but in certain cities they include sizable numbers of Puerto Ricans, Mexican-Americans, and Appalachian whites. They live in neighborhoods with large proportions of men without jobs or with jobs that do not pay enough to support a family and of families headed by women subsisting on welfare payments. Their schools are seemingly incapable of instilling fundamental skills of literacy in children. Much of their housing is overcrowded and dilapidated. Their neighborhoods also have extremely high rates of crimes.

True, census statistics suggest that the number of dilapidated housing units in all large cities combined has been declining, unemployment rates have been dropping as a result of the overheated economy, and the official count of persons subsisting on incomes below the poverty line has also been decreasing. But the proportions of dilapidated housing, unemployment, underemployment, and incomes below poverty level in certain large city neighborhoods are still two and three times the national average. According to the Kerner commission, in the worst neighborhoods, up to 91 per cent of the housing units are dilapidated, up to 15.6 per cent of the working force is unemployed, and as high as 47 per cent is underemployed. And although skilled, "successful working-class" and middle-class Negroes have recently been increasing their incomes rapidly and moving out of those slums, their places are constantly filled by the arrival of new unemployed migrants. These migrants, together with those "unsuccessful" slum-dwellers that are left behind, form a permanent contingent of two million hard-core urban poor. The Kerner commission found that during the current period of general prosperity the incomes of these hard-core poor "have not risen at all ... unemployment rates have declined only slightly, the proportion of families with female heads has increased, and housing conditions have worsened even though rents have risen."

Furthermore, even for those black slum-dwellers whose conditions have been improving, the improvement in the standard of living of middle-class whites (and even blacks) has been so much faster, that the gap between their life in the slums and what they see depicted as the "normal American" style of life on the mass media has been widening.

And unlike as recently as a decade ago, black slum-dwellers no longer believe that their color requires them to accept a permanently inferior standard of living or that governmental action is incapable of improving their situation. However much their conditions are getting better, they are still demanding more services and more benefits from city governments since their conditions have not yet reached equality with those of white Americans.

What many persons would probably consider to be the most critical evidence of ungovernability of large cities is their incapacity to stop increases in street crime and to contain mass violence. The chief victims of street crime are, of course, the people living in the lowest-income slum neighborhoods, where the rate of victimization is in some instances up to thirty-five times what it is in upper-income areas. But with the general spread of low-income neighborhoods in different parts of the city and with the mobility afforded by the automobile, middle-class areas have also experienced an increase in serious crime.

The outbreaks of riots by ghetto-dwellers that began in the summer of 1964, thus far have been directed primarily against police and stores in the ghetto areas. There is, however, increasing talk and apparently some preparation among the extremist black militants of starting citywide "urban guerilla warfare," which presumably would involve terroristic acts against white persons and property anywhere in a city. There has also been an increase in mass disruptions, vandalism, and arson of such places as welfare offices and schools and colleges. Until very recently, the participants in riots and disruptions have gone almost completely unpunished, as police have not made arrests or been largely unable to produce sufficient evidence in court to support successful prosecutions.

Drifting into the "Black Tinderbox" Future

Given the continuation of existing trends, the most likely outcome, at least in many of the older large cities of the Northeast and Middle West, is to turn them within the next few decades into "black tinderboxes." First, the proportion of Negroes in the country's thirty largest cities has been increasing rapidly since World War II, almost doubling between 1950 and 1966. By 1985 Chicago, Philadelphia, St. Louis, Detroit, Cleveland, Baltimore, New Orleans, Newark, and Washington, D.C., are expected to have black majorities. Second, with a continuation of present discriminatory renting and selling practices in housing, the bulk of this population will be concentrated in the older, racially segregated, all-black neighborhoods, and in "changing" neighborhoods on their periphery. As these changing neighborhoods inexorably shift toward heavier Negro occupancy, "massive racial transition" will take place and the ghetto will spread. Third, without a sharp increase in the present level of effort to enrich schools, increase job skills and motivation, and provide greater job opportunities, the number of dropped-out, unemployed, and underemployed young Negro men will continue to be large and possibly larger than at present. Fourth, at the present level of building-code enforcement and renewal of central city housing, and with the present ability of slum dwellers to pay rents sufficient to enable landlords to keep their buildings in good repair, more and more blocks of older residential properties will continue to deteriorate and become dilapidated, and larger parts of central city populations will be forced to live under slum conditions. Fifth, as the number of tax dollars required to provide even the existing level of benefits and services to the poor and otherwise disadvantaged increases, and as the number of tax dollars available grows slowly or actually declines as still larger numbers of middle-income taxpayers move to suburbia and business volume and property value also go down, city governments will be caught in a constantly tighter fiscal squeeze. Even present levels of standard housekeeping services might have to be reduced.

The combustibility of a city with these conditions would obviously be very high. Nothing would be going on, as the Kerner commission put it, "to raise the hopes, absorb the energies, or constructively challenge the talents of the rapidly-growing number of young Negro men in central cities. . . . These young men have contributed disproportionately to crime and violence in the past, and there is danger, obviously, that they will continue to do so." An even more serious possibility in this kind of "black tinderbox" city is that a rising proportion of older blacks with better educations and higher incomes, strong majorities of whom according to opinion surveys still reject separatist thinking and violence, might also become embittered. Many of them might well come to look on continued poverty and oppressive slum-living of their lower-class racial brethren in the midst of plenty and on continued discrimination in housing or job opportunities for themselves as so outrageously unjust that they might decide to support not only riots and other violent protests, but also the tiny minority of revolutionaries who advocate outright rebellion and general urban guerrilla warfare.

Providing further fuel for combustion of the "black tinder-box," incidentally, will probably be those lower-middle and working-class whites not affluent or mobile enough to become suburbanites. These whites would in all likelihood feel increasingly alienated and deserted in what was becoming a predominantly Negro city, perceiving themselves as "penned-in" and "declassed" as Negroes moved closer to their neighborhoods and in increasing danger of losing their jobs to black competitors.

Despite the tightness of municipal budgets and the need for compensating contraction elsewhere, the resources allocated by city governments to police forces will almost certainly be steadily increased. The police will, therefore, probably be developing ever-greater capacity, with occasional assistance from the national guard, to respond quickly and with sufficient manpower to outbreaks of violence to be able to cut down sharply the frequency of the prolonged, multiday riots. And also, as city officialdom with strong black representation responded to precipitating incidents of violence in ghetto neighborhoods with what by then could be more heavily black police, the interracial character of the confrontations might be blurred and the possibility of escalation reduced. On the other hand, probably no amount of increase in police power will be sufficient to prevent sudden, "hit-and-run" burnings, lootings, and vandalism confined to small areas, nor is it likely to prevent periodic sniping at the police themselves.

Whether augmented police power, including an increase in the amount and quality of infiltration and undercover work, will be able to prevent serious outbreaks of terroristic violence directed against the white community generally remains an open question. If such violence were to begin — and it could be sustained at a highly disruptive level by even small numbers of determined nihilistic revolutionaries who were not concerned about their own eventual safety and apprehension — the nine-to-one white majority in the population would most likely retaliate massively and indiscriminately against all blacks, both through vigilantism and through the use of official governmental force.

Among the measures that might be resorted to by an angered majoritarian democracy or by the right-wing dictatorship that might conceivably emerge if democratically elected politicians fail to act repressively enough are the formalization of the urban *apartheid* alluded to by the Kerner commission and the drastic curtailment of civil liberties and procedural due process for all Americans, but particularly for Negroes.

If this kind of garrison-state "black tinderbox" future for large cities appears wildly fantastic and implausible, one should consider the following aspects of existing harsh realities: The rhetoric of revolution and guerrilla warfare and the display and some use of weaponry and fire-bombing are already increasing by extremist black militants. Opinion surveys[1] conducted over the past few years furthermore show that there is a hard core of Negroes who essentially hate all whites and are so alienated from the white community that they believe "close friendships between

[1] The opinion surveys primarily relied on for this paper have been reported by Angus Campbell and Howard Schuman, "Racial Attitudes in Fifteen Cities," *Supplemental Studies for the National Advisory Commission on Civil Disorders*, Praeger Edition, New York, 1968; by William Brink and Louis Harris, *Black and White*, New York, 1967; and by Louis Harris in the daily press. Specific citations will appear in my book *Urban Political Systems*, Englewood Cliffs, forthcoming.

Negroes and whites are impossible" and that "there should be a separate black nation here." The percentage of Negroes who hold these views is small — only 5 to 12 per cent — but their absolute numbers are sizable, amounting to tens and possibly hundreds of thousands in each large city. Some 15 per cent of a sample of all Negroes, 20 per cent of the men, and up to 30 per cent of the youngest men believe that in order to gain their rights, black people should be "ready to use violence." Large minorities or majorities among Negroes believe that riots have been helpful to their cause, feel sympathetic with the rioters, and define the riots as essentially condonable protests against legitimate grievances. Finally, when asked after being specifically reminded that they were in a one-to-nine minority whether in any all-out confrontation with whites they would not lose, only 27 per cent of a national sample agreed, while 24 per cent of the overall sample and 15 per cent of the Northern ghetto contingent were not sure, *and 49 and 54 per cent respectively denied that they would lose in such a confrontation!*

There is already an increasing hardening of white attitudes toward blacks. Restrictive legislative action in Congress and various state legislatures and mounting electoral support for candidates who take strong "law and order" positions in the past two years all reflect this hardening. Recent opinion surveys of white attitudes also reveal, for example: Some two-thirds of a national sample believe Negroes "had gone too far in their demands," and 60 per cent feel an increase in themselves of anti-Negro sentiments as a result of the riots. Although there had been a long-term continuous downward trend in the acceptance by whites of unflattering stereotypes of Negroes, since the major riots of 1967 that trend has been reversed. Whereas as late as the summer of 1963, preponderant white majorities believed that demonstrations by Negroes were aimed at legitimate goals like "equal rights," "to be treated as human beings," and "equal education," only a minority of whites currently define riots as mainly spontaneous protests against unfair conditions, while varying-sized majorities characterize riots as being in part looting expeditions, planned and organized by "outside agitators" or "Communists" and calling in the short run for stronger police control. Some 5 per cent of all whites, 8 per cent of the white males, and up to 21 per cent of the least-educated white males believe that if Negroes rioted in their city, they themselves should engage in counterriot violence against Negroes.

Strong support exists among the American public for certain kinds of curtailment of civil liberties and safeguards of procedural due process. Political scientists have long documented that although Americans almost unanimously agree with various principles of free speech and legal procedure when stated in abstract terms, substantial minorities do not support various logical corollaries of those principles. Indeed, even majorities do not support specific applications to protect individuals or groups that become widely unpopular.[2] In early 1969 there was already serious consideration at the highest levels of American government of proposals for "preventive detention" of recidivists accused but not convicted of new crimes. The purpose of such detention would be to prevent the possibility of the accused committing further offenses while free on bail, as presumably permitted by the Constitution. Recent public opinion surveys on curtailment of Negro rights find that over a quarter of whites believe that even "orderly marches to protest against racial discrimination" are unjustified. More than two thirds think that nonviolent sit-in protests are also unjustified, and over a third are of the opinion that there is no "real difference" between nonviolent protest marches and demonstrations on the one hand and riots on the other. Majorities of two-to-one disagree with the Kerner commission findings that persons arrested during riots should have been given better legal counsel and fairer trials. A narrow majority believe that the "courts have been a major cause for the breakdown of law and order," the latter phrase being widely understood as code words referring in large part to Negro street crime and rioting.

Governing the City Toward a Healthy, Multiracial Future

It is not inevitable that large cities become less and less governable and drift into "black tinderboxes." Admittedly city governments with only their own tax resources and present level of grants from the states and the federal government cannot develop the governing capacity to deal with the most serious problems within their jurisdictions. This is particularly true of the "tangle of pathology" associated with slum poverty. And, of course, some of the major causes of city problems, like suburbanization, black migration to cities, the unemployability of the unskilled, the high cost of new housing, and the loosening of inhibitions on the use of forcible tactics are national in scope or origin and are beyond any particular city's legal reach.

But certainly the American political system as a whole does have the capacity to brake the adverse trends affecting large cities and begin to actually "govern" them toward a healthy, multiracial future. Properly governed cities could have upgraded housekeeping services and sharply reduced levels of unemployment, underemployment, and poverty. Deteriorating neighborhoods could be rehabilitated and new housing

---

[2] See, for example, James W. Prothro and Charles M. Griggs, "Fundamental Principles of Democracy: Bases of Agreement and Disagreement," *Journal of Politics*, XXII (1960), 276–294, and Herbert McClosky, "Consensus and Ideology in American Politics," *American Political Science Review*, LVIII (1964), 361–382.

constructed. More highly effective public schools could be developed to enable the next generation of slum ghetto children to break out of the "culture of poverty." The economy of these cities could still retain a fair share of top national firms and their downtown sections continue to be attractive as diversified shopping centers and as cultural and recreational hubs of their metropolitan areas. Such cities would also enjoy a greatly improved quality of law enforcement to control street crime in all areas of the city and to deal more effectively with riots and other mass violations of the law. Even though this "healthy" city would have a disproportionately high percentage of Negroes, and especially working-class Negroes, in its population relative to its surrounding suburbs, that percentage would be steady. Instead of increasing ghettoization there could be an expanding number of multiracial residential neighborhoods.

This future for large cities does not postulate any reversal of basic trends toward suburbanization of population and jobs or any re-emergence of the central city as the overwhelmingly dominant force in the metropolis. It simply assumes that even within the limits set by those trends, the large city could be viable enough to be the preferred choice for work or residence or play for a substantial portion of the metropolitan population, whether white or black, low, middle, or upper income.

The large city could be revitalized if massive sums of money were fed into it for upgrading of housekeeping services, expanded job-creation and job-training including the guarantee of jobs by government as "employer of last resort," improved income supplementation, a concentrated attack on slum conditions, and sharply strengthened law enforcement efforts, and if strong efforts were made to stop increased ghettoization. Stopping ghettoization would not be easy. It would require some combination of reduced black in-migration to central cities, large-scale suburbanization of Negroes already there, a slowing down of mass white exodus to suburbia, and deliberate "managed integration" of central city neighborhoods.

Obstacles to Improved Urban Governability

Given the unquestionable advantages of healthy, multiracial cities, why is not the American political system improving their governing capacity? Part of the answer is that there are important jurisdictional, organizational, technological, and fiscal obstacles that currently stand in the way of adopting and implementing the policies and programs required. The circumscribed legal powers often granted to city governments by their states, for example, prevent them from reaching some of the causes of the problems that they face, particularly those that are metropolitan in scope. The fragmentation of authority in most city governments often retards decisive, innovative decision making. The limited legal powers and staffs usually available to mayors, who normally are less parochial than the city bureaucracy, do not permit them to impart forceful direction to the city governments. The severe shortage of talented administrators limits the capacity of all governmental levels to design and operate complex urban programs at a high level of efficiency. The narrow channels for public participation in city-government decision making sometimes interfere with its being responsive to the problems of the ghetto poor. The inadequate design, lack of coordination, and mismanagement of some existing urban-oriented federal programs prevent their making as great an impact on urban conditions as they should.

Also, complete knowledge is not available about psychological or sociological processes to permit the design of programs that get at the basic causes of such complex social phenomena as the "tangle of pathology" associated with slum living or the failure of ghetto children to learn. Moreover, under present tax rates and expenditure commitments, there is not sufficient money available to city governments to fund at the required level the various programs necessary to reverse trends toward a "black tinderbox."

It is reasonable, however, to assume that a country which twenty-five years ago could fight successfully a world war, supply logistically a worldwide alliance, and develop a nuclear weapon, and today can place a man on the moon, has sufficient organizational, legal, and administrative ability and can assemble sufficient knowledge to deal successfully with the most seriously oppressive symptoms of urban problems. And if there were a decision to do so, enough additional revenues could be extracted out of an overall economy of some $850 to $900 billion in gross national product to go a long way toward paying for the cost of healthy, multiracial large cities.

Admittedly, in many city governments, which rely primarily on the property tax, further sharp tax increases might prove counterproductive by stimulating an even faster flight of industry and middle-income taxpayers to the generally lower-tax suburbs. Though, to be sure, those city governments that are currently taxing their residents only one-third as much as others could probably make a greater local effort. The states making the highest tax efforts also must consider whether still higher rates will not lead to an erosion of their tax base to other jurisdictions. The federal government, however, need not fear the flight of tax-paying industries and individuals to lower-tax jurisdictions. Moreover, the federal revenue system, based heavily on income taxes, is highly growth-responsive so that in a prosperous economy a given tax rate takes in more money each year than the automatic rise in federal expenditures. This difference constitutes the so-called "fiscal dividend." There are, therefore, no fiscal reasons to prevent the federal government from providing most of the financing necessary to produce healthy large cities. Former U.S. Budget Director Charles L. Schultze estimates that if the Vietnam war were to end, there would be available within two years a "fiscal dividend" of about $10 billion and within four or five years one in the range of $35 to $40 billion, even if the 1968 ten per cent surcharge were discontinued.[3]

The most intractable obstacles to improving the governability of large cities are political ones. The political forces that oppose the courses of action necessary to solve city problems are stronger than those that support them. This political opposition is directed to three separate aspects of the strategy required: increased spending, stepped-up integration, and strengthened law enforcement.

Opposition to the increased spending necessary probably results first of all from the "optimistic denial" by most Americans of the seriousness of the urban situation and from the failure to recognize the consequences of present trends. Opposition also comes from public officials responsible for approving expenditures and raising revenues. Their opposition presumably reflects the widespread reluctance of the public to pay increased taxes, especially for financing programs that are perceived as being of greatest direct benefit only to the minority of Americans who are poor, black, and residents of large cities. It is important to recognize that while some 56 per cent of the American people live in metropolitan areas, only 30 per cent of Americans live in the central city portions and only 20 per cent in really large cities of 400,000 or more in population.

The opinion data suggest that there is probably little ideological opposition to spending money for improving the *physical* condition of slums. There is, however, such ideological opposition among some officials, particularly the great majority of Republican and Southern Democrat members of Congress who form the "conservative coalition," and much more among the public to improving the *social* conditions of the slum poor by having governmental programs redistribute income through increased welfare payments, negative income taxes, or rent supplements. Opposition to these programs is strongest among those parts of the white population closest in income, education, and status to groups who would receive the expanded benefits.

Political opposition to the residential integration of central city neighborhoods comes not only from those white racists who are against residential integration in principle but also from that much larger group of whites who incorrectly attribute to all Negroes the life style of lower-class slum-dwellers. Their fear is that integration will lead to a

[3] "Budget Alternatives After Vietnam," in Kermit Gordon, ed., *Agenda for the Nation*, Washington, D.C., 1968.

deterioration in the quality of their children's education or the character of their own neighborhoods. Such opposition is likely to be strongest in those central city neighborhoods closest to the ghettos. Since suburbanization of Negroes sizable enough to halt the ghettoization of large cities would create a five- to ten-fold increase in the current growth rate of the Negro suburban population, suburban whites are opposed. Some are racists, but others simply fear that the problems of cities will be transferred to the suburbs.

Incidentally, some better-educated Negroes with higher incomes living in large cities also oppose these integration measures. Part of Negro opposition is based on their desire to turn large cities into black ghettos. Some of them are motivated by black racism and a commitment to separatism; others by an expectation of greater opportunities in such cities to capture top political offices and take over other major central-city institutions. Other Negro opposition is based on objection to the use of such means as "benign quotas" to maintain white dominance of white central-city neighborhoods. Such quotas are considered unacceptable and demeaning, even though their purpose would be to achieve real racial integration.

Finally, there is a considerable amount of sheer hostility among some whites toward all Negroes, which motivates them to be against anything that might benefit black people, even if no money had to be spent. Part of that hostility is no doubt based on the kind of long-term white racism cited by the Kerner commission, but opinion data suggest that probably more has been generated lately by the anti-white and violence-laden rhetoric and activities of the extremist black militants and by the rioting in black ghettos.

The political obstacles to strengthened law enforcement to reduce street crime and mass violence come from four diverse sources: the "antispenders," the police, the slum ghetto community, and some members of the liberal community. Slum conditions are not, of course, a sufficient cause for engaging in street crime and mass violence. Yet, slum living within the "culture of poverty" is highly conducive to criminal activity and does generate an underlying reservoir of grievances that provides fuel for crime and disorders. Thus the forces opposing spending for drastic amelioration of slums and poverty are perforce also obstructing law enforcement by preventing the removal of one basic cause of street crime and mass violence. Opposition to spending also blocks strengthened law enforcement in a much more direct way. It prevents the expenditure of the large additional sums of money necessary for expansion of police forces, for additional prosecutors and judges, and for expansion and improvement of correctional institutions to give them capacity not only to incarcerate, but also to rehabilitate convicted criminals.

The political obstacle to strengthened law enforcement provided by the police themselves is based on the hostility many feel toward ghetto slum-dwellers and toward persons who defy, or sometimes even question, police authority. Varying proportions of police officers in different cities act out their hostility against black slumdwellers by using insulting or abusive language during routine police contacts and chance encounters. Varying proportions of police also lose self-control when faced with rioting or nonviolent mass demonstrations, employing excessive gunfire and engaging in "police riots." This unauthorized verbal and physical brutality by police is, of course, no less illegal than any other crime. Furthermore, the resentments and hatred generated by this kind of brutality stimulate sniping and other violence against the police, and interfere with the kind of community cooperation that could help the police to reduce street crime.

The obstacle to strengthened law enforcement presented by the slum community is its deep hostility toward the police. Part of this hostility is, obviously, generated by police abuses and by the low level of protection afforded ghetto residents. But probably a larger part of that hostility is misdirected, with the police becoming the target for grievances felt against the shortcoming of city governmental performance in improving conditions, simply because police officers in the slums are the city's most visible and continuously available representatives. As a result, even when police are engaged in perfectly proper actions in black neighborhoods, such as stopping a speeding motorist or raiding an illegal business or intervening to stop an assault, bystanders will frequently treat the police officer as an enemy. This lack of support, indiscriminate hostility, and sometimes actual interference with the police when performing their legal duties predictably increase the sense of threat police feel and strengthen their belief that slum-dwellers are not really interested in better police protection. This in turn further stimulates their hostility toward the black community and makes them less likely to act in a restrained and discriminate manner.

The political obstacle to strengthened law enforcement that comes from the liberal community is based on the temperamental antipathy of many liberals to police as an intrinsically repressive force for whatever purpose used, but most especially when used against those perceived as unjustly deprived and downtrodden, like today's black slum-dwellers. This antipathy appears to be further buttressed by feelings of guilt over being part of the society responsible for allowing deplorable conditions like slum ghettos to exist. And these anti-police sentiments are often supported by an intellectual position that seems to hold that since by police action city governments can deal only with symptoms and not basic causes of urban problems, municipal governments should do neither until they can do both.

Prospects for Ending Urban Ungovernability

What possibility exists for overcoming the political opposition that currently exists to spending massively larger amounts of money on the problems of cities, to racially integrating central city neighborhoods as well as encouraging large numbers of central city Negroes to resettle in presently almost exclusively white suburbia, and to strengthening law enforcement sufficiently to control various forms of illegal violence without simultaneously curtailing nonviolent dissent, civil liberties, and procedural due process? Realistically speaking, the answer is "none" unless there develops a conscious and deliberate, long-term national commitment to alleviate the problems of cities much like the long-term commitment made for rebuilding the European economy after World War II through the Marshall Plan. And it is probably necessary that any expanded national commitment to aid cities be a part of a still larger one aimed at eliminating poverty and improving the quality of life of the less-affluent third of the population, whether urban or rural, black or white.

Actually, the supportive constituency for commitments to back the integrated package of policies and programs to bring about the healthy, multiracial future for large cities is potentially very broad. In terms of individuals and groups who stand to gain specific, tangible benefits, such a constituency would include:

Black slum-dwellers looking to improved incomes and other living conditions.

Other urban and rural poor, currently largely ignored, who would benefit from any general upgrading of incomes and quality of life for the nonaffluent.

Local and state elective and appointive officeholders, whose fiscal capacity to cope with demands and problems in their jurisdictions would be enhanced by federal absorption of the cost of welfare and poverty programs.

Large-city downtown retailers, bankers, utility and newspaper owners, restaurant, hotel, and theater operators, and other businessmen whose enterprises are largely "locked in" the central city's downtown section and whose economic success and survival depend on a healthy large city.

White upper-middle and upper-income devotees of apartment or townhouse big-city living, whose enjoyment would be increased by greater safety on the streets and by fewer slum sights.

Middle-income whites who prefer big-city living and who, with improved public safety and schools, might indulge these preferences.

White blue-collar and white-collar workers, who could see increased long-term security through "managed integration" against massive transition of their neighborhoods and who could also expect improved city services once poverty-related costs were absorbed by the federal government.

White suburbanites who want to patronize the recreational, cultural, and business facilities of the large city.

Persons who are highly disturbed by the increase in crime and riots and would be attracted by the strengthened law enforcement.

Incumbent national politicans of high visibility and competitive constituency, particularly the President, but also House members of the Administration party from close districts, who know that their reputations and reelection prospects will suffer if repeated outbreaks of violence occur during their own or their party's Administration.

On a higher level of generality, support for the package of policies and programs conducive to the healthy, multiracial city could come from all those whites who, regardless of actual place or residence, are ideologically or emotionally attached to large cities. They regard large cities as the nation's traditional centers of population, business, and culture, and oppose their becoming predominantly Negro possessions, particularly as this would entail the possible permanent loss of those specialized facilities necessary for a highly urban style of life. For such facilities require a metropolitanwide clientele and probably cannot survive economically except at the geographic center of the area's population mass.

Finally, on the highest level of generality, a supportive constituency for a pro-city national commitment is potentially forthcoming from the great mass of middle-class Americans who have feelings of humanitarianism, justice, and fairness predisposing them to help the underprivileged and guarantee a minimally decent standard of living for everybody. These Americans do not feel comfortable with the prospects of an increasingly racially segregated society. They recognize that allowing large cities to drift into "black tinderboxes" and improving public order exclusively through strengthened law enforcement do not solve the problem of cities or race but merely postpone dealing with them until some time when their dimensions will be still larger. An optimistic opinion survey finding is that white majorities by five-to-one believe that "thinking about the next five to ten years ... the best thing to do about the problem of riots" is *not* simply to "build up tighter police control in the Negro areas," but to "try harder to improve the condition of the Negroes" or "do both."

To say that support for a new pro-urban package will be forthcoming assumes that most white Americans, particularly younger, middle-class, and college-educated white Americans, are not unmitigated racists. Admittedly they are limited in the extent to which they are enthusiastic about converting their humanitarian feelings into actual sacrifices for the benefit of the black downtrodden. And they still harbor irrational prejudices against certain kinds of very close social contacts with Negroes. But there is no evidence to show that most white Americans are firmly committed to keeping Negroes in a position of permanent economic and social separation and inferiority. In this respect it was probably a mistake for the Kerner commission to refer to the racial prejudice interfering with Negro advancement by the term "white racism," with its strong implications that such prejudice is an inherent characteristic of all whites, all-encompassing in the relationships to which it attaches, and somehow fundamental and unchanging.

Whether or not the broad array of individuals, groups, and publics with tangible, ideological, and moral stakes in a healthy future for cities can be mobilized and their combined political resources brought to bear in support of a strategy necessary to bring it about is an open question. The answer will depend in great part on the kind of leadership that emerges, especially from national political officials such as the President, from large city mayors, from universities, from the mass media, and from business. Such leadership would have to instruct the American public in terms that will dispel its "optimistic denial" and capture its attention and sympathetic understanding about the harsh realities of the current urban situation and about the even harsher likely consequences of not changing present policies and allowing existing trends to continue. It would also have to explain that strategies, policies, and programs are available that when funded at a sufficiently high level can ameliorate current conditions and shift adverse trends. The most important targets of this kind of instruction will be that small stratum of politically active or attentive individuals who have disproportionately large influence over governmental decisions, especially solid working majorities in Congress for the authorization of necessary programs and the appropriation of sufficient funds.

The answer also depends on whether strong, responsible, and courageous black leadership will explain to the black community other harsh realities of the situation: that black time perspectives need to be lengthened as dramatic improvements in the most oppressive physical conditions are technically impossible to bring about immediately regardless of the sincerity and magnitude of the efforts made; that extremist antiwhite rhetoric and outbreaks of large-scale mass or guerrilla-type violence are almost certain to produce a backlash. For such black rhetoric and violence breed anxiety and hostility among whites that inevitably contract support for ameliorative urban policies and provide backing for different political leadership that is oriented toward responding to urban problems solely by imposing order through repressive force.

How receptive either white or black publics would be if this leadership emerges depends on a number of additional factors. If national and local officials demonstrate clearly that they regard the problems of cities as urgent, if reasonable demands of responsible, nonviolent and nonseparatist black leaders are being met, and if ameliorative change is visibly taking place, the vast majority of the urban black community may well accede once again to pleas for more patience and keep relatively "cool." Similarly, if the national economy is experiencing rapid growth and the nation is not engaged in large-scale military operations, much or all of the huge monetary costs of the new policies could be borne "painlessly" out of the "fiscal dividends" generated by the federal tax system. Under those circumstances the dominant majority of the white public might well provide support for decisions by officials in the White House, in Congress, in various city halls, and in state houses to engage in an overall national commitment to achieve a better future for large cities.

If, on the other hand, the national economy should be less prosperous or the military budget remains high because of war or major new weapons-procurement programs or if any "fiscal dividend" were to be consumed by expansions of nonurban, nonpoverty related programs, the costs of achieving the healthy, multiracial future for cities would fall more painfully on much of its potential supportive constituency. Increased taxes might be required and, depending on how fast personal incomes were rising, even cuts in existing standards of living. Sustained support for any national commitment to improve the "governability" of large cities would then depend on how successful politicians and other leaders were in convincing the more affluent two-thirds of the American public to forego some personal income for a society whose cities would be healthy and multiracial and whose poor no longer had to live under conditions that might nauseate the average member of the middle class. And success in that task would depend ultimately on how receptive most Americans were to the idea that in such a society, a somewhat smaller income could actually lead to a more enjoyable life than a larger income in a society whose large cities had become "black tinderboxes," whose poor continued to live in degrading circumstances, where the two-thirds of the population that lived in or near those cities felt some degree of Hobbes' "continual feare, and danger of violent death," and where there existed for all Americans a risk of the ending of the present form of American democracy. It is not inconceivable that Americans might prove receptive.

Urban America and the Urban Coalition

ONE YEAR LATER

"The deepening racial division is not inevitable," the [Kerner] Commission said a year ago. "The movement apart can be reversed. Choice is still possible. Our principal task is to define that choice and to press for a national resolution." The following summarizes the national response to that task. . . .

1. Civil disorders increased in number but declined in intensity in 1968. A significant drop in the death rate was due primarily to more sophisticated response by police and the military, resulting directly from the work of the Commission.

2. A wave of disorder struck the nation's high schools in 1968–69 and is continuing. At the same time, turbulence on college and university campuses has taken on an increasingly racial character.

3. A genuinely alarming increase in crimes of violence contributed to an atmosphere of fear inside and out of the slums and ghettos. There was little evidence of change or reform in the criminal justice system sufficient to stem this increase.

4. Incidents involving the police continued to threaten the civil peace in the slums and ghettos. There was some evidence of a hardening of police attitudes and a weakening of traditional civil controls over their activities.

5. Structural change in local government to make it more responsive was rare. The number of black elected officials increased substantially throughout the nation and particularly in the South, but remained disproportionately low.

6. There was no evidence that any more than a small minority of the nation's Negro population was prepared to follow militant leaders toward separatism or the tactical use of violence. This minority, however, continued to have an impact beyond its numbers, particularly on the young.

7. There was striking evidence of a deepening of the movement toward black pride, black identity, and black control and improvement of ghetto neighborhoods. There were repeated suggestions that efforts toward

Reprinted from *One Year Later* (New York: Praeger, 1969), pp. 114–118, with the permission of the authors and the publisher.

417

community control and self-help had been a major contribution to the relative quiet of the summer, 1968.

8. White concern with the problems of the slums and ghettos mounted with the Commission report, the assassination of Martin Luther King, and the April disorders. It was subsumed by concern for law and order in the months following the assassination of Senator Robert F. Kennedy, and continued to decline during the Presidential campaign. Outright resistance to slum-ghetto needs and demands intensified during the same months.

9. Black and white Americans remained far apart in their perception of slum-ghetto problems and the meaning of civil disorders. The gap probably had widened by the end of the year.

10. The physical distance between the places where blacks and whites lived did not diminish during the past year and threatens to increase with population growth. The most recent trend showed a virtual stoppage in black immigration and a sharp increase in the rate of white departure; the ghettos, meanwhile, were growing in area while declining in population density. There was an increase in suburban Negro population, but there also were indications of growth in suburban ghettos.

The nation has not reversed the movement apart. Blacks and whites remain deeply divided in their perceptions and experiences of American society. The deepening of concern about conditions in the slums and ghettos on the part of some white persons and institutions has been counterbalanced — perhaps overbalanced — by a deepening of aversion and resistance on the part of others. The mood of the black, wherever it stands precisely in the spectrum between militancy and submission, is not moving in the direction of patience. The black neighborhoods in the cities remain slums, marked by poverty and decay; they remain ghettos, marked by racial concentration and confinement. The nation has not yet made available — to the cities or the blacks themselves — the resources to improve these neighborhoods enough to make a significant change in their residents' lives. Nor has it offered those who might want it the alternative of escape.

Neither has the nation made a choice among the alternative futures described by the Commission, which is the same as choosing what the Commission called "present policies." The present policies alternative, the Commission said, "may well involve changes in many social and economic programs — but not enough to produce fundamental alterations in the key factors of Negro concentration, racial segregation, and the lack of sufficient enrichment to arrest the decay of deprived neighborhoods."

It is worth looking again at the Commission's description of where this choice would lead:

"We believe that the present policies choice would lead to a larger number of violent incidents of the kind that have stimulated recent major disorders.

"First, it does nothing to raise the hopes, absorb the energies, or constructively challenge the talents of the rapidly growing number of young Negro men in central cities. The proportion of unemployed or underemployed among them will remain very high. These young men have contributed disproportionately to crime and violence in cities in the past, and there is danger, obviously, that they will continue to do so.

"Second, under these conditions, a rising proportion of Negroes in disadvantaged city areas might come to look upon the deprivation and segregation they suffer as proper justification for violent protest or for extending support to now isolated extremists who advocate civil disruption by guerrilla tactics.

"More incidents would not necessarily mean more or worse riots. For the near future, there is substantial likelihood that even an increased number of incidents could be controlled before becoming major disorders, if society undertakes to improve police and National Guard forces so that they can respond to potential disorders with more prompt and disciplined use of force.

"In fact, the likelihood of incidents mushrooming into major disorders would be only slightly higher in the near future under the present policies choice than under the other two possible choices. For no new policies or programs could possibly alter basic ghetto conditions immediately. And the announcement of new programs under the other choices would immediately generate new expectations. Expectations inevitably increase faster than performance. In the short run, they might even increase the level of frustration.

"In the long run, however, the present policies choice risks a seriously greater probability of major disorders, worse, possibly, than those already experienced.

"If the Negro population as a whole developed even stronger feelings of being wrongly 'penned in' and discriminated against, many of its members might come to support not only riots, but the rebellion now being preached by only a handful. Large-scale violence, followed by white retaliation, could follow. This spiral could quite conceivably lead to a kind of urban *apartheid* with semimartial law in many major cities, enforced residence of Negroes in segregated areas, and a drastic reduction in personal freedom for all Americans, particularly Negroes."

The Commission's description of the immediate consequences of the present policies choice sounds strikingly like a description of the year since its report was issued: some change but not enough; more incidents but less full-scale disorder because of improved police and military response; a decline in expectations and therefore in short-run frustrations. If the Commission is equally correct about the long run, the nation in its neglect may be sowing the seeds of unprecedented future disorder and division. For a year later, we are a year closer to being two societies, black and white, increasingly separate and scarcely less unequal.

Edward C. Banfield

THE PROSPECT FOR
THE UNHEAVENLY CITY

It is impossible to avoid the conclusion that the serious problems of the cities will continue to exist in something like their present form for another twenty years at least. Even on the most favorable assumptions we shall have large concentrations of the poor and the unskilled, and — what, to repeat, is by no means the same thing — the lower class in the central cities and the larger, older suburbs. The outward movement of industry and commerce is bound to continue, leaving ever-larger parts of the inner city blighted or semi-abandoned. Even if we could afford to throw the existing cities away and build new ones from scratch, matters would not be essentially different, for the people who moved into the new cities would take the same old problems with them. Eventually, the present problems of the cities will disappear or dwindle into relative un-importance; they will not, however, be "solved" by programs of the sort now being undertaken or contemplated. On the contrary, the tendency of these programs will be to prolong the problems and perhaps even make them worse.

For the most part, the problems in question have arisen from and are inseparably connected with developments that almost everyone welcomes: the growth and spread of affluence have enabled millions of people to

Reprinted from *The Unheavenly City* (Boston: Little, Brown and Company, 1970), pp. 225–263, with the permission of the author and the publisher.

move from congested cities to new and more spacious homes in the suburbs; the availability of a large stock of relatively good housing in the central cities and older suburbs has enabled the Negro to escape the semislavery of the rural South and, a century late, to move into industrial society; better public health measures and facilities have cut the death rate of the lower class; the war and postwar baby boom have left the city with more adolescents and youths than ever before; and a widespread and general movement upward on the class-cultural scale has made poverty, squalor, ignorance, and brutality — conditions that have always and everywhere been regarded as inevitable in the nature of things — appear as anomalies that should be removed entirely and at once.

What stands in the way of dealing effectively with these problems (insofar as their nature admits of their being dealt with) is mainly the virtues of the American political system and of the American character. It is because governmental power is widely distributed that organized interests are so often able to veto measures that would benefit large numbers of people. It is the generous and public-regarding impulses of voters and taxpayers that impel them to support measures — for example, the minimum wage and compulsory high school attendance — the ultimate effect of which is to make the poor poorer and more demoralized. Our devotion to the doctrine that all men are created equal discourages any explicit recognition of class-cultural differences and leads to "democratic" — and often misleading — formulations of problems: for example, poverty as lack of income and material resources (something external to the individual) rather than as inability or unwillingness to take account of the future or to control impulses (something internal). Sympathy for the oppressed, indignation at the oppressor, and a wish to make amends for wrongs done by one's ancestors lead to a misrepresentation of the Negro as the near-helpless victim of "white racism." Faith in the perfectibility of man and confidence that good intentions together with strenuous exertions will hasten his progress onward and upward lead to bold programs that promise to do what no one knows how to do and what perhaps cannot be done, and therefore end in frustration, loss of mutual respect and trust, anger, and even coercion.

Even granting that in general the effect of government programs is to exacerbate the problems of the cities, it might perhaps be argued that they have a symbolic value that is more than redeeming. What economist Kenneth Boulding has said of national parks — that we seem to need them "as we seem to need a useless dome on the capitol, as a symbol of national identity and of that mutuality of concern and interest without which government would be naked coercion"[1] — may possibly apply as

---

[1] Kenneth Boulding, book review in the *Journal of Business* (January 1963) : 121.

well to Freedom Budgets, domestic Marshall Plans, and other such concoctions. That government programs do not succeed in reducing welfare dependency, preventing crime, and so on, is a rather minor objection to them if in fact without them the feeling that the society is "not worth saving" would be widespread. One would hope, however, that other and better means — a useless dome on the capitol, for example — would serve the symbolic need well enough. Moreover, there is an evident danger that the failure of urban programs to contribute to the attainment of our objectives will make them symbols not of national identity and mutual concern, but rather of national divisiveness, confusion, and unwisdom.

That government cannot solve the problems of the cities and is likely to make them worse by trying does not necessarily mean that calamity impends. Powerful accidental (by which is meant, non-governmental and, more generally, nonorganizational) forces are at work that tend to alleviate and even to eliminate the problems. Hard as it may be for a nation of inveterate problem-solvers to believe, social problems sometimes disappear in the normal course of events.

One powerful accidental force at work is economic growth. Because capital tends to increase by geometric progression, a rich country becomes exceedingly rich in the space of a few years. If Americans in the future take no more of their income in the form of leisure than they do now, the national income should increase from $713 billion in 1968 to $2,628 billion in the year 2000. If there has meanwhile been no great amount of immigration by people who are slow to adapt to the ways of industrial society, the end of urban poverty, in the sense of hardship, will be at hand even if the pattern of income distribution remains substantially unchanged.

A second such force is demographic change. The presence of large numbers of adolescent boys is (along with the presence of a large lower class) mainly responsible for school, job, crime, and disorder problems. This troublesome part of the population is now increasing at an extraordinarily rapid rate (in the ten years ending in 1975 the number of males aged 15 to 24 will increase from 15,540,000 to an estimated 20,296,000). The increase will almost stop before long, however (in 1985 there will be about 21,107,000 males in this age group), and the proportion of boys and young men in the population will be smaller than it is now. A decline in the relative importance of the young male part of the population will do more to relieve strain on city institutions, it is safe to say, than even the most "massive" of government programs.

A third such force — perhaps the most important of all — is the process of middle- and upper-class-ification. For [a number of] reasons . . . it does not seem likely that the lower class will be absorbed into the culture of the larger society. With this important exception, however, there will no doubt continue to be a general upward movement all along the class-cultural scale. This will mean a softening of manners, better performance in schools, less violence (but not necessarily less nonviolent crime and disorder), and a reduction in racial prejudice and discrimination.

The decline of prejudice and discrimination should proceed with gathering momentum because of the operation of what Gunnar Myrdal, in An American Dilemma, called "the principle of cumulation."

White prejudice and discrimination keep the Negro low in standards of living, health, education, manners and morals. This, in turn, gives support to white prejudice. White prejudice and Negro standards thus mutually "cause" each other.... Such a static "accommodation" is, however, entirely accidental. If either of the factors changes, this will cause a change in the other factor, too, and start a process of interaction where the change in one factor will continuously be supported by the reaction of the other factor.[2]

It is impossible to judge how much effect these accidental forces will have on the lower class.... [I]t makes a great deal of difference how much of the present-orientedness of that class is cognitive, how much situational, and how much volitional, but this is a question for which answers do not exist at present. If, as many social scientists want to believe, present-orientedness is mainly or even entirely situational, rapid economic growth may before long offer the lower class the incentives — especially job opportunities — needed to bring its members into normal culture. On the other hand, increasing affluence may have a contrary effect: overgenerous welfare programs may destroy more incentives to look ahead and provide for the future than improved job and other opportunities can provide. For this and other reasons that have already been discussed, an increase in the absolute (if not the relative) size of the lower class is by no means out of the question. Unless the increase were very large, however, it would not necessarily lead to a radical worsening of the situation or precipitate a crisis in the life of the nation.

Although the *objective* situation does not warrant the alarmist tone of much that is said and written about the city, the *subjective* one may. However much the accidental forces may reduce the *real* importance of the problems that have been under discussion, they may have no impact on their *seeming* importance. Indeed, this is likely to grow, for some of the very same factors that improve the objective situation also raise people's standards and expectations, thus leaving the subjective situation

[2] Gunnar Myrdal, *An American Dilemma* (New York: Harper, 1944), pp. 75–76.

no better — and perhaps even worse — than it was to begin with. What people *think* a situation is may (as sociologist Robert K. Merton has pointed out) become an integral part of that situation, and therefore a factor in its subsequent development. A false public definition of the situation may, as Merton says, evoke new behavior that makes the originally false definition come true, thus perpetuating a "reign of error."[3] In short, wrong public definitions of urban problems may lead to behavior that will make matters worse despite the ameliorating influence of the accidental forces.

This possibility is most painfully apparent in the case of the Negro. That racial prejudice has long been declining and may be expected to continue to decline at an accelerating rate counts for little if the Negro *thinks* that white racism is as pervasive as ever; that his opportunities to improve his position by acquiring skills are at last fairly good counts for little if he *thinks* that "massive" government welfare, housing, and other programs — and *only* these — can help him. If he misperceives the situation in these ways, he is likely to do things that are counter-productive (for example, to cut himself off from "white" schools, jobs, and politics and to enter the fantasy world of black separatism). Such a course, if carried far enough, may validate his original (false) hypothesis — that is, he may become in fact as dependent upon government programs as he (wrongly) supposed himself to be and may revive the fact of white prejudice by giving it some objective grounds to feed upon.

Nothing could be so tragic and ironic as the acceptance of a false public definition of the situation that proves to be a self-fulfilling prophecy of racial hatred. Even if nonracial factors had not in recent years superseded the racial ones as the Negro's main handicap, it would be well to pretend that they had, for a self-fulfilling prophecy of the unimportance of racial factors would be as great a blessing as its opposite would be a curse.

Except as they create, or reinforce, counterproductive public definitions of problems and thereby encourage a "reign of error," wrong governmental measures are not likely to lead to catastrophe or even to any very significant worsening of the situation. Most wrong measures will lead to nothing worse than some additional waste and delay, usually a trivial amount. . . . The governmental measures having the largest effect upon the city since the turn of the century are probably subsidization of truck and automobile transportation and subsidization of home ownership for the well-off; these measures certainly hastened the departure of the white middle class from the central city and, *a fortiori*, the entry of the

[3] Robert K. Merton, *Social Theory and Social Structure* (New York: The Free Press, 1949), p. 181.

administrators and therefore also by journalists. It would not be surprising if the conventional wisdom were to be very much revised in the next decade or two as a consequence of these developments. Turnover within the small world of opinion-makers is rapid, and the young newcomers in that world tend to be open to new ideas and even in search of them. Because communication within the small world and between it and the public-at-large is excellent, a new definition of the situation, once formulated, could catch on very quickly.

It would be pleasant to be able to end this discussion on that relatively optimistic note. Unfortunately, another side to the matter requires mention. Technically trained persons have their own characteristic biases, and if their view of the city is different from that of the commuter on the Long Island Railroad it is not necessarily more realistic. Moreover, as the technician comes to play a more important part in policy-making he is bound to come more and more under the discipline of large organizations, especially foundations and government agencies, whose maintenance and enhancement depend in some way upon the elaboration of an alarmist, or at any rate expansionist, public definition of the situation. That young newcomers to the small world of opinion-makers tend to be open to new ideas is not altogether reassuring either, for they may tend to accept new ideas *just because they are new*. To the pessimist, the prospect is that a new conventional wisdom about the problems of the city, the product of many millions of dollars' expenditure on research, cast in the language of systems analysis and the computer, will only compound the existing confusion. The optimist, however, will see reason to believe that facts, rational analysis, and deliberation about the nature of the public interest will play a somewhat larger part than hitherto in the formation of both opinion and policy.

...ny, the black poor — on a large scale, but they did not significantly change the pattern of metropolitan growth; this was determined by accidental forces — the demographic, technographic, technological, economic, and class-cultural imperatives. . . .

Although it is easy to exaggerate the importance, either for good or ill, of the measures that government has adopted or might adopt, there does appear to be a danger to the good health of the society in the tendency of the public to define so many situations as "critical problems" — a definition that implies (1) that "solutions" exist or can be found and (2) that unless they are found and applied at once, disaster will befall. . . . Although there are many difficulties to be coped with, dilemmas to be faced, and afflictions to be endured, there are very few problems that can be solved; it is also that although much is seriously wrong with the city, no disaster impends unless it be one that results from public misconceptions that are in the nature of self-fulfilling prophecies.

Insofar as delusory and counterproductive public definitions of the situation arise from biases that lie deep within the culture (for example, from the impulse to DO SOMETHING! and to DO GOOD!), they are likely to persist in the face of all experience. To exhort the upper classes to display more of the quality that Trilling calls moral realism would be to offer a problem-begging "solution," since the very want of moral realism that constitutes the problem would prevent their recognizing the need of it.

The biases of the culture limit the range of possibilities, but they do not determine fully how the public will define the situation. This definition is in large part the result of a process of opinion formation that goes on within a relatively small world of officials, leaders of civic associations and other interest groups, journalists, and social scientists, especially economists; from this small world opinion is passed on to the public-at-large through the mass media, books, classroom instruction, campaign oratory, after-dinner speeches, and so on. Needless to say, a vast amount of misinformation, prejudice, and illogic enters into the process of opinion formation. (The agony of the cities, someone has remarked, is what the network executive and his fellow-commuters on the Long Island Railroad see out the window as they make their agonized way to and from their offices in Manhattan.) Within the past decade or two, developments have occurred that could make for a more realistic view of the urban situation — for example, the number of technically trained persons working on urban problems has increased greatly, their resources for gathering and manipulating data and the analytical apparatus that they can bring to bear upon policy questions are much improved, and what they have to say is taken much more seriously by politicians and